Michael Schumacher
THE WHOLE STORY

Other books by this author include

Ayrton Senna
The whole story

Michael Schumacher
The greatest of all

Memories of Ayrton

Ayrton Senna
As time goes by

Grand Prix Century
The first 100 years of the world's most glamorous
and dangerous sport

Murray Walker
The last word

Murray Walker
The *very* last word

Ken Tyrrell
Portrait of a motor racing giant

Hitler's Grands Prix in England
Donington 1937 and 1938

Inside the Mind of the Grand Prix Driver
The psychology of the fastest men on earth: sex,
danger and everything else

Michael Schumacher

THE WHOLE STORY

CHRISTOPHER HILTON

Haynes Publishing

The hardback edition was first published in November 2006, comprising some text previously published by Haynes Publishing in:
Michael Schumacher: Defending the Crown (1995)
Michael Schumacher: Controversial Genius (1997)
Michael Schumacher: The Ferrari Years (2000)
This paperback edition was published in September 2007

A catalogue record for this book is available from the British Library

ISBN 978 1 84425 448 4

Library of Congress catalog card no 2007931169

Published by Haynes Publishing, Sparkford, Yeovil, Somerset BA22 7JJ, UK
Tel: 01963 442030 Fax: 01963 440001
Int. tel: +44 1963 442030 Int. fax: +44 1963 440001
E-mail: sales@haynes.co.uk
Website: www.haynes.co.uk

Haynes North America Inc., 861 Lawrence Drive, Newbury Park, California 91320, USA

Designed and typeset by James Robertson
Printed and bound in Britain by J. H. Haynes & Co. Ltd, Sparkford

CONTENTS

Introduction   6

1   The Journey   17

2   I'd Like That   35

3   The Explosion   66

4   A Remarkable Young Man   81

5   Rattling Senna   116

6   Scared, Really Scared   160

7   The Bronco   178

8   Almost There   229

9   Creating His Own Era   287

10   Total Domination   314

11   The Singularity   352

12   All time high   365

Appendices

The Races   393

The Grand Prix years   397

Index   457

INTRODUCTION

Michael Schumacher was tired but you'd never have known. Down all the long years he'd never *once* looked tired – not racing, testing, travelling, skiing, running up mountains and sometimes climbing them, giving interviews, shaking hands, getting off long-haul flights, playing a lively game of soccer or training as hard as an Olympic athlete. After hot races he didn't even sweat, never had.

It was a particular kind of tiredness, a mental weariness as much as the physical.

That's why you didn't know about this, as he flowed across the shadows which carpeted Interlagos on the late afternoon of 22 October 2006 to complete the Brazilian Grand Prix. For one hour 32 minutes and 17.845 seconds he'd driven the race of a young charger, frisky and feisty and impatient. He'd driven the race you get at the beginning of a career but this was precisely at the end when, as a 37-year-old, he had nothing further to prove to anybody anywhere on planet earth.

To compound this, the actual Grand Prix had long been plucked from him and with it his chance of an eighth World Championship. He'd announced his retirement 42 days before, although the circumstances were so unclear as to be frankly mysterious. He'd dropped a hint or two but not more, and to understand the tiredness we'd have to wait until a while after Brazil.

He could have stroked the Ferrari round Interlagos for the hour and a half waving endless farewells to the crowd as he went, blowing them kisses if he'd felt playful, smiled a last time for the immense, voracious tribe of cameramen and gone to the airport. By a huge distance he was already the most successful Grand Prix driver who'd ever lived, whatever did or did not happen at Interlagos.

He had family responsibilities, he was immensely wealthy – people spoke of $400 million, others spoke of much, much more – and now he'd fly back to the rest of his life, the one nobody knew about or why.

What he did at Interlagos revealed all the aspects of the public man: he would remain exactly true to himself. Waves and kisses? He would attempt, however hopeless the circumstances, to *win the race*. He had never gone to any other race in his life with any other intention.

An engine failure in Japan a couple of weeks before had made the Championship impossibly remote; after qualifying in Brazil it was more remote still. All Fernando Alonso in the Renault had to do was finish in the top eight and the Championship was his.

In the first sudden-death session of that qualifying, Schumacher's Ferrari team-mate Felipe Massa, an Interlagos specialist, produced a lap of 1m 10.643, almost a second faster than Schumacher, next. Although of course you can't carry times forward to the second and third sessions it looked likely to remain unbeaten, however academic that would be.

With some seven minutes of the second session left Schumacher became the only driver to dip below 18 seconds in Sector 1. He'd begun to make a big statement. Alonso had just done a 1m 11.148 and here was Schumacher as we had seen him down all these years, holding the car in perfect control so that even the G-forces did no more than make his head nod.

The gloved hands worked the steering wheel with minimum movement and maximum efficiency, creating as they had so often done a single impression: inevitability. He came up the hill and brought the car easily over to the left-handed curve which feeds the start-finish line and by then we knew it was going to be fast.

He rounded the left-hander and crossed the line.

1m 10.313.

Nobody would get near it, not Massa, not any of them.

Everything after that moved to pathos. Schumacher led the column of cars out to begin the third session for the front of the grid. He travelled slowly and half a dozen cars fled past him. He had a fuel pressure problem 'and all I could do was cruise round slowly back to the pits.' He did not emerge from them for the remainder of the session and, because he had no time, would have to start from the fifth row. Massa did take pole with a lap of 1m 10.680, Alonso fourth.

It was the first finality. For the rest of his life Schumacher would have 68 pole positions, the 69th now gone forever.

With complete justification he might have regarded the Grand Prix itself as a milk run.

He nosed the Ferrari on to the fifth row of the grid knowing that for the rest of his life he'd have 249 Grand Prix starts, and not one more. It was the second finality. The lights blinked off releasing the 22 cars and *immediately* he was probing down the inside as they all rushed the first corner, the left-downhill-right. He got squeezed onto the kerbing in the left, making him ninth. He held that through the right and now they were on a short straight. *Immediately* he flung the Ferrari to the side of the track to try and overtake the BMWs in front. When that was blocked he *immediately* flung the Ferrari full across the track and, into a curve, both BMWs drifted wide. Schumacher put the Ferrari inside them *immediately*.

He was making another statement and that was when

everybody knew he was staying true to himself, that he would be a racer to the last moment regardless of Championships lost and won, regardless of race positions, regardless of retirement. The young, angular man who stepped into a Formula 1 car for his first race at Spa in 1991 was exactly the same man who dealt with the BMWs and faced 71 laps at Interlagos with a lot more overtaking to do.

He went past a Williams like a knife and completed the opening lap seventh. The Safety Car came out after a crash and, as they circled, Schumacher eyed Giancarlo Fisichella, Alonso's team-mate, with a predatory eye. When the Safety Car pulled off Schumacher stalked him, attacked on lap nine into the left-downhill-right and out-muscled him. This too was from Memory Lane: speed, judgement, nerve and risk, brought together with lethal precision. He had made this move on virtually every Grand Prix driver of his generation.

Suddenly he slowed, a rear tyre punctured, his race now in utter ruins. He got the Ferrari all the way back to the pits and although the tyre was wobbling and bulbous it had not shredded completely. The car was undamaged. He was stationary for 11.1 seconds and emerged twentieth. That was right at the back.

Still Michael Schumacher remained true to himself.

The first pit stops began on lap 24 and he, of course, had already made his. As the others peeled off, lap after lap, he swallowed places: within ten laps he was ninth and attacking a BMW into the left-downhill-right and here it was again, the same speed, judgement, nerve and risk. It worked, just the way it had always done, worked again when he overtook the other BMW for seventh at the same place.

With 24 laps left he made another pit stop. It was the third finality because he'd never make another one. This lasted 7.7 seconds and dropped him to eighth. Others pitted so that he ran seventh and set a new fastest lap. He stalked his former team-mate Rubens Barrichello in a Honda and moved into Memory Lane again: sixth.

He stalked Fisichella again, Fisichella resisted but skimmed off onto the grass. Fifth. He stalked Kimi Räkkönen in the McLaren, Räkkönen of sublime pace and hard ambition, Räkkönen who was taking Schumacher's place at Ferrari in 2007. Schumacher tried to overtake on the *outside* of a left-hander and now Räkkönen resisted. Schumacher lined him up into the left-downhill-right and thrust the Ferrari inside. Räkkönen squeezed and here were two racers measuring everything they had against each other. Räkkönen gave him just enough room and Schumacher seized it. The mechanics in the Ferrari pit were on their feet brandishing fists in triumph, just the way they'd done in so many places down all these years.

Massa led comfortably from Alonso, Jenson Button third – and, two laps to go, Schumacher set a new fastest lap. From the speed of the Ferrari into the last lap the crowd sensed he was trying to end his career by hammering even that time. He couldn't but there was a kind of nobility about the attempt, as if he was trying to make a last, thunderous, echoing statement.

As he flowed to the finishing line across those shadows of afternoon which carpeted Interlagos he'd reached to within sight of Button.

The line was the fourth finality. There would be no more.

He handled the aftermath as he had always done, keeping his emotions locked down even now. This is what he said: 'I am very happy for Felipe who drove an amazing race. It is great for him to be the first Brazilian to win at Interlagos since Ayrton Senna. It would have been nice if I could at least have made it to the podium alongside him. I would also like to congratulate Fernando. Today, my race was compromised after the puncture I picked up on lap nine when I had just passed Fisichella. I was unaware of it until the team told me about it on the radio. I had a good climb back up the order, thanks partly to an amazing car and exceptional Bridgestone tyres. Today my racing career comes to an end. Obviously it is a special moment for me and I am proud to have lived my career with some fantastic people, namely everyone who is part of the Ferrari family. There is so much I could say about them, but it is difficult to find the right words.'

Long before this I'd said to Ferrari tactician Ross Brawn *I could never see Schumacher, any more than I could ever see Senna, become a sort of 30-something-year-old midfield runner. They'd have left F1 by then because they could no longer do it at their level.*

Brawn replied: 'You're right. There will be a point when Michael will decide that he can't do it the way he wants to do it, and that's what people didn't understand about his injury [in the 1999 British Grand Prix when he broke his leg]. It was nothing to do with him being physically capable of driving the car.'

He'll be able to do that when he's fifty five, to take one round.

'Yes! It's not being able to undertake the fitness regime and the training that he normally does in order to ensure that his fitness is not a consideration during the race.'

Brawn was vindicated. When Schumacher announced his retirement – at Monza, those 42 days before Brazil – he said: 'I can see it becoming harder. Getting older does not make it easier to keep strengths for a whole year. I just do not see I have this. It is also nice to go at this point, when you are strong – rather than at the other end.'

That was the clue, the big one as it turned out.

In time he'd tell his press spokesperson Sabine Kehm for publication (she was writing a book on him, *Michael Schumacher*) about the tiredness. 'I kept having to push myself to do testing or appointments that I didn't really want to be going to any more.' He stressed that this was not about the core of his career – the race weekends – but 'all the other stuff.' He began to question how he'd been able to sustain it for so many years. 'I often counted the minutes until I could go home.'

A feeling grew within him that the time was coming.

He spoke of Ayrton Senna and how 'emotional' he was thinking about that – and by implication the weekend at Imola in 1994 when Senna died after Formula 1 resident doctor Professor Sid Watkins had tried to talk him into retirement on the day before the race.

At Bahrain in 2006 Schumacher equalled Senna's record of 65 pole positions and that's when the feeling began.

What he did *not* do after Interlagos revealed many aspects of the inner man. He didn't linger as a constant presence in the no man's land between what he had been and where he was now, hanging around, looking awkward. He had a role with Ferrari but it was never disclosed what this might be. He did appear selectively, and quietly.

He attended the launch of the new Ferrari in February and Todt asked him if, looking at the car, his desires weren't stirring. 'No, not at all,' Schumacher replied. 'If I ever feel that then I can go and drive my karts.' He attended testing at Barcelona but this was *so* low key that the Ferrari Press Service, who send out daily bulletins, didn't mention the fact and it rated a paragraph in newspapers.

Evidently he contacted the drivers after races and, at Melbourne, as Räikkönen – who'd won on his Ferrari debut – went to the podium, someone gave him a mobile phone. 'I think it was Michael but the signal was bad and I couldn't hear.'

In spring 2007 Schumacher was in London – looking, as he always could, impeccably well dressed in jacket and scarf – as part of a United Nations campaign *Make Roads Safe,* to try to cut the 'horrific waste of life' of young men being killed on the roads: 400,000 under-25s every year. Schumacher joined British Prime Minister Tony Blair in deploring the carnage.

'Road crashes kill on the scale of malaria or tuberculosis, yet the international community has not woken up to this,' Schumacher said. 'That is why I strongly support the *Make Roads Safe* campaign and the proposal that the United Nations organise a first-ever UN ministerial conference to tackle it.'

This was his first official engagement since he retired and The Question was asked, as it had been and would be, about him coming back. He replied that he was 'a happy man' and although he remained in close touch with Formula 1 'I'm not missing driving at the moment.'

Nobody wrung too much out of that last phrase. He might or might not miss it one day, but that didn't mean he'd get back in a racing car: maybe just keep missing it.

He went to the fourth Grand Prix of the 2007 season, Barcelona, and remained both determined not to get in the way and defensive. 'I have my job but it is not my job to make that public.' He said he was there to help Ferrari in any way he could, and that didn't involve passing judgement on Massa and Räikkönen. 'I'm looking more at the team structure, what is going on in the team as well as road car development.'

He added: 'It is very obvious that there is life after Formula 1. It is interesting to wake up every morning and not think about Formula 1.'

In an interview he'd given before the 1996 season for a BBC profile, called simply *Schumacher*, he said: 'To know Michael Schumacher personally up to now was difficult because I didn't feel free to give away what I'm really like. What you had was a professional base and you worked at the racing circuit: that's what the English know. They don't know who Michael Schumacher is really.'

A decade later, discussing Senna, he told Kehm that he did get emotional when 'confronted with the history of Ayrton' but 'obviously you don't want to admit that and you try to hide your emotions so you don't show the others you're vulnerable.'

Prof. Watkins can take us behind this. At Monza in 2000, Schumacher equalled Senna's total of 41 wins after a difficult period at Ferrari. He produced a tear not just for the win but for a marshal who had been killed. He was asked about what the questioner called his 'human side.' He said this: 'I find the question a bit strange. It sounds as though I haven't been a human before or after, and I obviously had a lot of memories of Ayrton Senna that day, and it just broke out.'

Watkins says: 'Immediately afterwards he came to see me and said "would you get the name and address of that poor chap's widow so that I can make sure she can be financially safe for the rest of her life?"'

Watkins was close to Senna. 'Michael and Ayrton were totally different characters but the result was very similar. That's because of exceptional talent.'

Who was Schumacher? Who is he?

'You remember his crash at Silverstone in 1991 when he broke his leg? He was totally normal in his reaction. He's ice cool, isn't he? He's really totally composed most of the time. He was a bit uncomposed when journalists were asking him stupid questions at Monza when he announced his retirement. That was irritation. He was getting fed up with being asked "what do you feel about doing this?"

'He's a very warm-hearted chap, actually. Ayrton detached himself from the Press as much as he could and Michael does the same. When you ask Michael a question you get a fairly rapid and lucid answer, with Ayrton he used to think a long time before he opened his mouth. He composed himself first.'

Because of the demands on Schumacher, to maintain normality he has had to throw up an armoured protection around himself and we conclude there's nobody behind the armour – but there is.

'Oh, absolutely. He's got a façade, no question. I think that is necessary for survival in the modern pressures of the media. He lives in a hostile environment.'

Bernie Ecclestone captured this aspect of Schumacher in a single word. He had a sense of 'mystery' about him.

The mystery wore many cloaks. There was the native Rhinelander, and Rhinelanders are known to be open but he seemed closed. 'I have a healthy scepticism, that is my general attitude. I must admit, though, that it was reinforced by certain events in my life. Certainly Formula 1 has formed me in this respect, too.'

There was the ordinary background, not penury but not wealth either, and – as a youngster – neither knowing nor caring about Formula 1. He dreamed of being a goalkeeper.

There was the talent in a racing car which came at you as the most explicable thing in the world – produced by the logic of diet, fitness, attention to detail, team-work, the ubiquitous Formula 1 word 'motivation', tactical acumen and so on. Just when you thought one of the cloaks had been drawn back and you were murmuring *now I understand what I'm looking at* a different cloak was pulled across and you were murmuring *I don't understand this at all:* the mind-over-matter races, the stunning laps conjured on command from who-knew-where, the wet races when he walked on water while the others drowned.

There were the contentious crashes down all the years, and some of them were still reverberating long after the late afternoon of shadows in Sao Paulo, as people surveyed the career and tried to reach a proper conclusion. Was he the greatest Grand Prix driver of the modern era? How did the crashes fit into that? If he wasn't the greatest, how did 1369 points, 68 poles, 91 wins and the seven Championships fit into *that?* Once upon a time drivers kept the points from only so many races each season. Before Schumacher, the two most successful were Alain Prost, *counting* total 768.5, and Senna, 610. That's 1378. Schumacher finished a mere nine points from beating *both of them together.* Where does that fit?

This is the story of the ordinary lad from the ordinary

background, who failed to become a goalkeeper and ended up provoking those questions. I hope some of the cloaks will be coming off all along the way.

My sincere thanks to Martin Brundle, Julian Bailey, Marc Goossens, Alessandro Zanardi, Johnny Herbert, Heinz-Harald Frentzen, Jochen Mass, Eddie Jordan, Dave Price, Albert Hamper, Allan McNish, Otto Rensing, Josef Kaufmann, Peter Hantscher; Wolfgang Schattling of Mercedes, Peter Sieber, Dick Bennetts, Keke Rosberg, Elmar Hoffmann; Gustav Hoecker for his memories and providing race facts; Werner Aichinger of Formula Koenig for his memories and for providing a wealth of material including photographs; Wolfgang Neumayer who handles German Formula 3 statistics; Manfred Hahn of German Formula 3; Daniel S Partel of EFDA; Graham Jones of Ford Motorsport Britain, and Helga Muller of Ford Germany; Dietmar Lenz of German karting; Maurice Hamilton of *The Observer*; Derick Allsop formerly of *The Independent*; Malcolm Folley of *The Mail on Sunday*; Tony Jardine and Victoria Flack of Jardine PR; Mark Burgess for permission to quote from *Karting* magazine; Simon Taylor of *Autosport* for permission to quote from that; Stephanie Chassagne of TAG-Heuer, the company whose statistical service is invaluable; Angela Hof of the Deutscher Motor Sport Bund; Inge and the late Barbel for translation; the Ferrari Press Service for daily bulletins throughout the season; Professor Dr. Ralph Jessen of the Cologne University History department, Professor Sid Watkins; Ross Brawn and Rory Byrne of Ferrari.

Chapter 1

THE JOURNEY

With hindsight everyone can believe in predetermination. Foresight is a lot more difficult and yet there is something insistent, and consistent, about this story of the son of a working man from a small German town. In the beginning, in fact, it was two stories seemingly unrelated because they were happening in different places and to different timescales.

On Friday 3 January 1969 a boy, Michael, was born to Rolf and Elisabeth Schumacher. They were entirely ordinary people – Rolf was a builder, good with his hands – and the chances were that their son would be ordinary too. He'd grow up in Kerpen, a solid Rhineland town of industry, banking, graceful church spires and a little agriculture, within commuting distance of Cologne. Kerpen was built round an old church and modest in its pretensions – no tourist office or tourist maps even.

This was flatland Germany and the mighty north–south autobahns ran like arteries through it. This was heartland Germany, threaded with the villages and little towns you've never heard of – Erftstadt, Elsdorf, Düren – and their own old market squares, their own solid buildings, their own spires. This was crossroads Europe. You could be in Holland or Belgium in under an hour, France in a couple. An authentic flavour of the Kerpen region: the locals say you go to Aachen, over by the Belgian border, and they're boring; you go south to the Eifel

Mountains and they're boring; but here we like to live, that's how we are.

On the Saturday, 4 January 1969, a fresh-faced driver called Chris Amon won the New Zealand Grand Prix at a place called Pukekohe, driving a Ferrari. The race was the start of the Tasman Series and nothing to do with the Grand Prix World Championship, but entries for the opening round of Formula One – at Kyalami in South Africa on 1 March – were being announced: two cars each from Lotus, McLaren, BRM, Brabham, Matra, and Ferrari. Evidently the latter caused mild surprise because a short time before this, Enzo Ferrari said he'd only be entering one car for most of the Championship. Now, without explanation, he had changed his mind.

He nominated one driver, Amon, the latest in a dynasty drawn to Maranello, the town near Bologna where Ferrari were based, to tame the Prancing Horse – the symbol of the team. Taming is an apt word in several senses because the Ferrari team contained a great deal more than a seductive mixing of money, facilities and tradition. There was Enzo himself, patrician and in-house politician, prey to great passions and rages. There was a regal court of people scheming all around him. There was the Mediterranean temperament everywhere: creative, explosive. There was the backdrop of all Italy regarding Ferrari as their team enacting their fantasies.

And now the two stories are interrelated because Kerpen was the central axis of a hub of little linked communities, including Horrem, the other side of the Aachen–Cologne autobahn. From there, in 1957, went aristocratic, popular Wolfgang von Trips to try this same taming at Ferrari and become Germany's first World Champion, but he died in a terrible crash at Monza in 1961, and 13 spectators died too.

Amon had been trying since 1967 and others would follow, coming from several continents.

In 1969, as Rolf and Elisabeth organised their lives to accommodate baby Michael, Amon was partnered during the Grand Prix season by a Mexican, Pedro Rodriguez. They managed just seven points between them.

A year later the neat Belgian Jacky Ickx might have won the title after the Championship leader – Jochen Rindt (Lotus) – was killed at Monza, but he didn't, and was glad not to rob a dead man of his due. Ickx's Swiss partner, Clay Regazzoni, came third. Across the early 1970s Ferrari were descending, and in 1973 Ickx finished with only 12 points. His new partner, the Italian Arturo Merzario, had six.

In Kerpen the Schumachers gave four-year-old Michael a go-kart powered by a motorcycle engine. The boy would remember it well. His father 'loved to be messing about in the garage and one day he decided on a strange idea: to take my go-kart, a kids' go-kart which I wasn't using any more, and take an old motorcycle and put its engine in the kart. That's how it happened.' On this the lad puttered around the streets. Rolf told his son 'drive carefully and not too quickly' but mythology insists that Michael lost control on a corner and used a lamp post to stop.

In 1974 Lauda came to Ferrari – Lauda of exalted Viennese extraction who'd remember being taken to Fiorano, near Modena, where Ferrari tested and 'suddenly I saw all the technical marvels: a private race track with automatic time-keeping, with closed circuit television and computers'. He saw 'a comparably vast team of fitters, engineers, administrators. I couldn't imagine how such a set-up could fail to win.' It was an exact distillation of what others before him had felt and others after him would feel. Lauda won the Championship in 1975.

In June that summer a brother was born, Ralf Schumacher.

Lauda nearly died defending the Championship when his Ferrari crashed and exploded into a fireball at the Nürburgring in 1976. Instead he became The Living Legend and won the title again in 1977. Face forever seared, Lauda deepened the Ferrari mystique.

Far into the future Lauda would refer to the kid from Kerpen as 'the talent of the century' but now Michael was living 'the childhood of any other boy, playing football, climbing trees, getting into a little trouble. Absolutely normal.'

Lauda left Ferrari after a furious political row and a young Canadian, Gilles Villeneuve, replaced him. Villeneuve was intuitively audacious in a racing car but had a simple, direct honesty which disarmed everyone and Italy prepared to surrender to him, although not quite yet because 1978 proved difficult. His partner, the Argentine Carlos Reutemann, finished third.

Part of Horrem spread up a hillside. Narrow streets followed this contour, side streets to right and left. Along one, detached houses nestled in the bosom of respectable suburbia. At the end you climbed a curving path into woodland. Here a tiny kart track – a ribbon of tarmac – contorted between trees and clumps of bushes. Long grass grew. Michael was nine and felt drawn to this place. He couldn't compete, of course, because he was too young.

In 1979 an erudite and single-minded South African, Jody Scheckter, came to try the taming. It made for a good balance, Villeneuve pouring uncalculated passion into every lap he covered, Scheckter calculating a route to the Championship which he took at Monza. That late afternoon of 9 September was hot and dry. Scheckter rounded the Parabolica curve and accelerated along the wide start-finish straight, Villeneuve holding back to give him the moment. People spilled from the pits to witness it, brandishing fists in intoxication. A common impulse seized the whole of Monza. Thousands in the grandstands opposite the pits were on their feet, their Prancing Horse flags flapping like birds on the wing. Scheckter thrust his right forearm from the cockpit and held it rigid in salute. He flowed past the official who, positioned almost mid-track, cleaved the air with the chequered flag. In a few moments Scheckter would be up on the presentation platform, the crowd below out of control. The police waded in with batons and riot-shields. The crowd hardly noticed, not even someone with blood cascading down his face. *Jo-dee, Jo-dee, Jo-dee* they chanted. Scheckter was Ferrari's seventh World Champion and clearly there'd be many more.

In fact, in the next 27 years there would only be one: the ten-year-old watching the karts go round and round at Horrem.

Michael was lean, slightly angular, but he had balance. 'When I was ten or twelve, I couldn't do serious racing because I was too young. Over the weekends, when other people were at the track and it was raining and nobody wanted to drive, I always said *come on, let me drive, let me drive*. I enjoyed those conditions, playing with the kart, making 360-degree turns. That's the best way for getting the feeling for a kart or a car. Racing in the rain is difficult, that's true, but you just have to be careful and handle the situation.'

There was a problem, however. Far in the future he'd remember 'we were quite poor, to be honest. When I was ten we didn't even have the money to continue karting.' The fledgling career was saved because Rolf started a modest business renting karts.

Scheckter lingered at Ferrari in 1980, the car a disappointment. Even Villeneuve could only wring a couple of fifth and sixth places from it.

Along the side street at Horrem, middle-class sensibilities were irritated by the angry howling which go-kart engines made. The residents decided to enforce noise abatement and the karters departed, leaving the little track to become overgrown. Of a weekend, model cars would be raced round it by remote control. They were much quieter, much more in keeping with suburban decorum. (One of Kerpen's little communities, Manheim, had a proper kart track. Many years later he re-visited it because a group of supporters wanted to salute his achievements. They agreed that he didn't really come from Manheim but so what? An old woman took him to one side and said 'there is a candle burning for you in the chapel whenever you are racing'. Schumacher, meanwhile, said he hoped they'd forgive him for all the noise from the kart track…)

The Italian Grand Prix, at Imola, in September 1980, somehow typified Ferrari's descent. Villeneuve's rear tyre exploded early in the race, flinging him into a crash so heavy that he was concussed and temporarily blinded. Scheckter, who'd jarred his neck in final qualifying, slogged on to the finish, which he reached a lap behind the winner.

Three days after Imola, karters gathered at Nivelles, a circuit some 20 miles south of Brussels, to contest their own World Championship. An interesting gathering, it included Ayrton Senna. Michael, aged 11, was taken by his parents to watch – Nivelles was no great distance from Kerpen – and ever afterwards he'd be asked if this was when it all really began. He'd say no, he was still a kid, he was just watching. He must have seen, among the karters hammering round, a quiet, polite Italian called Ivan Capelli who would, when drawn to the taming of Ferrari, be almost broken by it. Michael might have watched Senna being punted off in a late round but wouldn't have seen Senna imploring a British official, Alan Burgess, to find some way to get him reinstated and, when Burgess couldn't, bursting into tears. None could doubt however that Senna had strong and sometimes overwhelming emotions, as the 11-year-old would one day find out – physically. Anyway, the Schumacher family drove back from sleepy Belgium to quiet Kerpen after a good day out.

In 1981, Villeneuve conjured two victories from the Ferrari, an extraordinary feat, while his new team-mate, Didier Pironi, settled in. Pironi was a stylish Parisian with a taste for beautiful women. In a racing car he was hard, ambitious and, at least once, unprincipled. He thought he was the one chosen to tame the Horse.

The track at Manheim (not to be confused with the big town further south) was set in countryside, in a bowl scoured by open-cast mining. It had a slightly pastoral feel and one of the corners flowed round a copse of tall trees. Rolf went to work there looking after the track and paddock, renting out karts, and he found a house just up the winding lane from the track, behind the warehouse of a delivery firm. The 12-year-old had an invaluable advantage over other karters. Proximity.

The chance to drive regularly feeds on itself. The more mastery a youngster acquires the more the satisfaction and desire will extend that mastery. Karting, an exciting pastime, may lead nowhere in particular. Later, in adulthood, there'll be a job to find and protect, and the only evidence will lie in a drawer somewhere – curling amateurish photographs of the boy buzzing round some track on a hornet of a thing. In time, however, Schumacher's parents would manage the track at Kerpen...

At that age 'I never even knew about Grand Prix racing, only about karting. Racing was a hobby. I had no fantasies about Grands Prix. And I didn't set out to become a German sports star like Boris Becker or Steffi Graf, but more just to enjoy myself. My hero was Toni Schumacher (no relation), the goalkeeper who played for Cologne and the national team. I always wanted to be like him. I took my football very seriously, especially between the ages of 12 and 15 when I copied him and played in goal all the time.'

The beauty about karting is that it is comparatively cheap and if you're good you move up in a natural progression without risk of total bankruptcy. Of all forms of motorsport it is arguably the most democratic because (generally speaking) merit is more important than money; and if you move up to national championships and international competitions, you'll be meeting strangers whose careers will follow yours into adulthood.

In 1982, at Imola during the San Marino Grand Prix, Pironi betrayed what Villeneuve considered a moral obligation by overtaking him – against team orders – on the last lap when they were running first and second. Villeneuve never spoke to him again. Two weeks later Villeneuve was killed in final qualifying for the Belgian Grand Prix. Three months later Pironi was crippled when he crashed in practice for the German Grand Prix. The taming passed into the hands of Frenchmen, the urbane Patrick Tambay and the feisty Rene Arnoux. They finished fourth and third in the 1983 Championship and Tambay departed letting in Michele Alboreto, a delightful man with an elfin smile and the first Italian that Ferrari had hired since 1973. The mythology proclaimed that Enzo hadn't hired Italians because he didn't want the risk of Italian blood on his hands, although – inevitably – nobody seems really to have known.

The 14-year-old Schumacher played a lot of football, did a bit of judo and a lot of karting. Once he had a choice between a judo competition and the karting, chose the former and quickly realised his mistake. He'd become a racer now and in 1983 drove in the World Junior Championships. He didn't have far to go, just down the hill past the warehouse. The Championships were held at Manheim. An ambitious young Scot, Allan McNish, remembers that. 'I went to the Championships as a spectator, at the circuit his father ran,' McNish says. 'That was the first time I'd seen Michael race. He raced the year after – 1984 – but I was ill and couldn't compete.'

In 1984 Ferrari were as far away as ever from the next title.

The 15-year-old Schumacher won the German Juniors and everybody seemed to be saying that he was good, very good, but not touched by anything more.

In 1985 Alboreto finished second in the World Championship and that was as near as anyone had come since Scheckter.

The 16-year-old Schumacher was second in the World Juniors at Le Mans, home of the 24-hour sports car race. The karting is, as McNish points out, opposite Maison Blanche and the Porsche Curve, two famous landmarks on the full circuit.

Le Mans ran to a complicated format, which for simplicity can be described as two self-contained days of racing. On the first, *Karting* magazine reported that 'the driver who dominated the heats was Allan McNish, with three excellent wins and a second place from row four. Section A: Although McNish was on pole, Schumacher shot straight into the lead never to be headed. Allan threatened occasionally but never looked likely to get past.

'Pre-Final. The group winners, [Yvan] Muller, Schumacher and [Gianluca] Beggio lined up at the front with Muller on pole. McNish was on the second row. The first corner saw a six-kart pile-up, due in the main to the very fast starts that were allowed. Muller led with Beggio, Schumacher, McNish and the rest chasing'. Muller won from Schumacher.

'Final: Schumacher was away, followed by Muller, Beggio, [Andrea] Gilardi, McNish and [Massimiliano] Orsini and for the next five laps or so the leaders chopped and changed.' Gilardi won from Schumacher.

In the last of the qualifying races on day two, 'Gilardi, trying to make it seven victories out of seven starts, led them away. Gilardi briefly lost his lead to Schumacher, but successfully recaptured it. Later Schumacher was off at the end of the main straight but managed to restart in tenth. He started to fight his way back when he was given the mechanical malfunction flag and made to retire'.

Leading qualifiers, in order: Muller, Gilardi, McNish, Schumacher. A certain Christian Fittipaldi, who'd journeyed from Brazil for the Championships, didn't make it.

In the Pre-Final 'Gilardi made yet another of his good starts with Muller, Schumacher and McNish following, and then pulled out a substantial lead. Schumacher overtook Muller and the latter retired soon afterwards. By lap 7 McNish was all over Schumacher and then got past but was unable to shake off the very determined German who kept up the pressure'.

McNish says 'my inexperience took over, or the experience of the rest took over. I didn't make a very good start, I wasn't quite up to speed. Schumacher passed me and got into second place and from then on it was Gilardi, Schumacher and myself to the flag. I was with him but I couldn't do anything about it. All the way through the meeting we had been closely matched'.

Karting reported that 'at the start Schumacher tagged onto Gilardi and squeezed in front of McNish. Schumacher was desperately trying to get in an overtaking position but Gilardi looked in absolute control of the race. By their sheer pace they had opened up a small gap over McNish. In the closing stages Schumacher gave all he had but still Gilardi held him off and took the flag, a worthy retainer of the title. Schumacher looked bitterly disappointed but on the day didn't have quite enough to stop the flying Italian. McNish had impressed everybody'.

What sort of a chap was Schumacher then? 'Quite different to now,' McNish says. 'We were both 15 or 16, pretty young. He drove very much on natural talent and whereas he still has the same flair he uses his mind a lot more and he is strong technically as well. He drives like an extremely mature man. In karting he hadn't developed that aspect. He was a quick, hard racer – as everybody was at that stage – and he was the one you knew would be there or thereabouts in the races. I competed against him again in 1985 in the Italian Grand Prix, as it was called, at Parma, one of the most famous kart tracks in Italy. Schumacher was second again and I was third again.

'I can only really remember speaking to him at the Junior Worlds very briefly after one of the pre-finals or one of the races I'd just won. I had a little chat. He spoke very much broken English but, to be honest, none of the drivers really socialised.

One reason was that we were so young and our native languages were the only ones we spoke with any confidence. It's only later, when an overseas driver's career begins to rise, that he learns English.

'The other reason is that we were competing against each other and battling hard against each other. For major meetings we didn't tend to be social about it – we took it extremely seriously. It was probably as serious then as Formula 3 is now. It's quite funny, because I only did the European and World Championship events [outside the UK], so every time I went it was different people to beat, although Gilardi was usually the one. A couple of years ago I looked back through a Formula 3000 grid and it was extremely strange. Basically all the people I'd raced in karts were on that grid, people like Gianni Morbidelli and so on.'

Elmar Hoffmann, a German official, remembers that 'Schumacher was never a brilliant kart driver – very good but not as a young man so good that you'd say he would become a Formula One driver, but what we know is that drivers who are not so good in karting can be very, very good in car racing. He worked hard and he was a funny boy, he made jokes with his friends, but he was never one who worked against the rules, not a type who is tricky or who tries to cheat. He was always correct, fair and correct. And always polite.'

A fellow karter, Otto Rensing, watched Schumacher grow. 'For long years I had the lap records at Kerpen, all the lap records, and then suddenly that changed. Michael Schumacher beat them. People said he was good and I could see he was good because he broke my lap records. I met him and spoke to him but, because of the difference in ages, there was not so much we had in common.

'At karting meetings I didn't know all the other 30 drivers, only the ones who were good. That is normal in karting and normal in some other forms of racing too. Later on I met people in Formula 3000 and all the young guys like Sandro Zanardi knew me but I didn't know them – because I was quite a central figure in karting, I was the one they looked out for. I didn't remember them because they were growing up.'

In 1986, Alboreto and a pleasant Swede, Stefan Johansson, could not rejuvenate Ferrari: Johansson fifth in the Championship, Alboreto joint eighth. Alboreto would stay, Johansson go.

The 17-year-old Schumacher came third in the German Seniors and people in single-seater car racing were wondering about his potential. He had more mundane considerations on his mind, like a three-year apprenticeship as a mechanic in a Cologne garage.

The German Seniors were spread over six rounds and he only finished in four. A certain Karl Wendlinger, from Kufstein in Austria, came 15th.

'That season,' McNish says, 'the European Championships were over two rounds, the first in Sweden and the second in Germany. In Sweden – Gothenburg – I hate to say it but Schumacher finished second and I finished third again! We both went on to Dunlop tyres, which weren't the ones for the circuit. A Danish driver caller Gert Munkholm won on Bridgestones. Schumacher and I both struggled with understeer.'

Karting, reporting the final, said that 'McNish in second place was obviously struggling to hold off Schumacher and eventually succumbed to a nice out-braking move on the hairpin. Schumacher pulled out a few lengths but couldn't quite get away. The rest of the field were well back so Frank Van Eglem (a Dutchman) could concentrate on the job in hand and towards the end of the race passed both Schumacher and McNish. But spurred on by Terry Fullerton [an experienced karter and McNish's mentor] leaning over the fence and making threatening gestures, the young Scot got back into contact and, when Van Eglem was demoralised by Schumacher doing the out-braking trick at the hairpin, pulled the same move on him the next time round.'

At Oppenrod, which someone described as a 'very convoluted track' near Frankfurt, Schumacher won the heats from Zanardi and Emanuelle Naspetti, McNish 42nd. 'Allan had a dreadful set of heats for various reasons,' *Karting* said, preferring not to elaborate.

'To be honest,' McNish says, 'I can't remember who came where in the final because my brake disc broke and I didn't finish, so it wasn't a real interest to me. I do remember Schumacher didn't win because a Swede did.'

That was Linus Lundberg. *Karting* reported that 'Schumacher made the most of his pole position and went streaking away. Lundberg grabbed second. Once free of the others, Lundberg reeled in Schumacher and put him under tremendous pressure. Lundberg's relentless pressure brought forth fruit as he squirmed past Schumacher to then open up an enormous lead which he never looked like losing. [Ralf] Kelleners challenged Schumacher. For six laps they fought until Kelleners got through. Schumacher was again put under pressure, this time from Munkholm, but managed to hold on to take third'.

In 1987 a genial Austrian with a wicked armoury of practical jokes, Gerhard Berger, partnered Alboreto at Ferrari. Berger liked Enzo and Enzo liked Berger. Berger scored a couple of victories late in the season to be fifth in the Championship and promised to be the chosen one – or was it just another turn in the cycle of new beginnings which led nowhere? Alboreto came seventh and would stay another year then leave, his energy seemingly exhausted. By now a gifted designer, John Barnard, had come to Ferrari – or rather not come. He'd design the new cars from the calm of his UK base in Guildford, Surrey.

The 18-year-old Schumacher, beginning to fill out and sometimes sporting a tiny moustache, was now a leading karter. He came second in the European Championship Northern Zone heat, this time at a circuit called Genk 'which is actually situated at a little sleepy town called Horensbergdam'. *Karting* reported that 'the pits could have been better, with most teams situated in a field some distance from the dummy grid and having a long trek on a muddy path'. In the opening time trials section 'the surprise package of the day was the pretty young girl driver, Lotta Hellberg from Sweden, whose second timed lap was all that prevented her from gaining pole position for all her races'.

Fifteen heats followed. In the third 'Schumacher gave us an indication of what he intended to do this weekend when he disappeared into the distance early on'. In the final, 'after one false start it was [Rene] Bollingtoft who took the lead from Conny Eriksson, Schumacher and [Robert] Valkenburg. On lap 3, Schumacher passed Eriksson on the infield loop and set about catching Bollingtoft whose advantage was slowly disappearing. On lap 10 Schumacher made a daring move on the back straight and took the lead. Next time round Bollingtoft tried the same, but to no effect as Schumacher firmly shut the door in his face.

'The gap between the two packs at the front had again narrowed and when Bollingtoft tried to pass Schumacher at turn one, [Martijn] Koene slipped up the inside of both of them and pulled away slightly. Schumacher was to have none of this and pulled away from Bollingtoft. Koene and Schumacher now had command at the front and, try as he might, Schumacher could not pass Koene who drove some of the best blocking lines I have seen for some time to take the flag after 24 gruelling laps.'

The European Championship Final, drawing the Northern and Southern Zones together, was at Gothenburg, with an entry of more than 100. Schumacher led after the heats and in the pre-final took a comfortable lead. In the final 'from his pole position Schumacher again took the lead, followed by Frederico

Gemmo and Bollingtoft. On lap three Orsini and Zanardi were in the lead and started a fight that will go down in karting history. Several times they overtook each other and several times they went through bends side by side. At the beginning of lap 22 of a 24-lap race Zanardi was in the lead.

'Orsini was faster on the long straight so Zanardi tried to keep him behind by driving to the right on the straight. But this did not stop Orsini. He attacked where there was not enough room for both of them and the two Italians took each other off the track. Zanardi wanted to finish the race and pushed his kart to restart it. Orsini's father ran out and tried to stop him by kicking him in the back. With the two Italians out of the race, the victory and the European Championship title was handed to Michael Schumacher who tactically concentrated on keeping Bollingtoft and Gemmo behind him'.

Kicks in the back? Zanardi remembers them. 'We did all the race, Orsini and I, passing each other and on the last lap, well, he did a small mistake in the corner before the straight and he knew that it was his final chance to take the lead. I saw him about 25, 30 metres behind me. I thought, "that's it, I've won", because I knew he wouldn't be able to overtake me on the straight. Then he did a desperate manoeuvre. He didn't brake at all! He went directly into my kart and we both went off. I was trying to restart because I had a big advantage – 27 seconds – over Schumacher and if I'd been able to restart I could still have won. His father came along and started to kick me, that's absolutely right.'

Karting reported that 'after the race a calm Schumacher commented "I regret the outcome. I waited lap after lap for the two fighting Italians to do something stupid, and they did".' Directly after the final, Bollingtoft protested Schumacher. 'After two warm-up laps the German driver had noticed that his engine was loose on the chassis. He had tightened it up before the start but the rules say that you are not allowed to get any help on the track. The Stewards rejected the protest due to the fact that Schumacher tightened the bolts himself and did not receive any outside help. Bollingtoft said afterwards that he was satisfied with the decision and added that he would not have wanted to be Champion in this way.'

Zanardi made a protest against Orsini 'and then the Italian Federation came to me because he was one of the top Italian drivers. They said "well, you know, if you go through with this protest it's going to be a big problem", so I retired the protest and then what happened? In the Italian Championships he ran me off and I lost that one too...

'Schumacher was a very good kart driver, although obviously not as good as he is now in Formula One. For me he used to be a good challenger but, quite honestly, I have to say that in karting I had very good material and that's why I was quicker than him all the time. Also, most of the material was made in Italy so we got the chance to do a lot of testing, maybe two or three times a week, which helped.

'The atmosphere between the drivers was like a big, big family. The drivers knew each other and, especially before the races, we socialised very, very well. We stayed together even the evening before a race, we played billiards and things like that. Basically we lived at the circuits and you didn't have all of this pressure you get from the Press and so on in Formula One. Many times you'd sleep in the motorhome or in a van.' (Compare with McNish and 'none of the drivers really socialised'. It depends on who you were, how you were, and what you remember.)

The Schumachers produced a single page publicity sheet in 1987 to advertise his potential. Michael Schumacher sits bareheaded on a kart, his face serious. The kart bears the number 1 and the caption says 'European Champion'. It lists his karting record and directs anyone interested to contact Rolf Schumacher at their address in Kerpen. Potential sponsors, no doubt.

That season Schumacher locked into a struggle with a driver called Peter Hantscher in German Senior Karting. Schumacher won the opening round at Kerpen, Hantscher the second round at a place called Geesthacht. 'How? Easy. I was a bit faster than him! I'd known him before the season, although I began karting at Munich and he at Kerpen, but I'd seen him literally take his first faltering steps into the sport. That season was the biggest fight of my life and exceptional in that two Germans were struggling for our own Championship.' The Dane Munkholm had won it the season before. 'It was the best time of my racing career and maybe the best time for Schumacher too, a very hard fight but a very, very fair one and, if you want the truth, tremendous fun measuring each other's strength. We always shook hands in friendship.'

They approached the eighth and final round at a place called Walldorf with Hantscher needing to win and Schumacher needing a single point for the Championship. 'He set fastest time in qualifying and I set second-fastest time,' Hantscher says. 'I was absolutely determined to win or have an accident. I would not give in, I really wouldn't give in. I repeat: I would have preferred a collision.'

Before the race Schumacher murmured to himself: 'Don't do anything wrong, make sure you finish'.

Hantscher remembers what happened next. 'It was tense, wheel-to-wheel – no, tyrewall-to-tyrewall – and then Schumacher fell back a little. To show you what we were drawing out of each other, the third driver finished 150 metres behind. When it was over we were still friends and we still shook hands.' Schumacher, second, had the Championship from Hantscher, 127 points to 112.

'Schumacher was a very upright young man, friendly, ready to help' Hantscher said [in 1994]. 'I'm still active in German karting. I stopped competing for five years to build up a business dealing in karts but I'm competing again now in the

German Championship. If we meet we greet each other just like we did in the old times, despite the fact that he's in Formula One. Schumacher's hobby became Formula One and Hantscher's hobby became his business!'

On that subject, Schumacher would say early in his Grand Prix career 'people keep asking me how it is I can come into Formula One and establish myself so quickly near the top level and for me there is a simple answer: experience. Although I am very young compared to some of the other drivers I have spent a long time in motorsport, 19 years altogether, and I have had really good preparation for the job.

'After all, I did 15 years in karts from 1973 to 1988 and in that time I drove a lot of races, got myself into so many situations and learned so many things like driving wheel-to-wheel, close to other people and fighting and so on. I got used to it [fighting is race shorthand for dicing]. We had tyre situations too, with soft compounds which I had to learn about as well, how to take it easy and not push them too hard in the beginning or they would be finished at the end; and also a lot about tactics. All the lessons were well learned and I used them in my further career. I enjoyed karts because you drive bumper-to-bumper and this is real racing.'

The world of single-seater racing beckoned. This world contains many names – circuits, drivers, cars and championships – and readers will almost certainly be unfamiliar with most of them. More than that, the names come at you quickly and in profusion because young drivers are apt to compete as often as they can. However, a thread runs through, the young driver drawing from all this unfamiliarity a way to launch a career.

That, starting at the bottom, was what Schumacher was preparing to do.

Chapter 2

I'D LIKE THAT

A Lamborghini dealer in Germany, Gustav Hoecker, was poised to go into a junior category of car racing, Formula Koenig, with his own car, and he'd need a driver. He'd been impressed by how Schumacher was 'a nice guy' who handled a kart 'perfectly'. Peter Sieber, who'd been mechanic to a young hopeful, Heinz-Harald Frentzen, in karting and was now heavily involved in a Formula Ford team called EUFRA, noticed Schumacher too. Sieber said to Schumacher, 'Maybe you'd like to try a single-seater one time', to which Schumacher replied, 'Yes, I'd like that!'

'Michael had already had contact with a couple of teams,' Sieber says, 'but that came to nothing because, I think, he had no money. Towards the end of 1987 – I remember it was a cold day – Michael came to Hockenheim to drive our Formula Ford 1600 car, his first time in a single-seater. I said to one of the team owners "OK, you drive the car and then Michael drives it and if he is quicker than you, we have to do something for him." Michael was quicker. He told me what he felt in the car, and I thought, "Oh, he feels a lot of things in the car, he doesn't just drive it."'

Schumacher remembers that suddenly he 'got the offer of a Formula Ford test and it went from there. I was warned that karters sometimes don't adapt well to FF1600 but I was on the pace straight away. I did 25 laps and the only comparison I had was with the EUFRA owner, who used to be quite quick and raced with Keke Rosberg. After I'd done a time, he said that it must be a very good day for driving, got in the car and was 2.5 seconds slower. We got down to some negotiations and that was it.'

McNish had moved into the Formula Ford category of single-seaters, driving a car made by a company called Van Diemen. 'In November, December time I went over to a circuit in France to demonstrate the Van Diemen to various teams there [potential customers for Van Diemens] so that they'd see the 1987 car was quicker than the 1986. The '87 car came straight from Hockenheim and the driver who drove it there was Schumacher, his first run in a single-seater...'

The career was getting serious.

In 1988 Berger was third in the F1 World Championship, Alboreto fifth and going to Tyrrell. In five years at Ferrari he'd won three races. Ferrari had consumed what should have been his years of plenty and the Horse had remained untamed since Scheckter in 1979.

Schumacher had a busy introduction to car racing, with 15 races between April and October. As well as the ten Formula Koenig rounds, he'd compete in rounds of the German Formula Ford 1600 Championship and the Formula Ford 1600 Euroseries and finish at the celebrated Formula Ford Festival at Brands Hatch. This is the way it begins: the youngster faces a ladder and if he climbs it rung by rung – and doesn't fall – he'll reach Formula One. Karting is invariably the first step; Formula Ford 1600 the second rung. Formula Koenig was a variation on that.

Werner Aichinger, who ran Formula Koenig, charts the background to the Championship. There was a man called Richard Koenig who made car and sports seats and also had 'a great big heart for pushing new drivers. He was in Italy in 1986 and saw Formula Panda running there. He said to himself "this is a formula we don't have in Germany". He asked who built the cars and was told it was a company in Milan. He went there and said "build me 40 cars but keep them in kit form so that the guys who buy them can learn about them as they put them together".

'He bought the 40 cars and sold them and in the middle of 1987 we had the first Formula Koenig cars, as they were called. They had Fiat engines and Fiat gearboxes, just like in Formula Panda. In fact, the only thing he changed was the bodywork, which was completely new – everything underneath remained Formula Panda. The cars had wings on the front and rear, which really work: you can completely change the set-up of the car from understeer to oversteer by altering them.'

Hoecker bought one and built it, but he still needed a driver as the Formula Koenig season approached – first race at Hockenheim on 24 April. 'I really can't remember how I first came across Michael and now, since he's made it big, everybody wants to know! Another problem was that I couldn't have a driver who was too tall – anyone of two metres wouldn't have fitted into the car. Michael was the right size [1.74m/5ft 7in].

'Time was short, literally two weeks to the first race of 1988. The decision wasn't made because time was so short, however. I wanted to win. I'd seen his promise in karts, I'd seen what I thought was potential. I rang him and he was delighted, he accepted immediately. He hadn't been in a single-seater race before, but he took to it in a completely natural way and enjoyed success straight away. The car was right, the team was right and he was right. With hindsight, things look so different because at the time Formula Koenig could have been seen as insignificant.'

Aichinger expands on this, seeking its true context. 'Formula Koenig is not very far from karting. The cars are smaller than Formula Opel, smaller than Formula Renault, but you don't drive them exactly like a kart and it wouldn't be correct to say you do. It is, nevertheless, the perfect way to take your first step on to a real race track after karting.

'I began to know Michael then. I had not met him before. You have hundreds of karters but you never know how good they might be in single-seaters. In the first race he did look good. He started in a good team and they tested and so on, so he was well prepared. He won that first race [at Hockenheim] and he looked natural, he could drive easily, yes, yes, yes. Michael always looked completely natural. I think this feeling for a car is something you are born with, but Michael is fortunate in that he has the ability to learn very, very quickly. He's like a sponge, you know, he soaks everything up.'

Hockenheim wasn't easy and wasn't a smooth progression to victory. Hoecker remembers that 'Michael's gear lever broke during the first few laps – the race was over 20 – and he could only engage gear with what was left of the lever. In doing that he hurt the palm of his hand.' A driver called R. Koester finished first in 26m 36.17s, Schumacher was second in 26m 39.39s, but Koester was disqualified and so was Helmut Schwitalla, third.

'The first three cars were tested for legality,' Hoecker says, 'and as far as I can remember the disqualifications were because the valve setting of their engines was not within the regulations.'

Aichinger, seeking the context again, says 'there were ten rounds and Michael won them all except Zolder, where he had a little technical problem and finished second.' He was beaten at Zolder by Andreas Baier, who later raced a Porsche. Baier won it in 24m 58.42, Schumacher finishing in 25m 07.07 (average speeds of 76.30mph and 75.57mph respectively).

'To win nine of the ten rounds was absolutely outstanding. He actually won the Championship at Hockenheim (another round there, the ninth of the series) in a race I organised, and you should have seen how happy he was, absolutely happy. He hasn't changed at all, he's the same guy now as he was then, calm, very – how can I put it? – well, you could talk to him about everything and if you asked him something you'd get a really intelligent answer. In that sense it was the same as now, although of course now at a deeper level. He was never a guy who said "I am the greatest, I am a future Formula One Champion". Never. And I noticed that he always did his best. He had the chance to do some Formula Ford 1600 races in the middle of the season and he took it. He was successful there, too.'

Thereby hangs a tale. Albert Hamper ran an FF1600 team: 'Schumacher's father rang me up and asked if I'd give his son a drive. His father said Michael was very, very good but the problem was that they didn't have any money. I said, "No money, no drive!"' A tale of what might have been – like so many. 'Schumacher went to the EUFRA team, who gave him a drive without him having to pay.' Mind you, Schumacher's long-time mentor from Kerpen, Jurgen Dilke, had been active in raising some funds, as he had done when Schumacher was in karting.

Sieber remembers that 'Dilke was a good guy, almost like a second father to Michael. He said, "You must learn English", and he taught him about racing. Really, Michael had no money of his own. He had an old Audi – his first car – and he slept in the truck. A real guy. We ran three drivers and Michael became friendly with one of them and in testing they'd practise slipstreaming on each other so they knew what it was about. You must remember that a Formula Ford car has no wings, no special tyres [one type, the same for everyone] but you can learn so much about setting a car up, about understanding it, about finding the right balance. You have no real grip and it's easy to get too much understeer, too much oversteer and you have to understand these problems. Michael did.

'I said to him, "Once you get in front in a race you will always be a front-runner". He did it in, I think, the fourth race, and he has been a front-runner ever since. We did the German Championship and four rounds of the European Championship where we had a big fight with Mika Salo, and Michael finished second. You need a bit of luck, you know.'

In that Championship – the EFDA Formula Ford 1600 Euroseries, sponsored by Bridgestone – the Finn, Salo, was outstanding, winning four of the five rounds, although Schumacher didn't compete in the first, Zandvoort, in June. Paradoxically the one round Schumacher did win – the last, also at Zandvoort – Salo didn't compete in. He didn't need to because he had the Championship already. This does not alter the fact that Schumacher could push Salo: at the Österreichring, Schumacher's Euroseries debut, he got to within 0.687 of a second at the end of the ten laps.

One of those Formula Ford 1600 races was at Salzburg in August.

'In practice we had our three cars in front, 1–2–3, but Michael wasn't that quick,' Sieber remembers. 'It would be a wet race – very, very wet – and I said to him, "Look, I can do an experiment on the car and if it works we win, if it doesn't we lose". Michael said "OK, Peter, do it and if I lose I'll go and have a beer!" He was nearly like a brother to me. If, say, the car broke down he'd say, "Forget it, we'll do better next time". At Salzburg Michael told me, "Everybody will go to the outside, I'll go to the inside. Plenty of space there." He got away sixth or seventh but he was really quick, two or three seconds a lap quicker than anybody else. He said, "I looked in my mirrors and I couldn't see anybody behind me so I thought: now I'll drive with my head." He won by 20 seconds.'

Josef Kaufmann, a benevolent and wise Formula 3 practitioner, as driver and then team manager, watched fascinated. 'We'd done the Formula 3 race and then came the Formula Ford 1600. It was wet and I saw one of the drivers was fantastic but I didn't know him. I got a programme and looked and his name was Schumacher. I thought *there is one very, very good driver*. I can't remember if he won or came second but I do remember he didn't have a particularly good start. He ran sixth or seventh and worked his way up. To be able to do that is not normal with only a little Formula Ford experience. He'd only done a few races.'

Sieber remembers that afterwards Kaufmann 'came up and said, "You can bring him into my team and you can come too!"' A lot of people were talking about this drive, including a former racer called Willi Weber, running a Formula 3 team...

That autumn, Schumacher contested the Formula Ford 1600 Festival at Brands Hatch, an annual gathering of dozens of youngsters from all over the place. The Festival carries prestige and produces plenty of action, some of it wild. Previewing the meeting, *Autosport* profiled 24 drivers, including Schumacher. 'Highly-rated by Jochen Mass, who wants him for the works Opel-Lotus team but has F3 aspirations.'

Schumacher went out in Heat 7. 'There was soon mayhem [behind the leaders] as Andrew Guye-Johnson and Schumacher collided at Graham Hill Bend, the local driver running wide over the grass, while the German retired with a wheel hanging off.' That was 30 October. The same day Ayrton Senna, driving a Marlboro McLaren Honda, won his first World Championship at the Japanese Grand Prix. In this one paragraph you have the two extremes of motor racing, the very bottom rung and the very top: the interweaving was to come.

That autumn, too, Weber, a driver for two decades and now running the WTS team in Formula 3, offered Schumacher a test session at the Nürburgring. Kaufmann was there with 'my driver, Frank Biela. We'd done the German Formula 3 Championship with him and he finished third but actually he'd had a chance to win it. At the Nürburgring, Biela went round and for five or six laps the Reynard of the WTS team followed him with, I thought, their regular driver Frank Engstler in it. Yes, I thought it was Engstler with the Alfa engine, though that seemed strange because Engstler wasn't that quick in

Formula 3, always one and half, two seconds slower than Biela. I didn't know it was Schumacher driving the Reynard...

'Biela stopped and asked me, "What times did I do?" We showed him the lap times and he said, "These cannot be correct because Schumacher was constantly right behind me. How?" I said, "Well, your times are correct and because he was right behind you he must have been doing the same times." And that was the first time Schumacher had driven a Formula 3 car, you know. I couldn't believe what I was seeing. He didn't have any experience and he could stay with Biela.

'Like the Formula Ford at Salzburg, it was not normal that after only 10 or 15 laps in an F3 car you do the same times as a driver like Biela – and the times Biela did were good. Biela was habitually amongst the first three in the races and he led a European round against Gianni Morbidelli and the rest.'

Schumacher remembers that 'after 20 laps I was faster than Engstler, I was faster by two seconds, so they made me sign a contract immediately.' Weber would become Schumacher's manager and mentor, forming a strong partnership. They'd contest German Formula 3 in 1989 and Schumacher could bid farewell to Formula Koenig and those he'd raced in it.

I quote from Formula Koenig's programme notes before the decisive Hockenheim race: 'The first year shows quite clearly that this "new blood" formula has a place in motor racing. It has established itself by finding Michael Schumacher and Helmut Schwitalla. That you can go straight from it to Formula Ford 1600 or the Opel Lotus Challenge is clear because Schumacher also won in Formula Ford.

'Only once has Schumacher been beaten in Formula Koenig, by the ex-mountain trials specialist Andy Baier when Baier raced like a man obsessed at Zolder. Schumacher's hardest opponent was the 24-year-old Schwitalla, also from kart racing, who was often rather wild at the beginning and sometimes had bad luck. Nevertheless he often got close to Schumacher and often enough finished only a few metres behind.

'Further drivers like Markus Hofmann, Kurt Gewinnus, Georg Hutter, as well as racers from karting like Thomas Kracht and Thomas Gellerman, played themselves to the fore and made life difficult for fast talents like Frank Kremer or the powerfully advancing Detlef Schmalgemeier. That's how it should be. Because the regulations and controls are so tight, everyone has the same chance and success has to be won on the track. The mixture of drivers who form "Koenig's children" increases the attraction.'

Hoecker says that 'the car used by Michael in Formula Koenig is still in my possession and has never been driven by anyone else but Michael.' Schumacher adds his own touching footnote by judging Formula Koenig the 'ideal entry class' because it was comparatively inexpensive and rewarded merit.

In 1989 Nigel Mansell came to partner Berger and soon enough would be called *Il Leone* – the lion. He won his first race for Ferrari, in Brazil, and priests in Modena came out to ring church bells. The mythology proclaims it happened thus, anyway, and surely it did. Mansell finished the season fourth, Berger seventh and going to McLaren. Alain Prost would be the next. He'd spent six lush seasons at McLaren winning three of his four world titles there but, as McLaren boss Ron Dennis sensed with great clarity, the attraction of being the tamer proved too strong.

The 20-year-old Schumacher moved up into German Formula 3 with Weber. They'd be together from this time on. It was a strong field, including two drivers destined for Grand Prix racing, Heinz-Harald Frentzen and Karl Wendlinger. The season finished in an agony of suspense: one point separated the winner – Wendlinger – from the two losers.

'I first met Michael in karting at Kerpen when I was 15 and he was 12,' Frentzen says. When he split up with his girlfriend

Corinna Betsch she moved in with Schumacher. 'I did the German Junior kart championships in 1981 and the next year I raced against Michael at Kerpen,' says Frentzen. 'He only did that one race and was what you might call a "guest starter". I didn't race against him again until Formula 3.'

'It is not right to say we grew up together,' says Otto Rensing, who'd also become a Formula 3 rival, 'although in one sense we did. I started karting in 1977 and I knew about Michael, I knew about the circuit at Kerpen that his parents ran. I live about 25 kilometres from there. I started at another circuit and won club races. The new circuit at Kerpen opened in 1978 or 1979 and I changed clubs and went there. That's when I got to know Michael. What was he like then? A "little giant" of the man who ran the circuit, his father. I was 17, he seven years younger. At one point I think I can say I was very successful in karting, the most successful in Germany, and I did that up to 24 when I started motor racing, so the last years of that I saw Michael growing up.'

Formula 3 is a major rung on the ladder and highly competitive. Kaufmann would run a driver called Michael Roppes, 'not at all bad but it was one of those years when you have a lot of good drivers. Schumacher was one of the best but Heinz-Harald Frentzen wasn't much slower, and you had Karl Wendlinger and Michael Bartels. All the season they were very close. Sometimes in Formula 3 you get an outstanding driver in a poor year and he wins everything and you can't be sure how good he really is. Sometimes you get four or five guys who can really handle a racing car and even if you finish second or third it could be better than winning it in another year.'

Schumacher, Bartels and a driver called Frank Schmickler drove Reynards, Wendlinger a Ralt, while Frentzen began in a Dallara.

Schumacher demonstrated his speed in two 1989 pre-season races at Hockenheim. Race one: he qualified third, 2m 20.05s against Schmickler's pole of 2m 14.03 but finished a strong second, Schmickler 18m 32.31s, Schumacher 18m 32.59s – and fastest lap. Race two: he qualified on the second row and won. The Championship, over 12 rounds, would be harder. I'm indebted to *Autosport*'s correspondent Wolfgang Schattling for the words which bring the races alive because, as Schumacher says about doing so well so quickly in Formula One, each race represented a gathering of experience.

Round 1, Hockenheim: front row, finishing third. 'Michael was immediately on the pace in F3,' Frentzen says.

Round 2, Nürburgring: third row, third. *Autosport* reported that 'the second round was deservedly won by Michael Bartels. The best start, however, was made by Victor Rosso, who came through from his sensational fourth grid position in his partly Russian financed Tark Aleco-Spiess. For eight laps the Argentinean managed to stay in the lead. At first he was followed by Frentzen, Schmickler, Bartels and Schumacher. Soon Frentzen's ill-handling Dallara was demoted to the back of this slipstreaming group and finally finished sixth.

'Bartels fought his way up to Rosso and outbraked him. He steadily pulled out his lead and came home more than three seconds ahead of a happy Rosso. Schmickler had an enormous high speed spin at the fifth-gear Veedol chicane when attacking Rosso on lap 10 (of 20). Although his Reynard was undamaged he could not get out of the wet grass, leaving third to Schumacher.'

Between the Nürburgring and the next round, the Avus circuit in Berlin, Schumacher wanted to take part in the Formula 3 support race at the Monaco Grand Prix but 'I was considered too inexperienced – and then the following year when I was in Group C [Sportscars] I was told I wasn't allowed to drive because I had too much experience!'

Round 3, Avus, twin carriageways of autobahn linked by loops next to the East German border in West Berlin: third row, third. *Autosport* reported that Wendlinger 'was the winner of a terrific slipstreaming battle. From the start, a group of six comprising Wolfgang Kaufmann (no relation to Josef), Schmickler, Schumacher, Frentzen, Frank Kramer and Wendlinger slipstreamed away from the rest of the field. The lead changed several times on every lap, with Kaufmann's Dallara and Frentzen's newly-acquired Reynard leading for most of the race. After poleman Schmickler had crashed out and Frentzen fallen back, a quartet consisting of Kramer, Wendlinger, Schumacher and Kaufmann remained to fight it out to the finish. They went into the last lap almost four abreast across the start-finish line. Wendlinger took the lead on the run to the last chicane ... somehow the foursome made it through to the finish.'

'That was an exciting year,' Frentzen says. 'At the beginning it was difficult. I had an uncompetitive Dallara and my season only really began after I got the Reynard and became competitive.'

Round 4, Brunn: fourth row, fifth.

Round 5, Zeltweg: pole, first, beating Frentzen (34m 57.803s against 35m 03.105s). Schumacher's pace 'spread the rest of the field'. A subtle undercurrent flowed at the lovely, pastoral Austrian circuit. Frentzen explains that 'the ONS [*Oberste Nationale Sportkommission*, equivalent to the British RAC] backed both Michael and I and they promised that if either of us won this race we'd get a test drive in a Formula One car. We were both perfectly well aware of that so we had a hard battle. He had more speed and I needed to gain a tenth of a second in the Bosch Kurve [a spoon-shaped right-hander at the back of the circuit].

'The tenth enabled me to close up on him after the exit. I took the shorter inside line – there were only two lines, the inside and the outside because the middle was very slippery. Michael came from the outside, closer and closer, we banged and I spun off but I managed to finish second. That was the first time we'd crashed. Sometimes he was quicker than me, sometimes he wasn't, but we had a good relationship, fighting but always fair.'

Round 6, Hockenheim: front row, Wendlinger pole (2m 12.46s against 2m 12.59s) but Frentzen won from Wendlinger, Schumacher third. His consistency, however, gave him the Championship lead with 98 points, Wendlinger and Frentzen 83, Bartels 82.

Round 7, Wunstorf: the third row, twelfth on aggregate because heavy rain stopped it, the track partly flooded, and a second part was run later. Schumacher 105, Frentzen 103, Wendlinger 98.

Round 8, Hockenheim: second row and out on lap 10 of 14, the water hose having failed. *Autosport* reported that 'pole position setter Frentzen made a blinding start followed by Schumacher ... but Schumacher spun at the Ostkurve and had to call it a day later on with overheating.' Frentzen 121, Wendlinger 118, Schumacher 105.

Round 9, Diepholz, an anti-clockwise airfield circuit near Bremen: second row, fourth. 'Schumacher closed up on the leading group after a disastrous start. On lap 10 he was fifth and the following lap he outbraked Peter Zakowski to take fourth.' Frentzen 141, Wendlinger 134, Bartels 124, Schumacher 120.

Round 10, Nürburgring: third row, fifth. Frentzen 153, Wendlinger 152, Schumacher 135, Bartels 130.

Round 11, Nürburgring: pole, beating Kaufmann by almost ten seconds. *Autosport* reported that 'Schumacher kept his Championship hopes alive with a lights-to-flag win. Championship protagonists Wendlinger, Frentzen and Bartels were involved in a first corner crash when Bartels pushed Frentzen from behind, sending him into a wild spin. Schumacher was in a secure lead after the first lap.'

Frentzen remembers the crash. 'I'd made a good start and gained two places, that is to say Schumacher led, then me, then

Bartels, who came into the back of me and pushed me off. Going into the race I'd been leading the Championship too.' Wendlinger 164, Schumacher 154, Frentzen 153, Bartels 130 and out of it.

Round 12, Hockenheim, and a tight finish – only 10 of the 12 rounds counted, a driver dropping his lowest scores after that. It meant Wendlinger must finish higher than seventh to score points, Frentzen higher than 11th, Schumacher higher than 12th. But the permutations resolved themselves into a simplicity. If Wendlinger finished third he had the Championship regardless. Schumacher and Frentzen had to think in terms of winning and hoping. 'So we go to the last race,' Frentzen says, 'and Bartels has no chance of the Championship. It had become a battle between Schumacher, Wendlinger and me. It was all a little bit nervous – Karl was certainly a little bit nervous. It was very difficult for him but we were all under different pressures.' Grid:

Frentzen	
1:01.61	Schumacher
	1:01.62
Zakowski	
1:01.77	Bartels
	1:01.90
Werner	
1:01.91	Wendlinger
	1:01.97

'I had the pole,' Frentzen says, 'and it was right for me because if the race finished in grid order I was champion.' Bartels made the best start, reports *Autosport*. Frentzen, Schumacher, Zakowski, Marco Werner, Kaufmann and Wendlinger 'tucked in behind on the run to the first corner. When the long train of cars had entered the stadium section there was drama as Wendlinger had a coming together with Kaufmann. Both continued at the tail of the field. Up front Bartels and Frentzen were already in a race of their own, steadily pulling away from Schumacher, Zakowski and Werner. Frentzen desperately tried to get close enough to Bartels for a successful attack but every time he had put the nose of his Reynard under Bartels' wing, Bartels put some breathing space between himself and Frentzen.'

Frentzen remembers that. 'The race was on the small Hockenheim club circuit, very difficult to overtake. Bartels did make a fast start from the second row and I *had* to overtake. For a long, long time I tried but it proved impossible. I drove knowing that if I didn't overtake Bartels, Karl was champion.'

Autosport reported that 'in the meantime Wendlinger had charged through to ninth but then had another "off" trying to pass Kramer's Opel-powered Schubel Reynard. He had to settle for a minor placing (14th) which nonetheless secured him the title'.

Bartels	36m 55.00
Frentzen	36m 56.93
Schumacher	37m 07.41

This translated to Wendlinger 164, Frentzen and Schumacher 163. 'I'd lost the Championship but I had many plans that day,' Frentzen says, 'so I was motivated towards the next step of my career. I was disappointed of course but I was thinking only of the future.'

A hard season. Bartels says that the leading four didn't socialise because the racing was so serious. 'I won most races [three, the same as Frentzen; Wendlinger and Schumacher two] but I had the most crashes. We were all young, all a little crazy. We always drove with a knife in our mouth.'

(Amusing what-might-have-been: Albert Hamper wanted to run Schumacher at the Formula Ford 1600 Festival at Brands Hatch. Schumacher wanted to drive in it, but as Hamper says,

'They wouldn't let him because he'd been in Formula 3 – so he never did drive for me, even once.')

In November, Schumacher took the Reynard to Macau, a Formula 3 race of prestige run over two heats. Here he'd meet international competition, the ambitious among them eyeing Formula One itself, including McNish with a Ralt Mugen-Honda. 'This was the first time I'd raced against Schumacher since karts although, because I had raced him, I'd watched his career and his rise through Formula Koenig and German F3 when he finished joint second to Wendlinger.

'I can't remember speaking to him at Macau. To be honest, Macau was quite a different sort of event because I was racing with Theodore, we used separate garages and we stayed at Teddy Yipp's hotel. [Yipp, a benefactor of the event, had taken Theodore into Formula One in the 1980s.] We tended not to be with the other drivers at many stages.'

On the first day Schumacher qualified seventh, doing three hot laps and then plunging off. 'I like the circuit,' he said, 'but it's not easy. Next time I must wake up.' He improved to sixth next day.

In the first heat, McNish says, 'I was in it for a period of 100 yards or so. Otto Rensing crashed at the first corner.' A Swede, Rickard Rydell, struck Rensing, McNish struck Rydell, Eddie Irvine struck McNish, and the crash rippled on back. The heat stopped. At the re-start Frentzen took the lead and forced out a 2.14 second gap to Paul Stewart by lap 1 before Schumacher took Stewart by diving past him. Frentzen hit a wall but struggled forward, evidently 'delaying and blocking' as Schumacher tried to lap him. Later David Brabham advanced on Schumacher who – and here is a glimpse of the future – increased his pace in a controlled way and won by 2.79 seconds. Schumacher led the second heat from Julian Bailey but Bailey took him. Schumacher drifted back and stopped with mechanical problems.

'Yes, I beat him at Macau,' Bailey says, 'and obviously he was good but I remember two things. We'd do the qualifying and then he'd go off and play tennis for four or five hours, keep on until late at night for his fitness. He was the fittest then, and in Formula One he's the fittest now. As a driver he was on the limit and you could see the car was alive, the back end working. That is a sign of supreme confidence. Senna could do the same, dance a car round a circuit. You see Alesi do it. Others seem to have their cars on railway lines, which isn't the same thing.'

And that was 1989, Schumacher's career moving in an entirely orthodox way, step by step.

In 1990 Prost, precise, prudent and driving a Barnard car of real capability, got as near to succeeding Scheckter as anyone. He conjured a wonderfully evocative phrase about winning at Ferrari – it produced 'a crisis of optimism'. He forced the Championship to the second last round in Japan, where he and Senna crashed. Mansell was fifth, and going back to Williams. Barnard was leaving, too.

That season everything changed for Schumacher. The man in charge of Mercedes motorsport, Jochen Neerpasch, introduced a junior drivers scheme in the World Sportscar Championship, hiring Frentzen, Wendlinger and Schumacher to (in turn) partner the mature and experienced Jochen Mass. Neerpasch left undisturbed the partnership in their other car, Jean-Louis Schlesser and Mauro Baldi.

Classically Schumacher ought to have gone to F3000, the last rung before Formula One. The Sportscars, called Group C, tended to be populated by three kinds of driver – the mature ones who'd done Formula One thank you, those never intending to go near Formula One, and those who temporarily couldn't get into Formula One.

Schumacher explores his reasoning at the time: 'The normal way is F3, F3000, F1, but it is not so easy to get a good car and a good team in F3000. My way is more safe. It's normal that only the top two drivers in F3000 get Formula One contracts but I can win races for Mercedes, which is important, and get paid. Then maybe Mercedes will go into Formula One.' Moreover a second season in German F3 could be threaded in with the sportscar races.

Frentzen chose a variation, combining Group C with F3000. 'I already had the chance to do F3000 for Camel Germany. I'd the budget and the sponsors and I wanted to do it.'

Mass charts the background: 'I knew Michael before Group C because at one stage I had an Opel Lotus team and I'd invited a number of drivers, he one of them. He refused it, saying, "No way am I ready yet". He was in Formula Ford then. The Opel Lotus would have been something new for him but he wouldn't do it because he didn't think he'd be able to do it justice. That's one of his strong points: he would not easily be persuaded to drive something in which he didn't feel comfortable. He was very open in admitting this was too fast for him. "I am not used to racing cars yet so I don't want to do it." I accepted that and I was impressed, absolutely. I thought it a very mature attitude. So we had Frentzen and Marco Werner, a German guy who did a lot of F3 and who was also very good. Anyway, that was the first time I'd had contact with Michael.

'Now, in Group C, I was given very little time to make up my mind whether I'd partner the three youngsters and it took me less than an hour to decide if I should do it or not. The idea was Neerpasch's. Mercedes took a big step in accommodating these youngsters. I was prepared to partner them – Schlesser didn't want to bother, Baldi didn't want to bother. I said, "OK, I'll do it." I judged it would be interesting, I liked the kids anyway and I had nothing particular to prove.

'If you're a kid and you come from F3 you want Formula One but you know that, to start with, it's out of the question unless you have a lot of money.' This does not mean sportscars need be a dead-end. They can be an alternative route although, as Mass says, 'nobody takes you to Formula One from sportscars because you are very quick. Something else needs to transpire: that you are *better*. Once, everyone scoffed at sportscar drivers, and suddenly people realised that the drivers weren't that bad, suddenly people believed. That was the chance Michael took and he was wise to take it. He thought a works contract with Mercedes had some value behind it.

'They partnered me as it fitted into their other racing schedules. In the beginning the three were approximately the same although it took them different numbers of laps to get there. The easiest in was Frentzen but Schumacher was the most analytical. Frentzen had an abundance of talent, probably more than the others, but his work capacity may not be the same as his analytical ability. I say may not. I don't want to beat him with a stick if he doesn't deserve it.

'He didn't make so many mistakes in German F3 and Schumacher also made his few mistakes. What I'm saying is that one guy – Schumacher – is maybe more focused than the other guy, maybe he feels he has to work harder. That's just the way Schumacher is. Maybe it's a subconscious reaction to his feeling of his own ability. Schumacher was an extremely good learner and he makes decisions, which is another strong point, whether they are right or wrong – usually right but sometimes wrong. If they are wrong he admits it but he also learns from it and he stamps them out. He doesn't repeat them.

'I helped the kids but I didn't say *don't do that again*. I didn't need to do much of that sort of thing. Their own abilities pretty much enabled them to see through the problems and find the answers. I always helped. I was always very open with them because there was no reason to hide anything and I never worked in a way of trying to gain an advantage by being a little more knowledgeable. I'd never deliberately have led them the wrong way. Actually it proved to be fun and you could see how these kids developed.'

Schumacher tested the Mercedes and 'sure, it had a lot more power than I was accustomed to but after six laps everything was all right. After 40 laps on the first test I was 0.2 of a second slower than Mass. The team was pleased. Frentzen was fast, too.'

Dave Price, race engineer, attended the test at Paul Ricard and 'it was bloody cold. The youngsters came and I was a bit sceptical of Schumacher. He's going to get into a 700 horsepower machine which weighed three times as much as a Formula 3 car with three times as much power. He wasn't smooth, he was all over the kerbs, spinning it – ragged. But they have to be that if they are to get their act together, if they are to find out how to do it. You could see that he had something, however.'

Frentzen says: 'We were immediately under pressure to beat each other because all three of us shared one car. Therefore no excuses. It was like holding a hand of cards but everybody could see the hand, everybody could read the hand. The telemetry told everything so we could study each other very well. We knew why Michael was quicker on one day, I was quicker on another day and Karl was quicker on a different day. It was a bit difficult between three young men. Michael and I had a better relationship than either of us had with Karl, who was always a quiet guy. He didn't want to speak, he didn't trust so much, he kept it inside himself.

'Group C was a big test for me, a real test, that's right. The three of us were quick because we were pushing from the beginning, pushing each other. We were really motivated. You had to be quick without using too much fuel and that proved another challenge, that was more tension. You knew you had to be quick so you gave it everything in some corners, tried to save the fuel in others or save it on the straights. You try different tactics, think more about your line when you're driving in such a way and that proved a further challenge to us.'

Wendlinger, like Frentzen, didn't do German Formula 3, but

Otto Rensing returned to it. Josef Kaufmann says 'everybody thought, "now Schumacher looks good to win the Championship," but in the first race at Zolder he made a bad mistake and spun. He damaged the car. Maybe that was inexperience.'

Schumacher had taken pole after, as a contemporary account puts it, 'a handful of laps, and then sat contented in the pits'. He made a 'peach' of a start to the race. *Autosport* reported that he was 'well clear by the first corner, into the chicane. Rensing dived inside [Peter] Zakowski for second, only to have his wings run over. As Rensing slowed, the field bunched up behind, and Schumacher and the undamaged Zakowski were more than five seconds clear of the pack by the end of the first lap.

'By lap 7 Schumacher was a clear six seconds ahead and looked totally unbeatable but going into Turn 2 the car understeered into the tyres and his race was run. Schumacher made his way back to the pits on foot, to be met by his Mercedes sportscar team-mate Jochen Mass. On the outside he kept his disappointment well hidden but he will obviously rue throwing away such a comfortable lead.' Wolfgang Kaufmann won, Rensing was ninth after a pit stop for repairs.

'I focused just on Michael during the season because he was the one to beat and nobody else; and it was the same for him the other way round,' Rensing says. 'Sometimes it felt very funny for me because we had a good relationship, we did workouts. At the circuits we raced for the Championship but away from them we did do things together and that was nice.

'He was a very high-level racing driver. He worked hard for it and he thought about racing all the time – as I did – but there were very few others like that. Michael thought about everything which could make him win. People said that about Senna as Senna grew up. Michael was exactly the same and, as I followed his career, I always said he was the one who would beat Senna.'

At Hockenheim, Schumacher took pole, Rensing on the fourth row. The race was stopped on the first lap when, in the wet, cars spun off like tops, Schumacher – leading – among them. He rotated over the kerbing and suffered minor damage, rejoining far back after a pit stop. Rensing worked his way up and won, Schumacher was 19th.

At the Nürburgring, Schumacher started from the rear of the grid, the car penalised for being 1.8kg underweight. He finished fifth after lively duelling which might have taken him to third; Rensing was second.

'I made a good start to the season,' Rensing says, 'but then I had problems, real problems, technical problems. I was in the lead at the Avus [the round after Hockenheim] and I fell off and Michael won. I took pole but it was tight [Rensing 1m 33.00s, Schumacher 1m 33.04]. I led, Michael running third, and my ignition failed: a part which in England would cost 50p.'

Two weeks after the Avus, Schumacher ought to have made his sportscar debut at the Sportscar World Championship at Silverstone, partnering Mass. In the Saturday untimed session Schumacher was travelling along the start-finish straight when the gearshift broke as he changed into fifth. He parked it on the infield by Copse, the mechanics sprinted there and did hasty repairs. Schumacher 'rammed' it into third and circled to the pits. Officials excluded the car from the race for work done 'outside the pits' and excluded Schumacher for circling with his seatbelts undone.

Schumacher offered atypically vehement views about that. 'They say I don't have seatbelts but I get into the car, start it, close the door, and then I close the seatbelts. Then I come to the pits and before I stop the car I open my seatbelts, and then I open the door and the guy can only see that the seatbelts are open then.'

In German Formula 3 at Wunstorf, Schumacher took pole, Rensing on the fifth row, and Schumacher won from Rensing.

'We couldn't work out exactly what the problem with my car was,' Rensing says, 'but it happened again here. I didn't fall off but the ignition didn't work properly either.'

Schumacher made his sportscar debut at Dijon, he and Mass qualifying on the second row. Mass says 'I remember clearly that first year at Dijon. In a Mercedes C11 the track was a difficult one and the car not particularly comfortable to drive. They were finicky. He was a bit slower than I was – maybe I was in better shape or stronger and I could manhandle the car more – but I could see how he was coming along.'

It was a hot raceday and the track offered little grip. Schumacher circled nicely at racing pace not using too much fuel, so that, after leading for three laps, he pitted and handed the car over to Mass with fuel to spare – so much so that Mass was able to turn up the turbo boost in the run for home. Schlesser and Baldi won, Mass and Schumacher under four seconds behind them after the 127 laps.

Reflecting, Schumacher says: 'It was only when I was 20 and went to Mercedes in their young driver squad that I said "Hey, maybe this is what you do for a living".'

At the Norisring in German Formula 3, Rensing took pole, Schumacher second row, and Rensing beat him, 39m 16.30s against 39m 23.48s; at Zeltweg Schumacher took pole, Rensing sixth row. Schumacher won, Rensing sixth. 'It was very bumpy,' Rensing says. Schumacher won Diepholz, Rensing third; Schumacher won the Nürburgring from Rensing (30m 55.99s against 30m 59.06s). Schumacher 123 points, Rensing 105.

Schumacher drove the Mercedes at the Nürburgring, although Mass put in the quick lap for a place on the front row alongside Schlesser and Baldi. In second qualifying *Autosport* reported that Schumacher went out on intermediate tyres 'just as the incessant drizzle turned to hard rain. On the first lap he lost it at the right-hander onto the fast sweeps behind the pits. The car pirouetted across the wet grass and thumped the barrier hard, with front and rear. Along the pit lane there were a few references to the junior team concept, but it was the first slip-up made by any of the talented threesome this year.'

Schumacher admitted the mistake. 'I pushed a little bit too much on the gas and I couldn't hold the car. There was a lot of damage.' In the race he and Mass ran strongly to be second.

The next German Formula 3 race was at ... the Nürburgring, where Schumacher could take the Championship. Qualifying:

Schumacher	Rensing
1:36.63	1:37.70

A wet afternoon. Schumacher led, but at the first corner he and Rensing touched. 'That put Michael in the mid-field,' Rensing says, 'but in the corner after that I spun because my front wing was bent. I had to let the whole field go past. I really "started" from the back. I knew that if I finished in front of Michael the Championship stayed open, if he stayed in front of me he won it.'

A struggle developed at the front, Schumacher on a charge up to fourth and challenging Kaufmann for third, Kramer hard on Schumacher and taking him on lap 14 (of 23). At the right-hand corner before the pit straight on the second to last lap Schumacher and Kaufmann tangled, but they kept on and hadn't lost any places. However, Rensing was up to fifth and because of the 'mayhem at the front' took Schumacher, who counter-attacked, spun, and finished fifth. Zakowski won from Kramer, then a gap to Kaufmann and Rensing. Subsequently Rensing was disqualified for reckless driving and overtaking under waved yellows. Schumacher had the Championship.

Rensing says that 'it was very close and afterwards we had the drama. They disqualified me for something which never happened. They complained about my water gauge or something, they blamed me for running over a marshal but this marshal never appeared. Then they said, "OK it was not a marshal but you passed under yellow flags". I still have the legal paperwork…'

Before the last round, Schumacher partnered Mass at the SWC in Mexico City. Late in the race it rained – Schumacher had done a blistering stint to take the lead – and Mass misjudged his pit stop, tiptoeing round in 4m 17s to regain the pits. By then the lead had passed to Schlesser and Baldi, and Baldi brought the car safely home. Some 30 minutes later it was disqualified for a refuelling offence. At the last stop they'd taken on 246.1 litres: 0.1 over the allowance. Mass and Schumacher had won…

The German Formula 3 season finished at Hockenheim. Among the entries:

'M Häkkinen   Marlboro West Surrey Racing Ralt RT34 Mugen'

Häkkinen won. 'That was the joke,' says Dick Bennetts, who ran the team. 'We'd gone to Imola and beaten 42 Italians in their Formula 3, and Graham Bogle of Marlboro Switzerland jokingly said "I want you at Hockenheim and I want you to be across the finishing line before anyone else comes on to the pit straight."

'Why did we go to Italy? Marlboro asked us if we could. I think they were getting flak. They were spending money in England but questions were being asked about the amount when they couldn't advertise on the cars [due to British tobacco advertising regulations]. Graham replied that the British Championships were the strongest and to prove that he paid us to do three rounds in Europe, at Imola, Hockenheim, and the French at Dijon.

'At Imola Mika stuck it on pole and won by seven seconds, then we went to Hockenheim and suffered dreadful problems, a misfire in the first 30-minute practice – and we'd the wrong ratios because we hadn't been to Hockenheim before. It was embarrassing, British Champions arriving at Hockenheim and something like 22nd quickest. I remember someone coming up to me and saying "you Brits are not as good as you think, are you?"'

Schumacher compounded that by going quickest.

'In first qualifying we jumped to sixth, still with a slight misfire, still with the wrong ratios and the chassis not handling the best,' Bennetts says. 'Overnight we took a long shot. We played around and got the gears right. We took all the electrics out of the spare car and put them into the race car. On the Saturday we sent Mika out with old tyres and he came round and gave us the thumbs-up – the misfire gone. He came into the pits and said, "The gears are good, the chassis is good, so bung a new set of tyres on." He stuck it on pole by a second.'

Häkkinen 2m 08.35s, Schumacher 2m 09.36s, Rensing 2m 10.19s.

'We didn't know Schumacher at this stage except that he had just won the German Formula 3 Championship. We'd heard of him but we hadn't seen him. I didn't speak to him, no, not really. Schumacher had done the 2:09, so I said to Mika, "Just bring your tyres in gently for a lap." He did that and went for it and we couldn't believe 2:08. A blinding lap...'

At the start Zakowski slotted into second place behind Häkkinen but fell back into Schumacher's clutches and Häkkinen hammered out such a lead that he reached the Stadium section – where the circuit uncoils between curved concrete grandstands before the start-finish line – 1.1 seconds before Schumacher. Rensing, who'd also overtaken Zakowski, ran third and took Schumacher on lap 3. You know what Schumacher did, don't you? Counter-attacked, retook Rensing next lap. None of this interfered with Häkkinen's stately and solitary progress to a new lap record and a 5.3 second victory over Schumacher, hobbled by a slow puncture in the closing laps. Rensing had been deep in Schumacher's slipstream but a rear wing mounting broke.

'I ran under Michael's gearbox [clinging close to him] and I did it with a broken rear wing,' Rensing says. 'The last four laps I had no rear wing.' That was third place.

The season culminated in Formula 3 races in Macau and Mount Fuji, Japan. Schumacher took his Reynard-Spiess VW and prepared to tackle Häkkinen again, not to mention Rensing – but Rensing hit a wall in qualifying, ending his meeting. Bennetts says, 'Because we had beaten Michael at Hockenheim, the story was that they were going to get us back at Macau.'

The qualifying was in two groups, Schumacher in the first, Häkkinen in the second. Schumacher did a 2m 22.00. 'I looked at my pit board and I couldn't believe the time. It didn't feel any quicker than the other laps and I didn't even get a tow.' Häkkinen countered with 2m 20.88.

The race was in two heats. 'We stuck it on pole,' Bennetts says, 'and won the first heat. From memory, when Mika crossed the line to begin the last lap he was like four and a half seconds in front of Schumacher and then he backed off and only won by around two and a half seconds [Häkkinen 35m 44.07, Schumacher 35m 46.73]. I gave him a bollocking for that. I said, "Why did you back off? The bigger the lead you take from heat one, the more of a cushion you have in heat two." "Ah," Mika said, "no problem." Typical Mika.'

Before the start of heat two Chinese dragons 'writhed and wriggled' on the grid to the beat of a drummer and firecrackers were set off. There were firecrackers in the race, too. At the start Schumacher hounded Häkkinen hard and between R Bend and Reservoir (the fast return section) surged through into the lead like a 'slingshot'.

As the race unfolded Häkkinen looked 'wild' at Fishermans and Reservoir and took the car dangerously close to the wall. Schumacher looked smooth. Häkkinen, however, was faster through the speed trap – readings taken at a specific point on the circuit – and the additional speed enabled him to squeeze Schumacher at each approach to the corner at the end of the straight.

'Mika made a mistake or he wasn't pushing, and Schumacher slipstreamed past him,' Bennetts says. 'I'd told him "as long as you sit within two and a half seconds of him you've won the race overall, don't take any risks". Apparently around the back he'd drop away to seven or eight car's lengths and then close up to Schumacher's gearbox. Schumacher told me this on the Monday after the race. He said, "Mika was playing with me." They came past and Mika was sitting one and a half seconds away, a good, comfortable distance, not any risk with the two and a half second cushion.

'Then the gap started to come to 0.9 of a second, then 0.8 of a second, then 0.6 of a second and, with only one lap to go, Mika was like 0.2 – right on his gearbox. I thought Mika would sit there and cross the line directly behind Schumacher. Then we heard a huge shout from the crowd...'

Autosport reported that Häkkinen was 'closer than ever before to Schumacher's gearbox as they rounded the right-hand kink past the pits. Then he pulled out to the right, to jink past Schumacher but Schumacher moved right a fraction to block him and Häkkinen clipped the rear of the Reynard, his Ralt then spearing left into the barrier and spinning across the track to retirement. A cry of shock rent the air. No one could believe what they had just witnessed. Häkkinen hopped from his car, then hurled his gloves at the ground in a display of titanic despair. Quite simply, he had cocked up.

'As a tearful Häkkinen wandered about in a daze, Schumacher whooped it up with the WTS Racing crew. "I think he was crazy," he grinned jubilantly. "Nobody takes anybody on the last lap. Not without a fight. I spent the whole race thinking he would win [overall] so I am even more delighted now."'

Bennetts says: 'Schumacher struck me as a very, very fit man, a very sharp driver, mentally alert and a nice guy. We were talking and I wanted to get his side of the story, and he said, "Of course I wasn't going to make it easy for Mika to pass me. It would have been good for him to finish second."'

Question. For a proud and confident young man to confess that the driver behind is so good he's playing with you stands as unusual, doesn't it?

'Yes,' Bennetts says, 'it does.'

Rensing judges that 'some people – how do you say it? – are lucky people, some people aren't lucky. Michael was lucky. I'll never forget him winning at Macau. I was in the hotel room watching the start of the second heat on TV and I said to someone, "Everyone talks of Häkkinen winning the race. He has the better car, he won the first heat by a distance but I bet Michael wins the race." It is a feeling, you know, a feeling about Michael. During the season I'd raced hard against him and early on I was in the lead but he's so strong he does give you a feeling...'

Schumacher dominated Fuji. 'We wrote the car off at Macau,' Bennetts says, 'and we had to build a new one. It had to be flown to Fuji and built in a hurry. It wouldn't handle, of course, and Schumacher walked off with a £20,000 bonus for winning both races. From memory, that was the year Schumacher was lucky. Steve Robertson [a Brit in a Ralt-Spiess VW] had a misfire and could have won Fuji.' Robertson and Schumacher contested the lead until the misfire.

'When Michael won the German Formula 3 Championship,' Josef Kaufmann says, 'the Reynard really was not the best car – and he won at Macau and Fuji with it, too. I am sure that that car was not good. Right after Schumacher stopped driving it you could see it was not good. I think in all the victories he had it was not the Reynard car, only Schumacher.'

Reflecting on the season Schumacher said that 'all the

lessons I learned in karting I used when I went through Formula Koenig and Formula Ford 1600. I could use my experience not to slide too much and so on. It was the same in Formula 3 and when I went into the Mercedes school with sportscars. There I learned a lot, too, about power, G-forces and power-braking. I was a lot quicker after this again.

'I was not used to this until I went to Mercedes and afterwards when I went back to Formula 3 I felt I could brake as late as possible and still have the car under control. I was used to speeds by then and it felt good. Driving the Mercedes you get another style and you can use *some* of this in Formula 3. It helps a lot, especially for finding the feel of the car and for using the tyres in the best way.

'I find the power of the Mercedes normal. Sometimes the team thinks I'm mad because I come in and say the engine isn't working properly when it is really. The best time is when you can use the big boost. It is so much fun. Driving with Jochen, Jean-Louis and Mauro has been fun, too, because they are so funny but serious in the race. I learned also, because I was working in a team which was in every respect like a Formula One team, a big team, the technology very advanced and the car quick; and there was pressure.'

Schattling, who covered German F3 for *Autosport*, reflects gently and perceptively. 'Could I see that he was outstanding? If you're talking about the 1989 season when he raced against Frentzen and Wendlinger, no, I couldn't. I saw good talent – he'd come straight from FF1600 and Koenig – but he didn't make a big impact that first year. I thought Frentzen was the quicker one despite the fact that he made more mistakes. Schumacher was more reliable. You knew that mostly he would finish in the top three.

'The second season, 1990, he was outstanding. He was mature, experienced, a young guy in Formula 3 with an old head. He knew what he wanted to do. If nothing happened he won the races. He learns quickly and he admits that. From 1989 to 1990 he'd gained a lot of experience and he used it. Once he has acquired the data he needs he uses that to the best effect.

'He was a shy, introverted guy. I spoke to him at the races, for sure, and it wasn't difficult. If you approached him he was quite open but he didn't come to you. He didn't make remarks except about what you'd asked him. He was very straightforward, he didn't get into discussions with you but told you his opinion and that was it.

'My first surprise was when I saw how quickly he went in the Group C car. He took a big step from Formula 3 into such a car and he outclassed the old, experienced drivers like Jochen Mass, Schlesser – they were looking foolish – and even Baldi. Jochen accepted early that Michael was outstanding. To go to Group C is an extremely unusual step for a young driver but Michael knew that with Mercedes he was on the right street, gaining all the experience you need in developing a car with the technicians.

'And it was the right street for him to develop quietly, not in the limelight of single-seater racing at the highest levels. The experience he gained from this helped him a lot in single-seater racing. He'd had a great opportunity to develop himself by driving these fast cars during the winter before he ever raced one. He had 5,000km of testing during the winter, most at the Paul Ricard circuit but also Jerez – testing, testing, testing.'

And learning, learning, learning.

We are now leaving German single-seaters. The career accelerates very quickly onto more familiar territory, and something else begins to happen. Schumacher will conjure masterstrokes – sudden, devastating – to exploit specific moments and, in time, he will conjure masterclasses to control whole races. I'll be using these two words throughout the book because they provide powerful evidence in the arguments of the final chapter.

Chapter 3

THE EXPLOSION

If you've won a Formula 3 Championship you don't stay to have another go, you move on. In the spring of 1991 Schumacher seemed to be moving full-time to Group C, where Mercedes paired him with Wendlinger and Mass with Schlesser.

Jean Alesi, of Sicilian extraction but French by upbringing (a heady combination), went to Ferrari to try and tame the Horse and was seventh in the Championship. Prost was fired. He'd been criticising Ferrari, something which only ever ends one way: the door is over there.

In Schumacher's first race, Suzuka, *Autosport* reported that 'with his tyres going off, Karl headed for the pits on lap 21, signalling the start of the first round of pit stops. Alas, a potentially good race fell apart in a matter of minutes. As Schumacher prepared to return in the C291, the fuel filter valve on the venting side failed to close properly, sending petrol onto the hot engine. There was a flash fire as the car left the pits, which grew more spectacular when Michael turned into the first corner, much to the consternation of spectators in the grandstand and the crew members viewing the pit TVs. Schumacher was urged to stop over the radio and he pulled off with the rear well ablaze, having to encourage some tardy marshals to direct their extinguishers properly.'

In the next race, Monza, the engine let go after 20 laps; in the following race, Silverstone, they finished second to Teo Fabi and

Derek Warwick (Jaguar); the race after that, Le Mans, they finished fifth, Schumacher setting fastest lap.

From this frankly mundane season Schumacher now moved towards a frenetic six weeks which astonished motor racing. He drove respectively a Ralt-Mugen, the Mercedes, and two different Formula One cars. The career exploded – no other word will do – and the fallout hurt some. It demands to be explored in great detail because what he did and how he did it opens a window onto so much that he achieved afterwards.

On 28 July he contested the Sugo All-Japan Formula 3000 race with the Ralt-Mugen (Sugo is a 2.3-mile circuit 180 miles from Tokyo; Ralt – in the guise of Ron Tauranac – built the car and Honda offshoot Mugen built the engine). He had not driven an F3000 race before. He came second in his qualifying group and ran fifth in the race, needing time to get past the Japanese driver Ukyo Katayama for fourth. He achieved this by overtaking Katayama on the *outside* at the first corner. A Swede, Thomas Danielsson, lay ahead and seemed able to hold Schumacher, but late in the race he suffered an engine misfire and, with the engine cutting out, Schumacher breezed into second with four laps to go. Ross Cheever, an American, won it with Schumacher more than ten seconds behind him.

'The race was crazy hard for me,' he said. 'It was the first time when I must give 100% for myself – sometimes over 100%. The car is not easy to drive. You have suddenly oversteer, suddenly understeer. The car is not really consistent.'

Shortly after that Mercedes tested at Diepholz. Josef Kaufmann 'spoke with Michael and I asked how it was, the race in Japan. He told me he'd had a very good chance to win but he couldn't overtake. He tried to overtake but he lost too much downforce, there were some extremely quick corners and he couldn't close up enough. Michael is like that, honest. He's a normal man, just a normal man with a big talent. If he won races he was happy and now when he wins Formula One races he is happy. He didn't change.'

Schumacher and Wendlinger contested the fifth round of the Sportscar World Championship at the Nürburgring. *Autosport* reported that 'Schumacher tried really hard to find a way by Baldi but he was to suffer from a problem which has blighted anyone who has chased a Peugeot this year. The 905, it seems, bears some resemblance to 007's Aston Martin, coating all followers with a screen full of Esso lubricant. Indeed, after just four laps it became so bad that Michael had to dive in for a clean-up, losing fifth place and 40 seconds in the process. Schumacher ran strongly to regain the lost ground but it became academic when he pitted after ten laps. It was a terminal engine fault caused by a failure in the throttle butterfly mechanism.'

Careful, knowing eyes watched Schumacher that day. They belonged to Eddie Jordan, then in the first season of running his own Formula One team, and nursing a problem. His driver Bertrand Gachot wouldn't be available for the Belgian Grand Prix at Spa a week after the Nürburgring. He'd had a disagreement with a London taxi driver, sprayed a canister of gas in his face and was headed for Brixton jail.

Ian Phillips, the Jordan commercial director, had already been taking steps to find an experienced driver to replace Gachot. He'd talked to Keke Rosberg, Warwick, and Johansson.

Eddie Jordan had been a driver of modest accomplishment in the junior formulae but when he founded his own team he was quickly successful and he accompanied that by managing drivers. He was a talent-hunter of rare intuition and reasoning. By 1991 he'd taken his team into Grand Prix racing and at the second race of that season – Brazil – he saw Willi Weber. 'I'd known him because we competed against each other in Formula 3 and I was always friendly with Gert Kramer, a Mercedes guy who spent some time telling me how fantastic this Schumacher was. I'd spoken to Dave Price, too. It was our theory always to have good information.'

Price, who'd been at Mercedes, can't remember exactly where the conversation took place 'although it was probably in Spain because I've a place there and Eddie has a place there. "What's he like?" "Bloody good." The conversation would have been as simple as that.' Price had 'great respect for Eddie' and how he went racing, how he found drivers. He and Jordan talked a lot.

More than that, Weber had been ringing Jordan in Spain telling him how quick Schumacher was.

Did Schumacher's performance at Sugo in F3000 sway Jordan? 'The Sugo thing? Michael was just a replacement there and he didn't do a particularly great job. That wasn't what turned me on to him. What did was what he'd done in Formula 3, his approach to racing, the way he went about things. I'd seen him in the Mercedes Junior Team. I'd spoken to Dave Price, I spoke to Neerpasch, and that's how it went.'

Jordan had consulted his team manager, Trevor Foster, and Foster pointed out how difficult it was to do well in Japan. Jordan inclined towards Rosberg because, as a former World Champion, he'd bring great credibility to the little team making its way into Grand Prix racing. 'Yes,' Foster said, 'but he's 43.' To which Jordan said, 'Is he? I thought he was about 38.'

At the Nürburgring, Jordan met Weber and Neerpasch and, as he said a little later, 'all the details were agreed.' Jordan rang Phillips, explained what he'd done and then Phillips rang Rosberg, Warwick, and Johansson to say Schumacher would be in the car. Rosberg said, 'Who?'

Eddie Jordan told me at the time: 'I'd always try and look at different angles but, of course, until then it was unknown that anyone would come into Formula One direct from a sportscar never having driven Formula One before. It was quite unusual to take someone directly out of Formula 3000 into Formula One (unless they'd done a lot of testing, say). Probably my closest friend in racing, Stefan Johansson, wanted the drive at Spa but, you know, in the history of Jordan we have always tried desperately to do something with the young drivers if they have passion and commitment and fire and absolute devotion to what they are trying to do. Following that theme we said, "OK, we'll go with Schumacher".'

Foster says: 'Well, we did the deal for Michael to drive the car in Spa at the Belgian Grand Prix and hopefully for the rest of the season. He came here to the Jordan factory one afternoon [the Tuesday] the week before Spa because it was the only chance we had to do a seat-fitting – remember, we'd very limited resources in those days, very limited number of engines. If we burst one before a race that was it, we were an engine down for the next race. We couldn't go to Cosworth and say, "Well, here's another £30,000, can we have a fresh engine?", because we didn't have it.'

The car designer, Gary Anderson, remembers that after the seat-fitting Schumacher sat on a bench and asked him how he should drive the car, what its strong and weak points were – Schumacher knew he ought to be maximising the strong points, ignoring the weak ones. That impressed Anderson. 'It's the right way to do it.'

Foster says that 'we made the seat and we said we'd give him 25, 30 laps on the South Circuit [half the Grand Prix circuit with a link section from Abbey curve across to Becketts] just to acclimatise himself to a Formula One car because he'd never been in one before. So we put him in there, I went through it all and he was very cool, very calm. I said, "Look, this is not the spare, it's your race car and as of this afternoon, when we finish bedding it all in and making sure the seat fits and everything else, it's going in the truck for Spa."'

Schumacher: 'Yeah, yeah, yeah, no problem.'

'So he got in the car and he had the pressure of never having been in one before, the pressure of the race coming very quickly

– it was the Tuesday – and the additional pressure of *don't damage it*. In those days we had a mechanical gearchange. It was very easy to over-rev the engine on the downshift or you missed a gear, and if you did the engine would have to come out. It wasn't a question of, "OK, we'll risk it." Cosworth monitored all that and if it happened it came out. End of story.

'Now obviously here was a young boy in the car, very easy for him to mis-shift first time. He did an installation lap, we checked it all out and I said to him, "Right, off you go, do a four or five lap run," and all the time we were repeating "This is the car and this is the engine you've got to use on Friday at Spa. Take your time because if we don't use this engine we haven't got one!"'

The dramatis personae: Schumacher in the car, Foster, Anderson, Phillips, three mechanics and Weber standing beside the Armco.

Anderson watched as Schumacher pulled away and began to accelerate. Anderson could see instantly that 'the car control, the finesse' was already there. As Schumacher completed his opening lap at speed he approached the little group at 150, 160mph – there was a kink and a chicane. Ordinarily, as Phillips says, drivers lifted off at the kink for the chicane but Schumacher came at them flat out. Instinctively they stepped backwards. Schumacher was gone into his second lap.

Foster says: 'Within three laps the brakes were glowing into the chicane, he was flicking it through and I remember to this day turning to Weber and saying. "We've got to call him in, slow him down by getting him out of the car!" He'd been immediately on the pace, immediately, like bomp-bomp-bomp. Three laps, there he was. No question of "I'll feel the brakes in because they're carbon brakes and I've never driven with them before," no, just bomp-bomp-bomp.'

Once Foster had told Weber this he said to Phillips, 'Go and ring Eddie in Spain and tell him we've found a star!' Phillips went off to do that – the factory was just across the road from the circuit.

Schumacher would say that 'the first three laps were quite impressive – in the impression they made on me – but then it was normal. Sure it was something special, but not over-special.'

They brought Schumacher in and, Foster says, 'Willi talked to him and came back and said. "Michael doesn't understand what the problem is. He's in control." Anyway, we did another three or four runs of five laps and it was a toy, it was just a toy, there was late braking, he was flicking it through – effortless, that's the word you would have to use: effortless. Yet the car looked loose, loose but in control. When he did overstep the mark it was an almost immediate correction – and not a single over-rev.'

Jordan had, naturally, been concerned that Schumacher actually knew Spa rather than having to learn it *and* cope with a Grand Prix car in race conditions at the same time. Weber assured Jordan that Schumacher had driven it plenty of times…

On the way to Spa, Weber and Schumacher discussed the fact that Jordan had been told Schumacher knew the circuit and they agreed that all would have to be confessed. Weber exited beautifully, telling Jordan he thought he meant Zolder!

'We went to Spa,' Foster says, 'and our other driver, Andrea de Cesaris, was a bit of a Spa specialist and knew the circuit well. Michael hadn't ever driven it. I asked Andrea to give Michael a couple of laps in a road car but Andrea was negotiating with Eddie for the next year's contract. Michael said, "No problem. I have a bike in the boot of my Mercedes, a fold-up bike which I've brought with me. I'll go round on my bike." He'd had the foresight to take a fold-up bike in the boot of his car to be able to go round the circuit. Didn't come and say to the team, "Have you got a bike I can use? Can I borrow a scooter? Can I use somebody else's hire car?" He'd thought coldly: what will I need when I get there?

'At the end of the first day we de-briefed and Andrea was going on about a couple of bumps on the very fast section into the Bus Stop – "Ah, it's very difficult, the car's very nervous there." Michael didn't say much, just sat there. Eventually I asked him, "Did you have the same problem, Michael?" He said. "Well, I did for a couple of laps but if you lift off the car becomes nervous," – it was one of those places which was marginal flat – "but then what I did was, I'd go through the first bump in fifth, then I hit sixth in the middle and I just left-foot brake. That calms it all down for the next corner." And Andrea didn't know that at all. Michael hadn't even mentioned it because for him it was totally natural.'

In free practice at Spa on that Friday, Schumacher covered a couple of exploratory laps, getting down to 2m 12.382; on his second run he covered six laps and got down to 1m 59.254; on his third run he covered five laps, warming up on the first and then:

1:59.511
1:59.265
1:58.318
1:57.333

The context of that is astonishing. He was already faster than other drivers would be in the session, including a driver with as much experience as Thierry Boutsen – a Belgian who knew Spa intimately. On his fourth run he covered three laps, warming up on the first and then:

1:57.593
1:57.654

On his fifth run he covered two laps, warming up on the first and then:

1:55.322

The context of that is equally astonishing. It put him 11th fastest *and in front of thrice World Champion Nelson Piquet*. Berger, quickest of all in the Marlboro McLaren Honda, did 1:50.343.

To familiarise himself with the car and the circuit, Schumacher covered 26 laps in first qualifying, quicker and quicker, climaxing with 1:51.071 on the 25th – provisionally eighth on the grid *and still in front of Piquet* (1:53.371).

Journalist Joe Saward wrote naughtily: 'Schumacher is not well known in F1. Even Eddie Jordan, that famous talent-spotter, seemed to be getting confused about his driver. "Where do you think Schneider will qualify then?" he asked on Thursday as he organised a sweepstake among British journalists on where Schumacher would qualify. In the end, everyone was wrong and, before long, clumps of German journalists were talking about "the best talent since Stefan Bellof". Eighth fastest in your first F1 qualifying session is quite an achievement, particularly if you have no real F1 experience and have never raced at Spa. As a result of Herr Schumacher, much of the other action on Friday was forgotten.'

Schumacher said: 'On the Friday I never tried Eau Rouge flat. I nearly braked, and firstly I took it in fifth gear, and then sixth. That was a problem, to get used to a part of the circuit like this where you can do it flat, but without experience you do it slowly and then step by step. With my first set of qualifiers I was just on my lap when Eric van de Poele went off and practice was stopped. The second time, I tried with the same set of tyres and Prost blocked my lap. He was starting his quick lap. I braked at my limit but he braked a little bit too early for me and there were only two possibilities: crash into him or use the escape road. I thought it better to use it…

'On my second set of qualifiers the time was not at the limit, not 100%, but maybe a really good 98%. I liked to take it easy because I wanted to qualify the car and not more. I didn't want to take any risks'.

On the Saturday, Schumacher got down to 1:51.212 (Piquet 1:50.540), worth the fourth row of the grid. In the Sunday morning warm up, Schumacher went an astonishing fourth quickest.

Patrese (Williams)	1:55.211
Mansell (Williams)	1:55.392
Senna (McLaren)	1:56.752
Schumacher	1:56.986

Riccardo Patrese, affable Italian, was at that point the only man to have won the World Karting Championship and reach Formula One. In the race Schumacher jumped the start – only slightly and understandable in the circumstances – but he burned the clutch and retired without completing the lap. Monza lay two weeks distant and what might Schumacher do there in the Jordan? The answer will never be known and the whole affair must be approached with caution.

After Spa, Schumacher tested the car at Silverstone, again on the South circuit, and did a lap of 54.4, faster than *it* had achieved before. Foster said, 'We were not running the optimum set-up for a really fast time so it was an impressive result.'

Because what followed is complex and occurred at racing speed, I set it out in chronological order, remembering that the Italian Grand Prix would be on Sunday, 8 September.

Eddie Jordan described the backdrop. 'A full contract was presented to Schumacher and his advisers on the Monday before Spa, following a meeting at the Nürburgring Group C race between Willi Weber, Jochen Neerpasch and me. All the details were agreed. Jordan Grand Prix had two letters of intent from Schumacher, one in German and one in English, which were signed before the Belgian Grand Prix and confirmed the intention to sign a full contract with the team prior to the Italian Grand Prix at Monza. This contract was to cover the remainder of the 1991 season, 1992, and 1993. There was a buy-out clause in 1993, and in 1994 Mercedes had the first option for his services.

'During the week before the Belgian Grand Prix, Mercedes Benz Competitions Director Jochen Neerpasch confirmed to the Jordan team by telephone that he was in agreement with the conditions and terms of the contract. He added that he would be at Silverstone with Schumacher at 11am on Monday, 2 September, to sign the contract.'

At one point at Spa, Jordan had noticed 'Neerpasch take Schumacher off for talks with people from IMG and I wondered why,' IMG being a powerful international company managing leading sportspeople.

Friday, 30 August. Neerpasch confirmed the meeting to Ian Phillips. Later, Neerpasch rang Eddie Jordan and asked if the meeting could be moved to London, but Jordan had a second, unrelated meeting that day with Cosworth and declined to go to London.

The weekend of Saturday, 31 August to Sunday, 1 September. Neerpasch telephoned Tom Walkinshaw, the team manager of Benetton, and Walkinshaw remembered him asking 'whether we had any interest in Schumacher for 1992. I was surprised. I thought he was committed to Jordan, so I said, "If he's not committed then I am interested in talking." I wanted to try him in the car. It was decided that he would have a run and we would negotiate something or not based on that.' The run would be at Silverstone on the Wednesday.

Monday, 2 September, morning. Jordan waited at his factory opposite Silverstone and the clock ticked to 11am. Neerpasch didn't come and neither did Schumacher. 'He was at Benetton having a seat-fitting,' Jordan said. 'When Jochen [Neerpasch] didn't turn up at the agreed time I'd chased round after him and had found him at IMG.' A further meeting was agreed, at the Jordan factory.

Monday, 5.40pm. The meeting began. 'When he [Neerpasch] turned up with Julian Jakobi from IMG instead of Michael and Willi I was surprised, and now I knew why. Michael wasn't allowed to attend. Neerpasch produced a contract and asked us to sign it. That was most unusual because it is usually a team's contract that is signed, not a driver's. In any case, the contract was all in Michael's name and made him responsible for the money, not Mercedes. We could never have signed that as it stood. The IMG contract needed some amendments and I didn't have a lawyer present. I hadn't thought I'd need one. We agreed to reconvene at 10am the next day.'

Monday, evening. Walkinshaw had 'a phone call from them [Neerpasch and Jakobi] saying they had been at Jordan and had failed to reach terms. Would we be interested? We got together late on Monday evening.' They agreed to meet again on the morrow.

Tuesday, 3 September. At 'almost exactly' the time for the 10am meeting at the Jordan factory, Eddie Jordan said that 'a fax arrived from Neerpasch saying that negotiations with Jordan were at an end. Neerpasch did not turn up.' The fax informed Jordan that all Mercedes' guarantees for Schumacher's sponsorship and contract had been withdrawn. Jordan received another fax, this one a legal document which Schumacher had signed, which informed the team that he would not be driving for them.

Walkinshaw and Neerpasch met. Walkinshaw said that it 'culminated in us making an agreement subject to the confirmation that Schumacher was free in all the areas that I wanted.'

Tuesday, afternoon. Walkinshaw attended a meeting of Midlands businessmen and then flew in his helicopter to Silverstone to talk to Jordan. 'I told him what was going on. Needless to say he was a bit excited. I said, "You must do whatever you think is right for you. I can only ask for all the guarantees [from Neerpasch] and I have to take those at face value. I cannot believe that a corporation like that [Mercedes] would make a statement to me that the guy was free if it wasn't the case. I signed him on the basis that he was free."'

Flavio Briatore, Benetton's Managing Director, met their number two driver, Roberto Moreno – who held a contract with the team to the end of the season – at Nice airport and fired him. Moreno decided to take recourse to the law 'to defend myself'.

Wednesday, 4 September. Schumacher tested the Benetton on the South circuit at Silverstone and in six laps got down to 54.6, after 30 down to 54.3, a fraction quicker than he'd done in the Jordan at his very first test. 'I was not surprised by his speed,' Walkinshaw said, 'but I thought he coped very well with all the pressure on him, in view of the fact that he's only 22.' Walkinshaw also said: 'Schumacher got in the car on Wednesday and we were happy with him. We signed on Wednesday afternoon.' He'd partner Piquet.

Thursday, 5 September. Jordan went to the High Court seeking an injunction to restrain Schumacher from driving for anybody else. It was refused. Walkinshaw said, 'I had no problem with Eddie applying to the court. He tried on several counts and the judge dismissed every one. I think there's been a lot of nonsense on this. The fact is that the fellow, for whatever reason, had no contract with Jordan. He was a free agent. How anyone can allow a talent like that to be walking around the paddock I don't know. That's their business. When we were informed of that we went about the proper way of securing him.'

While Jordan's application for an injunction was being heard the teams reached Monza for the Italian Grand Prix. Moreno defended himself by seeking an injunction in Milan that either he drove the second Benetton car or nobody did. It was upheld and the verdict reached the paddock at Monza at 6.30pm.

Someone described Moreno and Schumacher as 'tearful and confused'. Jordan said publicly: 'I want to stress that I hold no grudge whatever against Michael who is completely blameless in all this and just doing what he's told.'

Friday, 6 September. Lawyers moved to and fro among the motorhomes until 2.30am, when a compromise was hammered out, with the knowledge overhanging it that Jordan had obtained a waiver from FISA that they didn't have to nominate their second driver until 8am, no more than two hours before the opening untimed session. The compromise: Moreno secured $500,000 compensation from Benetton for an agreement not to enforce his injunction and Jordan got Moreno in place of Schumacher.

Neerpasch said, and natural justice demands that he be heard, 'Michael Schumacher signed an agreement with Eddie Jordan on the Thursday before Spa. It was an agreement to talk about an agreement. What he signed was a letter of intent. Eddie Jordan offered him the drive but he needed money. Mercedes-Benz agreed that money and asked for sponsor space. We talked with Eddie about the rest of the season and also the future, but only on condition that our money would guarantee a certain space on the car.

'I went to see Eddie Jordan on the Monday morning and we could not agree. A number of teams were interested in Michael and we went to Benetton. They wanted him and it is a straightforward deal. He is paid as a driver. I think the Jordan is a very good car for this year. There was no need to change. Michael wanted to stay with Jordan but Eddie would not agree with our requirements for sponsor space and wasn't prepared to discuss our contract. He wanted Michael to sign before Monza.'

Jordan, reflecting a couple of years later, said, 'I hope Michael realises what we did for him and I hope one day he'll recognise that publicly. That would be ... the right thing to do.'

In that Friday untimed session, 6 September:

| Schumacher (sixth) | 1:23.662 |
| Piquet (eleventh) | 1:24.146 |

After qualifying Schumacher was seventh, Piquet eighth, and in the race he finished fifth, Piquet sixth. His local newspaper, the *Kolner Stadt-Anzeiger*, hoisted the headline: 'Mansell wins but everyone's talking about Schumacher'. In Portugal he finished sixth (Piquet fifth) and at Autopolis, Japan, he and Wendlinger won the last round of the Sportscar Championship. In simple terms the end of the season comprised a sixth in the Spanish Grand Prix, a retirement in the Mercedes in Mexico City, a retirement in the Japanese Grand Prix, the win in the Mercedes at Autopolis, and a retirement in the Australian Grand Prix.

A footnote from Mass. 'It only took the kids one year and after that they were on a par with me and then quicker than me. Did that upset me? No. What I thought and what I said was they have to be quicker if there is something there. They have to be. I was happy for them, because if they'd been slower I'd have thought, "Jeez, they're not good enough".'

They were, especially Michael Schumacher. He would now prepare for Benetton, his first full season of Formula One and the 16-race slog. Karts, Koenig and FF1600, F3, F3000, and sportscars were already curling photos in the drawer of memory; and anyway, like so many modern drivers, Schumacher habitually looked forward not back. He had a lot to look forward to.

Chapter 4

A REMARKABLE YOUNG MAN

Diary of a season, part one – 1992 as the year happened, everything in the present tense. This is the young man exploring the complexities and complications of Grand Prix racing, and it led him to this conclusion: 'In one year Formula One can be so filled and so intensive it is more than the equivalent of five years for normal people.'

He flew to Johannesburg overnight suffering a minor irritation familiar to every long-distance passenger, 'someone next to me who seemed to have to get up and go for a walkabout nearly every two hours. That meant I did not get a lot of sleep.'

He spent a couple of days soaking up the sun, keeping fit and enjoying himself with his new team-mate, Martin Brundle, who'd joined from Brabham, Piquet having departed for IndyCars. 'Martin is probably not as keen on the water as I am, so it will be no surprise to learn that he took at least one unscheduled dip when he was not dressed for it – and I was! Of course, he tried to get his own back…'

The circuit of Kyalami had changed beyond recognition. The 'old', brandishing its fearsome, seemingly endless straight, lay among distant memories. The 'new' offered itself as custom-built in the modern style but it demanded that the drivers become familiar with it, hence an introductory session on the Thursday. 'I tried to spend at least two hours training on those days before we began driving. I liked to train at the same time of day as a qualifying session so my body gets used to it.'

Brundle, it seemed, could relaunch his career and of Schumacher he'd say 'he's ten years my junior and I wish I'd had his confidence at that age. He's a remarkable young man. He seems very fast but he hasn't got my experience. We're working well together because that's what Benetton needs but I'll have my hands full beating him. We're going to be pushing each other along. He'll want to beat me as I want to beat him – badly – but that must be constructive, not destructive.' On Brundle a merciless weight of comparison would fall.

On the Thursday Mansell made the Williams go decisively faster than Berger and Senna in the McLarens. Schumacher wasn't satisfied. 'We had a frustrating sort of day. The car felt very sensitive and lively, not the same as usual. Luckily the team were able to sort out the problem on Thursday night while Martin and I went out and enjoyed ourselves at the Heia Safari Ranch where the Zulu dancing was something special. We were both presented with Zulu spears! Willi [Weber] told me he had found a good use for it. He said he'd throw it after me when I came past the pits to make sure I was going fast enough.'

First qualifying settled, as it transpired, the whole season.

Mansell	1:15.57
Berger	1:16.67
Senna	1:16.81
Patrese	1:17.57
Schumacher	1:18.25
Brundle	1:19.88 (17th)

'I felt physically good in spite of the heat and the altitude. I knew my training would pay off and that I was really fit. I do not like to do any jogging because it shakes up my knees. Instead I do a lot of bicycle work and build up stamina.'

At the green light Mansell made a fast start and Patrese sliced between the McLarens, leaving Schumacher to move on Alesi. Berger was travelling comparatively slowly and Alesi thrust by, Schumacher thrust by. Schumacher tracked Alesi lap after lap, but 'it's a track where passing is difficult'. The field stretched, Mansell clear of Patrese, Patrese clear of Senna, Alesi and Schumacher together. Schumacher took Alesi on the 39th lap and ran fourth to the end. 'My only other trouble [apart from overtaking Alesi] was with my rip-off visors. I accidentally pulled three off at once and because Alesi's car was pumping out a lot of oil I found it difficult to see but this is the best result of my short Formula One career.'

He'd been to Mexico 'twice before and I knew what to expect. The least said about my feelings for Mexico City the better.' The irritations of travel aren't confined to aeroplanes, either, whether you're a Formula One driver or not. 'I always stay at the Fiesta Americana Hotel near the airport. When I arrived I was given a room with the runways on one side and loud music on the other so I had to change that straight away. Luckily I was able to get a quiet one.'

In first qualifying only Mansell went quicker (1:16.34 against 1:17.55), and although Patrese accelerated in the second session it still left Schumacher on the second row of the grid, Brundle alongside. Schumacher had outqualified Senna (sixth) for the first time. That must be tempered with the knowledge that 18 minutes into first qualifying Senna crashed at the dreaded Peraltada corner bruising his left leg and suffering shock. 'I had just gone on the track when it happened,' Schumacher says, 'and I saw it. In my opinion there is not enough run-off area and it is very dangerous because of the concrete wall.'

Senna recovered enough to do 16 laps in the second session, peaking at 1:18.79 while Schumacher improved to 1:17.29. Schumacher described the circuit as 'a challenge in a Formula

One car. I like it in one way because it is very different from all the others for the driver but you have to watch very carefully and it is very bumpy. I found it was also very slippery because so much of the track had a new surface, and altogether it is a dangerous place to drive.'

No containing Mansell in the race, Patrese following, then Senna, Brundle and Schumacher. On lap 2 Schumacher took Brundle – 'Martin pushed hard at the start but then he disappeared [engine overheating] and I began to have trouble with my front right tyre, but as soon as Berger started pushing I found I was able to go quickly enough to control his pace.' Because Senna dropped out on lap 12 Schumacher found a clear run to third place and the podium.

In Brazil Senna qualified third, Schumacher fifth, and at the green light Schumacher went hard left to a vacant part of the track, tucking in behind the Williamses. Senna responded instantly in the first corner, the left. 'I really felt very cross in the race and my anger was directed at Ayrton Senna, the three times World Champion, and I will tell you why,' Schumacher said. 'I'd made a really good start and got ahead of him but he came round the outside of me [they almost nudged] at the first corner. After that I was quicker but even though he was slower than me he chose to play around and I don't know what sort of game he thought he was playing. He braked in the slow corners where I could not overtake and then on the straight he accelerated and drove away. I was upset and it was not necessary.'

When Schumacher said this he was not perhaps aware that Senna drove like that for a reason. 'During the early stages of the race,' Senna said, 'my car suffered a serious and intermittent engine cut-out. The effect of this was totally unpredictable and could occur four or five times on one lap and/or not at all on the next. At times the cut-out was so bad that it felt as if I had applied the brakes. I continued with this problem, trying to cover it in the hope that it would eventually go away.'

Senna had already waved to Schumacher, signalling *I'm in trouble*, while he 'waited for the cut-out to go away. I raised my arm to warn drivers behind of my problem. The cut-out did not go away and was the reason behind my retirement.'

You can easily miss the undercurrents – nothing to do with a little argy-bargy (physical and verbal) between a couple of drivers that could be replicated at almost any time anywhere but the singular fact that Schumacher in his eighth race felt enough self-assurance to criticise the great Ayrton Senna da Silva. Few others dared, except those who held the shield of long experience. Schumacher could have been announcing *I fear no man, fear no reputation, I am what I am*.

Spain might have been nasty. Towards the end of first qualifying the Benetton snapped out of control approaching a right-hander. The back whipped round and the car went backwards off the circuit, lifted and rotated on the grey-gravel run-off area, ploughed into the wall shrouded in dust, struck the wall hard.

'I'd been trying different set-ups on my race car and T car [or spare; 'T' = training] in the morning and in the end I chose the spare. I preferred it. The problem arose when I tried to do one lap too many on the first set of tyres. My left rear blistered. We changed them over, putting the left on the right, for one more lap but it was too much. The rear left blistered again, I lost it and the car spun. It was my fault and at least I walked away unhurt. The car was not able to be repaired. This was annoying for me because I am sure I could have gone quicker.'

With the Saturday washed out Schumacher lined up alongside Mansell (pole). At the green Mansell and Patrese moved away fast, Alesi sneaking in front of Schumacher into Turn One. A wet race – 'the track so slippery I just could not find any grip or get going in the early stages.' He pursued Alesi for seven laps and made his move, placing the Benetton inside at a right-hander, Alesi turning in so that they almost touched. Schumacher held on. Mansell ticked off fastest lap and shed Patrese by lap 16.

Patrese went on lap 20, braking for a slower car at the quick chicane, losing downforce through the chicane and thumping the wall. Schumacher trailed Mansell by 22 seconds on lap 21 but rain fell. By lap 34 Schumacher had cut the lead to 15 seconds and kept on cutting until it reached 7.01. With 15 laps to go Schumacher loomed into view through the spray. 'I did not notice how near I got to Mansell until it was down below five seconds. I thought he must have spun or something but then he pulled away again, nothing I could do. I concentrated on finishing in the terrible conditions. During the last laps I tried to wave to get it stopped. It was a battle to try and stay on the circuit.' Mansell beat him by 23.91 seconds.

Imola caught Schumacher out. 'I made a mistake in the race and I had to pay for it. My fault, nobody else's, that's all there was to it but it bears out what I have been saying for a long time now about myself and what people have been forgetting. I am only 23, I have driven in less than a dozen Grands Prix and I am still learning. I am bound to make some mistakes and I hope people understand that. It is no surprise to me even though I try my best not to make them.

'All in all Imola taught me quite a lot. Grip and tyre wear are critical factors, just like engines and brakes, because it is a technical circuit and a very tough one. I found that the car handled a lot better on some corners than others on the Friday and I felt disappointed not to be better than fourth [behind Mansell, Senna, and Berger]. I suppose one of my most memorable moments came when I produced a complete 360-degree spin. I was trying too much.

'Saturday was even more difficult. We made various changes as we went along but none supplied the answers we were looking for in qualifying trim. At least I felt we were in good shape for the race. Martin made a good start and I was right with him on the opening laps when I made my mistake. I simply lost the car and it was damaged when I spun off.' The Benettons ran in tandem until Schumacher exited on lap 19.

Rosberg, World Champion in 1982, was an acute observer of everything about Formula One and I rang him to ask for an evaluation of Schumacher. Did Schumacher show signs of immaturity at Imola? 'No, not just there. He has destroyed four Benettons up to now – I don't mean engines, I mean cars. That is immaturity, but what we have to agree on is that the guy is phenomenal. That he is also immature is only logical.

'I want to look at it the other way around and say some of his performances are incredibly mature, like Spain in the rain. Bearing in mind the limited experience he has, to be immature is only natural and shouldn't surprise us. What does surprise me is how mature he is on occasions, in fact on several occasions.'

Brundle has said publicly that Schumacher is better now than Senna was at the same stage.

'Brundle has been talking about Senna now for the last 13 years. With all due respect to Martin how can he compare them? Senna didn't start in a Benetton, did he? Senna was in a bloody Toleman, so you tell me how you can make the comparison? You cannot. Looking back over all my years I judge that Schumacher is very good but [Gilles] Villeneuve was very good very quickly. On the other hand what I'd like to look at is who last got straight into a car which is capable of finishing in the top six all the time?

'OK, Villeneuve is the last one who did that, Alesi to a certain extent at Ferrari, but don't forget he had a season behind him with Tyrrell. But straight in with competitive machinery? Villeneuve. It didn't even happen to Prost, because McLaren had a miserable season in 1980. And if you do get a podium-finish car straight away as a young kid you get self-confidence.

In my day mechanics used to describe this as "he thinks he can walk on water", and that's the phenomenon you're seeing now.

'Therefore I absolutely don't want to take anything away from Schumacher. He's looking very, very brilliant, but to whom do you compare him? Senna didn't have the machinery at the start, as I've said, and anyway he's a phenomenon. You have to remember his 60 pole positions in different cars, which nobody can take away from him. In Senna's case we were never impressed with his maturity, were we? He made a million mistakes at the beginning but he was brilliantly quick.

'Schumacher often makes mistakes when they don't count except now at Imola where he made a mistake for which there is no excuse. Absolutely none. It was a bad, bad mistake. I hope the people around him will tell him that. He needs that to mature, to learn, to become even better. The problem with someone like Gilles, for instance, was that he was at Ferrari and when he went off nobody told him it was a mistake. The whole of Italy went *wow*. When he continued on three wheels [in the Dutch Grand Prix] they thought he was superhuman and that will never develop a racing driver.

'What Schumacher needed after Imola was a slap on the wrist. They should say, "My friend, you've now destroyed four chassis. In Barcelona you went off three times, in Imola you have spun during practice and you went off in the race."

'Mansell said very cleverly about a month ago in an interview – and I think it was very fitting – *the only thing Schumacher has to learn is how to drive slowly. Everything else he can do already.* And that's true.'

Your career was a struggle but you learned how to handle Formula One.

'Age also comes into that because he hasn't had time for the learning and it's difficult at that age to handle it all, isn't it? Tennis players probably have the same thing. You're into a big, big business and you're on top of it: big publicity, big pressures, big everything. I would say that all the responsibility rests in the first place with the individual himself but secondly with the people around him in his management. We have to remember the international media is already saying that his feet have lifted off the ground. We've seen this in everybody although probably less in Gilles than anybody else. His lift-off was only visible on the circuit. He was a really down-to-earth bloke who never walked three feet off the ground in the paddock, did he?

'Will the pressure swallow Schumacher? I had a similar discussion with Nigel Mansell a long time ago. I was very conscious that the biggest danger in racing – and I think Gilles taught me this lesson – is a kind of vanity. In '85 when I did that quick qualifying lap at Silverstone I was really mad with myself because it was totally unnecessary. OK, there was a goal, there was a 160-mile-an-hour barrier which I wanted to break for me. I wanted to demoralise the opposition, everything.

'In the same way I have to accept and understand Nigel on the Saturday at Imola last weekend and what he did in second qualifying [trying to beat his own provisional pole lap in first qualifying] but then you look at it from the other side: is it so necessary? He went off, he spun, he was on to every kerb. Why? He was already on pole by a second, one whole second. Anybody could have given him a written guarantee that he wasn't going to lose pole. At that stage what clever team management should have done is give him full tanks and start doing race testing.

'Anyway, what we discussed is that the biggest risk in Grand Prix racing is you get carried away. You lift off because you can get to a point where you believe you can do anything with the car – and you can't, it's going to bite you. That was a risk with Gilles in the beginning: he started by going off and then he learned to calm it a little bit. It was a huge risk with Alesi when he joined Ferrari but that went fairly well because Prost was there to dampen him. It is a risk that we have with Schumacher now.

'You have to say about Michael that for his age and experience he performs very good interviews, he handles it well, but there's another pressure. More than any other country in Western Europe, Germany is so hungry for success because they haven't had it for ages, if ever. I hope this pressure doesn't push him too far. I come back to the point: find me another successful driver since Villeneuve who has destroyed four cars in seven races. The risk of injuries starts being at a very high level, and he's had spins on top of that. It's time to de-tune the performance just a touch. A 23-year-old is braver than a 35-year-old. Mind you, Nigel is bloody brave for his age, isn't he? He's good value. And Nigel knows how to look after himself, Nigel knows you can get hurt.'

Monaco would be a particular test because Schumacher hadn't driven its tight geometry before. In the free practice he covered 29 laps, exploring and discovering. He spun at the Loews hairpin and might have been answering Rosberg, because he said, 'You find me a driver who can drive this track on the limit and not have any spins. It's that sort of place. I knew what to expect and that is why I came here early and spent a lot of time going around on a motorbike. I like to learn a circuit carefully, doing it in my own way. I am quite quick at doing this. I break the track down and learn it in sections. For Monaco I had five different parts to learn and I think I did a pretty good job with them.' He expressed disappointment that on this Thursday he hadn't qualified higher than sixth.

'Having a rest day on Friday [Monaco is unique in that the meeting starts on the Thursday, with Friday free for R and R and/or promotional activity] was good because we had time to work on the cars and I went off for a relaxing day. I went for a drive up the Corniche to see the Cote d'Azur with my manager and Corinna. We were so hungry we stopped for a hamburger in Nice! There we were on the French Riviera surrounded by so many great restaurants and we ate a burger, but at least it was a very good one.'

In the race Schumacher ran fifth behind Alesi for 28 laps before Alesi went, gearbox. 'I chased after Patrese but I had the same problem with him. I could only hope for a mistake but he didn't make any.' Schumacher finished fourth, 39.29 seconds behind the winner, Senna.

Schumacher hadn't driven Montreal before. He qualified fifth and ran fifth behind Berger. 'I felt much quicker but I couldn't pass him in traffic and when the fuel load went down he seemed to run a little quicker than me.' Senna, leading, went to lap 38 when the engine cut. Patrese went to lap 44 when he lost sixth gear, then fifth and fourth. Brundle had taken Schumacher. Order: Berger, Brundle, Schumacher. It lasted only a lap – Brundle's transmission failed, Berger 8 seconds ahead of Schumacher. The hunt was on.

Despite gear-change problems Berger stayed in the 1:22s, Schumacher matching that but not bettering it. 'As the race went on I began to wonder about changing tyres but I didn't feel I had enough time in hand [over Alesi, third] so I stayed out to make sure of finishing second even though I had no grip.' He crossed the line 12.40 seconds after Berger. 'In the last ten laps I really didn't try to catch Gerhard because I wanted to finish second and even if I'd got close I knew I wouldn't have been able to pass him.' Maybe he was learning the last trick: to drive fast slowly...

At the green light at Magny-Cours Patrese wrenched his Williams clear of Mansell, Berger third, Senna fourth, Schumacher hustling in fifth. 'I made a bad start,' Senna said. 'Gerhard and I ended up side by side at the first corner. It was close but OK. I followed him down the straight, he braked very late so I was being careful.' This was approaching the Adelaide hairpin, a hard right. Schumacher tried the inside and punted Senna. 'Schumacher came and hit me from behind,' Senna said. 'I think he totally misjudged his speed and his braking point for that corner, considering it was the first lap. He could not stop and hit me on the right rear.'

'I tried to go past in the last part of the braking area,' Schumacher said, 'but he came in and I could not stop my car in time. We were very close and, almost inevitably, we touched. It was my fault. There was nothing I could do. I came in for repairs and rejoined.'

Rain fell, stopping the race after 20 laps but at the positions on lap 18. By then Schumacher had set fastest lap. 'I have never been worried too much by driving in the wet.' At the restart, and at the Adelaide hairpin again, Schumacher and Stefano Modena (Jordan) collided, Schumacher briefly airborne. 'It was so tight. I tried to pass Modena on the outside because I thought he was going to the inside, but he didn't. He came across and we touched wheels and that was it. I went off and I could do nothing about it, but I can have no complaints. That is what happens in motor racing.'

At Silverstone 'the crowds are absolutely incredible and there were so many autograph hunters everywhere you went. If I were to go outside the motorhome I would not be able to move and although I love to see people it is very difficult because I have to concentrate on my driving. It does make me sorry that I have to upset people in this way. I would like to give them some more but sadly I cannot because of the pressures. There was no problem learning the track as I had raced on it before in the Mercedes but it was a different experience in the Benetton, particularly the wind down Hangar straight.'

Schumacher qualified fourth on the Friday, falling back to seventh on the Saturday, but that was wet and the Friday times stood.

Mansell

Patrese

Senna

Schumacher

'There was some worry from the press that there would be problems between Senna and I following our crash at Magny-

Cours because we were starting on the same row of the grid. Senna and I get on far better now than before the incident and I have learned a lot since then, especially that a race cannot be won on the first corner. My attempt on Senna could have worked, of course, and people would have said that I was a great star because I outbraked Senna – but sadly it didn't.'

The British Grand Prix belonged entirely to Mansell and the nationalistic engulfing: when he'd won the crowd poured like a ragged conscript army on to the track with cars still going round. Who remembered Schumacher, fourth? 'The start was not too bad but not good enough because Martin was quicker. I passed him at Becketts but I was going too fast and went into the gravel and then over a kerb. When I got close to Senna I lost downforce and locked my front wheels twice but at least I didn't hit him. I stopped for tyres when I felt some vibrations and at the end I really felt I could pass Berger and I pushed hard. Luckily for me his engine blew on the last few corners and I passed him for fourth.'

Of the crowd invasion, Schumacher said, 'It was very dangerous. I was going flat out through to the start-finish line when I saw all the yellow flags. I thought there had been an accident off the circuit or something, then I saw all the people and I had to brake really hard. It was very frightening.'

Between Silverstone and the German Grand Prix ten teams tested at Hockenheim, McLaren and Benetton among them. Senna felt Schumacher balked him at one point, Schumacher felt Senna balked *him* at another point. Senna journeyed to the Benetton pit and 'grabbed me by the collar – probably to give me a little message'. A couple of McLaren mechanics, sensing trouble, followed Senna and dragged him off.

'It was a simple misunderstanding on the circuit,' Schumacher said. 'In fact it happened twice. Once it was his own misunderstanding and once it was mine. Afterwards he was very angry and he came to me and I was angry, too, but after a bit of a disagreement – it was almost a fight, but not quite – we were able to talk and sort it out. In my heart and my mind there is no problem between us any more.

'It all started after Brazil, really, and I was glad that after scrapping again we had time to sit down together and talk about it. I think our talk helped change his mind a bit and it also changed my mind. I don't want any more fights with anyone. People have suggested all sorts of things about my relationship with Ayrton simply because he made an impression on me when I was much younger. That, of course, was when I went to a kart race in Belgium where I saw him in action and he really was very impressive, but it is not true in any way that I then said I wanted to follow his career and emulate him or anything like that. I never made him my idol or chose to copy him. I saw him driving his kart and never saw him again until I was driving in Formula One.'

I fear no man, fear no reputation, I am what I am.

He faced Hockenheim, his first German Grand Prix and rampant nationalism himself. 'I guess I was feeling a bit more pressure in the build-up because it was my home Grand Prix but I don't think that this pressure has had any influence on my driving. One thing I have learned is that I need to have a better overview of all situations and to have a bit more control of everything in the job. It is in this that I am inexperienced and I need to learn.'

He qualified sixth and ran fifth behind Berger early on although he rattled a kerb at the first chicane, putting two wheels over it and digging dust. The car bucked and twitched and 'I think I damaged the oil radiator'. On lap 14 his long pursuit of Berger brought reward. Berger pitted for tyres and the order became Mansell, Senna, Schumacher, Patrese. Patrese attacked hard, crowding, probing, Schumacher resisting. Patrese drew level once, twice, thrice, but Schumacher held steady and held him off.

On lap 33 Patrese did get through at the chicane. 'Three or four times I locked up the right front wheel when I was in passing situations with Riccardo,' Schumacher said when he'd caught his breath. 'We had a great battle, you know, and I think we both enjoyed it.' By 'passing situations' Schumacher meant Patrese overtaking him! Patrese duelled with Senna but with a couple of laps to go spun off, opening the way for Schumacher to finish third. He hadn't expected that.

He reflected on his partnership with Brundle. 'In the last few races before Hockenheim I made a few mistakes, just as I said I would, but this was not due as some people have said to increased pressure from Martin. Where Martin is concerned I must say I do not feel particularly threatened or pressured in any way.

'I am still quicker than him in qualifying but I have to admit that in racing Martin is fantastic. He is doing a great job but for some reason he cannot do what he is doing during a race in a qualifying session. I don't know why and I don't think he does. We have a good relationship and it has been even better since his successes in Magny-Cours and at Silverstone [third, third]. It has made things more equal and he is more relaxed, as we both are.'

Hungary belonged to Mansell who by coming second won the World Championship. Schumacher ran fifth early on. 'I had been fighting with Martin for a few laps. I tried to go wide to overtake Gerhard Berger and I think Martin touched me. After that I lost my rear wing and I spun off.' That was lap 64, Schumacher third, and reaching towards the end of the long start-finish straight. The rear wing failed and was plucked violently into the air making the car undrivable. It rotated with a fury, smoke belching from all four wheels, skimmed on to the grass, belly-flopped across the gravel beyond the grass; and sank there.

Without labouring the point Schumacher had now constructed a sequence – fourth, third, third, second, retired, fourth, second, retired, fourth, third, retired – on circuits that either he'd never seen before or had never driven a Formula One car round before except Spain. In a sense the run-in to the end of 1992 – Belgium, Italy, Portugal, Japan, and Australia – would be at least familiar, and he liked Spa anyway, although 'when I arrived I had a funny sort of feeling. It is a circuit I do not know terribly well, having driven there for the first time only when I made my debut. Just as 1991, I rode my bike to the track. I even stayed at the same place and tried to stick to a similar routine but I had a very different feeling about everything. It was strange. I had a strong impression it might be one of those weekends for me. The feelings got stronger as the race came nearer and nearer. I don't know why. When I was in the motorhome before the race I had it in my mind that I might have my first victory – and the first by a German since Jochen Mass in 1975 – but I hardly dared to think hard about it.'

He'd qualified third behind Mansell and Senna but the logic suggested that Spa would embrace Mansell's Canon Williams Renault as eagerly as all the other circuits of 1992. The Belgian Grand Prix of 30 August proved a wonderful example of the illogical (and simultaneously Ayrton Senna's perception of the logical) as the weather taunted, teased and tantalised every driver.

Schumacher closed on Mansell in the Sunday morning warm-up: Mansell 1:55.40, Schumacher 1:56.57. In the motorhome Schumacher began to have the good feelings...

A dry start but Berger's clutch failed on the line. In the jostle to La Source hairpin Alesi, behind Schumacher, took the inside, elbowing Schumacher to mid-track while Senna angled across Mansell. The order exiting La Source: Senna, Mansell, Patrese, Alesi, Schumacher. Out in the country Häkkinen (Lotus) pressed Schumacher who pressed Alesi and took him. On lap 2 rain began, Mansell pressing Senna, moving through on the inside in the Blanchimont loop, and soon enough Patrese moved by too. The Williamses were poised to give a demonstration run.

Mansell led the race and led the rush for wet tyres on lap 3, Schumacher in a lap later. Senna stayed out because 'gambling on staying out on slicks was my only chance'. Order at lap 6, the stops completed: Senna, Alesi, Mansell, Johnny Herbert (Lotus), Patrese, Schumacher, Brundle. The rain fell harder, mist rising and gathering in the trees that hemmed the circuit. Alesi and Mansell nudged, letting Patrese into second place, Mansell third, Schumacher close in fourth. Senna's gamble failed and quickly, quickly, Mansell re-took Patrese, swallowed the gap to Senna. Mansell drew Patrese and both Benettons with him. Mansell flicked by Senna into the Bus Stop, the artificial 'chicane' before the start-finish line, and beyond Eau Rouge Patrese followed. Schumacher probed in the murk, Senna covering each move, but an inevitability hung over it. Schumacher went by, drawing Brundle with him. That was lap 13. Could Schumacher catch the Williamses?

'People had asked me about driving in the wet beforehand,' Schumacher said, 'and I thought back to Barcelona where I finished second behind Mansell in the heavy rain. Maybe I am lucky in the rain…'

He stalked Patrese and as the rain stopped the rush for dry tyres began, Schumacher pitting first. 'It was my decision to come in when the track was drying on the racing line. That was the most important part of the afternoon. It came after my only mistake [on lap 30] when I went wide and off at Stavelot. I missed the apex and when I turned in it was too late so I turned wide. I was lucky not to have an accident and go into the barrier. Martin got past me. I could see his tyres were blistered and that helped me make my decision to go immediately for new tyres.' Order at lap 31: Mansell, Patrese, Brundle, Schumacher – and only Schumacher on dries. 'Perfect timing,' Schumacher said. Brundle pitted that lap, Patrese on 32, Mansell on 33.

Schumacher's lap 32, at 1:59.82, was the fastest so far and it proved pivotal, Mansell still on wets, Schumacher now at racing speed and producing a difference of nearly eight seconds. When Mansell did pit Schumacher moved smoothly into the lead and as Mansell worked towards racing speed himself the gap stood at 5.7 seconds beginning lap 35 of the 44. On lap 36 the margin was shaved to 4.7 seconds. Schumacher responded by breaking the lap record (1:54.76, although Senna, sixth, promptly beat that, 1:54.74). Mansell shaved the gap again, to 3.0 on lap 39. Schumacher responded by re-breaking the lap record (1:53.79) and now Mansell suffered an electrical problem, the gap suddenly yawning to 15.0, the race settled provided that Schumacher could complete it.

Winning your first race is a compound of many factors, not least mastering the realisation in the final few laps that you are going to win it. Schumacher controlled that absolutely, the car felt 'better and better' and he'd done it, beating Mansell by well over half a minute.

'My only regret, if I have one, is that my mother was not there. She was at home in Germany. It was very special, too, because not only is Spa the track where I began my Formula One career but the circuit nearest my home at Kerpen. It's only 100 kilometres while Hockenheim is 250 so I always feel that Spa is like my home Grand Prix circuit. Perhaps that is why I felt so emotional. I could hardly believe it. I had tears in my eyes for the first time at Hockenheim but I have to admit I really did cry after Spa.'

In the Italian Grand Prix, Schumacher charged… from last place. 'I made a terrible start with too much wheelspin and I had an accident on the opening lap when I touched the rear wheel of Thierry Boutsen's Ligier. It meant I had to make a pit stop for a new nose at the end of the opening lap.' Here, using laps and positions, is the young man confronting and mastering an entirely new complication:

Lap 2: 25	Lap 9: 16	Lap 15: 9
Lap 5: 22	Lap 11: 15	Lap 18: 7
Lap 6: 20	Lap 12: 14	Lap 19: 6
Lap 7: 19	Lap 13: 11	Lap 27: 5
Lap 8: 18	Lap 14: 10	Lap 42: 4.

He reached third on lap 50, where he finished, behind Senna and Brundle. It made him second in the Championship: Mansell 98, Schumacher 47, Patrese and Senna 46. In the background much unravelled, Mansell leaving Williams for IndyCars, Honda withdrawing – exercising a direct bearing on McLaren and Senna – Brundle to be replaced by Patrese at Benetton, Prost returning to Williams. It suggested that Prost would be the man to beat in 1993, Schumacher the man to beat him.

Two days before Estoril Schumacher went karting at Kerpen. 'That shows you how much I like it. It helps to keep me sharp and, contrary to many people's views, I think it is a really good thing to do. I often kart during the season.'

Estoril? 'The engine cut out, leaving me to start from the back of the grid. I also picked up a puncture and a damaged nose wing when I ran across debris left behind after Riccardo Patrese's accident [Patrese struck Berger's McLaren as Berger slowed for the pit lane entrance]. At that time I had climbed up to seventh but the pit stop effectively ended my hopes of getting into the points.' He worked his way from tenth to seventh at the end, only the fourth time he hadn't been in the points across the 14 races thus far. The Japanese Grand Prix would be the fifth because the gearbox failed but he moved to a strong second place in Australia behind Berger.

Of the season, Schumacher said, 'The hardest thing has not been on the track but off it. I have had to work very hard to get used to all the pressure, the people, the media, the television all the time. The driving is no problem but the pressure increases. I feel I am getting more used to it and finding it better to cope with. The worrying point is that if I wanted to just sit alone in the paddock at a table in the sunshine to eat something I would not be able to. I would have to disappear and that is something I don't like to do. I feel I want to relax at times but that is not possible – that is partly why I have moved to Monte Carlo. In one year Formula One can be so filled and so intensive it is more than the equivalent of five years for normal people!'

How do you put Schumacher's driving into context in 1992, even hearing echoes of Rosberg and a podium-finishing car immediately? I'll confine myself to the era that Rosberg's words covered. This is what the drivers achieved in their first full seasons:

	Team	Year	Races	Points	Best finish	Points finishes
Villeneuve	Ferrari	1978	16	17	1	4
Prost	McLaren	1980	11	5	5	4
Mansell	Lotus	1981	13	8	3	3
Senna	Toleman	1984	14	13	2	6
Alesi	Tyrrell	1990	15	13	2	3
Schumacher	Benetton	1992	16	53	1	11

Accepting Rosberg's argument about the quality of the Benetton, you still have to do the races, bear the weight of expectation and deliver, and this at so many unfamiliar places. Great drivers tend not to tarry in securing their first victory. Villeneuve did it in Canada in 1978, his 19th race, Prost in France in 1981, his 19th, Senna in Portugal in 1985, his 16th. Mansell took until the European Grand Prix at Brands Hatch in 1985, his 72nd. Schumacher did it in 18.

And the merciless comparison? Schumacher third in the Championship with 53 points, Brundle sixth with 38 and leaving.

Brundle gave me a lengthy interview a couple of years on from 1992 and his words moved into several interrelated areas.

'I realised he was an exceptional talent and that there was no point in blowing my brains out over it. Anyone would struggle to keep up with him. I have felt for some time that he is the fastest out there and, even before Senna died [in 1994], I had become convinced that in terms of raw speed he was. He'd got his feet on the ground. He's refreshingly down-to-earth. He's got values, family values. He's close to his parents and does all he can to help his kid brother's racing. I've got a lot of time for him as a person and, as a driver, there is no limit to what he might achieve.

'I first met him in Group C when I was driving the Jaguar but I didn't know him very well. The only real time we spoke was when I lost ten minutes in the pits at Silverstone [in 1991 – a throttle cable broke]. I then drove back up through the field to finish third and I took three laps out of him. The other Jag won, he was second with Wendlinger and I was third. I drove the whole race [rather than use a co-driver] and when I told Michael he said, "You drove the whole race?" thinking maybe he could do the same himself. And that was it, the only recollection I have.

'Unless you're a Senna or someone like that you don't really pick your partner in Formula One. The partner may be a stranger. What always surprises me is when you get chatting to someone like Mika Häkkinen and you discuss other drivers they'll say, "Yes, well, when I raced against him in karts he did this and that, then when we got to Formula 3 he did this and that," and you realise some of these guys have known each other since they were 16 – because they've been racing against each other from that age. It's one aspect of being partners if they find themselves in a partnership. Whilst these people are not necessarily close to each other they've known each other's driving for a lot of years; but in the majority of cases you know very little about your partner other than his reputation.

'The relationship depends on the personalities and the chemistry and the contracts. Nothing revs you up more than when you can't get into the spare car because the other guy's got that in his contract, or if he starts getting the new bits, not you. It's a very competitive environment and different people react in positive or negative ways. I enjoy a good relationship with my team-mates because I think that in Formula One you might as well work together up until the green light, but other people thrive on the aggravation. From what I understand, Senna used to ignore his team-mates and that created a problem for them in their heads, and then of course he was so incredibly quick, which created a bigger problem for them.'

The real tension is that the only person you can compare yourself with is your team-mate, because he has the same equipment. True…?

'Michael was quoted recently in a French magazine as saying, "I could outqualify Brundle," – he did, 16 meetings out of 16 – "but in the races it was different." I rattled him away from the start of the races and during the races, which has always been my strong point. There's no doubt about it: in the first four races of the season I had two mechanical failures and I made two driver errors, and the driver errors were forced because I had a team-mate who could pull laps out of the bag which I couldn't do. But he couldn't necessarily pull a whole race out of the bag.

'He was a bit immature at the time and it was, "Oh, I'm a young man and you're an old man" [Brundle 33]. He was very rude in the early days but by mid-season I think he realised that he could learn a lot from me in many respects. We get on extremely well now and I think we got on well at the time once I'd come to terms with how fast he was. I hung on in there and worked on other aspects of my driving that I was good at. Benetton haven't found anybody since who could get remotely as near to him as I did.

'It's very difficult. Most drivers go trundling along in the belief that they are either the best in the world or potentially the best. If you are to achieve that goal you have to believe it. Then suddenly one day you have to accept that someone is blowing your doors off [blowing you away]. Some people recover from that situation, as I did, and in the next 12 races after the mechanical failures and the errors I outperformed him.'

Brundle says that while some do recover from finding themselves pitted against a quicker driver 'some other people just seem to collapse. It's a mind game. There are no bad drivers, there are no idiots, because you cannot drive those cars unless you are supremely skilled...'

Once upon a time the writer Eoin Young arrived after the start of a qualifying session and asked another writer, Denis Jenkinson, who was quick. 'They're all quick,' Jenkinson said. 'It's just that some are quicker than others.'

Martin Brundle chuckled when I recounted that to him, chuckled at the truth of it.

In 1992, Ferrari fielded three drivers: Alesi, Ivan Capelli – who got so lost, and felt so abandoned, that he began to doubt his own ability – and Nicola Larini. Alesi scored 18 points, Capelli 3. The total of 21 was their lowest since 1980 and stood in direct contrast to young Schumacher with 53.

Something else happened. Designer Barnard rejoined. 'It's a very long and difficult story,' he said. 'They had a car which was fairly disastrous but it wasn't just that. They'd been on a slope since 1991, cruised slowly downhill until they arrived at 1992 and asked me to go back. I was very nervous about that because I knew what could happen and I expressed it very clearly.' This was to Luca di Montezemolo, President of Ferrari. 'We had lots of meetings. I said, "Look, last time I was here I was in charge of everything and you can't run it from England, don't make that mistake again. If you want me back, let me set up a complete facility in England where I can design – and even build – a prototype. Then we can be working ahead. You need a team in Italy who can run the car and develop it." Harvey [Postlethwaite, himself a designer] was in Italy and they even arranged for Harvey and I to sit down and have a talk because there had been a lot of history between Harvey and myself the previous time I was at Ferrari. I said, "Look, you run the car, you develop it and I'm going to look down the road." That was the deal.'

In 1993 Berger returned to partner Alesi and they managed 28 points between them after what Barnard describes as 'a fairly horrendous year. These were the days of active suspension and we had been wildly left behind. It was "We've got to put an active suspension on there in next to no time" – which you couldn't do: horrendous trying to sort it out.'

Approaching the season Schumacher felt 'much better mentally prepared. This is what comes from a full year's experience of Formula One.' He felt the racing might be more open. 'Last year was quite boring, particularly for the spectators, with Nigel Mansell and Williams so far in front.' More open? Everybody mouths that incantation every newborn season, although when they mouth it most drivers are conforming to Oscar Wilde's description of a second marriage: a triumph of hope over experience. Not so in the case of Schumacher. The Championship itself did not seem beyond him, depending on Prost and the Williams and perhaps also depending on Prost's partner Damon Hill. McLaren had Ford engines (but not the state-of-the-art version in the Benettons) and Senna would only commit himself to the season race by race. Schumacher liked Patrese immediately, as so many others have, but on Patrese like Brundle before him a merciless weight of comparison would fall.

Diary of a season, part two – 1993 as the year happened, everything in the present tense. This is the young man consolidating because so many of the complexities and complications of Grand Prix racing are by now familiar: 'In the last year, since I had my first taste of these big crowds at

Hockenheim, I think I have mentally matured. I understand it all a lot better and I feel that everything in my own life is harmonious. I have no problems, no pressures, just motivations and ambitions.'

In South Africa he put the Benetton on the second row behind Prost and Senna, Patrese on row four. Senna led from Schumacher and Prost – Prost seeming in no particular hurry, a familiar tactic. Prost understood that races last a long time. He also understood that a 16-race season lasts a long time. Prost knew all about driving fast slowly. He moved prudently up to Schumacher and on lap 13 went by. 'Alain was quicker than me down the straight so it was only fair to let him overtake.' Prost jousted with Senna and, given their past, it wasn't for spectators of a nervous disposition. Prost got through safely enough and so did Schumacher who felt understandable elation at running second behind Prost. Not for long. Schumacher pitted at the same time as Senna who emerged quicker. Across the next 26 laps Schumacher hunted Senna. 'I struggled to overtake him, but at one point I felt the time was right. I went on the inside, touched his wheels and spun off.'

Of Brazil he said, 'I often find I cannot sleep at nights at tests, and sometimes at races, because my mind is running over the problems with the car. It was a little like that on Friday in Sao Paulo. I had been disappointed with our progress and woke up on Saturday with a new plan. It worked. Even Riccardo copied my set-up and we improved quite a bit.

'Fourth on the grid was not too bad and I felt pleased with my situation, particularly after I had passed Ayrton in the race [on lap 24 to take third place]. I did not want any further tangles with him after what happened in Brazil last year and at Kyalami, but then came the first pit stop. To say it was not quite as good as I would have liked would be a massive understatement. The car fell off the jack, which meant it was left lying on the concrete and it needed two mechanics to lift it for the tyre change. If that was not bad enough it was further complicated by problems in fixing the nut on the right front wheel.'

Schumacher emerged third but rain began and the pace car came out. 'I thought it was a good idea, but one which might have been timed a little more carefully. I'd have preferred to see it out a lap or two earlier when the track was very wet. My second pit stop, to change back from wets to dries, was trouble-free, but not long after that I was brought in for a 10-second time penalty.

'To be perfectly honest I had no idea what it was for until long after the race when it was explained to me that I had overtaken someone while under a yellow flag. I was not the only driver to suffer for this and, since I believe I was passing backmarkers at the time and they were easing off to allow me to lap them, I feel it was not the right decision. I know Ayrton had some very strong words to say about this [he'd been given ten seconds on lap 24 for the same 'offence'] and I do agree with him. After that I did not think I had any chance of a podium finish or even the points, but I set about fighting back.'

With seven laps left Schumacher reached Herbert – third – and 'had a great scrap. I got past him once, he re-passed me and I nearly spun off on some dirt. He is a very fair driver. The next lap I tried again and this time he spun and I went through to third place.'

'I saw him coming when he first caught me, yeah, yeah, yeah,' Herbert says. 'What did I think? If he wants to try up the inside or wherever, well, he can but I'm not going to give him any room and if he takes me I'll try and take him back immediately. I don't like drivers who do mega-weaving and I'm not a weaver at all. If I'm going to be lapped I'll move over but I'll always try and let them overtake at a place where I won't lose too much time. I'm still in the race, don't forget. If I can do a couple of corners with them behind I won't hold them up that badly and then I'll let them go.

'My thinking was: I'm going to get as tight as I can at the mid-corner so that at the exit I can re-take him. I lined that up before he tried to overtake because I knew he would try to overtake. You have to think like that beforehand. To the watcher it happens simultaneously but I believe you drive a Formula One car with your brain working much quicker than it normally does. I know that after, say, a qualifying session when I'm driving home I can go round corners miles quicker without even thinking about it because my brain is working at the Formula One pace…

'Anyway, I did re-take him and, ooooh yes, it was a great moment. I did nearly stop and cry [naughty chuckle]. It's a nice feeling to do that to someone like that and, in a way, you can laugh about it. *You don't get me that easy. Have another go.* You know he'll do it at some stage for sure. Michael is fair, he's not a weaver-weaver. He'll lean on you but he won't actually weave, and he won't give you the full push on to the grass.'

The European Grand Prix at Donington belonged entirely to Senna. Only Hill finished on the same lap. Schumacher rose briefly to fifth (twice) but 'when I was shifting down to third gear my wheel locked. I was running on slick tyres in wet conditions at the time, pushing right on the limit. I lost the car.'

At Imola, Schumacher's Friday qualifying time was taken from him because the team used 'evaluation' Goodyear tyres. 'I knew very little about this. I went off to play football in a charity match with a lot of other drivers. That was fun except I was kicked heavily on my left leg. By the time I arrived back at the paddock I was told my times had been disqualified. Neither I nor the team could believe it. All I'd done was use some B tyres, which I thought we were allowed to use. There was a lot of talking and the next day my time was reinstated. I was happy to see that FISA was big enough to admit a mistake and put it right.'

Schumacher put it right in second qualifying, third again. Heavy rain fell before the start of the race and he ran fourth having 'a great battle with some of the cars behind me'. That meant Berger (now Ferrari) and Wendlinger (Sauber), 'enjoyable because I know Karl so well since we'd been together at Mercedes. He was really pushing me at one stage.' Schumacher tracked Senna but Senna had a hydraulic failure. Prost beat Schumacher by 32.41 seconds.

At Imola McLaren put pressure on Ford to get the Series VII engines, or rather share them with Benetton. 'A lot has been said and written about this,' Schumacher commented, 'and I have been mentioned in some places as saying that I would like to see Ayrton Senna have the same equipment as me. That is not what I have said. I only said that if it is in the team's best interests to have an agreement with McLaren I would be happy to race against Ayrton on equal terms. That is something different. I think it would be crazy just to give away something like that.'

Senna 26 points, Prost 24, Hill 12, Schumacher 10.

In Spain he suffered 'terrible vibrations from the tyres from about half distance. This developed into a serious gearbox problem which went away when I changed tyres, but then came back with a vengeance later on. I could not use second gear properly.' He accommodated this problem and lapped in the 1:22s except lap 60 (of 65) when 'I came upon Zanardi [Lotus] as his engine blew. I could hardly see for the smoke and oil but I knew he was still on the line so I pulled out wide to pass him. It was nearly impossible. There was so much dirt and gravel that when I turned the steering wheel the car went straight on over the gravel bed. I was happy to keep the car on the road after that to finish third.'

Schumacher's move to Monaco was 'a logical decision for business reasons. I had lost my normal lifestyle in Germany. When I was at home I didn't really feel I was at home. I had so much work to do and there were always interruptions and demands on me. I had nothing to lose by moving and Monaco was the obvious place. I could go out and relax properly at last. No one recognised me or made any fuss.

'In Monaco I am able to work much better on my conditioning than I would be in Germany, particularly during the winter. I am a regular at the Loews gymnasium and often work out there with friends or other drivers, particularly Aguri Suzuki. Mostly Corinna and I lead a pretty quiet life as far as we can. It is home for us now, with all our things, each other and our dog. I am even in a friendly football team which meets to play regularly and I also play tennis and badminton.'

He got traction control and on the Saturday morning drove with and without it and estimated the difference as 1.2 seconds, specifically a best of 1:25.59 without, 1:22.20 with. He lined up on the front row alongside Prost who jumped the start and the subsequent stop-go penalty gave Schumacher the lead from Senna. By lap 32 he'd drawn that lead to 15 seconds but at the Loews hairpin 'I think I had a failure on the active suspension system. I jumped out as it caught fire. There was smoke billowing everywhere and it looked quite spectacular.'

Before Canada he took a five-day holiday in Nassau then Florida. 'While in Nassau I even started reading a book, which is unheard of for me, and I completed it in one go. I quickly started another one and in two weeks I think I read more books than in the rest of my life! The books were called *The Company* and *The Judge*, by John Grisham.

'After my break in Nassau – where the beaches were beautiful but the food not so good – I went to Orlando to visit Disney World. It was fantastic. We went to see the Magic Kingdom, but Riccardo told me afterwards that we missed some even better places to visit. Unfortunately the food in the Bahamas was a problem for me because it was entirely different from what I need for my conditioning and fitness routine. I could not get my work done in the gym after eating hotdogs and cheeseburgers so I was glad to get to Orlando. The first thing I wanted to do was go to a German place and eat some proper food, and with my food a shandy.

'I felt happy to have found somewhere like this but the waiter, instead of taking my order, asked for my passport. I said, "Why?" He said, "You need to have a passport here to prove you are over 21 if you are ordering an alcoholic drink." I argued with him but I didn't have my passport with me. To make matters worse the guy was German too! This upset me the most, I think. A typical German with his rules. So I didn't get my beer and had to ask for alcohol-free beer, but he would not let me have this either because, he said, it had 1% of alcohol in it. I had apple juice with mineral water in the end.'

The start in Canada 'went terribly wrong', a problem with the traction control adjustment. He nearly stalled twice, was briefly engulfed – both Ferraris through – and in the left-spoon-right corners after the start-finish straight Senna rode the kerbing inside and they ran side by side, wheels twitching together. Senna moved ahead. 'Obviously,' Schumacher said, 'I had a big fight on my hands to make up the lost ground.' He enjoyed himself, 'particularly the fight with Ayrton towards the end. Then on lap 63 quite suddenly he began to slow down for a reason which I later learned was alternator failure. I don't think he could see me very well and we almost touched as I went around him at the entry to the hairpin.'

Senna said that 'the car suddenly started cutting out and I was so concerned about it that I didn't see Schumacher coming on the outside. I am sorry that we touched.'

Touched? Almost touched? Never mind.

Schumacher finished 14.52 seconds behind Prost.

In France, running fourth behind Senna, he made a second pit stop on lap 45 and set fastest lap two laps later. Senna said, 'I didn't change tyres for the second time because we felt it was best to wait and see what kind of pit stop Schumacher might have. Had it been a slow one I'd have come in, but lack of power didn't allow me to go in, be overtaken and then try to get back in front of Schumacher.' Order: Prost, Hill, Senna, Schumacher, Brundle. By lap 58 Schumacher caught Senna and five laps later went by, Senna visibly slowing. The race ended like that.

Schumacher changed apartments in Monaco. 'I have just moved out of my old apartment to a new one which is bigger but still rented. I know you think we drivers all earn vast sums but I don't have enough money to buy an apartment down there, I can tell you. In fact if my landlady had not put up the rent when I was hoping to talk it down I guess I might not have moved, but she increased it.'

A knee problem recurred. 'Unfortunately it is no better than it was. It felt particularly bad at Magny-Cours because I went running twice. I tried to do a long distance on my bike in training [at Monte Carlo] but I really suffered afterwards. I went to a museum with Corinna and her parents but I couldn't stay. I felt I had the knees of an old man.'

By now he regularly outqualified the McLarens and did so again in Britain but on the Saturday went off at Copse: 'Too much oversteer. I could handle it this morning but the wind direction changed this afternoon and the car just got away from me. I have to mention my team-mate and friend Riccardo Patrese. He was very generous and helpful. When I lost my car at Copse I knew Riccardo would let me have his. I felt very motivated. I could not have gone any faster.' Patrese fashioned a best of 1:22.364, but in three laps near the end in the same car Schumacher probed then accelerated from 1:32.362 to 1:20.865 to 1:20.401. Hill led the race until his engine blew and Prost stroked the Williams home for his 50th victory, Schumacher 7.660 seconds behind.

In Germany he rode the clamour and might have had provisional pole, 1:39.64 against Prost's 1:39.04, but to hold Hill in the second session would be difficult and he couldn't. Just before the race he switched to the spare because the race car 'had been jumping around a bit and I did not know why'. Deep into the race Hill led, then Prost, then Schumacher. 'I did not think I had much chance of overtaking him and I knew the first set of new tyres after the change had been worth two or three seconds a lap. It was almost an ideal race. When I was running about five seconds behind Prost towards the end I thought about making a second stop for tyres and decided it was best to talk to the team first. We decided to change again. It did not quite work out properly and I heard a strange noise in the car over the final eight laps. That made me decide to ease off and change gear earlier to preserve the engine and gearbox.'

Hill went out on lap 43 when a tyre exploded so that Prost scooped up the Grand Prix, Schumacher slowing to 16.66 seconds behind. The crowd adored it. 'I was as delighted for the crowd as for myself because there were 148,000 there on Sunday. I thought it was the best crowd I had ever seen and they were my motivation all weekend. Some people ask me if the crowd and the media attention at your home Grand Prix builds up the pressure and makes life more difficult. For me it is not that way at all, although I did get a bit tired of being stuck in the traffic and crowded in by people every morning as I came into the circuit.

'In the last year, since I had my first taste of these big crowds at Hockenheim, I think I have mentally matured. I understand it all a lot better and I feel that everything in my own life is harmonious. I have no problems, no pressures, just motivations and ambitions. I knew the crowd was there to see a German driver do well and I did my best. I felt that my mental self, my physical self and my driver self were together in harmony. We held a Press Conference earlier in the week and had invited 95 German journalists. I was amazed when 150 turned up.'

In Hungary he made a slow start and ran wide at Turn One, three cars going through. Out of Turn One into the short snap-right/snap-left Alesi moved inside. At the start of lap two Schumacher powered past Patrese at the end of the long straight and went for Berger, danced all over the back of him and at Turn One went outside, the car wobbling under the impetus. He caught that but almost immediately was on to the grass. 'After pushing hard I spun when the rear wheels locked up as I went down to second gear.' He churned the wheels and regained the track from a cloud of dust, tenth: burn from the stern but on lap 27 the fuel pump failed.

In Belgium he dismissed the fact that he was a second and a half slower than Prost, pole: 'We're quicker than McLaren and Ferrari and these are big names but the Williams is the one we are measuring ourselves against.' At the green 'I released the clutch and the revs were not there. I had only 2,000 to 3,000, enough to keep the engine going but not much else. I tried to get the revs back up but I couldn't. It was like starting a road car in sixth gear, very difficult indeed.' As Prost, leading, reached La Source Schumacher lay tenth. 'I stopped early for tyres,' Senna said, 'because I felt that would give me the best chance to fight with Schumacher.'

As Senna pitted – 7.11 seconds stationary – Schumacher passed, third. It had been 'especially difficult to get past Ayrton. He was a real problem. The team made a good decision to bring me in early [the lap before Senna] but I still found Senna difficult to pass and I thought he caused me some unnecessary problems. When I arrived at La Source after he came out of the pits he went straight out ahead of me and then to the left. I don't know why he did it. I nearly crashed into him and I would have done if I had not pulled right off and nearly on to the grass. It was not nice driving by him at all and I was not impressed.'

It settled Hill, Prost, Schumacher, settled to a lovely racing situation: Hill clear of Prost, Schumacher right on Prost. At Les Combes, a favourite overtaking place, Schumacher drew alongside, kept the power on and as the right corner loomed he stabbed the brakes, brought smoke from the tyres. He was through. Could Schumacher catch Hill, 2.75 seconds ahead? No.

In Italy 'we were never really in control at any time. The car was dancing badly, particularly over the bumps, on Friday and Saturday. At times I was really worried I was going to end up in the barriers and at a place like Monza, where the average speed is around 150 mph, it is a pretty unattractive proposition. On top of all that I had a truly horrible cold with a fever which made me feel awful most of the time. It left me with no voice by Sunday morning.'

Senna and Hill bumped at the first chicane, making Schumacher third. On lap four he took Alesi but around Monza's broad acres Prost drove into another dimension far beyond reach and Schumacher's engine went, 'a terrible noise from the back of the car just after I had left the first chicane'.

On the Friday in Portugal Prost took provisional pole and called a Press Conference to announce his retirement. Thus Schumacher's first qualifying – fifth – drowned in that. Schumacher fell back to sixth in second qualifying. 'I was getting understeer, oversteer and bumping. I stayed at the circuit until 11 o'clock at night. It was a worrying time for myself and everyone in the team. I can honestly say I have never worked so hard at a race. I am known to be a hard worker and I am usually one of the last, if not the last, to leave the circuit, but this was worse than anything I had known.' He went to bed with 'data about the car swimming before my eyes. I had no idea that we would be able to solve the problems.'

In Sunday morning warm-up 'we were going slower and slower' and in the wrong direction.

'It was one of those races where everyone was driving closely together from the start. You had to be careful and you had to conserve the car well and the tyres. To err on the side of caution we planned to make two pit stops, but once the race started it was a different story. And what a start. Who would have expected Jean Alesi to be leading in the first corner?'

Answer: Jean Alesi.

'I was trying to get past Prost in the early part, but I found it very difficult,' Schumacher said. 'The car was handling really well but we needed something else if we were to make up places. That is when I decided to come in and change my tyres early. It worked.' Senna went on lap 19, engine, and at lap 23, Prost leading, the Hill-to-Schumacher gap stood at seven seconds. A flash reading came up, Prost leading Hill by 15 seconds, Schumacher closing to within four seconds of Hill. In traffic Schumacher caught Hill, leaving him utterly vulnerable. Prost pitted on lap 29, was stationary for 6.82 and almost stalled; Hill pitted a lap later. Schumacher led.

'I suddenly found myself with a chance of winning *if I did not come in for the second scheduled pit stop*. I don't think anyone in the team wanted to argue about me staying out. I did my best to look after the tyres from then on. I tried also to control the gap I had ahead of Prost and it was not easy. It went from two seconds out to six and then back again, and at the end of the race Alain was definitely quicker.'

The laps melted, each like the other, the cars equidistant. Schumacher lapped Philippe Alliott (Larrousse) but Prost couldn't immediately, giving Schumacher respite, but not much. Next time he glanced in the mirrors Prost was back. In those last few laps Schumacher resisted whatever pressure Prost laid on him and won by 0.98 of a second.

In Japan he crashed. 'I was trying to stay close to Berger to stop Hill from moving inside but he did and I hit his wheel. The impact knocked my wheel off.'

In Australia he pitted early for tyres, but the engine let go shortly after. 'I'm sure I could have caught Senna [the winner] and maybe challenged him for the lead. It's a shame.'

The merciless comparison? Schumacher fourth in the Championship with 52 points, Patrese fifth with 20 and leaving.

Chapter 5

RATTLING SENNA

Everything seemed clear as January turned into February and February turned into early March amid the usual winter testing, launching of new cars and triumphs of hope over experience: Senna at Williams Renault to partner Damon Hill, J.J. Lehto at Benetton to partner Schumacher. Lehto and Hill were regarded as supporting cast and either Senna or Schumacher would take the 1994 Championship: Senna had the envied car, Schumacher the car nobody should underestimate.

On Lehto the merciless weight of comparison would fall.

The Ferrari improved, and Berger and Alesi totalled 65 points although few would remember that; or that Alesi was injured early on and Ferrari reached for Nicola Larini again. He did two races, crashed immediately in the Pacific at Aida and finished second at Imola. But Imola was shadowland.

January turning gently into February, Formula One appeared as ordered as it can ever hope to be. An array of electronic driver aids had been banned to return the art of driving from the microchip to the human being. Who would handle the art form best?

Benetton unveiled the B194 early in January (which was early) and it would have Ford's new Zetec-R engine. At the unveiling someone asked Schumacher if Lehto would push him. 'I don't think I've ever needed motivation of that sort, because I've had Senna in front of me, which is great motivation.' He'd undergone an operation on his knees and 'they are fine. I can walk normally.'

At Silverstone in testing Lehto plunged off at Stowe and hit a tyre barrier. He needed surgery on his back and injured his neck.

At Barcelona in testing Hill did 1:18.2 against Schumacher's 1:18.9, but that was the Monday. Later Schumacher did 1:17.60, which, as everyone noted, was faster than Prost's 1993 pole of 1:17.80. Senna wasn't at the test...

At Imola in testing Senna did 1:21.24 and in the final moments Schumacher did 1:21.07. Neither driver suggested that these times were definitive, Senna insisting that he hadn't stretched to the fullest, Schumacher accepting the insistence.

The Brazilian Grand Prix at Sao Paulo on the 27th would, as it seemed, be just another opening race to just another season, this one grouped around the expectation of Schumacher versus Senna. In Brazil Senna took pole but it was tight.

First Session
Senna	1:16.38
Schumacher	1:16.57

Second session
Senna	1:15.96
Schumacher	1:16.29

At the green Schumacher got the start wrong. He judged the left-hand side of the circuit, off the racing line, to have less grip. As he lurched forward Senna burst clear, Alesi slotting the Ferrari to mid-track, Hill following Alesi and crowding Schumacher who held him into Turn One, the left-hander. Senna legged it away through the loops and dips and climbs. At the Bico de Pato, a left horseshoe, Schumacher tucked inside Alesi but with such impetus that it drew him full across the track. Alesi tucked inside *him*.

Senna moved further and further away. On lap two Schumacher repeated the move at the Bico de Pato but kept the car tighter and Alesi could only follow. The gap to Senna: four seconds. Alesi made a feint or two but Schumacher eased from him and advanced upon Senna. The season tilted then, but only in retrospect. Senna could not escape and a flash reading put the gap at 1.89.

They pitted on lap 21, Senna stationary for 7.8 seconds, Schumacher – further up the pit lane – fractionally quicker. He emerged first and thus into the lead. Senna had to prove everything, catch and dispatch Schumacher, but Schumacher forced a gap of 4.33 and after the second pit stops 'never really felt under pressure. I could control the gap by pushing a bit hard.' It steadied at nine seconds and on lap 56 Senna spun out. 'My fault,' he said, 'pushing too hard.'

On Senna now the merciless weight of comparison had fallen. Schumacher lapped everyone.

It prompted Brundle, who'd joined Marlboro McLaren, to say that 'the guy is awesome. He and Senna were in a class of their own, but in Brazil for instance he got Senna rattled. Schumacher did his job without mistakes, did it brilliantly and won the race. I had a long chat with him there and I couldn't help but be impressed by his maturity and professionalism. He knows what he wants, where he's going and how to go about it.'

At Aida, a new track for a new race – the Pacific Grand Prix – Senna took pole from Schumacher again. Schumacher described how he approached the circuit: 'A bit like you drive a go-kart. It's tiny but very tricky and very technical.' At the green they veered towards each other, flicked away. Into Turn One, a right, Häkkinen bumped Senna and pushed him off, Larini (deputising for Alesi) in the Ferrari ramming him. By the end of the race only Berger stayed on the same lap, and only because Schumacher deliberately circled behind him in the closing laps. 'After the start I wasn't pushed very hard so I could take it very easy with the car, with the tyres, and could run the race home. That's the only intention I had after the start.'

In an interview in *Motoring News* under the headline 'Who is better – Senna or Schumacher?', Niki Lauda said that the main difference between them is 'their age. A big difference. Presumably God has blessed and gifted both of them with the same amount of talent; then it's only a question of time until Schumacher has the same experience as Senna. And then, thanks to his youth, he will beat – maybe even outdrive – Senna. But Senna will never sleep. Always he will go full throttle.' *Autosport* carried a front-page headline 'Senna: Can he take the heat?', with a sub-heading 'Crunch time in San Marino'.

Imola was the weekend of mourning, Austrian Roland Ratzenberger's Simtek veering off at 200 mph and hitting a wall on the Saturday. He died in hospital slightly over an hour later.

At the green on the Sunday, Lehto stalled and Pedro Lamy (Lotus), unsighted by a car ahead, struck the Benetton hard. Both drivers escaped serious injury but a wheel went into the crowd, injuring several spectators. Senna led Schumacher and Berger before the pace car came out and circled while the wreckage was cleared. At the end of lap five the pace car peeled off, releasing them.

Schumacher immediately pressured Senna and noticed that through the Tamburello corner Senna's car 'seemed very nervous. I could see that it was bottoming quite a lot and he nearly lost it.' Schumacher continued the pressure and on the next lap 'at the same place Ayrton did lose it. The car's rear skid-plates touched the ground, he got a bit sideways.' Senna braked and across the brief run-off area cut his speed by some 70 miles an hour but that still meant he struck the wall at the far side of the run-off area at more than 130 mph. 'It looked a very dangerous impact but I didn't have the feeling it was anywhere near what happened when Roland crashed,' Schumacher said.

Senna died in hospital.

Eventually the race was restarted and Schumacher won easily enough from Larini. He stood sombre on the podium, hands locked behind his back, his face drawn towards the dignity of bearing grief.

At the next race, Monaco, a British newspaper, *The Mail On Sunday*, quoted Schumacher as saying that if he'd lost the feeling for driving 'I would have stopped. This was the question to myself after Senna: "Michael, if you don't have back the proper feeling, then it is no use. Michael, you have to stop for good." Everything you would do in a car without this feeling of being certain would be dangerous.' Could he have walked away? 'I can't truly know because I have never tried it but I like to feel I could have been this strong in my mind.'

Weber was quoted as saying, 'He did suffer for a long time. We discussed. Then for hours, for days, he thought. I would not have been surprised if he had decided to walk away. For 20 years I was a race driver and I knew how serious he was. This week [Monaco] you see him more changed than ever before because for the first time in his life he has been put in touch with death.'

Each driver and each team approached Monaco in a personal way, essentially forcing themselves through it, and in Thursday's free practice Wendlinger crashed heavily, was taken to hospital in a coma. 'On Wednesday and Thursday in practice I drove with no feeling and I was not sure,' Schumacher said. 'Then on Friday it was different. Only then did I feel I could continue my job.'

He had pole from Häkkinen and Berger and the drivers observed a minute's silence for Senna and Ratzenberger before the race. At Ste Devote Häkkinen and Hill collided, Schumacher moving away from Berger in a decisive, devastating way. He led by nearly four seconds at the end of lap one and would have only one instant of anxiety when the engine on Mark Blundell's Tyrrell blew and 'I was right behind. I almost hit the barrier.'

Schumacher crossed the line 36 seconds in front of Brundle and as he walked to the podium he and Flavio Briatore, Benetton's commercial director, embraced with such emotion that Schumacher was lifted clean off the ground: a curious moment capable of many interpretations, not least that some sort of normality had returned, that a victory could again be celebrated.

Schumacher 40, Berger 10.

Hasty new regulations governing the cars were in force for the Spanish Grand Prix. Schumacher tested the 'new' Benetton at Jerez and said that it 'slides more and is more sensitive to drive. When you go on the throttle there is more reaction in the corner. It's going to be difficult for the teams which don't have the opportunity to test. We need to do something, but whether this [the change in regulations] is right I'm not sure. The accidents mainly happened because the cars were touching the ground and to improve things in that area would have been better.'

The Spanish Grand Prix meeting at Barcelona writhed with a turmoil of its own. On the Thursday the drivers gathered and discussed a new chicane which, using foresight during Monaco, Schumacher had asked to be built before the ultra-fast right-hander at the back of the Catalunya circuit. It hadn't been and some felt that Schumacher should have been at Barcelona early to make sure it had; but, as others pointed out, he'd been testing at Jerez and it's awkward to be at two ends of a country at the same time.

Whatever, the drivers made a clear demand. *Build that chicane or we won't drive.* The drivers won and got themselves twin tyre walls with a little gap in the middle. The gap was widened by two metres on the Friday after free practice, a free practice during which only five teams went out. The others were locked in talks with FIA (renamed from FISA) President Max Mosley over the implications of the new regulations.

They all went out in first qualifying, Schumacher quickest from Häkkinen and Hill; on the Saturday Schumacher moved down from the 1:23s to 1:21.90. At the green he led from Hill and increased and increased it. He made his first pit stop on lap 21 at the same time as Herbert in the Lotus. As they both exited the pit lane, Schumacher first, Herbert following, it seemed entirely ordinary. A new 50 mph limit in the pit lane had been introduced at Monaco and obtained here, too.

They reached the point where they could accelerate and Herbert surged past Schumacher. What could that mean? 'The car was perfect in the beginning and I was able to open up a good lead quite easily,' said Schumacher. 'Then the gearbox wouldn't select gears. All I know is that it was stuck in fifth. When I stopped at the pits I asked if there was anything that could be done but there was nothing.'

'I was completely unaware that he was stuck in fifth,' Herbert says. 'He'd been leading the race, but if he's slower than me I'll pass him. I looked in my mirrors and thought he'd dropped back quite a long way.'

Häkkinen went by, Hill went by, Schumacher third and crippled. He applied his logic to this problem. 'At first it was a bit difficult to take all the corners in fifth, but then I managed to find a good line and keep up reasonable lap times. My experience in Group C helped me in this because I learned many ways of running differently, of changing my driving style, usually to save fuel. I used that same style and it certainly helped me a lot.' The lap times after the stop chart Schumacher doing precisely this. Successively he moved through the 1:31s to the 1:27s in ten laps.

Häkkinen made his stop on lap 31 and Hill on lap 42, giving Schumacher the lead again. Häkkinen's engine let go on lap 48. By then Schumacher had made a second stop, fraught with hazard because he risked stalling as he pulled away. He didn't – astonishingly he looked smooth. 'I had to use a lot of revs and slip the clutch to get going. I gave the engine a lot of punishment but it kept working beautifully.' Hill led to the end,

Schumacher slowing to protect his clutch so that the final margin stretched to 24 seconds.

There are telling anecdotes about Jim Clark. Sometimes in a race he'd suddenly slow for a lap or two, then regain his former pace. He'd had a problem, adjusted to it and, in the motor racing phrase, 'drove round it'. For a generation only Senna had been compared to Clark...

Ford said that the 'telemetry confirms that following the gearbox failure, the Zetec-R in Schumacher's car was required to pull from a minimum 5,200rpm on each remaining lap and rev to its maximum 14,500rpm for long periods on the straights. With his Benetton Ford stuck in fifth gear Schumacher's best lap around the 2.95-mile Barcelona circuit was 1:26.17 seconds. There were only three other recorded laps better than that, one of those being Schumacher's own record-setting 1:25.15 seconds – with all gears operative [lap 18].'

'Under the circumstances we couldn't be more pleased with Michael's result,' said Steve Parker, Ford's Formula One Program Manager. 'The fact that he was able to carry on racing despite the loss of all but one gear is eloquent testimony to Michael's superb driving skills, the tractability and strength of Ford's Zetec-R V8 and the brilliance of the Benetton's chassis design. Some journalists were so surprised by this performance that immediately after the race we had to show them the raw telemetry data before they could accept that Michael really had driven the race in fifth gear only.' Here was the mastery and the masterclass.

For the first time since Senna's death Schumacher came under genuine pressure in Canada during qualifying. In the opening session Alesi hammered in 1:26.27 against 1:26.82. In the second session *Eurosport* enjoyed one of those moments you can't script. Martin Walters, Chief Engineer of Cosworth engines, went up to their commentary box and chatted to John Watson. Alesi came out and pitched the Ferrari at the circuit,

Schumacher also on the circuit. Alesi had the Ferrari twitching and darting and you could feel the effort. 1:26.73. Schumacher looked less nervy although at one point he locked the brakes. 1:26.33. He moved into another fast lap.

Watson: 'A big improvement from Michael Schumacher and he's looking to improve further. Now Martin Walters is sitting here beside us smiling at this performance...but Michael again locks up, his fronts this time. Martin, you must be impressed with how he's developed in the three years of your association with him.'

Walters: 'We're very impressed with Michael. I think this year he's more relaxed, we're working much better as a team. We haven't had any distractions from other teams and I think we'll see great things from Michael this year. As John said earlier, I think this is the first race meeting where he's been really pushed, and Michael is now trying as hard as he knows to get pole position.'

Watson: 'As an engineer, how do you explain that ability to convey information between you and Michael Schumacher?'

Walters: 'What you actually have to remember about Michael is that he can drive at this pace and still have enough capacity left in his mind to understand what's going on. At the end of the run he's able to relate to us exactly what the problems are. Are there any hesitations on any of the corners from the engine? Does it pick up cleanly? Does the gearshift pick up nice and clean? For instance yesterday we had a problem changing from fifth to sixth.'

[At this moment Schumacher completed his lap, 1:26.17, translating to 0.09 quicker than Alesi's Friday time.]

Walters, chuckling: 'I've gone quiet now because he's gone to the front.'

Schumacher stayed pole and led the race from start to finish.

Mansell returned for the French Grand Prix, generating a vast groundswell of hype, curiosity and, when he clambered into the Rothmans Williams Renault, respect. Young Scotsman David Coulthard had taken Senna's place in Spain and Canada but he couldn't hope to challenge Schumacher. Mansell might. His presence – although nobody was saying as much – also represented a challenge to Hill. Meanwhile Jos Verstappen replaced Lehto at Benetton, the team explaining that Lehto hadn't fully recovered from his testing crash in January. That merciless weight.

On the Saturday, Mansell and Hill traded fastest laps and for once Schumacher found himself on the second row. He blitzed the start, slicing between the Williamses, Hill clinging, Mansell falling back. 'I couldn't have made a better start,' Schumacher said. 'It was absolutely perfect. I went just as the red light went out. It was a very tough fight at the beginning but that is what we all enjoy.' This start became a cause of wondering rather than just wonder.

Silverstone, the Thursday, and the pressure hemmed Damon Hill. He faced the press and, head tilted downward, unloaded. 'What do you have to do? That's what I want to know. What do you bloody have to do for people to believe that you're any good? Last weekend I beat Nigel Mansell [in France] and the year before that I beat Alain Prost for pole position. I led the race, I came closer to beating Michael Schumacher than anyone's come all year other than Ayrton Senna [in this context Spain hardly counts] and all I get from the papers, all I'm reading about, is my bloody job's in jeopardy.

'I'm second in the World Championship, I've come here to beat Michael Schumacher and try and win this race and try and turn the Championship round. I've never heard such a lot of bollocks in my life as I've heard since last week. [Long pause.] I'm very pissed off. I don't get any credit for being polite and diplomatic so I'm going to ditch that tack because it's not getting me anywhere. [Pause.] I'm fighting a battle here with a car that is clearly not as good as the Schumacher-Benetton combination.

'I need 100% backing from Williams to do the job properly – which I've asked for – and I proved last weekend that I am getting the best out of the equipment. [Pause.] It's taken me ten years to get to this position in Formula One. I'm not going to relinquish it or give it up to anyone without a serious fight. I promise you I am here to stay. I have proved myself as a top Formula One driver and this weekend I will work again to prove that point. That's all I have to say.'

On the Friday, Schumacher took provisional pole from Berger, Hill fourth, and after the session Schumacher was leaving the pit area on his scooter. That involved, as it always does, squeezing through the crowd who gather at the gate. All unknowing Schumacher ran over the foot of 10-year-old Ian Foulds from Seaham, County Durham, who stood holding out his autograph book.

Ian was taken to the medical centre to see if any bones had been broken and I set off to Benetton to get some reaction. They expressed astonishment and in turn set off to tell Schumacher, in a technical meeting. He was 'stunned' and left the meeting immediately, jumped on his scooter bearing a tee shirt for Ian and reached the medical centre only to be told that Ian was fine and had been discharged.

Maybe that set the tone for a peculiar race meeting, Hill taking pole from Schumacher after a rush-rush-rush of a second session where they and Berger traded blows like heavyweights right to the bell. On the warm-up lap before the race Schumacher set off in a cloud of smoke from the tyres, leading Hill – a breach of the rules, which state that cars must remain in grid order. Coulthard couldn't get his engine to fire on the grid so the starting procedure had to be aborted. When they tried a second time Schumacher took the lead again on the warm-up lap and would subsequently claim that Hill was 'going a bit slow'. The rules are clear: Schumacher ought to have been ordered to start from the back of the grid. That did not happen.

Hill took the lead from Schumacher while the Stewards deliberated, decided on a five-second penalty and informed Benetton. Crucially the penalty did not include the words 'stop-go'. Briatore said that 'we were told of the penalty but the stop-go wasn't mentioned. Therefore we didn't ask Michael to come into the pits.' Benetton, and Schumacher when they told him over the radio, assumed that the five seconds would be added to his total race time and Schumacher faced the problem of overtaking Hill and getting five seconds clear of him.

After the early pit stops Schumacher was given the black flag on lap 21. The black flag has always been the ultimate sanction in motor racing and non-negotiable. The driver's number is displayed at the start-finish line and the black flag. The indicated driver must come in. This time negotiations – heated – did take place between Benetton and the Stewards, and for the next two laps Schumacher ignored the black flag. It was then withdrawn.

Schumacher did come in on lap 27 for the stop-go, essentially costing him the race. He was reluctant to discuss it afterwards and small wonder. The Stewards issued a statement culminating in a decision 'to formally reprimand the competitor Mild Seven Benetton Ford for a lack of a complete understanding of F1 rules and of the need for this to be corrected and for their meticulous application in the future. Michael Schumacher and competitor Mild Seven Benetton Ford were fined US $25,000 for breach of the applicable regulations.'

The turmoil was back already and, more than that, from being the absolute favourite to take the World Championship long before season's end Schumacher moved into a waking nightmare. Nothing like it had happened since 1976 when another native German speaker, Lauda, and another Briton, James Hunt, contested the Championship amid protests, hearings, appeals, disqualifications and reinstatements. Schumacher's nightmare came at him on a weekly and sometimes daily basis. Leaving Silverstone, Schumacher had 72 points and Hill 39. (Please note that in what follows Benetton referred to themselves by their official name, Benetton Formula.)

Week 1 (11–17 July): The FIA launched an inquiry into the events of Silverstone, raising the spectre that they might take Schumacher's six points from Silverstone away and, following the precedent of Nigel Mansell in Portugal in 1989, ban him from the next race. This was extremely intriguing because the next race was Hockenheim, already virtually sold out. Would the FIA dare? What would their reputation be if they didn't?

Benetton team manager Joan Villadelprat said, 'We messed up [at Silverstone] but so did the Stewards. The rule says we have to be notified within 15 minutes of the incident.' By now a timetable had been recreated minute by minute and it showed clearly that Schumacher's original offence – overtaking Hill on the warm-up laps – took place at 2.00, but the Stewards' decision did not reach Benetton until 2.27.

Week 2 (18–24 July): Benetton and Schumacher were summoned to a meeting of the World Motorsport Council in Paris on 26 July – the following week – over the British Grand Prix. Schumacher was quoted as saying, 'It is all a lot of hot air and I don't think it is right to interfere with the Championship like this. All the theatre is rather stupid.'

The following were also summoned: Rubens Barrichello (Jordan) and Häkkinen (who'd crashed on the last lap at Silverstone), Hill (who'd allegedly stopped on his slowing-down lap to gather a Union Jack, stopping now illegal), representatives of Benetton, and Pierre Aumonier, clerk of the course.

Schumacher took part in general Silverstone testing for three days. There were new regulations in force – a stepped undertray beneath the cars to reduce downforce and cornering speeds. 'The car is certainly more difficult to drive but it has been a very productive test session. You have to lift off the accelerator

RIGHT: *The German junior kart champion in 1984, and a world to win (Werner Aichinger).*

All pictures are from LAT Photographic unless stated.

BELOW: *The world was won. He stayed clean-cut and well-groomed to the end.*

ABOVE, LEFT: *Happy days in Formula Koenig* (Werner Aichinger).
ABOVE, RIGHT: *Triumph at the 1990 International Formula 3 round in Macau. Manager Willi Weber (right) looks as happy as Schumacher.*
BELOW: *And 1990 was a vintage year. Here, selected for the Mercedes junior drivers' scheme in the Sports Car World Championship, he moves to second place at Dijon.*

RIGHT: *Revealing moment. Schumacher, thinking ahead, brings his bike to Spa to learn the circuit before his Formula 1 debut with Jordan in 1991.*

BELOW: *The debut about to end at La Source, the clutch gone.*

ABOVE: *The extraordinary partnership born at Benetton: Schumacher and tactical guru Ross Brawn.*

BELOW: *Following Nelson Piquet in the wet, Adelaide 1991.*

OPPOSITE: *The athletic all-rounder: confident on snow at Madonna di Campiglio in the Alps, playing football, in a bike race at Silverstone, preparing to serve and playing table football with wife Corinna.*

LEFT: *The Schumachers at play: Michael, Corinna, Gina-Maria and Miki* (Action Press/Rex Features).

BELOW: *The start of the 1994 Australian Grand Prix – Schumacher versus the Williams cars, and global controversy to come* (ICN UK Bureau).

ABOVE: *The first championship, Adelaide, 13 November 1994. Schumacher with Flavio Briatore, senior team member Tom Walkinshaw and the rest of Benetton. He'd secured the title by one point from Damon Hill in circumstances that shocked the F1 world. Even his crew looks uncomfortable.*

RIGHT: *The uneasy relationship with Hill, always on–off.*

ABOVE: *The picture that distils Schumacher's time at Benetton: success, adulation and moments of wonderful joy.*

BELOW: *The inheritance: Ayrton Senna, giant of one era, talks seriously to Schumacher, giant of the next. Between them they would dominate Grand Prix racing from 1988 to the very end of 2006.*

considerably more now and it has been important to get good ride on the car.'

Week 3 (25–31 July): Schumacher, wearing a multi-coloured sports jacket (nice not garish) cut a path through the media and went into the FIA headquarters, Place de la Concorde, Paris, on the Tuesday. After the hearing he lost his six points from Silverstone and was given a two-race ban. The World Council didn't accept that he hadn't seen the black flag. He faced a dilemma. If he accepted the ban he missed Hockenheim. If he lodged an appeal – and he had seven days to do that – he could drive at Hockenheim but risk having the ban increased if the appeal failed. The talk was of precedents again. Jordan's Eddie Irvine had been given a one-race ban after crashing in the Brazilian Grand Prix, subsequently raised to three when his appeal failed. Leaving the Place de la Concorde, Schumacher 66 points, Hill 39.

Benetton were fined $500,000 for their failure to obey the Stewards' orders at Silverstone and a further $100,000 for being tardy in producing 'source codes' for their electronic systems, which the FIA had been demanding since the San Marino Grand Prix. This is a dark part of the nightmare. Benetton were found to have a system that *could* be in breach of the regulations. In essence, as we have seen, the regulations prevented computers from controlling the cars; but the FIA found no evidence that the system had been used. (This did not prevent fevered speculation on Schumacher's astonishing start in the French Grand Prix where, remember, he'd blitzed it.)

Two days later, Benetton announced: 'Both Michael Schumacher and the Benetton Formula team feel that the penalties inflicted on them were very severe. Together both parties have agreed to appeal in front of the International Court of Appeal of the FIA through the respective National Sporting Authorities, and therefore Michael Schumacher will take part in the upcoming 1994 German Grand Prix. This decision has been reached following the concern from both Michael Schumacher and the Benetton Formula team that Michael's absence from his home Grand Prix would unfairly penalise and disappoint all the German fans who have long awaited this event. Michael Schumacher and the Benetton Formula hope that this appeal will result in a decreased penalty. Their priority now is to prepare for a winning performance this weekend.'

So to Hockenheim, where, commenting on what happened in Paris, Schumacher said that 'obviously they didn't believe me that I didn't see the black flag. I'm really sorry that I didn't see the black flag, that I haven't taken care about the black flag, but if you don't see it you don't come in, you do your race. You continue.'

On the Friday an immense crowd watched Schumacher qualify third behind Hill and, gloriously, Berger in the Ferrari. In the nightmare it could not be so simple. During the morning untimed session Verstappen went off and in their zeal the marshals doused the car with so much extinguishant that it needed new wiring, engine and gearbox. The car could not be readied for first qualifying so Schumacher had a run, then passed his car to Verstappen and 'at the second chicane I suddenly spun on to the gravel. I feel really sorry having ruined Michael's qualifying.'

On the Saturday Schumacher went only fourth fastest, Berger and Alesi filling the front row. It put Schumacher on the second row with Hill. 'I don't really care about my grid position here. What I do care about is the job we've done, and that's been superb. It's been a hundred per cent effort by everyone in the team and we have improved the car a lot.' He talked of perhaps a podium finish.

Week 4 (1–7 August): Race day at Hockenheim and a wild start to the race. Berger got away fast, and so did Alesi, but mayhem towards the back of the grid. Cars bumped and spun: De Cesaris in the Sauber, Zanardi in the Lotus, Alboreto and

Pierluigi Martini in the Minardis. Häkkinen (McLaren) went deep to the inside, running along the pit lane wall looking for an advantage. Approaching the first, curving-right, corner Häkkinen moved over on Coulthard and tapped him. That pitched the McLaren full across the track and across the rest of the grid. It skimmed directly in front of Blundell's Tyrrell and, Blundell already on the brakes, Barrichello could do nothing but perform a battering-ram on the Tyrrell. By now cars were moving in bewildering directions and the real perspective is that – Alesi out with electrics – 11 cars had gone after a single lap. And Hill had been tapped by Katayama's Tyrrell on that first lap. He'd lose more than three minutes in the pits.

Schumacher hustled Berger, attacked, and Berger resisted. 'I tried very hard to overtake. I put the Ferrari under a lot of pressure and I felt sure I could have taken the lead eventually.' Schumacher pitted for tyres and fuel after 12 laps, resumed in second place. Verstappen followed into the pits three laps later. The car stopped but the fuel nozzle wouldn't go into the entrance to the fuel tank properly. Fuel belched out, became spray like torrential rain and the instant it touched the hot, hot, hot engine the car seemed to explode. Verstappen and the crew still changing the wheels were engulfed in a molten yellow wall of fire that rose ten feet into the air with a mushroom cloud of black smoke above it.

Some images you'll never forget.

That Verstappen survived with comparatively minor burns and only one of the crew was burned was frankly unbelievable. Like Berger's crash and fire at Imola in 1989, the more times you replay it on video the more you are sure, absolutely sure, that the driver cannot survive.

The race went on and after 20 laps Schumacher 'suddenly had a problem. I've no idea what it was but the engine seemed to lose power. I'm very, very disappointed for the supporters who gave me such great support during the weekend.' Hill finished second so that leaving tree-lined, concrete-clad Hockenheim, Schumacher 66 points, Hill 39.

The images weren't of any of that but of Verstappen.

On the Tuesday a team statement said that 'Benetton Formula are carrying out a thorough investigation into the events leading to the fire and until this investigation is complete we will not be making any further comment. However, Benetton Formula would like to commend the actions of their staff in dealing with the fire in such a professional manner. In common with other teams in Formula One, Benetton Formula staff had been trained in fire-fighting techniques, the benefit of which was clearly demonstrated. A small number of staff received superficial injuries in the fire and we wish them a very speedy recovery. Benetton Formula are aware that certain team members made comments following the incident and expressed their disapproval with regards to refuelling. We would like to point out that the comments made naturally came from the emotions provoked by the incident.'

That week Briatore said, 'When I went back to the factory and saw the faces of the mechanics who had been burned I said, "Jesus, we have to stop this." We could even do it immediately and if necessary have shorter races for the people who don't have enough fuel capacity. I saw that the mechanics are now scared, and when you are scared you make mistakes more easily.'

Intertechnique, who made the refuelling equipment that all Formula One teams used, were delegated by the FIA to examine that of Benetton on the Wednesday at Witney, Oxfordshire, the team's base. After the fireball, a time-bomb.

Week 5 (8–14 August): The FIA ignited it on the Wednesday. 'The fuel spillage was caused by the fuel valve failing to close properly. The valve was slow to close due to the presence of a foreign body. The foreign body is believed to have reached the valve because a filter designed to eliminate the risk had been deliberately removed.' One estimate (not the FIA's) estimated that, by removing the filter, fuel would have flowed in 12.5% faster, saving perhaps a second during the pit stop, and Formula One teams are always looking to save a second. Formula One teams *think* in terms of seconds.

The FIA statement implied in stark terms that Benetton had deliberately compromised safety, with all that that involved, to steal an advantage. Would the FIA banish Benetton from Formula One? Would that be the end of Schumacher's Championship? Benetton struck back immediately with an explosion of their own. They said:

Following the press release issued today by the FIA regarding the fire involving Car no 6 during a Pit Stop at the German Grand Prix, Benetton Formula Ltd would like to make the following statement:

Benetton Formula's concern for an investigation into the events surrounding the incident prompted us to contract an independent company specialising in accident investigation to carry out a study of the accident and to give an opinion on the method of refuelling.

This company is a specialist in the field of accident investigation and assessment of engineering failures and accidents. They particularly specialise in the aerospace field.

The company has conducted investigations into over 300 serious accidents worldwide, in addition to numerous less serious cases. Their work has included involvement in most major accidents since 1972 to public transport aircraft and helicopters in the UK, and surrounding waters, as well as overseas incidents where aircraft of UK registration or manufacture have been involved.

The company has also frequently served as technical investigator for military boards of inquiry into serious and complex military aircraft accidents.

Part of their report states:

'Consideration was given to the effect of the absence of the filter previously positioned at the point where the inner hose joins the nozzle unit (it is understood that this was removed for the Hockenheim Race after a lengthy period during which no debris was collected in any of the Benetton team's filters).

Any debris would, under normal circumstances, travel through the connection into the car tank. No evidence was seen, during the examination of scouring or of other effects, which could have resulted from debris fouling any of the moving parts. A study of the layout of the fuel path and of the evidence surrounding the incident did not suggest any way in which any feasible debris contamination from the fuel flow could have caused the failure of the nozzle to engage correctly.'

Given our concern over refuelling safety, we had hoped to be able to discuss this report with FIA and undertake the necessary actions to reduce the risks involved in refuelling. A written request has now been placed with the FIA urgently requesting such a meeting.

A copy of this report was immediately lodged with our legal advisers, Marriott Harrison of London, upon receipt of the FIA's press release.

The filter mentioned was introduced part way through the year in response to problems teams were having with debris entering the valve and car. Benetton was able to eliminate this problem.

The Benetton fuel rigs prior to Hockenheim had been thoroughly stripped and cleaned and there was no risk of debris entering the valve assembly. Benetton also pre-filter their fuel twice before it is placed in the fuel rig.

Benetton Formula concluded the filter was unnecessary and it was removed with the full knowledge and permission of the FIA Formula 1 Technical delegate, Mr Charlie Whiting. This permission was given on the afternoon of Thursday 28 July to Joan Villadelprat in the presence of Ross Brawn [Technical Director].

The consequence of attributing, in Benetton Formula's view incorrectly, the cause of this fire to the lack of a filter means that such an incident could happen again, possibly with far more serious consequences.

The World Motorsport Council summoned Benetton to the Place de la Concorde on 19 October. Only two races would remain after that, Japan and Australia. During Week 5 the season and the Championship had disintegrated into more or less anything you wanted it to be in your imagination; and if you enjoyed mental arithmetic – or even riddles – you could play endlessly. Schumacher was appealing against Silverstone, which might cost him more than missing two races; Benetton might be retrospectively kicked out of the Championship *when Schumacher had already won it*. Schumacher might win his appeal. Benetton might defend themselves well...

On the Friday in Hungary, Schumacher took provisional pole from Hill; and confirmed it on the Saturday. The boy could take pressure, could isolate every external influence and just drive. You can't if you can't, if you see what I mean. Some say the adrenalin and urgency of the act of driving at these speeds inevitably precludes every external influence. I'm not so sure. The most *aware* human beings you're ever likely to meet are Formula One drivers, and they prosper by isolating one train of thought from another train of thought; and they learn the mechanisms for doing it.

Week 6 (15–21 August): Hill made the better start to the Hungarian Grand Prix and, on the inside, found himself better positioned for Turn One. Schumacher drove clean round the outside and squeezed Hill so hard that he was half into a little tarmac run-off area. Nothing serious. 'I had a good start but then I had too much wheelspin and Damon was able to pull alongside going into the first corner. In fact, he was slightly ahead but I knew that if I stayed alongside I would be OK through the next corner and that's how it worked out. I then had some pressure because I did not know what the Williams pit-stop tactics would be. I was stopping three times and that meant I had to push hard to make sure I kept my advantage. Once I made my final stop I was able to ease off a bit. Winning this race has taken away much of the pressure on us.'

Only the juggle of pit stops took the lead from Schumacher (from laps 17 to 25), and thereafter he ran for home smooth and isolated as you like, beating Hill by some 20 seconds, Verstappen third. Schumacher no doubt revealed a bit and concealed a bit of his feelings when he said that 'after all the recent happenings this was a truly great result for the team. Everybody has been a little bit nervous all weekend but now we can relax and I was very happy for Jos to finish on the rostrum for the first time, which made it a very special day for everybody in the team.'

Well, yes, and not a protest in sight. What was this, just a motor race? We'd forgotten what they were. Leaving stately, earthy Budapest and its infuriating motor racing circuit in the bleached hillocks outside it Schumacher had 76 points, Hill 45.

Schumacher tested at Silverstone on the Wednesday, managing 20 laps when it wasn't raining. On the Thursday he stayed in the car a lot longer and towards the end got down to 1:27.16 against the next best, Hill, on 1:27.68.

Week 7 (22–28 August): Maurice Hamilton, writing in the London *Observer*, claimed that Schumacher was considering leaving Benetton over the fuel filter affair and quoted him as saying that 'for me, honesty is the most important thing'. Hamilton is the most meticulous of motor racing writers and completely uninterested in sensationalism so what he does write carries both authenticity and authority. Benetton wouldn't say a word about what Hamilton said Schumacher was saying.

On the Tuesday, Benetton announced that they had signed a three-year contract with Renault for use of their engines, thanking Ford for 'an invaluable and dynamic relationship'. Williams would be keeping Renault engines too – interesting for 1995.

On the Friday, Barrichello in the Jordan took provisional pole by waiting until the end of a wet-drying session and risking slicks. Schumacher was next, then Hill. Schumacher had risked slicks himself but spun on his last lap. He thought it would have been a pole lap if he hadn't. 'I made a mistake and it cost me. I hadn't adjusted the brake balance properly so I locked the rear brakes.' On the Saturday, wet again, no change to the top of the grid: Barrichello had become at 22 the youngest driver ever to take pole, and did a war-dance to celebrate the instant the session ended – but not an instant before it ended, just in case.

Week 8 (29 August–4 September): A dry race at Spa, Barrichello keeping his nerve at the green light, Schumacher behind and pitching the car right then left searching for an opening. Barrichello held Schumacher to Les Combes, the right-left-right out in the country. Schumacher powered round the outside of him. Order: Schumacher, Barrichello, Alesi, Hill. It became a typical Schumacher race, power and poise applied to maximum effect and only one moment of danger when, on lap 19, he spun and rode the kerbing, but gathered it up quickly and cleanly enough. He led the first lap by 2.5 seconds, forced that up to 4.2 after the second lap and beat Hill by 13.66 seconds. 'My car was really sensitive on the throttle this time and it was difficult but I think in the end it was difficult for everyone. Certainly we managed somehow to have a car which from the beginning was even more competitive.' Leaving the tree-lined Ardennes Schumacher had 86 points, Hill 51.

The Stewards checked the Benetton and whispering began

that all wasn't well. At 8.20 in the evening the Stewards announced that the plank under the Benetton had not conformed to the regulations and Benetton's points were being taken from them. The plank had to be 10mm deep with an allowance of 10% wear during a race, meaning that it must measure a minimum 9mm afterwards. The Stewards claimed that in some places it measured only 7.4 mm. In defence Brawn argued that it might have been Schumacher's spin that had ground down the plank. Benetton lodged an immediate appeal. Leaving a by now darkened and desolate Ardennes, Schumacher 76, Hill 55.

On the Tuesday, Schumacher tramped the familiar route across the Place de la Concorde (wearing a different jacket this time) and made his appeal against the two-race ban over the Silverstone black flag. It was rejected. Evidently when Schumacher saw his number – 5 – hoisted he assumed that it meant a five-second penalty. 'We thought we had good arguments but it turned out they were not good enough.' In the media scrum when he emerged, someone asked if he'd leave Formula One. 'I need a few days to think about a lot of things. When I make a decision, or need to make a decision, I will let you know but at the moment nothing has changed for me.'

In another sense, of course, a great deal had changed for him. Five races remained and if Hill won the two that Schumacher must now miss – Italy and Portugal – that cut the difference to a single point between them; with the Benetton explanation over the Hockenheim fire and the Spa plank appeal still looming, ghosts in the nightmare. Benetton might be out of it altogether or Schumacher might conjure ten points back from the darkness – which presumably would relegate Hill to second again at Spa, costing Hill four points. Yes, yes, I know that at most sporting events you don't need to wait weeks for the result, but…

The FIA had abandoned the absurdity of waiting until 19 October to adjudicate on the fire, and instead of hearing the plank appeal on Monday 5 September and the fire explanation at dear old Place de la Concorde on Wednesday 7 September, they'd do the two for the price of one on the Wednesday in Paris. At least nobody at Benetton would need a street map to find it.

Week 9 (5–11 September): The German newspaper *Welt-am-Sonntag* (*World on Sunday*) quoted Schumacher as saying that 'if it is established that the team have been doing things behind my back which are forbidden by the rules I would not accept that. By that I mean that I could move to another team.'

On the Monday, Benetton announced that Lehto would join Verstappen for the Italian Grand Prix at Monza, and presumably for Portugal, too.

Schumacher didn't go to Paris on the Wednesday, where the World Motorsport Council decreed that the Spa appeal had been rejected but there was insufficient evidence to take further action against the team over the fire.

Benetton said: 'The Mild Seven Benetton Ford Formula 1 Team is very pleased with the result of today's hearing in Paris, which has completely cleared its good name from any allegations of cheating. Whilst the team may not have been able to satisfy the World Council as to the precise cause of the wear to the skid board it was delighted that the FIA stated in clear terms that there was no question of the team cheating.

'The team has also been completely cleared of the charge of removing the fuel filter illegally. This should put an end to unfounded and wild speculations in the press that the removal of the filter caused the fire at Hockenheim. Before the hearing the FIA conceded that it was not alleging that the removal of the filter had caused the fire. In giving the World Council's decision, the President [Max Mosley] stated that its unanimous view was that the filter was removed in complete good faith and that it would be inappropriate to impose any penalty whatsoever.'

Briatore said that 'now the team's good name has been upheld we can concentrate on doing what we do best, winning races. We look forward to Michael Schumacher's return at the Jerez Grand Prix.'

A single task faced Verstappen and Lehto, to beat Damon Hill around Monza's parkland and Estoril's slopes to protect Schumacher's Championship lead until he returned to protect it himself from Jerez to the climax, wherever and whatever that would be. The nightmare could not be over yet because Schumacher was completely helpless until Jerez.

Hill won Monza and judged 'this victory was well deserved by the team', while Schumacher watched from a restaurant in Monte Carlo. During the following week Williams confirmed that Hill would be staying with them for 1995. That offered peace of mind because the presence of Mansell, returned from IndyCar racing in America, loomed. If Williams had signed Mansell instead – and with Coulthard progressing superbly in the Williams before Mansell's return – it might have cost Hill the drive.

Hill won Portugal, a race Schumacher watched on television in Germany. 'It's a magic result,' Hill said, 'and I have a great sense of relief because I know people have been considering these last two races, when Michael has been away, as a foregone conclusion.' Schumacher 76, Hill 75.

During the week after that, the suspension served, Benetton and Williams tested at Estoril. Reportedly Schumacher and Hill shared the same hotel but sat at opposite ends of the dining room during meals. Schumacher did a best time of 1m 18.75s, Hill next with 1m 19.33. 'I hope that gives Damon some sleepless nights,' Schumacher said. 'I had been looking forward to driving the car again for so long [four weeks] and it was great to be back.'

Incidentally, apart from watching Hill win his two 'missing' races on television, Schumacher had been turning the negative into the positive during his enforced absence. He went to Switzerland and worked, worked, worked on his physical condition, building his strength. 'I did six to eight hours every day at 2,000 metres and it paid off. I felt really great.'

Immediately before Jerez Schumacher launched an astonishing and untypical personal tirade against Hill, which was the equivalent of the world going wild in a quite different way. 'I don't think we would have been in this situation [in the Championship] if Ayrton Senna had been in the car. Ayrton would have been driving circles around me. That shows what I think about Damon as a driver. He has been thrown into the Number One driver position but he never really was a Number One driver. With Coulthard driving quicker than him after three races, it proves he is not a Number One driver. So the respect is certainly not as much as I have for other drivers.

'You always start to know when you are in trouble and he has not been very helpful when I was in big trouble. Every time we proved we did not cheat they found a way to turn it around and say "Yes, but there was something else." A lot of people were unhappy with what happened to us, only one or two thought it was right, and one person in particular. I did respect him more in the past because I thought he was a nice guy and a fair guy. A lot of drivers have said fair things but Damon was the opposite. I don't expect him to stick up for me and say what is happening is wrong, but I don't expect someone to make it even worse. He would have been better to say nothing at all.

'As soon as I saw what he had said I thought "OK, now I know how to handle it." This has made me more determined to win the Championship. I always get stronger when I am in trouble. I am certainly more determined because there is one point between us and if I win the title I will have done it in 12 races, not 16. If I don't win the Championship I think everyone will know why' — the 'missing' races, plus disqualification at Silverstone, plus Benetton's disqualification at the Belgian Grand Prix.

Hill guarded his dignity. 'I'd rather not drag the Championship down by trying to diminish the reputation of the opposition. I think that's sad. Formula One has been in that situation for too long, with the two protagonists seemingly hating each other's guts. I think that's bad for Formula One and bad for sport, especially in a season when we've lost such a great champion in Ayrton.'

The European Grand Prix turned on pit-stop strategy. Hill led from Schumacher, and Hill intended to make only two stops, Schumacher three. If you compute a pit stop as 20 seconds (slowing down, stationary for fuel and tyres, emerging slowly) Schumacher seemed very vulnerable. The Benetton action plan: give Schumacher a light fuel load from the start to burst off into the distance then make the subsequent stops at his leisure (if you can put it like that). Instead Schumacher was captive behind Hill and pitted earlier than foreseen, partly because his tyre pressures weren't quite right and this affected the Benetton's handling.

Williams responded by bringing Hill in three laps later and two problems arose simultaneously. Hill's stop was slower than Schumacher's, giving Schumacher the lead, and there was a fault with the gauge on the Williams refuelling equipment. It delivered 13 litres more than it said it had, which translated to six laps' worth. Those six laps would have been run at high speed, the fuel load lightening moment by moment – but the team couldn't know those 13 litres were in there. They did know something was wrong. Schumacher pitted again on lap 33 of the 69, Hill two laps later. The Williams crew (using Mansell's rig on Hill's car to circumvent whatever the problem was, but itself creating a logistical problem) gave Hill 105 litres to finish the race, but of course the unknown 13 litres were still in there, too. Hill had to haul this load to the end and quite possibly it cost him a second a lap.

Schumacher did make his third stop at his leisure and won by some 25 seconds. 'This result is exactly what I wanted after having to miss the two races. I knew I could pick up time when

I realised Damon was making two stops to my three and it worked brilliantly.' Schumacher 86, Hill 81.

They went to Suzuka, Herbert replacing Verstappen. The merciless weight of comparison: across ten races Verstappen had scored no more than ten points.

At Suzuka, Hill broke the Championship open by mastering insidious, invisible, stalking pressure knowing that *if* he failed to master it, *if* he finished second to Schumacher, he faced a mathematical morass at Adelaide.

Schumacher had pole, Hill alongside on the front row, but heavy rain, almost a storm, drenched and drowned the circuit. Schumacher led, Hill in behind, but Herbert, third, aquaplaned off on lap four – the fifth retirement. The pace car came out and those who remained followed it for seven laps before it peeled off. They raced again but by lap 14 another six cars had gone, stopping the whole thing. This created that nervous mechanism of mental arithmetic, the aggregate. Schumacher's lead of 6.8 seconds from Part One would be carried forward as a weapon into the 36 laps of Part Two after the re-start of the race.

Benetton made a crucial error because Schumacher pitted for fuel twice, Hill only once, so that after Schumacher's second stop, on lap 40 of 50, Hill led on the aggregate by 15 seconds. Schumacher, sensing that he could virtually settle the Championship now, attacked and cut this gap by a couple of seconds a lap. Ghostly, it was, two cars widely separated on the track but one catching the other *on time*. Physically they would never glimpse each other, mentally they both knew the shark-nosed Benetton was taking big, big bites. Not quite a feeding frenzy, but close. Schumacher chewed that gap from 10.1 seconds through 8.3, 7.0, 5.2, 4.2 to the denouement: as they fled into the final lap Hill led on the aggregate by 2.4.

Hill had handled it as to the manner born. 'I was on the radio every lap to keep myself informed of Michael's progress.' Hill held the Williams steady, the conditions still full of lurking dangers, and made no mistake; and he had a clear road on that last lap. Schumacher faced two backmarkers. They didn't slow him but equally their presence and the dispatching of them prevented him from going for the kill. Hill had it by 3.36 seconds. He was naturally unaware of that as he toured on the slowing-down lap. 'There were about four people trying to get on the radio to tell me that I was P1 [Position, First] but there was so much interference that all I could hear was "P-blah-blah". I had to tell everyone to calm down, shut up and tell me where I'd finished!'

And they did.

The gap between them stood at the single point but it magnified itself. If Schumacher finished anywhere in front of Hill at Adelaide he had the Championship. Hill had to think in terms of gaining two points over Schumacher, which meant winning or finishing second and holding Schumacher to third. The descending scale of points for the top six finishers in any race – 10, 6, 4, 3, 2, 1 – held Hill rigidly and a tie on points was useless to Hill because Schumacher still had it on the most-wins tiebreak, another rigidity. Approaching Adelaide, only a week after Suzuka, that stood untouchably 8–6 to Schumacher.

Hill arrived in Australia on the Tuesday and spent two days as a guest of former World 500cc motorbike Champion Barry Sheene, the cockney living on the Gold Coast in the north. Hill relaxed, swam, prepared himself and then, when he arrived at Adelaide, gave an amazing Press Conference, forcibly complaining that he was underpaid, that he sometimes felt the team wasn't fully behind him.

Patrick Head, the forthright Williams Engineering Director, continued the quiver. 'He's having a whine and a whinge and as far as I am concerned the sooner the first practice starts the better. Looking at the situation dispassionately we have to overcome the odds to win. If I were a betting man and I had 100,000 dollars I would be putting it on Schumacher; but that is not meant to undermine Damon.' Whether it undermined Damon or not it gathered a shriek of headlines.

In first qualifying, to complicate everything, Mansell took provisional pole.

Mansell	1:16.17
Schumacher	1:16.19
Hill	1:16.83

Two minutes from the end of the session, and going beyond the limit, Schumacher spun heavily into the barrier as he tried one last time to beat Mansell. Was the pressure reaching Schumacher? A filthy wet second session left these times undisturbed and now the pressure shifted, also, on to Mansell. He had to help Hill but if they ran in grid order in the race how could he orchestrate that? Someone suggested that he might – I am being diplomatic – indulge in the unethical, and Mansell controlled his anger with momentary difficulty. 'That is a disgusting question. I'm above that.' Meanwhile Schumacher murmured, 'No, I'm not bothered about Nigel being in front of me.'

In the build-up to each Grand Prix a publicity company called Proaction produced a lap of the forthcoming circuit. Before Adelaide they asked Häkkinen for his: 'I think they have changed the first corner so I am not too sure about that part of the circuit, but if we look at a lap it goes like this. Ignoring the first corner you then head for the first tight 90-degree right-hander, which used to be very bumpy under braking. Hit the kerb on the left-hand side and you lose control immediately. You can brake very late but it is tricky. The left-hander is again very bumpy and it is easy to lose the back end. It is particularly difficult as there is very little grip at the entry to the turn...'

Adelaide, of course, was a street circuit and although mercifully no rain threatened – which would have made overtaking all but impossible – the start might be the matrix of the complete race. Even in the dry overtaking was very, very difficult. At the green light Mansell's Williams wobbled under the whaaack of acceleration and that was enough to allow Schumacher to draw level. Mansell moved to mid-track but by then Schumacher was ahead, the three cars arranged in a stagger: Schumacher, Mansell, Hill. Leading, Schumacher twisted smooth and safe through the corkscrew of the chicane at the end of the start-finish straight, Hill nipping inside Mansell. They travelled down Wakefield Road to the 90-degree right, travelled to the bumpy left-hander and Mansell went off onto a wedge of grass so verdant it might have been a lawn, scrambled back – but fifth. It left Hill alone and friendless to pursue Schumacher. He had been there before, most of the season.

On lap two Hill set fastest lap and started to draw up. The gap crossing the line: 3/10ths and if you blinked you missed it. Schumacher forced it up to just under 2 seconds and held it there, sometimes a bit more, sometimes a bit less; but that wasn't the story of the race because Hill hadn't cracked. He applied a tourniquet of pressure on Schumacher lap on lap, keeping the Williams just there, always there, and Schumacher couldn't shed him.

They pitted together, emerged together, resumed in tandem. Hill sensed that Schumacher was 'feeling the pressure'. Hill lost nothing as they moved through the backmarkers, matching Schumacher move for move, nerve against nerve, in that particularly uncertain art. Fleetingly Hill thrust the Williams directly behind the Benetton but never close enough to risk an outright challenge. They travelled down Wakefield Road and through the 90-degree right followed almost immediately by the left.

The shark-nosed Benetton should have taken that left smooth and safe, just the way Schumacher had made it do 35 times before. Hill was some distance behind but anyway it wasn't an overtaking place. A moment later and without any warning everything changed very, very quickly. The Benetton turned in, but as Schumacher would say 'I got caught on a bump and the car went sideways.' It slewed out of control, scrabbled over multi-coloured kerbing, skittered across the wedge of grass and slapped into a concrete wall; it twitched on impact and bounded back, digging whispers of dust as it went.

The Benetton returned to the track diagonally and at that instant Hill *had* taken the left smooth and safe and was upon it. He had not seen Schumacher hit the wall, only Schumacher's returning. He did not have any chance to gauge the extent of the damage to the Benetton. Hill's impetus was so great that he had to make the Williams veer or strike the rear of the Benetton. The symmetry: both cars within touching distance and *both* diagonal. The mouth of the next corner, a hard right, sucked. In mid-track Schumacher regained control, straightening the Benetton but only when he was far over to the *left*. Hill, hypersensitive, had already straightened the Williams. A millisecond later that hypersensitivity told Hill that a broad gap had opened to the *right*, perfect for the beckoning corner. A flash reading in Hill's mind: *I have to go now*. If only he'd seen Schumacher strike the wall and been able to gauge, 'I wouldn't have gone...'

He angled the Williams towards the gap and straightened it there, feeling towards the corner. Schumacher began to turn in himself but that could only mean turning full across Hill and, under the laws of geometry, into him. The impact forced Hill over curved kerbing at virtually the apex of the corner, Schumacher airborne. The Benetton ran grotesquely, balanced only on the rim of its front and rear left wheels, its underbelly panoramically presented to Hill; but the Benetton was running from Hill and off the circuit again. It righted itself, bounced on all four wheels, skittered over a tight run-off area and head-butted the tyre wall.

'I went to turn into the corner and suddenly I saw Damon

next to me and we just hit each other. I drove over his front wheel and I went up in the air. I was afraid because I thought I was going to roll over, but the car came back.' Schumacher added that after contact with the concrete wall his steering wasn't working properly.

Hill continued round the corner, continued along the short straight and disappeared round the bend at the end of it. 'This was the worst moment,' Schumacher said, 'not being able to continue and yet seeing my rival still driving.' As Schumacher unbuckled his seat belts, levered himself from the Benetton and trotted off tugging at his gloves, Hill need finish only fifth.

On foot Schumacher reached another concrete wall and clambered over through a gap between it and the protective mesh fence above it. He could not know that Hill was limping back on the long journey to the pits, slowing. Schumacher removed his helmet and stood unconsciously chewing his lip. Hill reached the pits with a wheel locked. Worse, a wishbone on the front suspension had bent. He sat in the cockpit and the clock flickered, 7 seconds stationary, 8, 9, 10, 11, 12. At 12 he shook his head. He lifted the visor on his helmet and his eyes seemed enlarged, incredulous, saddened, resigned, perhaps embittered. The clock no longer held meaning. Mechanics, urgent uniformed figures flitting to and fro, gathered at the wishbone and felt it, probed it. A gloved hand, gentle as a caress, touched the wishbone where it had bent like a crease. Another gloved hand gripped it there, moved it up and down testing its strength or its weakness.

Hill sat motionless.

Schumacher stood behind the concrete wall so far away, the lip he had been chewing pursed now. He waited for Hill to come round again, waited to watch his Championship pass by.

They stopped working on Hill's car. Still he sat motionless.

Schumacher's tongue scoured his lip, moistening it because the tension had dried it so much. He watched a Williams come quickly, quickly, quickly towards him – but it had a red number 2 on its snout. That was Mansell, not Hill. Schumacher heard on the loudspeakers that Hill 'had a problem but I wasn't sure what kind of problem'. He watched Mansell go by a second time, a third, no sign of Hill at all. 'Then I thought, *that's it.*'

Hill waited in the pits in the car that could not be mended in time. He sat hoping something could be done, the only chance left that he had. Further up the pit lane the Benetton team watched. Hill got out and walked away by himself. The Benetton mechanics unleashed themselves from their rigidity, danced up and down, embraced, waved to the crowd.

Deep into the Williams pit Hill took his helmet off and the loudspeakers were proclaiming he was out. Schumacher wandered off shaking his head in wonder and initial realisation while a forest of spectators' hands reached out to him. He slapped a few affectionately, shook a couple. Schumacher wandered back to where he had been standing, his whole face lost in a grin and still the hands reached out to touch him. He leant against the protective wire mesh, his fist drawn like a shield to his forehead in order that the wire didn't cut it. In the Williams pit Hill raised his fist and levered his arm downwards in a compressed gesturing of despair and mouthed something – not an obscenity, which he didn't need, but a profound protest against fate which plays such melodies on human ambition.

A Championship lost and won, here and gone.

Hill faced the microphones and said, 'I've a bit of an empty feeling but I gave him a good run for his money. He was certainly feeling the pressure because he ended up falling off the road. I saw the opportunity and I thought *I've got to go here.* I didn't make it. That's motor racing. I am not going to be drawn on the interpretation of what happened. I am very disappointed for my family as much as myself. I want to say that everyone in the Rothmans Williams Renault team deserves a medal this year. They have been through a hell of a tough time and here we were fighting for the Championship and looking very strong and competitive.' He did not compromise on his natural dignity, which is what a big man does when the melodies have taunted; didn't cast deep into the well of perceived injustice.

Mansell won the Australian Grand Prix from Berger and Brundle although, as the new Champion, Schumacher joined them to face the world's Press. After some typical Berger banter – he computed that he, Mansell and Brundle had a combined age of '120 years' – Schumacher spoke. You couldn't miss that he was struggling to get the pitch right; he felt towards the occasion as he might have felt for the mouth of any corner, conscious of what a bump might bring. The interviewer said that presumably he would not have wished to see the Championship decided in this way. I set down Schumacher's response verbatim, and as it was spoken, because it ought to be so. I've only added a measure of interpretation in square brackets.

'Certainly. It was a great battle between me and Damon in the state of the race and I have to say he has done a really good job during it. We both didn't make mistakes and it was really, I would say, thrilling for you on the outside.

'I have to say I did make some comments this year about Damon that I didn't have the kind of respect for him that maybe I had for somebody else [Senna, no doubt], but I have to admit that I was wrong. What he has done in the last two races in particular – and what he did before – has been a fantastic job. He has been a great rival and I must say sorry for what I maybe said. I'd like to congratulate him.

'Nevertheless the feeling about the Championship, winning the Championship... I nearly won it earlier this year and then I got banned for a couple of races and couldn't continue. I lost a lot of points so I thought, "Now it's going to be very, very tough and difficult to make this Championship up again." Just sitting here now having won it, it's a dream, it's, it's...

'The emotions in me, I mean Nigel can talk about this as

well. You can't really bring it outside. I have them here but I can't express them…'

Mansell: 'It'll get better…'

'It will get better? I must also say that this year our team has done a really, really good job. With the package we had available we really squeezed out a hundred per cent. There was nothing left. As you saw it got more and more difficult towards the end of the season and I'd like to thank those people.

'I have something special to say about this whole season. The season started quite well, I would say, in Brazil. Aida was a good race and then we came up to Imola. What happened there is just a… if I talked about nightmares before that [I didn't know about nightmares]. All of us know what kind of feelings we had to make, particularly about Ayrton but as well for Roland, and for Karl after his crash at Monte Carlo.

'To me it was always clear that I was not going to win the Championship, and it was Ayrton who was going to win the Championship. But he hasn't been here for the last races and I'd like to take this Championship and give it to him. He is the driver who should have won it. He was the best driver, he had the best car and those are my feelings about him. It was difficult at the time to show those feelings because I am not somebody who likes to show their feelings to the outside world, but I always thought about it and it's the right time now to do something: to give something which I achieved – and he should have achieved – to him.'

Then it was time, high time, to put a Crocodile Dundee hat on and go dancing amidst a happy throng of a party.

Next day, composure regained, he was pressed about the crash of '94 and insisted in his quiet, methodical way, 'I was still in front of Damon. I drove over his front wheel. It was still my corner…'

Chapter 6

SCARED, REALLY SCARED

From late March to late April 1995 Michael Schumacher's career resembled a looking glass of chaos, confusion and controversy. At instants it deepened beyond even that. Could the crisp young man with the quasi-military haircut really be defending motor racing Champion of the World?

While all this was being played out the Horse remained untamed. Alesi would score 42 points and Berger 31, fifth and sixth in the Championship. Year upon year they rode but never reached the finishing post first never mind the taming. Alesi suffered enough misfortune to break a heart but kept forcing whatever car Barnard gave him to the edge, and over it. His passion flowed into that of the crowd, and theirs flowed back to him in a communion. It was just the sort of thing the mythology created – but Jody Scheckter was still the last Ferrari Champion, and that hot, dry Monza afternoon when they chanted *Jo-dee, Jo-dee, Jo-dee* was a long memory ago.

Barnard evaluates that year's Ferrari as 'actually quite nice, the 412 was a good little car, simple, basic. Alesi and Berger liked it. What we needed to do was improve the aerodynamic efficiency. One problem I had was that I kept being pushed by Montezemolo. "What are you going to do for us, what's new?" I shouldn't have succumbed to it but they wanted me to produce the miracle. "Where's the miracle?" They wanted something new, something different and I kept pushing to try and find it.'

It is true 1995 ought to have been the settled season governed by new rules to bring the purity of racing back to racing, and once the traditional driver-team arrangements had been struck the season did look primed with much more than the usual promise.

The drivers in the leading teams:

Schumacher was joined at Benetton by the precocious Herbert, now full time after doing Japan and Australia for the team.

Ferrari – Alesi, Berger.

Jordan – Barrichello, Irvine.

McLaren – Mark Blundell, Mansell then Häkkinen.

Williams kept Hill and gave Coulthard a contract rather than Mansell.

The kernel of the 16 races, beginning on 26 March, appeared to be Schumacher v Hill Part II, not least since Benetton now had the same mighty Renault engines as Williams.

Benetton unveiled their new car in February and Schumacher insisted he wasn't feeling undue pressure despite so many people telling him he was clear favourite to retain the Championship. This is the sort of thing drivers insist, anyway. Schumacher did concede he'd moved from being 'the hunter to the hunted'. Benetton tested at the Paul Ricard circuit in the south of France where he did a best time of 1m 9.01s but Berger ran him close, no more than nine-hundredths slower. Williams tested at Estoril and when Benetton went there it stayed close.

Schumacher	1:21.30
Irvine (Jordan)	1:21.67
Hill	1:21.75
Coulthard	1:21.75

The identical times of Hill and Coulthard are not, incidentally, a misprint, but one of those statistical astonishments that occasionally come along. Briatore paid a flying visit and during it Schumacher hacked out his hot lap. The team denied any 'conspiracy', insisting that it was just one of those coincidental astonishments that come along. Overall, and so far, nothing unusual.

With only a few days to the opener at Interlagos in Brazil events at McLaren drowned even contemplation of Schumacher v Hill Part II. To general astonishment McLaren admitted that million-dollar Mansell wouldn't fit in the cockpit of their million-dollar car and wouldn't go to Brazil or the following race, Argentina. Schumacher, meanwhile, spoke in measured tones of how sensitive it would be returning to Brazil, the first race there since Senna's death.

In sum he anticipated a lively struggle with Hill. 'I feel more relaxed because I am Champion.'

On the Thursday at Interlagos the drivers were weighed. In previous years the car had to be a minimum 515kg, but under one of those rule changes the car *and* driver must now be a minimum 595kg. This seemed straightforward and worked like this: the cars would be weighed again during the season but the drivers' weights from this Thursday taken as a constant – because they wouldn't vary much – and added. No point in weighing the drivers the whole time. Schumacher was 77kg, which seemed mildly curious because at the beginning of 1994 he'd been 69. (A kilogram is 2.2lb, so he'd put on over a stone.) Whatever, a man could clearly gain that over 12 months, as many of us know to our cost.

In Friday first qualifying he was sixth and pushing hard. In a corner he felt a 'little movement' from the car and in the next corner he had no steering at all. He missed the apex and the Benetton flowed onto grass. He reacted instinctively – so instinctively that subsequently he wasn't quite sure what he'd done – and changed down, making the car slew to strike a tyre wall backwards. The tyre wall shattered and scattered. Schumacher, shaken, said he wouldn't race unless the cause of the problem could be discovered and cured. It was, but only after much consternation at anticipating Schumacher v Hill minus Schumacher.

In second qualifying Schumacher went quickest, but not quick enough to dislodge Hill who'd taken provisional pole on the Friday. Schumacher led the race until he pitted on lap 18, ceding the lead to Hill, but on lap 30 Hill's gearbox seized and he spun off. Schumacher pitted a second time, ceding the lead to Coulthard, but regained it when Coulthard pitted, and never lost it. He beat Coulthard by some eight seconds. Nothing unusual, another Schumacher win. He'd set off any minute for a relaxing break on the coast.

Before that he was weighed again (a spot check) and the scales said 71.5kg. This would cause an eruption, although not before a different eruption. Five hours after the race – Schumacher long departed, and Coulthard too – the FIA announced that Elf fuel samples taken from the Benetton and Williams did not match the fuel samples previously submitted for approval. Schumacher and Coulthard were stripped of their points pending appeals by the teams. While Formula One tried to ingest this, word emerged of what the scales said and a ringing question was born that anyone who has ever dieted found fascinating. How could Schumacher be 77kg on Thursday and 71.5 on Sunday? Without the Sunday check, 77 would have been added to the car during the season rather than 71.5. Patrick Head, the Williams designer, estimated that pulling 5.5kg less meant around 14 seconds gained over a race.

Many mischievous theories were put forward but Heiner Bickinger, Schumacher's PR, countered. 'First of all he had a couple of days off before Brazil. He went to the Club Med and they have a pretty good French cuisine. He likes to eat and he likes to eat good. Therefore when he arrived at the racetrack he had one or two more kilos than usual. Secondly he didn't have his race helmet when he was on the scales, because that didn't arrive until Friday – but that's only a few hundred grams. He drank between two and three litres of water, and you can translate one litre of water to one kilo of weight, as part of his fitness programme. That was coupled with some salt tablets to keep the water in the body and make the blood thin. He's naturally losing between one and two kilos during the race, and if you watched I think you saw that the car wasn't good at all compared to the Williams and Ferrari. He had to work a lot harder than the other drivers.'

Schumacher said, 'I certainly did not go to the toilet before the weigh-in.' Surely billion-dollar Grand Prix racing hadn't come to this?

Following Brazil, Berger (third, a lap down, but promoted to first pending the appeals) caused an aftershock when he seemed to say in a British newspaper that 'cheating is cheating'. Berger pointed out that what he actually said was 'rules are rules', something self-evidently true and not the same thing. The 'cheating is cheating', however, stung Michel Bonnet, Elf's head of marketing, to a trenchant response. 'For a team to say that one of their competitors is cheating, and for the drivers to say that, I find shocking.'

Holidaying at Bahia, Brazil, Schumacher went out in a boat to dive a coral reef. Fiancée Corinna Betsch and manager Willi Weber remained on the boat while Schumacher made the dive – with an instructor, a hotel manager, and his trainer Harry Hawkela – eight miles off the coast. The boat drifted and when Schumacher came up it had moved out of sight.

'It was a terrible feeling. The waves were quite big. In the beginning I was screaming to get together and take hands, trying to get to the boat, but we didn't move and it was difficult with the waves taking us backwards and forwards. I felt I could go quicker by myself. I opened up the belt with the weights and threw that away and I was thinking of taking off the air bottle but I didn't know how to do that without losing the life-vest which was with it so in the end I tried to swim with the bottle. The other three guys were almost finished. They were just lying on the water with their life vests on. Corinna saw me first.' Schumacher had swum for an hour to make sure he and the others were picked up safely.

'For the first time in my life, I thought that was it,' Schumacher said. 'For the first time I got scared, really scared. When I had the accident in Brazil, for example, where I suddenly had no steering, it didn't scare me. It happened, we had an explanation for it, we resolved it. I feel comfortable in a racing car where I know what I'm doing but I've never thought about death before.'

No Grand Prix had been held in Argentina since 1981 for a variety of financial and political reasons. Coulthard took pole, Hill alongside, Schumacher on the second row. Coulthard led but had problems, drifted back, seemed to overcome the problems and drew up to Schumacher, outbraked him and overtook him. In the course of this move Schumacher appeared to back off. For a driver so strong and uncompromising this might be revealing. Hill drove a magnificent race to win from Alesi, Schumacher third. Schumacher made three pit stops and explained that 'there was a lot of variation in the performance depending on the tyres. On the first and third set of tyres I was nowhere but on the last set everything was perfect and I was able to set fastest lap of the race. If I had had four sets like that I think I could have won.'

By now the German Press had rounded on Schumacher, and the German Press, like the German Police, are not be to trifled with. He arrived in Buenos Aires and complained that 'no one talked about what a great race I had in Brazil. They wrote of other things. I am getting to the point where I find these accusations too much to take. There are limits. I have thought about going to IndyCars. I was thinking about it before Brazil but certainly thinking about it afterwards.'

On the Thursday after Argentina the FIA Appeals Committee met in Paris and reinstated the Schumacher and Coulthard points. Elf expressed satisfaction:

> 'After detailed examination of the technical problem which took place at the Brazilian Grand Prix and which brought about the disqualification of Michael Schumacher, Benetton Renault, and David Coulthard, Williams Renault, both teams and their petroleum partner Elf confirm, in the light of the information they have obtained so far, that the difference in the original fuel sample sent to the FIA for approval and the fuel used by the two teams at the Brazilian Grand Prix was due to a difference in the sampling procedures.
>
> 'They acknowledge that the chromatographic [dividing components of a mixture] procedures used by the FIA and the equipment which was used was correct and that some statements made to the press by Elf and the teams were based on information that was received prior to knowledge of the results of the new analysis.
>
> 'The FIA have confirmed that the fuel used by the two teams was completely legal and they acknowledge that no advantage was obtained by the fuel used by the teams and that there was no intention to infringe the regulation. The decision of the Stewards was based on the fact that the chromatogram of the fuel used at the event was not identical to the chromatogram of the sample that was sent by Elf for approval by the FIA.'

Another eruption, despite fines of $200,000 on Benetton and Williams. Lauda, currently Ferrari adviser, said, 'I cannot separate car and driver completely. If this is the new rule, you can build an illegal car and let the team pay for victory. The whole thing is only commercial and has nothing to do with sport any more. It's like scoring a half-goal in soccer – it is not possible. Either you score a goal or not. The decision for me is the biggest defeat for the FIA, who cannot govern the sport any longer.' Berger put it more bluntly, as well he might. 'I no longer understand anything. Formula One has become a joke.'

Table after Argentina		Table after Paris	
Berger	11	Schumacher	14
Hill	10	Hill	10
Alesi	10	Alesi	8
Häkkinen	6	Coulthard	6
Schumacher	4	Berger	5

Before Imola, Schumacher was quoted as saying that 'Berger should concentrate on racing instead of thinking how he can criticise me. If Berger drove with the talent he shows doing his own PR he would have won many more races. I have never understood how somebody could celebrate a victory like that [Brazil] one lap down and winning after someone else has been disqualified.'

Berger struck back a day later. 'I never criticised Schumacher. I only criticised the decision [to reinstate him]. I can live with Schumacher being angry. I was declared the winner by the FIA Stewards so I had every reason to open the champagne.' Berger also referred to the podium after the San Marino Grand Prix of 1994: the race had been restarted after Senna's accident and Schumacher won. 'I cannot understand how someone can celebrate a victory by jumping around when one of our colleagues has died.' Berger described this jumping around as 'like a clown' and also said he objected to champagne being sprayed. Schumacher struck back at that. 'Berger has a short memory. First, there was no champagne. Second, Senna's death was only announced later.'

Before Imola, Schumacher and Berger met in a gym in Monte Carlo and smoothed out their differences.

At Imola, Mosley gave a Press Conference and admonished Schumacher. 'I think it is unfortunate that the World Champion gets involved in a misunderstanding about how much he may or may not weigh at any time on a race weekend. It reflects poorly on the sport and shows lack of an adult attitude. It's not extraordinary that somebody should put on a stone over a year, particularly as weight no longer matters and they've been doing a lot of training and so on. What is extraordinary is that he should lose it in three days. It was a pity that it became a matter for public discussion, whether he drank a huge amount of water, didn't go to the loo or had a heavy helmet. It is just a pity he didn't take care that it didn't happen.' Schumacher struck back at *that*. During the weekend he met Mosley. 'I told him that in future it might be good if he had a word with me before [he said such things] so he can judge from the facts.'

Schumacher took pole although under the weight of Senna's memory confessed that he'd rather the race had been somewhere else. Pole was decided on the Friday because hotter weather on the Saturday precluded improvements.

It rained on race morning and the front-runners chose wet tyres. Schumacher made a mighty, monumental start, Berger tucked in behind. They threaded safely through, the cars nervy as the tyres sought grip. Schumacher felt confident that he could 'control' Berger. Soon enough a dry line appeared and Berger pitted for slicks on lap 5, leaving Schumacher 2.1 seconds ahead of Coulthard. Schumacher pitted for slicks on lap 10 and emerged third behind Coulthard and Berger. Moving towards Piratella, the hard left on the far side of the circuit, Schumacher lost the Benetton. It spun on the grass, struck a wall, spun on, bounded across a run-off area partially in the air and thrashed a tyre barrier. Schumacher clambered out quickly and trotted from the scene. 'After the tyre change I felt that the car was a bit unstable at the rear. It's not clear why I went off and we will have to investigate the reason. I was afraid because it's a really quick part of the circuit and it felt as if the spinning was never going to stop.' Hill won to be on 20 points, Schumacher 14.

One aspect seemed clear. The Benetton's chassis was not yet as good as the Williams, suggesting that Schumacher was having to dig too deep into himself to compensate. Another aspect did not seem clear. Were the accumulating pressure of this *and* the almost daily controversies exacting a toll? Schumacher's race engineer Pat Symonds said lustily, 'Michael knows damn well that if you get into a race and your car is not capable of winning but is capable of finishing second then you get six points and that's what counts at the end of the year. Maybe Michael did make a mistake – people do – but if he did I don't think it was necessarily the result of pressure. Leading the race then throwing it at the wall is not the sort of thing Michael does.'

In Spain, Schumacher gave his own answer but not before Hill had said of him, 'I know he has a certain amount of arrogance but I don't believe he is impervious to criticism. At the weigh-in in Brazil he was pushing the regulations and effectively stuck two fingers up at them. That is not the sort of behaviour you expect from a Champion. He has been making mistakes, too, which is the sign of someone over-driving.'

Schumacher's answer? He dug deep to take pole on the Saturday (1:21.45 against Alesi's 1:22.05, Hill fifth on 1:22.34) and – discounting the diversion of pit stops – led the race from beginning to end, making no semblance of a mistake. Hill, a distant second until the final lap when he lost hydraulic pressure, came fourth. That gave Schumacher the Championship lead 24–23.

At Monaco, Hill took a tight pole from Schumacher, 0.79 of a second between them but potentially decisive if Hill reached the first corner in the lead; he did. Schumacher pressured for a while then fell back for what seemed a pleasant Sunday afternoon run and six points. Hill pitted for new tyres and fuel – the first of two stops – and Schumacher would follow any lap now. Wouldn't he? Schumacher went hard to build a gap before his stop and this became wondrous to behold, the shark-nosed Benetton oscillating under power, quivering towards the metal barriers, bounding over the bumps as it searched out its prey; and that prey was time itself, the car swallowing the seconds that ought to have belonged to Hill. Lap after lap Schumacher did not come in.

Only then was the strategy clear. Schumacher intended to stop only once and if he could sustain his pace until then Hill faced a crippling disadvantage from which he could not recover – the time lost in his extra pit stop. Schumacher flew onwards and won it by 35 seconds. Yes, he'd say, a pleasant Sunday afternoon run, and pleasanter in the Championship, 34–29, Hill visibly downcast.

Hill would be more than downcast in Canada. Schumacher had pole and led comfortably from Hill, who fell back into the clutches of the Ferraris and was overtaken by them before the hydraulic pump failed after 50 laps. As he emerged from the cockpit his whole body was consumed by rage. He'd been third at the time, four points gone. Nor was he mollified when on lap 57 Schumacher crawled into the pits stuck in third gear; a new steering wheel (they contain the gear shift mechanism, of course) was fitted and Schumacher burned a path from seventh to fifth and two points. Schumacher 36–29.

Schumacher had been almost mechanical in his mastery at Montreal until circumstances beyond his control intervened. That was one aspect of him. Monaco distilled another aspect – not just the arguments and fines and suspensions but the supreme racing driver: *you are being educated in my masterclass.*

As much as you can pinpoint such things with any accuracy the Championship tilted towards Schumacher at Montreal and Hill wasn't able to stabilise it again. The French Grand Prix three weeks later confirmed that because although Hill took pole from him the race turned on tactics and Benetton were artists at that now. Hill led and Schumacher pressured him, almost hit him when Hill negotiated a backmarker – 'I am very angry,' Schumacher would say. Schumacher pitted first and, emerging, set fastest lap. Hill meanwhile now had to negotiate three backmarkers before his pit stop so that although it was a second quicker than Schumacher's he still emerged eight seconds behind him. End of story.

On Herbert the merciless weight of comparison had fallen, sixth in the table on 12 points.

When the pit stops were done in the British Grand Prix Schumacher led and Hill on fresh tyres gave chase, 20 laps to go. A great urgency held Hill because the advantage of the fresh tyres wouldn't last long. He knew that. Schumacher knew that. The gap was 2.3 seconds, and to maintain it – to keep Hill at bay until the tyres went off – Schumacher goaded the Benetton so hard he was locking wheels. The gap narrowed, 1.5, and across three laps virtually vanished: 0.4. Powerful stimuli were at work, psychological and physical.

Schumacher and Hill travelled into the Complex before the pit lane straight which contorts right under the bridge, left, left again, right. Between the bridge and the first left Schumacher went wide, positioning himself to turn in but – Hill thought instantaneously – creating a gap down the inside. Hill lunged into the 'gap' and Schumacher turned in. They thumped, scudded off. You can always have two views about these things and re-viewing in video slo-mo is instructive but hardly fair to drivers who had to make their decisions *now*. However, and accepting that Schumacher did go wide, at no stage was Hill near enough to claim the corner.

The rest was a mosaic of faces. A German television crew hovered to interview Schumacher and he looked stony, his eyes sharpened and locked into the distance. You couldn't even tell whether his gaze fell upon the track, where Herbert was winning the race. Afterwards Herbert could barely contain his delight and Schumacher was there to congratulate him, smile with him. Hill, surrounded by microphones and tape recorders, gave his side of it: 'I thought I saw an opportunity I could take advantage of and I'm afraid that Michael is a harder man to pass than that.' Schumacher gave his: 'It was completely unnecessary in my view what Damon has done there. There was no room for him to go there.'

Before Hockenheim, questions were asked in the British tabloid media about Hill's safety. Reportedly Hill had received death threats the year before. Schumacher said, 'I'm pleading for fairness. I cannot see that Hill wanted to take me off the road deliberately [at Silverstone] although I cannot understand his manoeuvre. I still feel bad [about the death threats]. We are doing a sport here. I have been fairly treated by British fans wherever I have gone so I expect the same from the Germans for Damon.'

In fact Hill had quite other problems, spinning out after the first lap while Schumacher simply flowed to the end unmolested. Schumacher 56, Hill 35.

Some time after Hockenheim something almost inevitable happened. Ferrari offered Michael Schumacher $25 million a year to tame the Horse.

He said yes. Ultimately, it was as simple as that.

Barnard explores the background. 'It was a case of this: you knew you wanted him, everybody wanted him – he was thunderingly quick – but how do you get him? I was there and at the time I was a strong enough pull. He was interested to work with me and we had programmes going at Ferrari. He went right above di Montezemolo, he went straight in up to

Agnelli level [Gianni Agnelli, head of Fiat which owns Ferrari]. He wasn't about to put himself in a situation where the President was changed after a year, which could happen very easily. He and his people made very sure about that.'

The idea was that the miracle would come from driver and designer working together. Barnard insists a driver like that 'wouldn't move unless he thought there was a chance of doing something with a team he was moving to.' Barnard is being factual, not fanciful, when he adds that although they hadn't worked together before 'he'd seen lots of evidence of what I'd done – he'd come to Benetton after I was there – and I'd got a reasonably good track record. I think he was keen to work with me. In fact that was in his contract at the beginning.' If Barnard left, he could leave too.

'It was strange because various people were talking to me, saying, "Well, of course, if you get on with him, if you really work well with him, the sky's the limit." That was true but the problem remained, and they didn't realise it: I did not expect to be and did not want to be on track 100% of the time looking after one driver. As everybody knows, I live here in Guildford and I do not intend to move.'

In Hungary the fuel pump failed near the end when he was second to Hill. Schumacher 56, Hill 45.

The sharpness of the season lingered. At Spa, the weather typically changing from moment to moment, Schumacher qualified 16th (which, for the record, was only the second time in his whole career so far that he had been outqualified by a team-mate). A grid of delicious prospect, then: Berger and Alesi on the front row, Hill the eighth, Schumacher lost so far back even from that. Hill needed until lap 14 to seize the lead but a lap later Schumacher was behind him, after which Hill pitted and Schumacher was in the lead. Schumacher risked all by staying out on slick tyres in the wet to gain a decisive advantage over Hill – he remembered seeing Senna do this here in 1992. At one moment, as Hill on rain tyres threatened, Schumacher outbraked him at Les Combes. It prompted a fellow Formula One driver, Gachot, to murmur, 'There are two things in this world that you don't want to do unless you have to. One is climb into a ring with heavyweight champion Mike Tyson and the other is race that guy.'

Williams felt some of Schumacher's tactics in keeping Hill behind were so questionable that they merited a protest. Schumacher received a one-race ban suspended over the next four races and said he intended to appeal. After due consideration he didn't. If you lose an appeal they tend to crank up the punishment. Meanwhile Berger signed for Benetton for 1996, insisting it wasn't because of Schumacher coming to Ferrari. 'That wasn't the case at all. Neither he nor anyone else counted in the decision. What I took into consideration was the engine side.' Alesi would join him at Benetton.

This August, Schumacher married Corinna in a ceremony near Bonn.

The lingering sharpness was reborn on lap 24 at Monza, a weekend of undercurrents. Schumacher ought to have been worshipped as the new Messiah coming, in 1996, to rescue Ferrari; Alesi ought to have been reviled for leaving Ferrari to join Benetton with Berger.

Monza's paddock is a fortress and an animated crowd stands ten or twenty deep at the entrance yearning for a glimpse of any driver but especially the two riding the Horses. The trick for the driver is to be as anonymous as possible and get inside the fortress as fast as possible. Alesi responded to such notions by arriving in the most publicly visible, and touchable, way – on his scooter with his girlfriend on the back. The people who'd chanted *Jo-dee, Jo-dee, Jo-dee* so long ago now chanted *Ale-si, Ale-si, Ale-si*.

Schumacher came in a car protected, as one source puts it, by a 'machine gun-toting police escort' and some of the throng called obscenities as he passed. The *tifosi,* the adoring supporters, are prey to emotion more than logic.

They'd treasured Lauda for his heroism and his Championships, flung rotten fruit at him in 1977 because he was leaving Ferrari; they'd thrown stones at Alain Prost and spread straw on the track during testing – so he'd go off – because his Renault was beating the Ferraris; they'd cheered Rene Arnoux, whose Renault had just won the Italian Grand Prix of 1982, because he was joining Ferrari; they'd jeered Patrese, a fellow *Italian,* because his Brabham went off leading the 1983 San Marino Grand Prix, allowing a *Frenchman,* Patrick Tambay, to win in a Ferrari. The dislike of Prost was so intense that, this same year of 1983, he arrived with the President of France's bodyguard to protect him; seven years later, when Prost came to tame, they openly venerated him. And so it went. The reaction of the *tifosi* was not fickle or contradictory but entirely consistent. If you were with Ferrari you might win their respect but what they really sought, in journalist Pino Allievi's delicious phrase, was 'people who have something to transmit from the heart.'

And if you weren't with Ferrari you represented the enemy.

Mario Andretti understood that perfectly when he was brought back to contest Monza in 1982, replacing Pironi, crippled. He'd last driven for Ferrari a decade before and was presently in IndyCars. Andretti wore a red Ferrari cap, Prancing Horse prominent, as he disembarked from an Alitalia jet in Milan. It meant *I care enough about this to show you I care*, it meant *I have come to be the expression of your passion.* The glimpse of the cap created hysteria.

Schumacher could easily silence the obscenities by winning in a Ferrari, and everybody knew that, but he might never enter those darkened, secret places every Italian holds sacred because as a matter of first principle he thought, lived, and drove rationally. The ones who'd transmitted from the heart –

Villeneuve, perhaps Arnoux, certainly Alesi, perhaps Mansell – had driven in the grip of their own passion, offering the blood red cars and themselves as flourishes against whatever fate brought. That created communion.

Berger led the Italian Grand Prix from Schumacher and Hill. A crocodile of cars crossed the line to begin lap 24, Berger already gone through, Taki Inoue (Arrows) about to be lapped, Jean-Christophe Boullion (Sauber) about to be lapped, Schumacher, Hill, Alesi. At the mouth of the first chicane Boullion flicked adroitly aside to form an open channel for Schumacher, Hill and Alesi. They threaded through nose-to-tail, no problem. Ahead the imperious Curva Grande carved its path through the parkland trees. Around it Inoue hugged the inside, Schumacher overtaking him on the outside, no problem. Hill followed Inoue nose-to-tail.

As the corner uncoiled and straightened into the lunge to the second chicane Inoue darted sharp left. He subsequently admitted he was unaware of Hill's presence and had made the move because the braking point for the chicane was 'coming very quickly' and he worried that, if he remained behind Schumacher, his aerodynamics would not work in the turbulent air created by the Benetton. At the mouth of the chicane, which is a left-right, Schumacher was to the right and on the brakes, Hill suddenly behind, Inoue away to the left. Hill rammed Schumacher and – it might have been Silverstone again – they scudded off. When they came to rest Schumacher sprang out and sprinted across to remonstrate with Hill, who still sat in the cockpit of the Williams. Schumacher was led off by marshals, shaking his head. Hill said that Inoue 'shouldn't have a licence. He changed lines twice in front of me. He let Schumacher by, blocked me, then moved out of the way again.'

In the sound and fury of the aftermath suggestions were made that Schumacher was entering the chicane more slowly than he had been before to box Hill behind Inoue. Benetton contested this strongly when they'd examined their telemetry, insisting that at the point of impact Schumacher was going slightly faster than on the previous two laps and he'd braked eight metres later.

Herbert won.

Coulthard took Portugal from Schumacher and Hill, then in the European Grand Prix at the Nürburgring Schumacher virtually settled the World Championship and summoned from himself a performance of such refinement, intensity and bravado that you knew you were witnessing something historic. Alesi led, Hill spun off and Schumacher, obliged to make a third pit stop for fuel, had 16 laps to regain 24 seconds to Alesi. The master went to work, creating a force which – mounting and gathering – carried him to Alesi and, outrageously, past him in the eye-of-a-needle chicane, the two cars intertwined, their wheels overlapping but not touching. It was one of the great overtaking moves.

Schumacher needed no more than third place in the Pacific Grand Prix at Aida, Japan, for the Championship and promptly won the race, Hill third. It couldn't be that neat and it wasn't. Schumacher accused Hill of naughty blocking and Hill mounted a robust defence. Schumacher won the Japanese Grand Prix at Suzuka, equalling Mansell's record of nine in a season, but crashed with Alesi at Adelaide, which Hill won.

Chapter 7

THE BRONCO

A November morning. Michael Schumacher flew in his Citation 2 plane from Nice to Bologna with Corinna and a friend. The twin-jet plane had eight seats, cost $1.9m and had belonged to Thierry Boutsen. It was flown by Schumacher's pilot, an American called Roger Giadone. Corinna and her friend set off into Bologna to do some shopping while Schumacher was driven to Maranello, 40km to the north-west, by Weber.

They toured the Ferrari factory, then Schumacher had lunch with his new partner, Irvine, and di Montezemolo. Irvine had signed a contract which bound him tightly to supporting Schumacher, not supplanting him. The consolation came in regular wage packets of large amounts. 'I have to tell you Eddie was very happy with his situation,' Barnard says. 'I'd been involved in that discussion: who do we get as a second driver?'

Schumacher became so engrossed in conversation with the engineers that he was 90 minutes late for a Press Conference. There Todt presented the two drivers. Schumacher wore blue jeans and a thigh-length anorak, Irvine a casual jacket.

One report, by Pino Allievi (under a joint byline, to report the report accurately), contained these words: 'The atmosphere in the team was said to be one of curiosity, but not particularly warm.' I asked Allievi to expand on that. He explained that that was the initial feeling about Schumacher. 'We did not know him.'

Nigel Stepney, Ferrari's Chief Mechanic, was present when Schumacher first came to the factory for a seat-fitting. Stepney has spent a lifetime in Formula One, working at Lotus with Ayrton Senna, and sees everything with a steady eye. 'I didn't know Schumacher before,' he says. 'It was the first time he came to Maranello. We prepared him in the November. I was doing the seat-fitting with some of the other people, the engineers and everybody. My first impression? Well, he's a very typical German. I say typically German because he's fresh, cold, clean, got a good image – a clean image – and he commands respect. He was very fit and very enthusiastic even for one of the top-line racing drivers.'

It really began on another November day in 1995, at the test track at Fiorano, when Schumacher prepared to lever himself into a Ferrari for the first time. He wore plain white overalls. Alesi and Berger had gone to Benetton, of course – normally drivers' contracts run to the last minute of the last day of December but, just this once, it made sense to allow Schumacher to test the Ferrari and vice versa with Alesi and Berger. To avoid the nightmare of clashing sponsors all three were bared.

It was a cool afternoon and an estimated 2,000 spectators pressed against Fiorano's perimeter fence to witness the moment. Irvine watched, too. Schumacher said emotion touched him that so many had come. You know the way the world is: he covered one lap before a driveshaft problem halted him. They worked on that and the shadows of early evening were drawing in when he put together a sustained but prudent run of 16 laps.

He didn't push it and that was interesting because mythology demanded each new leading Ferrari driver break the Fiorano lap record. Schumacher clearly did not feel the need to do that or bow before the mythology. 'I just wanted to get used to the car,' he'd say before he made all the right noises, about how proud he was, about his enthusiasm and the work to be done ('a lot but I am quite optimistic'). He'd explain how he anticipated race wins in 1996 but the championship wouldn't come into play until 1997. This was the Press Release-speak.

He tested at Estoril and at the end of the first day it rained. Out he went, loving it, then pronounced the Ferrari was the best car he'd driven in the wet. During the test, over four days, he did push – to within touching distance of the fastest man there, Jacques Villeneuve (Williams-Renault). Villeneuve did a 1m 20.94s, Schumacher a 1m 21.20s.

Estoril was fascinating but revealed a potentially serious problem. 'I'd not spoken to him before, no, not really,' Barnard says. 'We had two cars at the test, the 12-cylinder – the one we'd been racing – and the first 10-cylinder "mule" [workhorse] that we'd put together. Schumacher came along and drove the 12-cylinder, and of course first thing he was immediately quicker than Alesi and Berger, he was on the pace with the current latest crop of other cars testing at Estoril. He said, "I like this, it's a good little car. If I'd had this I'd have won the Championship easily." That's what he said. So we thought, "Bloody hell, this is a bit different."

'What came out of it was interesting. Through all the season we'd been dealing with the 12-cylinder engine and it had a lot of internal friction in it. Our drivers were finding it difficult to drive smoothly because of this internal friction. Every time you lifted off the throttle you'd get a big reaction from the engine and it would tend to upset the car. We were always struggling with this. Schumacher, on the other hand, drove a car very differently and it was the first insight I'd had into seeing just how differently. We thought, "Oh, he'll get in the 10-cylinder and it will be better," because the engine had less friction inside it – it was smoother to drive. You could lift off and it didn't have the massive reaction, and so on and so on. It was lighter at the back of the car and that would help.

'Not so. In fact Schumacher preferred the "12" because he drove it on the throttle and that's what I didn't understand until I was there. He had a front end that would turn into a corner like a go-kart: just flick it in and you're gone through the corner. What he did, he balanced the car on the throttle all the way through the corner and he needed the braking power of the engine to make the car react to the throttle.'

He played on the throttle – you'd hear it, baarp, baarp, baarp – very much as Senna once did; and needing the braking power means that if you change down a gear and don't touch the throttle you can feel the engine braking. It is a characteristic of all engines.

'The other guys had been saying, "Oh Christ, can't drive like this, every time you lift off it does this and it does that," so we'd been working on all kinds of strategies and electronics and goodness knows what. Then along comes Schumacher and says, "Yeah, I like that."'

Because this leads so directly to the immediate future, I intend to break the narrative and examine part of that future. Schumacher liked any car set up so that it turned in to corners with vicious suddenness. 'I think the main ability I have is a good and consistent feeling for the limit and I am able to run the car virtually a hundred per cent on the limit. That's probably the difference in style.' He'd broaden that by explaining a driver might have the ability to do that in the entry of a corner but not, say, in mid-corner or at the exit again – or combinations of these. 'I can almost do this all the way around the corner.'

Hence the problem for Barnard.

'By this time [the Estoril test] we had already gone down the road for the 10-cylinder, which was the correct decision anyway, but because of that we had to put a seven-speed gearbox in,' Barnard says. 'Schumacher wanted that braking capability and to get it he would run the corner in a higher gear. He said, "I need seven speeds because I need to be able to select exactly the gear I want through the corner, therefore giving myself the engine braking: if I can run the engine at high revs I've got more engine braking" – because there's more friction. And of course coming out of the corner with the revs up you are already nearer the peak power.'

A Grand Prix is about gaining fractions and amassing them so that the fractions become chunks.

'Where I fell foul of him really,' Barnard says with his customary candour, 'is that my experiences working with guys like Alain Prost and Niki Lauda and John Watson – all those people – was: to make a quick car you needed it to work off the back. In other words you had the aerodynamic load on the back wheels and effectively all the front wheels did was turn it into the corner. Prostie was the absolute 180 degree opposite of Schumacher and I have to say I think Prost was right, because time in a car is about having enough traction, grip and so on. You cannot underestimate the Prostie capability. John Watson used to tell me, "Look, I want the car to work from the back, I want to feel as if the back is nailed to the ground and then I'm not worried at all about the car. I can flick the car in."

'It was very, very difficult to get a car to work like that, and where I was unfortunate with Schumacher was that I wanted to try to do it. In a way that's really where we fell apart – about working the way I thought, off the back of the car and a low downforce front end with a lot of mechanical grip. I thought, "He's good enough, he's got such fundamental reactions and just natural driving skills." All the things that come naturally he'd got, but of course what he also had was a German brain. That meant there was no way he was going to even attempt to see another point of view. I thought, "*Blimey.*" It was an immediate problem, and this is before we ever get to 1996.'

Stepney explored this dimension. 'He drives a racing car like a kart. He does a lot of practising on karts at his track in Kerpen

182

and all of that. There's a circuit just over the Italian border from Monaco – Ventimiglia – and I know the guy who runs the place. Michael practised there a lot. He'd go with some friends and two or three karts. All the drivers do their exercises to keep fit and so on, but at the end of the day he still drives a kart. I don't think many of the other drivers do that. He hasn't lost that and I think it's how he makes comparisons, keeps himself concentrated and pushing. I don't know but there's *something* there. And it's good for fitness, too. I can't think of many other drivers I have known who've done that all the time.'

The new car, the F310, was launched in mid-February. New car launches are ritualistic, especially at Ferrari where, amidst the pomp and circumstance, the same question came back. *Is this the year?* Di Montezemolo dealt with it diplomatically. 'Ferrari is coming from a very long road but today we must say that we have reasons to be optimistic.'

The ritual is replaced by reality at the first race of the season. That was the Australian Grand Prix at Melbourne on 10 March. Incidentally, in 1996 Grands Prix weekends still followed their traditional ritual. Typically this was: Friday – untimed practice from 11.0 to 12.0, first qualifying from 1.0 to 2.0; Saturday – untimed practices from 9.0 to 9.45 and 10.15 to 11.0, second qualifying from 1.0 to 2.0; Sunday – warm up from 8.30 to 9.0, race at 1.0.

The drivers in the leading teams:

Benetton – Alesi, Berger.
Ferrari – Schumacher, Irvine.
Jordan – Barrichello, Brundle.
McLaren – Häkkinen, Coulthard.
Williams – Hill, Villeneuve.

Schumacher qualified on the second row of the grid (behind Irvine) and after the race had been restarted – Brundle crashed

– he ran fourth, Villeneuve leading from team-mate Hill, Irvine third. Irvine obeyed his contract and moved aside, Schumacher digging deep to get within 0.74 seconds of Hill, but you could see the Ferrari twitching and bucking under the demands he made of it. After 11 laps the front-runners ran equidistant. At lap 20 Schumacher pitted and rejoined fourth.

Breaking the flow of the narrative again, at least one pit stop for refuelling had been mandatory since 1995, although a team could make as many as they wanted. Stepney explained that 'the teams are under so much pressure now, they're putting each other under that pressure not only driving on the circuit but in the pit stops as well. You win or lose a race on a pit stop, and it never used to be so critical.'

At Melbourne the early stop meant Schumacher was on a strategy of two. The Williamses weren't and *that* meant Schumacher had been running with a low fuel load, and *that* meant the Ferrari could only stay with them when it was lighter.

No matter. His brakes were failing and he pitted again on lap 32 to see what could be done, sat in the cockpit explaining while, all around, the mechanics toiled. He was stationary for more than a minute, his race destroyed. He went back out but into a right-hander churned wisps of smoke as the wheels locked. The car coasted gently over a narrow ribbon of grass and he let it reach towards a multi-coloured tyre wall, twisted it and brought it to the track again, dust billowing; returned quietly to the pits and the mechanics wheeled the car into the darkness. As they did, a shadow – might have been of sadness – fell across the nosecone.

And that was the reality after the ritual.

He returned to Italy to test at Fiorano, working on the difficulties which Melbourne had revealed, then qualified on the second row again in Brazil. The Ferrari was, as someone observed, 'evil to drive', but the race would be wet-dry and he finished third. During it Hill lapped him and confessed to a 'wry smile' that he'd been able to do that unhindered after all the crashing and bashing of 1994 and 1995. Afterwards, sitting alongside Hill, Schumacher described being lapped as 'not very nice' and smiled sincerely, no irony anywhere. 'As soon as I went to dry tyres I picked up the pace again. I looked good but nevertheless [shaking his head] there is a lot of work in front of us.'

Di Montezemolo was less kind. He was quoted as saying: 'I am deeply unsatisfied by the chassis made by Barnard. I was expecting more performance.'

The pressure was gathering.

Qualifying for the Argentine Grand Prix at Buenos Aires seemed to confirm it, Schumacher wrestling and muscling the car onto the front row of the grid alongside Hill, who had pole. 'First of all,' Schumacher would say, 'we need to go into the wind tunnel to find the areas in which we must improve.'

He made a good start to the race by nestling in behind Hill, Alesi third. He began to press Hill, forcing him to fastest lap after fastest lap but the order at the front endured through the first pit stops: Schumacher summoning one of his sprint laps to ensure Alesi didn't get out in front of him.

The Safety Car patrolled after Pedro Diniz (Ligier) and Luca Badoer (Forti) crashed. When it withdrew Hill pulled away almost immediately and ran over debris from the crash, helplessly churning it at Schumacher. 'I saw something black flying towards me and instinctively I ducked because I thought it was going to hit me in the face.' Alesi, tracking Schumacher, saw the impact of the debris on the Ferrari's rear wing and rang his own team to tell them to go and alert Ferrari but the on-board radio wasn't clear.

'Soon afterwards,' Schumacher would say, 'the car got loose and I realised something was wrong.' Suddenly he was touring, his rear wing breaking up.

The pressure continued to mount on Barnard, who was quoted as saying that di Montezemolo's comments were 'disruptive' and 'unhelpful'. He also said he was 'fed up with the pantomime' at Ferrari. Reflecting later, Barnard says, 'It is true, it is true. Ferrari have got ways of getting rid of people which you can't imagine. A story comes up in an Italian paper or magazine or something like that – theoretically nothing to do with anybody but somebody's written something and it's all being fed, it's all being leaked. They operate like a grand opera and the country is the stage, not the factory: the *whole country* is the stage in the magazines and newspapers...'

Mind you, Ferrari pointed out that di Montezemolo's original comments were inaccurate and reiterated what he had actually said. 'I was expecting more from the F310 but I am quite satisfied with the beginning of this season. We are just behind Williams. My objective for 1996 is to win one more race than in 1995. In Formula One you cannot win from day-to-day.'

Di Montezemolo went public at the Nürburgring, where the European Grand Prix was run, giving his support to Barnard. 'I would like to emphasise strongly that I am the man who hired Barnard for Ferrari.' He spoke of the work to be done and said, 'I am very pleased to have Barnard with me rather than with someone else.'

Barnard evaluates the car. 'Unfortunately somewhere along the line we made a mistake in the aerodynamics with the 1996 car. I kept asking my aero [aerodynamic] guys to check it out. When we did full-size testing against our wind tunnel work our aero correlation was quite good but you had certain dynamic things going wrong on the track, car bouncing and so on. I am sure it was all to do with dynamic ground effects we got on track which we couldn't see in the tunnel.

'Fundamentally that car had an aero that was so different from the tunnel. We thought we were just making an efficiency step from the 1995 car but on track it behaved so differently. I knew the suspension geometry and all the rest of it was pretty much the same as the '95 car – OK it had a different engine in it and weight distribution was a little bit different – but it was clearly illuminated as an aerodynamic problem. There were a few things done to the car after a few races which made it a bit better and, to be honest, I'm not quite sure how good or bad it was but all I got was [expletive], I just got the [expletive]. I think part of that was Schumacher lining up the way to get his people in. Todt didn't want this place [Barnard's research centre] in England, anyway, he said it and he said it to me as well. That was his opinion and I got on with him fine. I didn't have major problems but I knew what was coming. At the same time there was the constant *barraging* of the car, although if you look at the record, at the end of the day it wasn't that bad.

'The way Schumacher drives the car, and the way he likes it, you tend to end up doing a car around him: its balance, its aerodynamics and so on – I'm talking again about the reason it had a seven-speed gearbox – all those things. Before you know where you are, you've got the thing built completely by Schumacher and that's fine so long as Schumacher's still there, but then lose Schumacher and you're...'

Stepney evaluates the situation, broadens it and unconsciously echoes Barnard in his conclusion. Schumacher, Stepney says, 'dragged the car round' to good effect. 'If the driver does that, and pulls the team around, everyone *believes* and it all starts to come together. We were at that point at Ferrari where we weren't quite ready for him – but we'd never have been quite ready for him to come until he did come to help us!'

The broadening: 'He takes you with him, not as much as Senna though. Senna was a lot stronger in that respect. Look at the way he dealt with Honda. He had a lot, lot more pulling power than Michael. That's the feeling I have. [Note: Stepney told me this in the late 1990s. It wouldn't be true into the 2000s.]

'The problem is that even though you have the best driver in the world you still have to have the best car. So you have to be careful – remember McLaren. They built a team round Senna and Senna left and they lost five years in rebuilding. You can end up with all the top drivers like that. You put all your eggs in one basket and somebody drops the basket...'

At the Nürburgring Schumacher 'dragged' the car to third in qualifying and said it felt better than in Argentina. Because this was a season dominated by Williams, he had Hill and Villeneuve in front of him on the grid.

He was about to show why he was worth the $25 million.

Villeneuve made a strong start, Schumacher fourth, Hill behind him. On lap 6 Hill took him at the end of the start-finish straight, Schumacher not resisting. Häkkinen (McLaren) came up behind so Schumacher faced twin problems: holding Häkkinen while trying to re-take Hill. Once he almost made it as Hill attacked Barrichello for third place. The pit stops broke all this up and, after them, Schumacher dealt with Coulthard (McLaren), holding the inside line through the left-right sweeping corners to a mighty roar from the crowd. He was third, which became second behind Villeneuve when Häkkinen pitted. It was lap 27 of the 67, the gap 8.7 *and* Schumacher had just set fastest lap. He sprinted.

	Schumacher	Villeneuve	Gain
Lap 27	1:21.97	1:46.73	(after pit stop)
Lap 28	1:21.98	1:23.40	+1.41
Lap 29	1:21.82	1:23.13	+1.30
Lap 30	1:22.01	1:24.23	+2.21

By lap 37 he was directly behind Villeneuve, so the second pit stops would decide everything.

He was stationary for 8.5 seconds and regained the track poised for two fast laps, but Coulthard happened to be in the way and each melting second he spent behind Coulthard battered the tactic.

Villeneuve pitted and as he moved away Schumacher came like the wind down the pit lane straight, closing but never near enough. Villeneuve retained the lead to the end despite pressure from Schumacher and a clutch of backmarkers to negotiate.

Arguably only Schumacher could have brought the car to second place 0.76 behind Villeneuve.

'I was thinking the whole time about last year,' Schumacher added, sporting that mouthful-of-teeth grin. He was remembering how, impudently and impossibly, he'd threaded past Alesi at the hairpin in 1995 and 'there should be that situation coming now [smile] where I can pass Jacques by making the same move, but obviously he did a fantastic race without mistakes and there was just no way for me to pass. He had the edge on top speed. But we had a great race together, very close fighting and I'm very pleased to finish. In the middle of it I was a bit worried because I got some noise at the back and I thought [grimace] "That's it," but I was able to finish. I think we have shown that we go step-by-step. Qualifying was really surprising but you'll have to wait a little bit longer until we are back on the winning road. We will, I am sure.'

And so he came to Imola for the San Marino Grand Prix, the first 'homecoming', the first possibility of communion. He was quickest on the Friday by 1.2 seconds and, in a climactic end to qualifying, wrung an astonishing lap of 1m 26.89 from himself (Hill next, 1m 27.10) although immediately after he'd taken pole the rear suspension broke, pitching him into a gravel trap. He did a tour of honour on an open-topped vehicle and waved frantically. 'It feels as if I won the race but that's what Italy's like.'

He made a hesitant start. On the run towards Tamburello, Alesi put wheels on the grass so Schumacher stole through but Alesi *flung* the Benetton across the width of the track and tried to retake him on the outside. That's what communicating from the heart meant, that was what the *tifosi* had adored about Alesi, that was communion. Schumacher blocked Alesi and braked so hard for Tamburello that he dug smoke from his front right tyre. The order: Coulthard, Hill, Schumacher.

Into Tamburello on the second lap Hill placed the Williams over to the right – the mouth of Tamburello snaking to the left – and Schumacher was inside. For an instant Hill *was* coming across, realised, swivelled away. Schumacher went through and chased down Coulthard, leant on him, but Coulthard pitted. Schumacher led a Grand Prix in a Ferrari for the first time.

He conjured a 1m 29.51, fastest so far, and pitted. He was stationary for 9.5 seconds and he'd done enough to keep Coulthard behind him, but Hill, who'd inherited the lead when Schumacher stopped, hadn't stopped himself yet and sprinted, set a new fastest lap and built a 20-second cushion. Schumacher followed him home.

On the last lap the Ferrari's right front brake disc exploded, locking the wheel solid. Schumacher rammed the car forward and over the line, smoke seeping from the tyre. The *tifosi* liked this. When he parked it on the grass at the little left-hander beyond the start-finish straight the *tifosi* flooded on and engulfed him.

'What happened? A good question. I don't know. Something in the front wheel broke, the bearing or the wheel itself. That was after Aqua Minerale into the chicane and I just had three wheels left to finish with. I was thinking I had to go another full lap [fleeting grin] and I was very lucky and happy that [chuckle] the race was finished when I crossed the line.'

The pressure continued to mount on Barnard. 'The problem was this: on the one side these people [Ferrari] had brought us all together, thinking, "Ah, what a combination, we'll get Schumacher and Barnard working together like father and son," sort of thing. It might have been brilliant except for a few difficulties. One, that wasn't what I had intended to do when I came back to Ferrari, and two, I suppose we just didn't get on. We just didn't click. You do or you don't, you can or you can't.

'I am very bad at disguising my feelings. If I like somebody I think they feel it, they know it and I have no problems, if I don't get on with somebody they also probably know it. So it was a combination of *I didn't want to be there* and *I didn't really click and get on with him*. I can't say that we really fell out. I think he was surprised that I didn't go to every test and every race and just spend my time working with him, but, I thought, once he realised that he was immediately pushing to get people who he knew *would* do it, people like Ross Brawn and so on. They would work for Michael and no one else, and Eddie [Irvine] would make sure the spare car was warmed up and ready to go, basically.'

Schumacher took pole at Monaco with a consummate lap half a second quicker than Hill and rationalised that by judging the track conditions must have improved and he'd got himself 'tuned in a little bit better'. A wet race, Hill into the lead, Schumacher – as it seemed – proceeding at a prudent interval behind him. He rounded the Loews hairpin and moved into the descending right-hander after that, riding the red-and-white kerbing on the inside. As the Ferrari came off this kerbing he felt it floating away from him towards the Armco over on the other side. He'd oversteered. In a desperate instant he churned the steering wheel right-right-right to miss the Armco but the car skated on and impacted. 'I made a mistake at the start and I made a mistake here, too. I'm very sorry for the team and very angry with myself.'

In Spain he qualified third behind (of course) Hill and Villeneuve, and here was the next irony because the race was run in a deluge which made Monaco look like a spring shower. The start went so wrong that he reached for a single word – 'disaster' – before amplifying the sequence of events. 'I went for the clutch and there was nothing. I nearly stalled, then tried it again. For some reason I just had an on/off clutch. Fortunately no one went into the back of me and I don't know how many positions I lost – even Diniz [starting seven rows behind] passed me, I think. Now I know how it is to start a wet race from the back. You just can't see anything. I was really afraid I'd go into someone.'

The key is *I think*. Imagine standing directly under a raging waterfall and looking up into it wearing goggles. In that wet, 20 cars churning, nobody could see much except Villeneuve, leading. It may be that on this opening lap Schumacher overtook three cars, it may be four. One of his masterclasses had begun. He crossed the line sixth, 6.251 seconds behind Villeneuve.

	Schumacher	Villeneuve	Loss
Lap 1	2: 00.51	1: 54.25	−6.25

Irvine skimmed off on lap two and didn't come back, the car sunk in sodden grass, its rear wheels spinning and spinning; and that was fifth.

	Schumacher	Villeneuve	Loss
Lap 2	1: 53.89	1: 52.77	−1.12
Lap 3	1: 53.40	1: 52.18	−1.2

Hill skimmed off on lap four and did come back – gently coaxing the car forward, not too fast, not too slow – but not before Berger and Schumacher had gone through; and that was fourth. The gap was out to 8.47, which is how it generally goes when the leader has the clear track and you're peering into the waterfall.

	Schumacher	Villeneuve	Gain
Lap 4	1: 52.14	1: 52.26	+0.12

Schumacher set fastest lap, moved cleanly past Berger and that was third.

	Schumacher	Villeneuve	Gain
Lap 5	1: 50.56	1: 52.59	+2.03

He immediately gained on Alesi, who now was with Villeneuve and trying to apply pressure. Somewhere in the walls of water the Ferrari hunted Alesi, and Alesi was known to be quick and brave in the wet. Alesi was hunting, too, hunting Villeneuve.

	Schumacher	Villeneuve	Gain/Loss
Lap 6	1: 49.04	1: 52.76	+3.71
Lap 7	1: 51.14	1: 52.35	+1.21
Lap 8	1: 51.46	1: 51.07	−0.39

Schumacher drew full up, darted out for a sighter, darted back. He loomed over Alesi. He took different lines through the corners. He left his braking late for a left-hander, forcing Alesi to concede; and that was second. Immediately he gained on Villeneuve, then drew full up, wielding the Ferrari with such dexterity that for him, and him alone, the track might have been dry. On lap 9 the gap was a meaningless 0.45 seconds and three laps later he did to Villeneuve what he'd done to Alesi; and that was first. He set new fastest lap and shed Villeneuve, who subsequently explained that Schumacher had been quicker through all the corners. Now he lapped devastatingly faster than Villeneuve.

The other 50-odd laps? Schumacher drove into his own mythology. That in the end he beat Alesi by more than 45 seconds seemed irrelevant because Alesi had been in a different race, and so had the other *four* who finished, and so had the 14 who failed to finish. More than that, Schumacher was now second equal in the Championship with Villeneuve on 26 points, Hill 43.

'It's amazing. If anybody would have asked me how much I would have bet on any of this I wouldn't even have bet a penny on it.'

Next morning *L'Equipe* carried a large headline: 'Schumacher, Ace of Aces'. Under it Johnny Rives, their very experienced correspondent, wrote: 'You have to plunge [!] into the history of Formula One and examine the Grands Prix contested under equally difficult conditions to measure the quality of the performance achieved by Michael Schumacher yesterday, setting it against the most famous epic drives.

'Jackie Stewart, at the Nürburgring, in 1968, in the rain and the fog, won by four minutes. In 1972, at Monaco under a deluge, J-P Beltoise held in check Jacky Ickx, considered *the* great master in the wet. Closer to us, there was Alain Prost and Ayrton Senna in 1984 at Monaco again. And this same Senna, at the beginning of 1985, at the Grand Prix of Portugal when he got the first of his 41 victories. Or, yes, Senna again, always him, at Donington in 1993 [at the European Grand Prix where he led by a lap]…'

Barnard gives a postscript. 'I wasn't in Spain but I was talking to [Giorgio] Ascanelli, the Chief Engineer. One of the things they did for that race – which other people didn't do, or didn't have available – was that we put maximum downforce on. I think in those days we pretty much generated more downforce than any of the other cars and that was coupled with Schumacher's amazing skills. He just drove round everybody and it was a classic Schumacher victory.'

Stepney was in Spain and gives another postscript.

Schumacher didn't know how many cars he got past on the first lap.

'You look at Senna in Portugal in 1985 or Donington in 1993. Take Donington. How many cars did Senna overtake? About five on the first corner. Some drivers just adapt quicker.'

What is it?

'Hmmm. I don't know. It's… feeling. [Pause.] It's down to…

feeling and confidence, but sometimes you can have too much confidence and then you go off.'

Because, as Rives has so graphically illustrated, the Spanish Grand Prix of 2 June 1996 assumes a legitimate place in the history of the sport, and because the season had unfolded through seven races, this is an appropriate moment to let Stepney evaluate Schumacher, again with the caveat that Stepney was doing this in the late 1990s.

'He's like all the great ones. There are differences between him and other drivers of other eras – and we are talking about a *completely* different era now – but these great ones have something about them. They don't need to push what they have on to the people around them. When he came he helped Team Ferrari out greatly in this respect: we had a lot of problems and we didn't have a competitive car as such, well, not a very competitive car. The other drivers we'd had caused more disturbance, they didn't calm the waters. Alesi put everything out in the open – in the Press, everything. Michael has never done that and when he started off he took people here by surprise because of it. Personally, I'd thought that's how it would be because he's not like Berger and Alesi: they open their mouths and think afterwards. He helped to calm everything down – because he knew he could do the job. He never had self-doubt and I don't think the good ones do have, they are always very positive because they *know* they can. And if you *know* you can do something you do it automatically. You don't have to worry about it, so you can worry about the rest of the things around it.

'I like to work with good drivers. The major problem at Ferrari as far as drivers are concerned is that they are baby-sat too much. That hasn't affected Michael as much as some of the other drivers. He's got the sort of mind that sees through all that and asks, "What are we really doing?" He cuts through that crap, he *knows* what he wants.'

Grand Prix racing mirrors real life (if I may phrase it like that) in at least one sense. It kicks you when you're up as well as when you're down. Canada was downbeat, third on the grid despite a revised version of the F310, but the engine died before the parade lap and he started from the back. He reached seventh but after his pit stop the driveshaft broke.

In France he took pole but the engine blew on the parade lap; in the British at Silverstone he ran third but retired on lap 3 with a gearbox problem and the talk was whether he'd extend his contract beyond 1997. Di Montezemolo weighed in with 'We are extremely pleased with Schumacher and for me it is important that the driver is pleased with Ferrari. We both have the intention of going on together. I would rather pay $20 million for Schumacher than the same amount for two drivers.'

In Germany he qualified third and complained about the car, finished fourth. In Hungary he took pole and led, finished ninth with a throttle problem. The promise of the season, the laying of a foundation for an assault on the championship in 1997, was ebbing away, and when the races are coming at you in their hectic rhythm every other weekend you can be running as hard as you can just to stand still.

In Belgium he qualified third again (behind the Williamses), and this after a major crash on the Friday when he turned in to a left-hander and the car danced away from him, swapped ends, bounced across a gravel trap and smacked the tyre wall high up. He bruised his knee. He made a better start to the race than Hill and crowded Villeneuve, pitching and pounding the Ferrari to stay with him, but each lap at the Bus Stop chicane he lost time to Villeneuve.

He forged fastest lap and pitted first on lap 14 but there was a measure of confusion for spectators and teams alike. The Safety Car was out ... Villeneuve pitted and emerged behind Schumacher ... Coulthard led Häkkinen but neither had pitted… they were on one-stop strategies. When the Safety Car pulled off and the racers resumed Schumacher felt 'a lot of play in the steering'. Spa is imperious in the speeds it allows and as a consequence this 'play' frightened him. 'I was close to stopping.' He radioed and the team reassured him that all would be well if he respected the kerbs by staying off them.

The McLarens came in, giving him the lead. He pitted a second time, passing the lead to Villeneuve, who passed it back when *he* pitted. Villeneuve emerged from his second pit stop as Schumacher was rounding La Source. The pit lane exit is further on down the incline. Villeneuve ducked across the track but Schumacher had the impetus of accelerating from La Source and went clean by. And that was the story of the Belgian Grand Prix. When it was done he conjured an evocative phrase – after the frightener with the steering, to win 'was just Hollywood life'.

A question remained, Monza and the Italian Grand Prix two weeks away. Was there communion? How much had been remembered or forgotten about the armed guard a year ago while Alesi scooted around on a scooter?

Qualifying obeyed the current of the season, third behind Hill and Villeneuve, but you can gain or lose position on the long, sustained surge to the first chicane when the race begins. The chicane is so absurdly tight that a hunting pack of cars braking for it and *still* trying to create positions remains an alarming annual spectre. In this Schumacher lost, not gained, and the order completing the opening lap was Hill, Alesi, Häkkinen, Villeneuve, Coulthard, Schumacher.

On lap two Coulthard spun off; and that was fifth. Into the Ascari curve he moved past Villeneuve, and that was fourth. Häkkinen ran into a loose tyre from one of the silly mini-tyre walls which decorated Monza this particular year and it broke his nose cone. Schumacher crowded him but Häkkinen had to pit anyway for repairs, and that was third. Next lap Hill clipped one of the mini-walls and that sent the Williams spinning down the track. He wrestled it until it pointed forwards but the engine had stalled, the suspension bent, and that was second.

The gap to Alesi was 2.99. He accelerated and ate into that, to 1.62 on the tenth lap. The *tifosi* appreciated this stretching of their emotions, the hunter and the hunted, Alesi still in their hearts, Schumacher absorbing their minds. Schumacher was impressed with Alesi's straight-line speed which prevented him getting close enough for proper assault, although he carried a heavy fuel load 'so we could stop quite late'. He worried Alesi might be doing the same. The hunt went to lap 31, when Alesi pitted. Schumacher pitted two laps later – after two fast laps – and emerged in the lead, won it by 18.26 seconds with only one alarm when he struck a mini-wall hard enough to pluck the steering wheel from his hands. He'd call it a stupid mistake. As he moved towards the line a last time he raised a clenched fist and held it rigid just above the rim of the cockpit, a curiously subdued gesture. Later on round the slowing down lap he began to pump the fist like a piston, but that's the maximum you can convey from a cockpit.

The *tifosi* became a mob. Was it communion or adulation born of the moment? The *tifosi* behaved like this every year. Now, in their thousands, they gathered beneath the podium balcony for the anthems, the champagne and the antics. Schumacher said he'd 'never seen so many emotions of so many people enjoying themselves. The way they celebrate is only possible in Italy.' He shook his head in bewilderment.

Grand Prix racing mirrored real life again. Portugal kicked a little (fourth on the grid, fourth in the race), Japan less so (third on the grid, second in the race). It gave him 59 points, third in the championship. Whether Ferrari were making real progress, or whether Schumacher was so good he masked that they weren't, remained unresolved. It would be resolved soon.

Wouldn't it?

The width of the chasm is graphically demonstrated by a table for the previous decade showing where Ferrari's leading driver finished each season against who won the Championship. Note that the points in brackets refer to the total a driver scored before he had to deduct because you could only count so many finishes.

Season	Ferrari	Pts.	Pos.	Champion	Car	Pts.
1986	Johansson	23	5	Prost	McLaren	72 (74)
1987	Berger	36	5	Piquet	Williams	73 (76)
1988	Berger	41	3	Senna	McLaren	90 (94)
1989	Mansell	38	4	Prost	McLaren	76 (81)
1990	Prost	71 (73)	2	Senna	McLaren	78
1991	Prost	34	5	Senna	McLaren	96
1992	Alesi	18	7	Mansell	Williams	108
1993	Alesi	16	6	Prost	Williams	99
1994	Berger	41	3	Schumacher	Benetton	92
1995	Alesi	42	5	Schumacher	Benetton	102
1996	Schumacher	59	3	Hill	Williams	97

The table needs only the briefest extrapolation because however sceptical you are about statistics the Championship is decided *only* by them and so they become the currency you have to use. Ferrari hired Schumacher *to win it*. In this decade of Ferrari effort only Prost came close. As the exotic and quixotic Grand Prix world folded its tents and departed Suzuka on 13 October, the 1996 season completed, Schumacher's third position and 59 points represented another year of being in no man's land; nor, that evening in Japan, were there any suggestions that this was more than just another year.

We've heard, however, Schumacher himself say it would take time and heard di Montezemolo backing him. Soon enough Schumacher extended his contract to the end of 1999 (and secured a pay rise!) so that demonstrably he was giving it time.

Rumours, always a permanence at Maranello – and delicious or damaging depending on who, what and where you happened to be – insinuated that Benetton Technical Director Brawn would be coming and, by definition, that raised questions about Barnard's future, questions heightened because evidently Rory Byrne, Benetton's designer, would be coming too. The crop flowered into November. Byrne was still leaving Benetton but to set up a scuba diving school in Asia while, simultaneously, Brawn was surrounded by a crop entirely of his own, insinuating he'd stay at Benetton, join Ferrari and – for good measure – join Arrows.

Brawn began work at Ferrari on 16 December, stayed until one in the morning and made Todt stay until then too. The latest attempt at the taming had begun, and begun as it would continue: seriously and *un*emotionally. The fervour – which fed on the rumours, just as the rumours fed on the fervour – was to be exploited by exercising great control over it. Not yet, but very soon.

When you went to Ferrari from Benetton for the 1997 season, was Schumacher instrumental? Did he want you or was this something Ferrari wanted?

Brawn: 'It was a mix really. The circumstances were that he and Ferrari had heard that I'd had one or two disappointments at Benetton – not Benetton directly but Briatore had made some commitments to me to change the structure of the team because I felt we needed to reconsider that structure for the future. At the end of 1995 Briatore made commitments that I felt were necessary. Although 1996 was pretty disastrous we were still competitive – we just didn't put it together, lost several races and so on. It was a particularly difficult year because of the new drivers [Alesi, Berger] and losing Michael. I became even more convinced that those changes were necessary but during 1996 Briatore didn't carry them out. By the middle of the season that became clear and therefore was technically in breach of the agreements we had. At the same time Michael was having a bit of a difficult time [at Ferrari].'

John Barnard has described some of those difficulties.

'I have to be honest. My time here at Ferrari with John was very good. I had no problem with John at all and he was very supportive. In the short period we had together I had no complaints at all.'

I think he felt that if you had been there from the start with Schumacher, and Barnard had been doing what he wanted to do from Guildford, it would have been the perfect arrangement – but he was being drawn back to the pit lane because they didn't have a Ross Brawn getting hold of it.

'Middle of 1996 Willi Weber was the first person to contact me and say, "Look, I hear some rumblings that things are not quite right at Benetton. If you do ever consider leaving would you contact us?" I gave it some thought and then got in contact with Willi and Jean Todt. It really went from there.'

There's nothing sinister about this. A man like Schumacher wants his own people around him and he will perform better.

'Yes.'

The new car, the F310B, was described by Barnard as 'conventional'. It was launched at Maranello on 7 January and the Marlboro Press Service caught the mood nicely because, just this once, there was a variation to the ritual: 'Despite thick snow on the ground, heavy rain and near-freezing temperatures there was a full house when Ferrari President Luca di Montezemolo and drivers Michael Schumacher and Eddie Irvine unveiled their 1997 Formula One challenger to 400 press and VIP guests gathered inside a huge tent that had been erected on the Maranello test track.'

Di Montezemolo said: 'The car is ready for two months of work and testing before the season and the team is now very strong, organised and maintaining continuity. Our drivers are fantastic and I am sure we have a good year ahead of us. I have said it for three years in a row but this sport sometimes makes you wait. The ways of God are complicated but 1997 will be good.'

Schumacher gave it some initial testing at Fiorano (31 laps) and made the noises about how much promise the car seemed to have, how small adjustments needed to be made.

Reflecting much later, Barnard said: 'We thought we had learnt from our mistakes on the 1996 car. It was getting very disruptive by that time because Todt had gone out and hired two aero dynamicists over in Italy and it kind of ruined our programme [in Guildford]. Effectively the development was switched off here and went over there. I think the 1997 car wasn't a bad car at all.'

A few days after the launch Schumacher was at the ski resort of Madonna di Campiglio where he met Italian ski slalom champion Alberto 'The Bomba' Tomba and where Irvine went snowboarding. Schumacher was in expansive mood, although never compromising his pragmatism, and he covered a lot of ground.

'Fiorano was beautiful in the snow but with the track so wet comparisons with last year's car are impossible. The F310B conforms to regulations, is easy to drive and hasn't caused any problems. It's a good sign. Reliability will be very useful this season. It's not possible to know whether we can start winning right away. We won't even know after we have tested against our competitors' – at Jerez. They wouldn't really know until the first race, Melbourne on 9 March.

He explained that 'a driver can make a technical contribution to the performance of his car. Last season I made a graphic to show how I felt in the car, what worked and what didn't. It was very helpful. We uncovered a lot of problems. But then it's up to the designers to find solutions. Aerodynamically Formula One cars are so complex today that even a very small thing may require a design overhaul.'

He also said, astonishingly: 'My team-mate Eddie Irvine could not work well last year because we only had one car for testing. This year we will have two.' He illustrated it by pointing out that at Melbourne in 1996 Irvine had let him through on the first lap 'because I was fastest. This year, if Eddie is fastest, I'll have to stay behind for the sake of the team. If he has a better chance for the title, I'll try to help him. He will do the same for me. And, if I have to retire [from races] he'll go for the points.'

The astonishing aspect was that Schumacher had written into his contract that Irvine would behave with the absolute obedience of a Number 2 unless Schumacher happened to be in trouble, in which case, and presumably still at the team's discretion, Irvine would be unleashed.

Schumacher went to Jerez, the car suffered three engine failures early in testing – and a fourth, later – and his happiness with the car, or lack of it, generated a fresh crop of rumours. These hardened to: exit Barnard, joining Alain Prost at Ligier, enter Byrne, exchanging the delights of the Thai coast for the shark-infested waters of Maranello. Thereby hangs a tale.

'I'd finished at Benetton and I was in the Far East to start the scuba diving school,' Byrne says. 'I'd worked flat out until seven o'clock of the evening of December 31 at Benetton and early January that was *it*, I was actually on an island right in the south of Thailand having a look at the prospects. I was going to spend a few months sussing out the various areas seeing what the potential was. I was staying in a little guesthouse right on the beach and the lady who ran the place called me off it. She said there was a bloomin' phone call for me and your first thought is, "Jeez, what's going on? Is it bad news of my family back in South Africa or what?" It was Jean Todt on the phone. He said they were looking at restructuring the whole organisation and bringing everything back to Italy and did I fancy the job of Chief Designer? I said, "Well, I'll think about it."

'The reason he had my number of course is that I'd been quite friendly with Ross and Ross had gone from Benetton in about October of 1996. I'd left him my phone number and said, "If ever you're out there this is where I'll be staying for the first few weeks. If you fancy a bit of diving, come out!" Obviously when he joined Ferrari he'd given the number to Todt and so I got this call. About ten days later I was in Maranello…'

What was the thinking behind the decision, because it's not like Benetton ringing and saying, 'We're in a bit of trouble, can you come back?' This is Ferrari you're talking about.

'The way I figured it, I was being offered the opportunity to design a car which would hopefully win a Championship for Ferrari for the first time in two decades. That is a unique challenge. You only get one such in the world. That was the first thing: I thought about the challenge and at the end of the day there was nothing stopping me doing what I wanted to do [the diving school], I was just delaying it a few years. Then there was the thought of working with Michael and Ross and I thought "Yes".'

Michael must have been pushing for you.

'I don't know. It's quite possible.'

He was going to surround himself with the people he knew.

'Sure. There must have been an element of that in it.'

Meanwhile, still at Jerez, Schumacher had handling problems, and although he murmured about improvements made he ventured coded criticism when he added not as many as he'd hoped. Berger in the Benetton was fastest at the end of the week with 1m 21.24s, Schumacher seventh on 1m 22.86s.

Barnard remembers Jerez as 'virtually the last thing I had to do with the car. I went down there on the basis of doing a few set-up changes with it and seeing how it was going to perform. The problem was Ross Brawn was there, Ascanelli was there, Todt was there and Schumacher was there. It was impossible. I stayed two days and then went. I said, "That's it, I'm finished, I've had enough." They were doing things which even Ross Brawn was sitting there saying "We shouldn't be doing this."

'They had an active differential in and all the experiences I have had of active differentials – over many, many years – is that you are never 100% sure what you've got. You can play with them and change a car and you can make a car so bad so quickly with them. The last thing I wanted was a brand new car with an active differential. I said, "Let's put the standard differential in and work from that." They said, "No, no, we know what it does, we are absolutely sure." In the end I thought: this is nonsense, this is ridiculous now, we have got to a farce situation. I could have stood up and said, "Stop, I have got control of the set-up of the car, I am still here," but I thought, "What's the point?" I knew it was over, I knew I was going. So I thought, "Just walk away." I said, "There's no point in me staying any longer," packed my bags and went. That was it, that was the end of it really.'

Meanwhile, Ralf Schumacher joined Jordan and reached it by virtually the same route as his brother. He'd started karting at three, been in club races at six, and became German Junior Champion in 1991. He graduated to cars in Formula 3, did some Japanese Formula 3000 and, towards the end of '96, tested a McLaren Mercedes.

There had been brothers in Formula One before (ten pairs) and, just for the record, fathers and sons (eight pairs), so the Schumachers were by no means unique. Speaking of family, a daughter – Gina-Maria – was born to Michael and Corinna on 19 January.

Ralf was asked the inevitable questions.

It is a problem or an advantage to have the same name as the best driver in the world?

'Listen, when the results are there the name has no importance. Clearly I am not able to escape the comparison with Michael but I feel I have the right to be a little slower than he is for the moment.'

Have you had the chance to discuss the racing with your big brother? Do you exchange information?

'No, not really. When we get the chance to talk quietly with each other we prefer to talk about things of everyday life.'

The drivers in the leading teams:

Benetton – Alesi, Berger.
Ferrari – Schumacher, Irvine.
Jordan – R. Schumacher, Fisichella.
McLaren – Häkkinen, Coulthard.
Williams – Villeneuve, Frentzen.

At Maranello, Byrne examined his inheritance, the 1997 car. 'Certainly early on it was difficult. I was faced with the car and we had to do two things. One, build up the design infrastructure in Italy because there wasn't any – R & D, everything, was in Guildford. We had to recruit most of the technical side of a Formula One team *toute de suite*; and two, design a car for 1998 with a very big rule change, so not only did we have to assemble the people but we had to get on with a car.'

Is there anything you can do as a designer when you are confronted with somebody else's car, in this case Barnard's?

'The first thing is try and understand the car. His design philosophy is different to mine, and understandably. All people's design philosophies are different, certainly to some degree. And there were quite a few fundamentals that were different to what I was used to doing. One thing I have learnt is don't steam in and rubbish what's there and try and put bits of your own ideas on because really that very seldom works. The first thing you've to do is understand the animal you've got. It took us a while. And there were one or two fundamental errors in the car which fortunately we were able to rectify in a fairly short space of time.'

Ferrari approached the Australian Grand Prix as they had approached the first race of every season since Scheckter in 1979, consumed by wondrous uncertainty. Schumacher qualified third. After a blast of a start Frentzen led from Coulthard and Schumacher. Frentzen was on a two-stop strategy and with a lighter fuel load drew away but his first stop on lap 18 made him third. He ran there until Coulthard and Schumacher, on one-stops, pitted and returned the lead to him. During Schumacher's stop the rig didn't deliver the full amount of fuel and that forced him to stop again towards the end for a splash'n'dash. He was stationary for 4.4 seconds. The order – Coulthard, Frentzen, Schumacher – broke up when Frentzen's brakes failed and he crashed, hoisting Schumacher to second although he finished 20 seconds behind Coulthard.

He qualified on the front row for the Brazilian Grand Prix at Sao Paulo (Villeneuve pole) and made a strong start into that corkscrew left-right at the end of the pit lane straight. Villeneuve moved to the theoretically commanding position of mid-track but Schumacher thrust the Ferrari down the inside and, as the corkscrew lured them in, they were abreast, Schumacher holding the advantage of the inside. Villeneuve had to go the long way round – outside. There he found no grip and went off on to the grass, bounced across that and came back on, but seventh.

Schumacher led.

Barrichello (now with the Stewart team) stalled on the grid, halting the race. Schumacher would have to do it again at the restart and did, producing enough power to lead Villeneuve into the corkscrew. Villeneuve tracked him, applied power of his own as they crossed the line to complete the lap and went by. Soon enough Berger did the same and after the pit stops he drifted back to fifth. Much ado about nothing.

Argentina became a cameo of what can go wrong. He qualified on the second row and into the first corner brushed against Barrichello, spinning the Stewart and ramming it, Schumacher's visor smeared with oil from the Frentzen of Williams so he couldn't see.

Three races into the season Villeneuve led the championship with 20 points, Schumacher fifth on 8. *Could* his abilities mask the superiority held by Williams and McLaren over a whole season? More poignantly, any assault on the championship would need to acquire momentum soon or Villeneuve, Frentzen, Häkkinen, and Coulthard would be too far away.

That squeezed the San Marino Grand Prix at Imola. Qualifying offered moments of hope because he was fastest early on but Villeneuve took pole from Frentzen – and Frentzen won the race, Schumacher second. 'I was basically happy,' Schumacher said. 'Second position was [face tightens into a grimace] more than I was expecting, I was expecting third.'

The Ferrari was clearly moving towards the pace although it was not there yet. I asked Byrne how important it is to have somebody like Schumacher when you are going through the process of reaching that and rectifying faults.

'Vital. That's one thing Michael is very good at, really knowing if you make a change to a car whether it's actually going to make it faster. There are quite a few drivers – well, all drivers are able to get the car balanced the way they want it, but there is always the question mark "OK, it's well balanced but does it have more grip? Is it potentially faster?" I've found with Michael that if you give him a car with more grip he can normally find a way to drive it. If the car's got the grip, even if the balance is not right, he adapts his style, finds a way. He has this ability to experiment with various lines round various corners depending on the car's handling and he is able to get the best out of the car even if the car's not 100%. That's unique. That's certainly not something all drivers have.'

Monte Carlo offered possibilities, as it does to the driver who harnesses pace, precision and persistence. Frentzen took pole from Schumacher. 'I did three laps all around the same time which just shows that we pulled the maximum out of the car. I tried again at the end but I couldn't improve. I just had too much understeer.'

Anyone who'd been to the Monaco Grand Prix on a regular

basis soon learned to pack waders, sou'westers and water wings. On Sunday 11 May the forecast reflected this, drizzle which would broaden to rain half an hour before the start and then stop fairly soon after. It was maddeningly inconclusive to each team now facing the critical decision about what weather to prepare the car for.

Williams gambled that the forecasters would be right and the rain stop, so they set Frentzen and Villeneuve up for the dry. In the pit lane Schumacher hesitated, weighing the case for and against. He had one Ferrari set up as the Williamses were, the other (the spare car) a compromise: intermediate. The decision could not long be postponed because he had to bring the chosen car to the grid. The decision on tyres, however, could wait until he was there.

Todt watched carefully. 'Michael hesitated a great deal. Finally, 20 minutes before the start [five minutes before the pit lane closes] he alone took the decision and moved towards the car chassis number 175' – the intermediate. A masterclass was coming.

Schumacher was circumspect, almost matter-of-fact. 'I decided to jump into that one at the last possible moment.'

On the grid he asked for more wing and selected intermediate tyres while at that moment Frentzen's car, alongside, was being fitted with dries. 'I was truly astonished,' Schumacher said, 'and it perturbed me a bit.' He'd had the feeling that the track might 'dry quickly' but nothing here on the grid could prove that and he knew 'if I'd made a mistake' it would bring an additional pit stop to change to the right tyres, a crippling disadvantage at Monaco where overtaking is so difficult to regain places lost.

Behind him Villeneuve's Williams was being fitted with dry tyres.

Stepney glimpsed Schumacher's face and it glistened. Stepney knew exactly what that meant.

They moved away on the formation lap and somewhere the far side of Casino Square the rain hardened. Each of the 22 knew their luck or their fate before they settled on the grid. When the red lights went off Frentzen felt his way forward and within perhaps 20 yards Schumacher had pulled ahead, long before Ste Devote ran decisively ahead. He drew Fisichella's Jordan, also on intermediates, through in his slipstream.

'Yes, I made a terrific start,' Fisichella says, 'especially considering that I had intermediate tyres and Michael had full rain tyres. That's why the Ferrari immediately took a big advantage but my thinking was only to do my best in these weather conditions. When you have to make pit stops, strategy is important and so normally you're thinking about your own race.' This is doubly interesting because Schumacher was, as we know, on intermediate tyres and would only switch to full wets at his sole pit stop (at the end of lap 32). Forgive Fisichella. As he says, you worry about yourself.

At the top of the hill Schumacher extended his lead, although exiting Casino Square, where the track looked like grey ice, the Ferrari tugged and twitched. He caught that.

He approached the little dip towards the right for the tunnel, approached the place where the year before he'd butted the barrier so ignominiously. 'In attacking this zone of the circuit on that first lap I was super-prudent. And anyway, from Mirabeau to the tunnel during the whole race I'd be in big difficulties. On the one hand I had the impression I was going so slowly that I could have got out of the car and walked alongside it, on the other hand that I'd not backed off enough.'

Fisichella did close the gap a little but after the tunnel Schumacher restored it. On to the start-finish straight the Ferrari tugged and twitched again, but that was from the power he was wringing from it. As he crossed the line *Fisichella was not yet in sight*.

The gap froze when eventually Fisichella did cross the line:

	Schumacher	Fisichella	Gain
Lap 1	1: 58.76	2: 05.44	+6.67

Stepney's reaction is revealing because it's how those closely involved think: not triumphalist, not clenched fist in the air, but feet firmly on the ground. 'You just hope the [expletive] thing's going to hang together…'

You can argue that Fisichella was young (24) and only in his second season of Grand Prix racing, that he had yet to score a single point and that however super-prudent Schumacher was Fisichella would be more prudent still. This was *Monaco* and he was running *second*. You can argue that he had only driven one Grand Prix here before, in 1996 for Minardi, when he'd qualified 18th and crashed on the first lap. Now, amidst all this grey-ice treachery and the Armco always so close, if Schumacher made any semblance of a mistake Fisichella might *win*.

No doubt that, partly, is the true context of the opening lap and explains the gap which, in real time, was a barely-believable chasm. No doubt the full immensity of Schumacher explains all the other parts of the context. Whatever, I want to explore this with an example. The 1984 race was filthy wet becoming monsoon, Prost (Marlboro McLaren) led Mansell (Lotus) by 0.94 – *not six and a half seconds*. Prost loathed the wet, Fisichella was no Mansell but even so…

Stepney casts a knowing gaze over Schumacher's achievement. 'Sometimes you see a twinkle in a driver's eye. Might not go particularly well in the Sunday morning warm-up, doesn't matter, in the race he'll perform. You can see when he's ready to do that. He's cool and his eyes are glistening and he's *loaded* for the race. You can *see* he's loaded, *see* he's ready for it. Some you never see it in but with Senna you could, too, and nine times out of ten they do something special when you do see it. They're all hyped up and *ready*. It's very difficult to read drivers but sometimes you can.'

I want to explore this opening lap further, by setting out in their various states of disarray the next four drivers to cross the line after Fisichella.

Ralf Schumacher	@ 8.51s
Frentzen	@ 8.71s
Barrichello	@ 9.93s
Herbert (Sauber)	@ 10.89s

'No, I wasn't intimidated by Schumacher's sudden disappearance [into the distance],' Fisichella says. 'You have to consider many parameters that can change a car's performance, fuel on board, tyres and so on. We were expecting the weather to change a little and so, with the intermediate tyres, we would have had an advantage. If the weather stayed the same – as in fact it did – it was pointless to worry about the Ferrari. You mustn't forget that my car had a dry set-up, with a few changes made on the grid. My thinking was simply to do my best to reach the best possible place and to keep other drivers under pressure. I was not at all intimidated by being second. I've always been fighting for top places ever since I started racing, and I'd won the Monaco Formula 3 race in 1994 so I was cool and calm. *If I did it in Formula 3 I can do it in Formula One.*'

The second lap heightened the feeling of disbelief, Schumacher reaching Mirabeau, which affords a view all the way back to Casino Square, and *Fisichella was not yet in sight*. By the end of this lap the chasm had widened to 11 seconds.

He settled to a rhythm but it was between *four and five seconds* a lap faster than Fisichella so that, completing lap three, the leader board had become a freak, as if two distinct events were being held simultaneously, Schumacher in one, the rest in the other.

Fisichella	@ 15.718s
Ralf Schumacher	@ 16.648s
Barrichello	@ 16.965s
Herbert	@ 18.614s
Olivier Panis (Prost)	@ 24.689s

Five cars had spun or crashed and they would not be the last. *Did it matter to Fisichella that Schumacher was literally out of sight?* 'No. With different race strategies cars can be very "different" at the starting line. You have to do your best – as you do in qualifying – but now do it between the pit stops, and only in the last part of the race can you directly face your opponents.'

How hard is it to drive Monaco in the wet? Herbert, who had been making such safe and steady progress, says 'the actual track itself is not too bad. The problem is the white lines, so many white lines [the normal road markings]. Over the years they have tried to burn them off – they've tried to do the crossings – and that is the trickiest part. Sometimes when they've burnt them off they are still slippery. And that year it was quite bad.'

And visibility? 'Cars have rear lights but you can't see them because there is so much spray and it is so dense. You see peripherally – you can see the Armco so you can see where you are, although not what's immediately in front if it's very, very wet. It's much easier when you are in the lead and have a clear road but he was pretty good. I think the drive he did in Barcelona was probably better...'

They'd stop the race after two hours, or 62 laps of the original 69, and Schumacher had but a single instant of alarm on the journey to that. 'During the whole race I had trouble braking [!]. At Ste Devote I was often locking my front wheels.' On lap 53 he 'couldn't slow down enough' there but reasoned *I can take the corner but I risk hitting the Armco on the exit. I'll go straight on into the safety of the escape road, I'll do a U-turn and return.* 'There was no problem.'

He beat Barrichello by 53.30 seconds.

I asked Stepney (in the late 1990s) for his favourite Schumacher race. His chuckle rumbled, subsided, and he gently mused: 'For me, Monte Carlo the year it was wet. That's personal, but to beat Monte Carlo is the best. Spain in the wet in '96 was fantastic but I just like to win at Monte Carlo. It's a place you have to go to, have to win and then get out. To do that gives me satisfaction.'

Rory Byrne was about to discover that all the Ferrari mythology was true. 'Here at Maranello on a Sunday night after Ferrari have won they have to have extra police out controlling the traffic, the church bells are tolling. The place just goes crazy. They're honking their horns and waving Ferrari flags. On a Sunday night after a race win, wherever I go I never have to pay for a meal. They refuse to accept any money.

'It's a totally different sort of atmosphere to England, amazingly different. The first win after I arrived was Monaco and I could not believe it. Incredible! I hadn't imagined anything like that would happen. These people are passionate about it. The Fiorano circuit is quite close to apartments and so on. Rather than complain about the noise – and we test sometimes up to nine o'clock at night in the summer – they are hanging out of the windows. They've got friends coming round, hanging off the balconies having a look! There'll be a traffic jam outside. There's a bridge going over a through-road and the bridge is jam-packed full of people looking at the circuit. Yes, amazing.'

Spain was the obverse of Monaco. Schumacher qualified on the fourth row and finished the race fourth nearly 18 seconds behind Villeneuve, who took the Championship lead back.

In Canada Schumacher had a tight pole from Villeneuve – 0.013 of a second. As Byrne says, 'by Canada time we were on the pace.'

For the core of the race it was a tale of two men, Coulthard and Schumacher. Coulthard maintained the lead to lap 39 when he stopped, Schumacher leading to lap 43 (his second stop), Coulthard leading to lap 51 and *his* second stop. Coulthard's clutch misbehaved and that passed the lead back to Schumacher, then Panis crashed heavily. The Safety Car came out and escorted the ten cars that were still running round to the finishing line, no overtaking permitted. Schumacher 37 points, Villeneuve 30.

He said you took no pleasure from winning a race where somebody had been injured and, as chairman of the Drivers' Association, spoke about safety and how it is always under review, how the drivers discuss circuits after the races, how measures put in place were working 'not too badly'.

Now the pressure twisted onto Villeneuve and in France that heightened because Schumacher took pole from Frentzen and brother Ralf – a uniquely Germanic grid the like of which had never been seen before – Villeneuve fourth; and that shaped the race, Schumacher from Frentzen, Irvine up to third, Villeneuve fourth. The order solidified although within that Schumacher smoothed the Ferrari through Magny-Cours' sweepers and constructed a gap of 4.16 seconds by lap five, Villeneuve far adrift and still fourth. The pit stops? Schumacher was on a *two* but so were Frentzen and Irvine; Villeneuve a *three*. Schumacher was travelling at such pace early on, however, that Frentzen assumed he was carrying a light fuel load and it must be a three. Wrong.

The leaders pitted at third distance and resumed, the order resolidifying. The sky was darkening, and a regular visitor to Magny-Cours soon learns to pack the waders, sou'westers and water wings they took to Monaco. Schumacher accelerated to build a big gap against whatever the rain might bring. On lap 62 the rain fell hard and Schumacher went wide at the first corner, put two wheels onto the gravel then all four but kept the car moving and rejoined. He didn't pit and neither did Frentzen. Seven laps remained and he navigated them safely enough, beating Frentzen by 23 seconds, Villeneuve fourth, to lead the championship with 47 points, Villeneuve 33.

Silverstone was straightforward – a Villeneuve win from pole, although at one point Schumacher led; a wheel bearing failed on lap 39 – but the German Grand Prix confused everything. From pole Berger in the Benetton led from Fisichella, Schumacher third and running the second half of the race without fifth gear. He adapted to cope, Fisichella had a puncture and he was second. Berger won it by more than 17 seconds but Schumacher wasn't concerned about that. He wanted to know where Villeneuve had finished and was told he'd spun out on lap 34. Schumacher 53, Villeneuve 43.

In Hungary Schumacher had pole but his tyres blistered during the race and he limped to fourth. Worse, Hill ought to have won but a throttle problem near the end let Villeneuve in. Schumacher 56, Villeneuve 53.

Six races remained. If you're going to Belgium don't forget the waders. He qualified third behind Villeneuve and Alesi, and that in the spare car. He wrung the fast lap out of himself – three-quarters of the way through the session he'd been down in seventh – and murmured about how much work needed to be done.

Twenty minutes before the start of the race it rained. His race car was set up for the dry and the spare a compromise with intermediate tyres and a lighter fuel load – and that would allow him to gain enough time to make an early pit stop for dry tyres if that was necessary. He went out and did a reconnaissance lap in the race car searching, monitoring, weighing, projecting. *Too much water*.

He made his decision to race the spare, leaving the decision so late that he was the final car to arrive on the grid. He looked around. Almost everybody else was on wet tyres. He thought that if this rain was only a shower, when it passed the intermediate tyres would be the ones to have and the other drivers crippled on full wets. Now the track was awash and the race began behind the Safety Car. He glimpsed sun emerging from the clouds.

They skated three laps in spray and when the Safety Car released them Villeneuve set off with Alesi somewhere in the waterfall behind and Schumacher close to Alesi. Into the next lap towards La Source they slithered in tandem across the standing water and Schumacher took the inside. By Les Combes Schumacher had caught Villeneuve and stole a glance down the inside but wasn't close enough. After Les Combes he went inside again and floated past Villeneuve in something approaching regal splendour, drew away. Villeneuve would not see him again. When Villeneuve pitted for intermediates Fisichella moved up into second place but the way it was developing Schumacher had enough time to nip back to Kerpen, take afternoon tea, motor back and still be in the lead.

He pitted for dries on lap 14, was stationary for 8.0 seconds and rejoined. He made a third stop at his leisure later on, eased off and won by 'only' 26 seconds from Fisichella (Villeneuve fifth). Schumacher 66, Villeneuve 55. In one of his wonderful exercises in understatement he described the result as 'satisfactory'.

The Ferrari was off the pace at Monza (Villeneuve fifth, he sixth) and off the pace in Austria, compounded by a stop-go penalty when he overtook Frentzen under yellow flags. Villeneuve won: Schumacher 68, Villeneuve 67, three races left.

He qualified fifth for the Luxembourg Grand Prix at the Nürburgring but the distance from the grid to the first corner, a right-hander, is long enough for places to be won and lost; and the first corner enjoys a specific notoriety. It can throttle a column of advancing cars. Initially Schumacher moved over to the right so that he had Fisichella outside him but Ralf drew up outside Fisichella and went past. Schumacher immediately darted away to the left, Ralf and Fisichella travelling abreast towards the corner. Ralf turned in, squeezing Fisichella so hard he put two wheels on the grass and Schumacher, now himself abreast of Ralf, turned in too. Fisichella tapped Ralf's rear and the Jordan was airborne, its right rear wheel passing very close to the Ferrari's cockpit.

Schumacher ploughed across the gravel run-off area and continued to the second lap, when he pitted and stepped from the Ferrari. He seemed to be stretching filial piety to its limits when he said 'It's a shame that the incident happened with my brother', but he did expand. 'I don't think anyone is to blame because it was not a deliberate move.' Villeneuve won and led 77–68.

Clearly Schumacher needed to win Japan and although Villeneuve had pole (from him) Villeneuve was racing into great uncertainty because he'd ignored a yellow flag in the Saturday morning session, his fourth similar offence of the season, and been excluded from the race, then allowed in under appeal. Whatever points he earned might, and almost certainly would, be subsequently taken from him.

Villeneuve decided on an obvious tactic, to lead the race *slowly*, hoping Schumacher would become embroiled in a jostling of the bunch which going slowly would create. Completing the opening lap Villeneuve had created the bunch because Berger, sixth, was only just over two seconds behind. On the second lap, approaching the curving right-hander, Irvine went past Häkkinen on the outside and stayed outside, moving past Schumacher too. If you didn't know, this looked like one of the great overtaking moves. If you did know, it looked like the consummation of the thinking team. Irvine caught Villeneuve apace, rasped out fastest lap and jinked past at the chicane. This was uncomfortable for Villeneuve who knew that at some point Irvine would obey team orders and aid Schumacher.

The pit stops shook it up, although during them Schumacher gained enough to be present and correct when Villeneuve emerged from his, and Villeneuve made a muscular move across the track. What Villeneuve did, Schumacher said, 'could have been very dangerous'. Irvine slowed and let Schumacher through then held Villeneuve back; Villeneuve pitted again but the refuelling rig malfunctioned and he finished fifth. The Schumacher win set up the finale in the European Grand Prix at Jerez exquisitely.

Leaving Suzuka, Villeneuve had 79 points and Schumacher 78 but the FIA stripped Villeneuve of the 2 points for fifth – he'd been racing under the suspended ban, remember – and Williams did not appeal for fear the FIA turned prickly and banned Villeneuve from Jerez. The new total, Schumacher leading 78–77, did not disturb the merciful simplicity of what would be happening amid the rolling, barren hills of Andalucia: whichever driver finished in front of the other became Champion. Finessing that, *if* Villeneuve was third, fourth or fifth and Schumacher a place behind then they tied on points but Villeneuve took the tiebreak on most wins over the season.

Grand Prix racing had not been to Jerez, a tight sort of circuit in the modern way demanding patience and accuracy, for three years. This interval meant that the track lacked the grip you get when rubber is regularly burnished from Formula One car tyres, laying a film of adhesion; and also meant that the Friday times carried dubious overall significance.

The Saturday morning practice session, or rather its aftermath, brought tension and temperament to the surface for the first time. Villeneuve made his way to Irvine, still sitting in the Ferrari, and berated him for baulking. Waving his finger and stooping over the cockpit Villeneuve told Irvine to stop behaving like an idiot. This was, Villeneuve claimed, the fourth time so far during the meeting that Irvine had slowed and waited for him. 'We all know he is a clown,' Villeneuve said. Later Irvine riposted that Villeneuve always talked like that and what's the fuss?

The qualifying session proved unique. Villeneuve did a hot lap and it seemed enough for pole.

The timing devices froze: 1m 21.072s.

Schumacher booted the Ferrari through the spoon of a left onto the finishing straight – the impetus hauling it onto the blue-white kerbing at the track's rim – and smoothed it to face directly ahead, forced it to the line.

The timing devices froze: 1m 21.072s.

To have *no* difference, to three decimal places, between the two fastest drivers was unknown. With ten minutes left Frentzen was booting the Williams into and out of the spoon, forcing it to the line.

The timing devices froze: 1m 21.072s.

The grid order was decided by *when* these three laps had been done, giving pole to Villeneuve, then Schumacher, then Frentzen. Irvine, seventh, accepted there wasn't much he could do to help Schumacher.

In Kerpen the Schumacher indoor kart track had been converted into a cinema and 800 guests, sitting on moulded blue plastic chairs in mini-grandstands, would watch the race. The solid burghers of the town itself prepared in their habitual self-control, hanging Prancing Horse flags beside their window boxes. In the square a pretty lady sold hats and tee shirts from a trestle table while, nearby, young men who'd already bought the tee shirts wheeled beer kegs away on trolleys. A little girl wore a Ferrari scarf and *Schumi* was painted on her face in mum's lipstick. A man banged a big bass drum which had a clown's face etched on it (not Irvine). A man had trimmed a bush in a giant pot to look like a Ferrari and it did, more or less.

German television was carrying pictures of Willi Weber showing off 'Michael Schumacher 1997 F1 World Champion' tee shirts, which might have been tempting fate.

In the square at Maranello autumnal sunlight cast long, precise shadows from the people who already waited. They'd grow to 10,000, watching the race on a giant screen. Prayers for a Schumacher victory were said in the old, ornate church, its spires pointing to heaven like fragile stalagmites. The flowers in the window boxes at the town hall were Ferrari red and from the upper windows of houses the Prancing Horse flags came, just like Kerpen.

Two communities, so different in so many ways, had found communion.

Jody Scheckter was at Jerez bearing his open and slightly quizzical smile as he moved about. He had the businessman's haircut, its shape and length conventionally modest. The years had touched him, but lightly. The years had touched his South African accent, too, softening it perhaps.

Autumnal sunlight fell across Jerez, also, but warm enough for Schumacher to peel off his overalls down to his white tee shirt on the short journey from the pits to the transporter. The tee shirt was decorated with Ferrari and Marlboro logos but *nothing* about being champion 1997. He looked as he always did approaching pressure, perfectly composed.

Brawn, standing somewhere near the Ferrari pit, smiled in his benevolent schoolmasterly way. 'Everything seemed fine in the warm-up. No problems. We're just getting ready for the race now,' he'd say, quick and clipped, revealing absolutely nothing. *What strategy do you think Williams will have?* 'I don't know.' Then Brawn was gone into the shadows of the pit.

At the kart track at Kerpen the German television channel *RTL* interviewed Rolf and Elisabeth. She was small, straw-blonde, and wore a yellow anorak. Curious. You could not see the lineage in her face or eyes. She masticated what appeared to be chewing gum absently, mechanically, perhaps as an aid to calming herself.

The combatants have been asked how they prepared for the great day. How do you as parents feel about it?

'I do not prepare myself and I am worried,' she said.

What time did you get up?

'Half past six.'

Had a coffee?

'Yes.'

Do you talk to Frentzen's mother or Villeneuve's mother?

'No, I don't do that. I don't know them. I have no contact.'

Rolf wore a hip-length coat and a blue shirt. He had white, receding, dignified hair and spectacles. Curious. The lineage to Michael was uncannily evident in his face, the set of his eyes, the curl of his mouth. 'It appears I am very composed but as a father you get quite wound up. First of all I want to wish every driver in the race good luck.' He pointed out that whatever happened Michael would be 'deputy' World Champion 'There are a lot of drivers who never made it that far...'

In Ferrari, across the decade before, only Prost.

The parents weren't unduly defensive and certainly not demonstrative, just caught up in something they could influence no more than Scheckter, ordinary people expressing themselves as ordinary people do.

On the grid a mêlée pressed closer and closer to Villeneuve's car, so dense that he and the car vanished within it.

Brawn stood beside Schumacher's Ferrari, minder of the munitions.

The width of the track melted into a shuffling semi-scuffling spread of guests, mechanics, officials and media, all playing human skittles as they gathered and dispersed and gathered again, peering, posing, working, trying to work.

Somewhere over there was Hill's Arrows, in the bay on the grid behind Schumacher and next to Frentzen. That had become a sub-plot. Schumacher said plaintively that he considered Hill the third Williams driver and 'I hope he stays out of the way.'

Scheckter was interviewed on this grid, the mêlée ebbing by, and explained that if Schumacher won, Italy would go wild. He added that when you drive for Ferrari you represent the Italian nation. He was philosophical about Schumacher succeeding him if it worked out that way, because it would be good for motor racing as a whole.

The 22 cars moved off into the formation lap, Villeneuve drawing them round slowly, taking his place to the left of the grid, Schumacher to the right. They faced 69 laps, slightly under 190 miles (305.5km).

Five red lights – off.

Villeneuve came over to mid-track but Schumacher had made a fine start, clean and swift, and taken the lead. Frentzen was past Villeneuve. Crossing the line to complete the opening lap, Frentzen was at 1.981 seconds and Villeneuve at 3.221 from Schumacher and it settled like that until Frentzen let Villeneuve through on lap eight. The first crisis of the race was at hand. Could Villeneuve catch Schumacher, 4.3 seconds ahead? At lap nine he'd reduced it by a fraction and pushed hard enough to set fastest laps but Schumacher responded, setting fastest laps, too.

They ran towards the first pits stops, Schumacher making his on lap 22, Villeneuve on lap 23. When Frentzen, Häkkinen and Coulthard pitted, as they would soon, Villeneuve could attack Schumacher. By lap 28 those pit stops had been completed, Schumacher back in the lead, Villeneuve back in second place. The second crisis of the race was at hand. Could Villeneuve mount the attack? He nibbled into the corner called Dry Sack, a spoon-shaped right, withdrew. That was just the opening salvo.

At lap 31 the gap was 3.1. Villeneuve, dogged as a terrier, set about drawing up again and by lap 34 had it to 2.3. He pushed harder and two laps later had it under two seconds, then under a second and a half. At lap 39 it was 1.04.

They weaved paths through backmarkers and ran tight to the second pit stops, Schumacher's on lap 43 (stationary for 9.4 seconds and enough fuel to go to the end), Villeneuve's a lap later (8.3 seconds, and enough fuel too). Villeneuve emerged behind Coulthard and maddeningly, maddeningly couldn't get past him. Instant by instant Schumacher escaped. It was only a lap before Coulthard pitted – but a long lap and, when he did, the gap had opened to 2.5. Villeneuve knew that tyre wear would become critical very soon: too worn to mount the attack. He estimated he had three laps to catch and despatch Schumacher or the championship was gone.

Villeneuve pummelled the gap and they came across the line to start lap 48 separated by 0.3 of a second. Villeneuve hustled him through and out of Expo 92, the right at the end of the pit lane straight, tracked him through Michelin, another right, tracked him on through the next left, closed up through the long, elegant right-hander after that. They travelled in lock-step down the descending straight to the right-twisting spoon of Dry Sack.

They were positioned over to the left, a ribbon of blue and white kerb coursing by at their elbows.

Villeneuve jinked right into the expanse of empty track, Schumacher level but outside him.

At the entry to the corner Villeneuve was nicely on the inside, Schumacher crowding him hard.

Villeneuve was half a car's length ahead but, with Schumacher to his left and the grass to his right, he had nowhere to go except ahead. The crowding was so hard that momentarily he put two wheels on the grass.

With shocking suddenness the Ferrari turned into him, its right-front wheel smacking the bodywork of the Williams beside the cockpit.

Villeneuve 'wasn't really surprised when he finally decided to turn in on me. It was a little bit expected so I knew I was taking a big risk [in trying to overtake].'

The Ferrari dribbled off into the gravel trap on the left but Villeneuve continued, amazed that the car appeared to be undamaged after the strength of the hit it had just taken. Schumacher sat beached on the gravel, his rear wheels spinning but finding no propulsion. He clambered out and marched away, hauled his crash helmet off and stood on a low wall watching Villeneuve go by, Villeneuve go by.

The crash looked damning enough for Schumacher from a distance but his on-board camera compounded that mercilessly. When the tape of it was played moments later every televiewer in the world could watch Villeneuve there on the inside, Schumacher crowding, then Schumacher's gloved hands twisting the steering wheel so that the Ferrari rammed the Williams. This was impossible to miss.

Someone on a scooter gave Schumacher a lift back to the pits while Villeneuve went by to the championship. It didn't matter that at the very end he ceded the lead to Häkkinen and second place to Coulthard. Third sufficed and Scheckter was still the last driver to do the taming.

The fallout reverberated.

Schumacher claimed Villeneuve's overtaking move was 'optimistic' and 'I was very surprised by what he did', but, paraphrasing these words, it was an extremely optimistic defence and ultimately untenable. At a Press Conference days later at Maranello Schumacher softened his stance, conceding that 'I made an error' and adding 'I'm a human, not a machine.'

Two weeks after Jerez the FIA's World Motorsport Council ruled that he be stripped of his second place in the championship but nothing more except the penance of doing a week's public relations on road safety for the European Commission. Max Mosley, president of the FIA, explained that the Council felt Schumacher's move was not premeditated but an instinctive action.

Schumacher revealed that he hadn't slept properly for three nights after the race 'because of the pressure I felt for what I had done. It was an instinctive action and it was important they decided it was not deliberate.'

The crash raised questions about the level of desire Schumacher worked to, and whether, if you are to win consistently in motor racing at its highest level, you have to find defeat intolerable. But hadn't Villeneuve just proved you can win and conduct yourself decently? Wouldn't Häkkinen move from this first Grand Prix win of his career to the 1998 Championship exhibiting the most becoming conduct?

The Jerez crash left other questions unanswered too. Did the strength of the modern car allow drivers to behave as they did, behaviour which could well have been fatal a generation before? Did the people who invest in Grand Prix racing for its television ratings *delight* in the crash and the fallout – nobody injured, and *wonderful* for those ratings? Did the FIA duck its responsibility by slapping Schumacher so limply on the wrist rather than kicking his backside all the way back up the autobahns to Kerpen?

Jerez was a mess of human weaknesses, Schumacher's the most visible, Schumacher's the catalyst.

Barnard was long gone from Ferrari but I was curious about his evaluation of Schumacher's strengths and about what Schumacher had that made good judges evaluate him so highly.

'How do you explain it? If you look at those top-top guys, and I'm talking about the Prosts and Laudas [as well], they have a dedication to it which the others don't understand. They have *such* a total immersion in what they are doing and an exclusion of *everything* else. They all have a natural skill at driving a racing car and that's second nature – going quickly *is* second nature.

'That leaves them a lot of capacity while they are driving to think about the car and the tyres and so on. *Where do I need it better? How do I make it better? I'll talk about this with my engineer,* and so on and so on. It's what they are all able to do, and they have this classic, mind-blowing dedication. It can grind the engineers into dust. Senna? I've known the technical people say "I can't keep up with him, I just can't keep up with him." They are so *into it* all the time.

'Schumacher was very similar, although perhaps less on the

car side [demanding to know every detail about the car] and more on the total dedication side, the whole keep-fit thing. He's going to be fitter than the next guy, he's going to be the fittest guy, he will make *sure* he's the fittest guy. Then he's going to have more of what he thinks are the right people round him to make *sure* he's going to do the job better. He's going to take everything one step more.'

I was curious, too, about Barnard's view on the strategy of mid-race sprints which Schumacher created to order, particularly since, by definition, the driver already seems to be going as fast as he can.

'The important part of the question is *going as fast as they can*. Sometimes you know for an absolute fact that they are not. It happens time and time again: somebody "falls off", there's a sniff of points or something and *bomp*, suddenly the stopwatch is going faster. You're asking about the driver "what have you been doing up to now?" It's all about motivation. The good ones are still motivated even when they are sitting on the back of the grid. They think: "OK, I know I am back here but I am going to do *this*, I am going to do *that*, and I know I can get up there." The other guys are out there just going round and round – and there's a lot of them doing it.

'Everybody talks about good strategies and marvellous strategies, and it's all very well being aware of what you need to do, all very well going on the radio and saying *you have so many laps to gain so many seconds* but [chuckle] it's no good saying that to the guy who can't do it! If you'd said something like that to Berger he'd have told you to eff off because he's going as hard as he can. Some of them would take a very dim view of being told to go faster and they'd think you were being [expletive] rude with "do you mind going quicker now?" Schumacher doesn't gear up to do a quick racing lap, he goes *over* his racing lap. Again it's dedicated concentration, the ability to switch everything else off and keep a focus on this one thing.'

Some sweat after a race, others – especially Schumacher – look almost fresh.

'That's the difference between the naturally talented guys and the guys who want it so badly and push themselves to do it. That's what Mansell was. For many, many years he wasn't considered to be worthwhile at all but they come to a point – Hunt was the same, Hunt had one year – where they feel that they've either got a car that can do it or they've got a team behind them that is big enough to allow them to do it. Whatever it is, they think the situation is good enough and they won't get too many chances like this again. They decide inwardly – in their own minds – *this is my chance, I have to do it now, I am going to drive over my limit to do it*. And that's what Mansell did. I saw him drive absolute blinders in qualifying and it was only because he's got enormous balls – and enormous balls are part of the determination built on *this is my chance, if I don't take it now forget it, I'm never going to do it at all*. Tremendous driver, old Nigel. He said to me on many occasions, "You get the car close enough, I'll fix the rest of it." He'd get in and big-balls it round.'

Barnard pauses, reflects, points out that Hunt was a 'one-time champion whereas Schumacher, Senna, Prost, they say "Ah, so that's how you win a championship" and they win more. That's the difference.'

Barnard pauses again.

'With Schumacher, the fundamental driving talent is there, the quickness, the reactions, the balls – it's all there. He's just bloody quick and all the good ones are that, just bloody quick. On to the top of that you can then pile all the baggage of peripherals, all the problems they have to deal with outside the car. The good ones kick that part into gear as well. *Then* you've got *it*.'

Chapter 8

Almost There

The Ferrari F300 was launched in early January amidst the habitual pomp and circumstance, but Brawn put a hard blade into that: 'This year only total success will be good enough.' Di Montezemolo put his own blade in too. 'Today is the first time we can say with belief that Ferrari can win the World Championship. We start the season absolutely aware that our objective is to win it.'

Schumacher tested the car at Fiorano and Jerez and had problems with, among other things, the gearbox electronics. He covered only 33 laps in two days. He tested at Mugello and described the car as having 'that certain kind of nervousness that a racing car should have.' Häkkinen in the new McLaren had broken the winter testing record at Barcelona on only his third serious lap…

This was Byrne's first Ferrari and his design philosophy is important because we have heard how Barnard preferred rear end stability in a car while Schumacher wanted the reverse (if you can put it like that). How did Byrne approach this? 'The way John wanted the car to be set up did not, I think it's fair to say, suit Michael. I am sure Michael would have got the best out of it but he felt the car would be potentially quicker if you set it up a different way, nervous at the front [see paragraph above!]. The thing is, if you think about it, front downforce comes fairly drag-free – you can actually set up a car so it's running more front downforce than, relatively speaking, how Barnard would want to set it up. And the overall downforce would be higher.'

This is not a criticism of him or you or anybody else, this is just different approaches to the same problem.

'Yes, sure, exactly. Prost wouldn't drive a car like that, he wanted to drive it the way John's described it.'

So you're now designing the 1998 car. Do you design it with all that in mind?

'Yes, but to be honest, I design the car the way I think it's going to have the most grip, it's going to be the quickest, the best balance, the best variation in balance. The driver ends up adapting it, setting it up to suit his style, but the fundamentals – the weight distribution, the aerodynamic distribution, the sensitivity – well, I design to what I think is going to produce the quickest car.'

But you have to bear in mind that he'll be the one driving it.

'Yes.'

And the more you give him what he wants, the quicker he'll be able to go.

'Yes, sure, but what he wants is exactly what you need to go fast so there is no conflict of interests.'

The leading teams:

Benetton – Fisichella, Alexander Wurz.
Ferrari – Schumacher, Irvine.
Jordan – Hill, R. Schumacher.
McLaren – Häkkinen, Coulthard.
Williams – Villeneuve, Frentzen.

At Melbourne, Schumacher went quickest in drizzle-shrouded Friday practice but 'the weather made it difficult to do any proper set-up work. This practice was more or less a gamble. I never managed a single clear lap.' He qualified on the second row, was happy with the car although 'it is not yet at the level we intend it to be', and ran five laps of the race before the engine broke. The McLarens finished first and second.

Brazil was better although he qualified on the second row again and said 'I think the McLarens will be unbeatable under normal circumstances but we should be the best of the rest.' Correct. Häkkinen won from Coulthard, Schumacher third and talking of how the team had maximised what they had.

Initially Argentina seemed like Melbourne and Sao Paulo. On the Friday he was second (Coulthard 1m 28.130s, Schumacher 1m 29.114s), saying, 'I am happy with the new wider front tyres from Goodyear. They have helped us to close the gap. We also have some improvements on the car. Looking at the section times, I was quicker on the first section and only a couple of tenths slower in the other sections.'

He sustained that in qualifying, putting the Ferrari on the front row. 'A miracle has happened. I am between the two McLarens and not so far from pole. I feel that maybe now we can go where we want to go.'

At the red lights he had a clutch problem and was third, stalking Häkkinen, got past in a right-hander, quickly shed him and reached towards Coulthard. He caught Coulthard by lap five and into the hairpin, a slow right, Coulthard was stricken by a gearbox problem, ran wide. Schumacher pressed the Ferrari's nose into the gap and Coulthard, turning in, turned into him. Coulthard spun, Schumacher continued.

'He had already run wide at that point on the previous lap so I went for the gap but he seemed to close the door. I did not want to lift off because I felt I had the momentum to get through. The car was damaged and it suffered from understeer in right-hand corners,' Schumacher said. To compound that he was on a two-stop strategy and the McLarens one, obliging him to gain 20 seconds. He didn't find them and lost the lead when he pitted on lap 28. Häkkinen stayed out for another 12 laps and when he pitted Schumacher assumed the lead again. He'd make his second stop in 11 laps and needed a sprint. He led by 17 seconds at lap 50 and forced that to 21 seconds three laps later. As he emerged from the pit stop Häkkinen was within sight but behind backmarkers. It was, or ought to have been, a milk run, but on lap 67 rain fell. Schumacher went off at the final corner. He ran across gravel and rejoined, and this is how it happened: 'I lost control where the track surface was shiny but I remember Johnny Herbert going off there in the warm-up and getting stuck – so I didn't try to brake, just headed for the escape road. I'd made sure I knew where it was when we went round on the parade lap.'

He beat Häkkinen by more than 22 seconds, Irvine third.

The San Marino Grand Prix appeared pivotal. Were Ferrari really able to match the McLarens? In Friday practice he was third and 'we are not too far from them but I don't know if they used new tyres. The situation is more difficult than I anticipated and my car is not yet set up properly. It was tricky to drive and unpredictable.' He qualified third. The race is simply told, Coulthard leading throughout, Häkkinen behind him until lap 17 when the gearbox failed, Schumacher moving into this second place.

Barcelona favoured the McLarens and he finished the race a distant third behind them. Häkkinen 36, Coulthard 29, Schumacher 24.

Suddenly you're a third of the way through the season and the catching up is still to be done.

At Monaco he crashed in Casino Square in practice ('I was trying too hard and lost control'), qualified fourth and spoke of perhaps a place on the podium. They ran in order Häkkinen, Fisichella, Schumacher to the pit stops, Schumacher's on lap 30. He was stationary for 7.4 seconds. Wurz in the Benetton, yet to stop, held second and Schumacher drew up. At Loews, Wurz seemed preoccupied with three cars proceeding nose-to-tail in front of him and seemed unaware that Schumacher was thrusting the Ferrari down the inside. The two cars rubbed wheels then Wurz's front left brushed Schumacher's right rear. In a reflex action Wurz re-took Schumacher, who thrust again, re-took him before the tunnel. 'I tried to pass Alex because he had left the door open. We touched, but very lightly. It was just a normal race incident and I definitely do not blame him.'

Wurz remembered this vividly. 'It was the last lap before I would have come in to the pits. There were three cars in front of me, slowing each other down. Then I saw Michael coming behind me. I thought, "OK, if I start to fight I will lose a lot of time" – I was racing for second position in the race at this moment. Then I saw Michael trying to overtake me. I wasn't surprised: I was going slowly because of the three cars in front of me.

'He went on the inside and normally I would have defended my line completely to avoid any chance of him overtaking but because, as I have said, I was to go into the pits I didn't want to lose time, especially overall time in terms of the race. That's because you do lose more time when you fight than if you just let him go. But when he came on the inside I said to myself, "Oh no, I can't make it that easy for him!" So there I was on the outside and I accelerated. We touched, I think, two times because there was no space. It was not done by him on purpose and it was not done by me on purpose! Then he left me just the space of one car – the width – so I re-took him. For me this was quite a normal thing to do but I was a bit annoyed because I had lost time while this was going on – but my ego was so big I wouldn't let him past!

'Then we came to the corner before the tunnel. I wanted to be too brave and come from the outside, taking the speed into the tunnel and I forgot about Michael because I thought he'd understand I wasn't making life easy for him. I was too brave and I didn't defend my line, not even a single centimetre. And he tried it again, too aggressive for my taste because he hit me very hard. I was already in the corner and the hit was so hard it knocked the steering wheel out of my hands. I went around the corner and I felt my car was OK but I had lost a lot of time. I went into the pits and my wishbone was a little bit bent, we put in 90 kilos of fuel – I was on a one-stop strategy – and my car was too low with the bent wishbone. It was touching the ground very hard and I couldn't steer round the corners.'

Here you are, a young man, and the great Michael Schumacher comes up behind you. What are you thinking? Are you intimidated?

'No, not at all. It's the other way round for me because with guys like Michael – or Jacques Villeneuve, for example – if you fight with them first of all they know what they are doing, and second they are quite fair because they leave you the space: enough but not a millimetre too much! They are not like drivers who are new to Formula One who make stupid things and you crash. Then when you fight with Michael or Jacques it makes so much fun because there is a special – well, not an agreement between us but an understanding that everyone has to live on the circuit and so we leave each other the required space: to that millimetre.' Or, as it happened, several millimetres short approaching the tunnel at Monaco…

Schumacher came into the pits prepared to retire 'but the mechanics managed to change the track rod and I continued.' Häkkinen won, Schumacher tenth.

Canada started gently, Schumacher qualifying third and 'I am happy, mainly because I am only two-tenths of a second behind pole. It's a long time since we have been this close.' Deep into the race he came out of the pits just as Frentzen was passing over on the far rim of the track. Schumacher moved across towards him…and across…and across, eventually forcing Frentzen into a spin and retirement. 'I do not know what happened,' Schumacher said after the race. 'If it was my fault then I want to apologise to him. I looked in the mirrors and saw nothing, then I looked to my right and still saw nothing so when I was called in for my penalty [a stop'n'go for what he'd done to Frentzen] I did not understand, as I knew I had not speeded in the pit lane.'

This penalty, on lap 35, put Schumacher third behind Fisichella and Hill. He caught Hill, but as he tried to pass Hill defended his position, even giving Schumacher the elbow. 'I want to have a strong word with Hill. What he did was unacceptable. To change line once is normal but to do it three times at 320kph down the straight is very dangerous. He braked early for the first chicane and I had to cut the chicane to stop hitting him. I am very angry. You do not want to hear the words I thought in that moment because that's purely dangerous. If someone wants to kill you he can do it in a different way – because we're going down there [at] 320kph and somebody moving three times the line, that's simply impossible.'

When Fisichella pitted on lap 44 Schumacher sprinted and made up enough time to keep the lead during his second stop. He won from Fisichella, Irvine third. Häkkinen 46, Schumacher 34, Coulthard 29.

After the race Frank Williams protested Schumacher and what he'd done to Frentzen. Williams wasn't particularly concerned when it was rejected because 'I was making a voice heard rather than seeking redress. I felt that Michael's behaviour was out of order on the Grand Prix track, and it's not the first time.'

(By a great irony, at the drivers' briefing before the race Schumacher had asked for particular care about exiting the pit lane and, if drivers were arriving at racing speed down the track, let them go. He also asked for a blue flag to be waved to anyone exiting the pits to warn them a car was arriving, but in his case no blue flag was waved. He did apologise to Frentzen, explaining that he'd seen Diniz and Villeneuve and 'then there was a gap.')

Hill had pungent things to say about Schumacher; but side-stepping these quasi-controversies Rory Byrne takes us on a fascinating and relevant detour of Schumacher's mastery, embracing Ayrton Senna.

Does Schumacher have an analytical ability? The difference between the great ones and the merely good is, as John Barnard has already underlined, that the great ones do it so naturally they still have brain space available.

'Yes, that's true, that's absolutely true.'

So he can come in and say X, Y or Z when he's done a really hot lap?

'Not only that but during a race. He can be turning in really quick laps *and* be on the radio asking questions or telling us various things. Most drivers don't really like to be bothered on the radio when they're really going for it whereas he's got the mental capacity to drive quickly and still consider the other aspects of the race or whatever it is to be considered.'

Even during one of the famous sprints?

'Yeah, oh yeah. He's got a bit of reserve in terms of speed and he uses it when he has to.'

And even during the sprints, when he comes on the radio or you get on the radio to him, does he still seem unhurried in his thinking?

'Sure. That's the incredible thing and that, to be honest, separates the World Champions from the others. What strikes me most is not his sheer one-lap speed, because relative to people like Ayrton he's not had that many pole positions. It isn't so much his ability to put in a quick lap, which he does, it's that in qualifying quite often his very first lap is his quickest. That means he is able to find the limits straight away.'

That's not all of it…

'There are countless races where he has produced something that no one expected. Canada, for example, when he was hauled in for that 10-second penalty and everyone said "Well, that's that", but he pulled back enough to win.'

Isn't it true that during a race the great ones never think they've lost, they think how do I pull it back?

'And that's how Michael thinks.'

Is he mentally strong?

'Yes he is.'

What is it that allows him to move from racing pace up to a different pace altogether...?

'...and he doesn't only do it for one lap, he can string together ten, fifteen laps like that. That's what I find really amazing.'

Could Ayrton have done that?

'I don't know. When Ayrton drove for us at Toleman in 1984, the racing – relatively speaking – wasn't as competitive. You couldn't race a car on the limit for the whole race, or people did very seldom. Nowadays it is much more competitive and often you do have to race pretty much on the limit the whole time. So I can't really say if Ayrton could have done it, although I think he proved when he did need to go faster that he could.'

Therefore, Byrne concludes, 'it means the great ones are racing at slightly under 100% and they can step it up to 100%. And as I say, Michael can keep it there for ten, fifteen laps if he has to.'

In France everything seemed to be changing. He qualified agonisingly near pole (1m 15.15s against Häkkinen's 1m 14.92s) and 'it's probably the closest gap we've ever had this year. I believe we are in a position to beat McLaren in a straight fight for the first time.' He led the race throughout except for a single lap when he pitted, passing the lead to Irvine; paid tribute to Irvine and said, 'We are the best team in the pit lane.' Häkkinen 50, Schumacher 44, Coulthard 30, Irvine 25.

That was halfway through the season.

The British Grand Prix assumed extreme importance because if Schumacher could win there the season would tilt towards him. He qualified second, albeit half a second slower than Häkkinen who initially led the race from him, Coulthard third, on a track surface which was drying. On lap five Coulthard crowded Schumacher and overtook him. Rain fell. The order remained undisturbed to lap 38 when Coulthard spun off. By then the leaders had pitted once and now pitted again, emerging with the order still undisturbed, Häkkinen far in the lead from Schumacher. The track was deluged. Häkkinen skidded off, wrestled the McLaren back.

At 3.15 Schumacher lapped Wurz under a stationary yellow flag: *danger, no overtaking, slow down*. To miss a flag in this grey water murk was understandable but still required punishment. In fact Wurz did not see the flag either. 'Honestly,' as he adds, 'I didn't know a lot of the things which were happening because it was such chaos. I was happy to stay on the circuit, and I knew that Michael was behind me so I even slowed down to give him the opportunity to overtake me. I was concentrating on my driving, I watched the mirror and saw him. I didn't race against him – if I had, I wouldn't have done what I did. So he overtook: I wasn't going really slowly but I wasn't at racing speed either. I had problems and I wanted to drive behind him because if you are behind another car and on their line there is not so much water. That was my idea. I didn't see a yellow flag at all. I was surprised [that Michael was punished]. Afterwards Jean Todt came to me and asked, "Did you see a yellow flag?", and I replied, "I'm very sorry, I didn't see any".'

At 3.16 the Safety Car came out and the racers bunched, followed it.

The Stewards debated what to do and from this moment on Article 57 of the rules came into (and went out of) play with chaotic frequency. Section *a* of the Article said the Stewards must inform a team official of any infringement 25 minutes 'after the moment at which the incident occurred.'

The Safety Car pulled off at the end of lap 49, the conditions marginally improved. Häkkinen tried to hold Schumacher but the McLaren was damaged and on lap 51 Schumacher moved through, nine laps to run.

The Stewards did not record their decision – to penalise Schumacher by ten seconds – until 3.39.

At 3.43, while the sodden and diminishing band of runners edged their way round lap 57 – three to run – the Stewards' verdict was delivered to Ferrari. Crucially, it was 29 minutes after the offence.

Article 57*a* also stipulated that notification of the penalty be displayed on the timing monitors (which all teams have). It wasn't.

Todt was quoted as saying that 'when the official handed us the document relating to the penalty he was unable to tell us which rule it referred to.' This provoked confusion, because the difference between a ten-second stop'n'go penalty – Schumacher slowing into the pits, remaining stationary, going slowly out of the pits – would give the race to Häkkinen, but if ten seconds were added to Schumacher's overall race time at the end he'd win, because he'd have enough time in hand.

Compounding the confusion, Article 57*e* stipulated that if an infringement happened 'with 12 or less complete laps remaining' the Stewards shall 'have the right to add the time penalty.' It would be no problem for Schumacher: *but* the infringement had happened on lap 43 when there were 17 to go.

Compounding the confusion even further, Article 57*b* stipulated that if the infringement happened with more than 12 laps left 'from the time the Stewards' decision is notified on the timing monitors, the relevant driver may cover no more than three complete laps before entering the pits and proceeding to his pit where he shall remain for the period of the time penalty.' That was the ten-second stop'n'go.

Three laps remained...

Brawn was described as frantically talking to the Stewards.

An ITV pit lane reporter, James Allen, observed and said: 'Ross Brawn is shaking his head, waving at the Stewards saying "No, no, no, you're wrong, you're wrong".'

Todt said that 'because of the doubt' about the penalty they decided to bring Schumacher in for the stop'n'go. Beginning lap 58, as Schumacher skimmed along the start-finish straight, his crew prepared for him to come in and pay the penalty: five red-uniformed men, one holding a round sign on a pole and positioned where Schumacher would come to a halt. He completed lap 58 and moved into lap 59, his tyres stirring little rosters of spray. He had 23.41 seconds in hand.

On lap 59 he sprinted (as best he could in these conditions) because he still might need all the time he could get, the Ferrari slithering wide and coursing through standing water as he goaded it forward. An interesting thought: the Ferrari pit, where now seven red-uniformed men stood waiting, was up towards the far end of the pit lane and you'd cross the finishing line (or rather its hypothetical extension from the track itself) to reach it...

At 3.47 the team brought him in, the Ferrari angling from the track to the long pit lane entrance. He travelled down that, travelled along the pit lane and, just before he reached his pit, crossed the 'line'. He'd won. Hadn't he? Few could be certain of that, least of all Schumacher himself. Motionless, he served his penalty and then went out and covered another couple of laps just to be on the safe side. When all that was over, Häkkinen brought his McLaren in and sat, eyes uncomprehending. He had no idea what had happened. Nearby Schumacher embraced the Ferrari mechanics who were waving clenched fists, consumed by delight. Häkkinen 56, Schumacher 54, Coulthard 30.

Before the Austrian Grand Prix he signed a four-year deal with Ferrari at $32 million per annum and explained that even though he'd had other proposals ('in some cases superior') he felt happy at Maranello, he and the team had done an awful lot of work and he felt optimistic about the Championship.

A turbulent first lap settled to Häkkinen leading from Schumacher; they duelled until lap 17 when, at the last corner – a descending arc of a right – Schumacher ran wide at the exit, bounding across grass and gravel, battering bits off the Ferrari. 'I lost control because I was going too quickly. It was a stupid mistake. As the car jumped through the gravel and I lost the front wing I thought there was more damage but the car proved to be very strong.' He was last.

He put together a sustained recovery so that by lap 34 he was in the points, and by lap 68 (of 71) on the podium – overtaking Irvine, who slowed with a reported brake problem. Team orders? But they'd been banned since Melbourne, when Coulthard allowed Häkkinen to win under a gentleman's agreement – hadn't they? Irvine was diplomatic and spoke of Inspector Clouseau solving this particular mystery. Häkkinen 66, Schumacher 58, Coulthard 36.

Layers of pressure hemmed him at Hockenheim, where he qualified ninth. In the race he finished fifth, 'the best I could do. My main problem was lack of grip in the Motodrom [the stadium section] where it was difficult to simply keep the car on the road.' Häkkinen 76, Schumacher 60, Coulthard 42.

Across the 77 laps of the Hungarian Grand Prix, Brawn and Schumacher would banish historical precedent, bend the rigidity of the circuit to their will and ultimately redefine the possible.

He qualified third behind the McLarens and both teams intended to pit twice. Häkkinen led the race from Coulthard, Schumacher third. Precedent held so far, the race static. At lap 14 Coulthard was at 2.4 seconds from Häkkinen and Schumacher at 3.6. Schumacher pitted first but emerged behind Villeneuve, Coulthard pitting next lap, Häkkinen two laps later. Häkkinen kept the lead, Coulthard kept second place,

Schumacher still behind Villeneuve and to underscore Schumacher's captivity Coulthard set fastest lap. The McLarens were romping it.

Brawn now made a profound decision: 'We'll move to three stops.' When this was radioed to Schumacher he thought *I'm not sure if it will work*.

Brawn conceded that the new strategy was aggressive but 'we had nothing to lose'.

Villeneuve pitted on lap 31, releasing Schumacher, who set fastest lap and cut into the gaps. Coulthard was 2.2 seconds ahead and Häkkinen 6.1. This was going to be arm-wrestling. By half distance Schumacher had pressed Coulthard up towards Häkkinen and three seconds covered them all. What happened next needs careful dissection.

Schumacher did a lap of 1m 21 and pitted on lap 43, Coulthard the lap after and, emerging, watched Schumacher go by.

Now he pounded the Hungaroring, on lap 45 going below 1: 20 for the first time – 1: 19.91, then 1: 19.59.

That was lap 46 – Häkkinen pitting. As Häkkinen, emerging, was halfway down the pit lane Schumacher went by. Schumacher led because he'd been stationary a shorter time – because the team didn't need to put enough fuel in to get him to the end, with another stop to come.

Neither of the McLarens were far behind.

The Ferrari radio crackled and Brawn said the fateful words which have passed directly into Grand Prix history. 'You have 19 laps to build a 25-second lead.'

Schumacher replied 'Thank you very much.' A masterstroke was about to reach an entirely new level. He forced the Ferrari as hard and far as it was possible to do: his phrase. He was about to put together one of the most sustained periods of speed which Grand Prix racing had ever seen. The struggle for the soul of the race was about to begin.

	Schumacher	Häkkinen	Gain/loss
Lap 48	1: 19.80	1: 22.28	+2.4
Lap 49	1: 20.64	1: 22.27	+1.6
Lap 50	1: 21.28	1: 22.21	+0.9
Lap 51	1: 20.30	1: 22.85	+2.5
Lap 52	1: 25.82	1: 25.59	–0.2

On that lap the depth of the forcing took him off the track at the right-handed curve onto the start-finish straight, across grass, smearing the tyres with dry mud as, ferocious, he came back on. He'd been forcing too hard: his phrase again. Even so, in these five laps he'd gained 7.3 seconds. He did not know that Häkkinen was finding the McLaren almost impossible to drive with some undiagnosed problem, nor that Coulthard – now past Häkkinen on this lap – had a problem with a rear tyre.

	Schumacher	Coulthard	Gain	Overall
Lap 53	1: 20.67	1: 23.67	+2.9	+13.8
Lap 54	1: 19.85	1: 21.67	+1.8	+15.7
Lap 55	1: 21.00	1: 21.25	+0.2	+15.9
Lap 56	1: 20 16	1: 21.47	+1.3	+17.2

He was flicking the Ferrari through the twitchy sequence of corners towards the curve to the start-finish straight, commanding it across the kerbs, skimming a little smoke from the tyres as the brakes dug. He was spreading mastery across the whole circuit.

	Schumacher	Coulthard	Gain	Overall
Lap 57	1: 20.10	1: 21.37	+1.2	+18.5
Lap 58	1: 19.62	1: 22.16	+2.5	+21.0
Lap 59	1: 19.96	1: 21.65	+1.6	+22.7

On lap 60 Schumacher forced the Ferrari towards what must have been the ultimate even he could draw from it. He set a new fastest lap and now you could see the consequences of the forcing. The car shivered and danced and vibrated, his helmet was bobbing, his hands were pumping. He was carving through the corners.

Even Brawn watched stunned: his word.

	Schumacher	Coulthard	Gain	Overall
Lap 60	1: 19.28	1: 21.21	+1.9	+24.6
Lap 61	1: 19.51	1: 21.42	+1.9	+26.6

The Ferrari mechanics trundled fresh tyres into position and began to man the refuelling rig. Schumacher dipped the car into the pit lane, was stationary for 7.7 seconds and as he accelerated onto the track Coulthard was on the horizon – *back* on the horizon.

To explain this astonishing result I'm quoting two men close to the heart of what happened at Ferrari, Stepney and Brawn, with an illuminating insight from Schumacher himself.

Stepney: 'You need to look more and more each year for advantages, and that's the problem, because there are a lot less now than there used to be. Hungary was down to strategy but that meant a *lot* of pressure on the driver. He was made to drive on the limit and his race became three sprints. That's the hardest thing. There's a lot of pressure in the strategies to push the driver as much as you can, and you are going to make mistakes because it's sprinting, it's not behaving as you do in normal racing conditions.'

If Brawn makes a specific demand Schumacher meets it.

'Yes, because Michael believes in that strategy and he goes with it.'

Stepney, like Barnard and Byrne, emphasises the absolute importance of the mental aspect and the advantage *that* brings.

'The top drivers spend very little time thinking about what they are doing. Their driving a racing car is as natural to them as you getting in your car and going to the shops. Other racing drivers are thinking about other things too much, they're thinking about everything – the person in front, the braking and so on. With Michael that's in a second memory, if you like. The rest of it is concentrated on pushing to get the best out of the car, and feeling the car, and getting the maximum performance out of himself as well.'

Speaking of this second memory, this naturalness…

'If you see Häkkinen when he gets out of a car after a race, he's been sweating a lot. Michael – not a bead. I've seen him sweat once, I think. He's *so* cool when he gets out of the car.'

Yes, but if Brawn gets on the radio and says you have 19 laps to gain 25 seconds, where do those seconds come from?

'You have to have the car…well, you have to have everything, the strategy, somebody with the potential to do that strategy, and the capability yourself.'

He doesn't just find it for one lap…

'No, no, he finds it all the time. Some drivers overdrive a lot and I'll give you an instance of what that can mean. We asked Michael to back off in one race and he went quicker, so we radioed and said, "We asked you to back off." He replied, "But I have backed off!" The reason he was actually going faster was that in backing off he suddenly had more momentum going on the car rather than pushing it and pulling it. This can work the other way. Sometimes the more you ask them to push the slower they go, whereas that time Michael relaxed it a little bit and he was smoother, using less fuel, less brakes and going quicker.

'For some drivers this sort of thing can be a problem in qualifying. You see some of them pushing like hell and they're pushing too much. If they just drove as they had in the morning session, when they weren't under pressure, 50% of them would achieve better lap times. The only people who can do banzai laps are the Sennas and Schumachers [*Banzai* = one qualifying lap of total speed]. Well, Berger did a few and Mansell could

245

produce them – Prost was quick but he couldn't do that. Senna always wanted to be quickest, *booof*. That's not true of Michael. For Senna it was a physical and psychological thing to be quickest, a need to give himself that push, and also psychological against his competitors.'

Schumacher explains that 'a logically thinking driver will usually try for the limit of the car's performance' but not push beyond that, because (a) you risk a crash and (b) if you go even slightly off the track you destroy the lap in competitive terms. 'I try to feel where the limit is at each corner. In order to detect the limit, I must however always try to drive faster than it seems the car can go.' He wanted to 'exhaust the efficiency of the car completely, meet exactly the point of where it performs best.'

Next Brawn:

Can you please unlock the door to the famous tactics? I watch races like Hungary in 1998 and when it's over I don't know how it was done. Lots of people are thinking he couldn't have won that, could he – it's impossible.

'The thing that is important to stress is that Michael is a driver who takes a great deal of time to understand the tactical considerations and the tactical options during a race. He will spend a great deal of time, particularly on a Saturday evening, with me and the other members of the team to contribute to those tactical considerations. There are direct things he can contribute in terms of how easy it is to overtake here, which way does the track "go" during a race – does it pick up pace, does it stabilise? – etc etc etc. There's information from him that we need in order to be able to make a decision, but he's astute enough to throw in proposals: have you actually thought about this, have you thought about that, what happens if we do so-and-so? He understands the principles behind reaching a tactical decision and he contributes as well. His strength is that he spends that effort on a Saturday, and sometimes on a Sunday morning, then when he gets into the race he listens to what we want to do – because he knows his part now is to drive the car with an understanding of what we want to do. We never get a discussion during the race: we have confidence in him and he has confidence in us.'

So you don't discuss it then?

'Very rarely, it's very rare during a race that we discuss it in order to make a decision. We discuss it in the sense of "right, Michael, this is what we are doing now, we're going to Plan B or Plan C and you understand what you've got to do".'

This is the part that's been discussed before, A, B or C?

'Yes.'

But what about when Ross Brawn says, 'By the way, we're going to Plan D, which I hadn't mentioned to you before, Michael'?

'We don't do that, to be honest, unless we've had something crazy go on – because all of the things we do in a race have been considered beforehand. It's only if the race falls apart that you have to start doing a few things purely by intuition, and those races generally aren't the races you win, they are the races where you are trying to salvage some points.'

If you ask him to do the unexpected, can he do it?

'Well, it's not unexpected any more. That's a little bit of a contradiction – because what he does know is what we expect him to do. You mentioned Hungary and his performance in the middle of the race. When we said, "Right, Michael, this is what you've got to achieve," he just lit up. That's his talent.'

John Barnard explained that if you got on the phone to, for example, Berger and said 'look, we want you to go faster for a certain number of laps,' he'd tell you where to go...

'...that's true...'

...because he's already driving as fast as he can, whereas Schumacher says 'OK' and seems to be able to go to a kind of qualifying mode at will and come off it at will.

'Like every driver, I imagine, Michael drives at a certain percentage during a race because there is a risk involved if you drive at the maximum every lap, but he does have more ability than anyone to drive at 99.9% of the car's limit for a long period. It was quite a shock to me when we had Jean [Alesi] and Gerhard [Berger] join Benetton after having Michael there – and even having Michael with Johnny Herbert and Michael with the other drivers we had – because when we got in to the race we'd see a tactical opportunity and we'd say, "Right guys, this is it, now you've got a clear track, you've got to pull the pace up," and nothing happened. Sometimes Jean and Gerhard went slower because they were then trying too hard. We'd become accustomed to getting on the radio to Michael and saying, "Right, you've got to find some time now," and then you'd start to see the times coming up. It *was* quite a shock, because that had become normal and it became abnormal when we lost Michael.'

…and then of course normal again when you regained it at Ferrari.

'Yes.'

What is this ability? Why can he do it, and Senna could do it, and others just can't?

'Well, the thing is the others are hanging in there by their fingernails. That's the reality. Some of the drivers are having to drive like that just to be respectable. Michael can drive a very respectable race with a lot of spare margin.'

Häkkinen 77, Schumacher 70, Coulthard 48, Irvine 32.

Belgium was the epicentre of several storms and the weather wasn't very good either. In Friday practice he was first, qualified fourth next day and wasn't happy to be over a second off pole. Race day was wet and on the first lap a vast, churning accident developed on the descent towards Eau Rouge. At the restart Hill led, but round La Source Schumacher and Häkkinen bumped, the McLaren spinning. Helplessly Herbert rammed it.

'I was on the outside and I tried to leave a bit of room,' Schumacher said. 'He was forcing me a bit wide but I had the better line and could accelerate better out of the corner.'

He advanced on Hill but the Safety Car came out, circled, and released them into lap 3. He advanced on Hill again and on lap 8 stole nimbly inside at the Bus Stop. Far, far behind – second last, in fact – Coulthard ploughed through the water. He'd skimmed off just before the Safety Car arrived. Schumacher pitted and resumed in the lead, Hill too far away to pose any threat. Cars loomed and lurked within the spray, emerging and returning. Somewhere in this was Coulthard, last because he'd just made a pit stop. Schumacher was almost 2m 14s ahead of him and seeking to lap him. Todt made his way down the pit lane to McLaren to point this out. Schumacher reached Coulthard, tried to hurry him and – according to one report – waved his arm, meaning *get out of the way*.

Subsequently Ferrari put this into words. 'For almost an entire lap Coulthard ignored the blue flags [another competitor trying to overtake you] and never allowed Schumacher to go by…on several occasions Schumacher moved off line to show Coulthard he was there.'

Schumacher's urgency was surprising, because he led Hill by 34 seconds, ample time to make his second pit stop (scheduled for the next lap). Ron Dennis radioed to Coulthard, saying *let him go*, to which Coulthard replied that in the spray he could see virtually nothing and asked exactly where Schumacher was. Coulthard then eased off and positioned the McLaren over to the right on the approach to the left-hander Pouhon corner. Unfortunately that was the racing line…

Schumacher ran full into the back of him, the impact a moment shocking enough to pluck the Ferrari's right-front wheel clean off. Schumacher continued to the pits on three wheels wild with rage. He sprang from the cockpit and marched down the pit lane, tearing his helmet off as he went, to confront Coulthard. A Ferrari employee tried to restrain him but couldn't. By the time he'd reached the McLaren pit a phalanx of five or six Ferrari people, Todt among them, formed a wall between him and Coulthard.

'Are you [expletive] trying to kill me?' he shouted across it to Coulthard.

The phalanx ushered him off and he walked stiffly back up the pit lane, his face now consumed by the rage.

Later he said Coulthard 'seemed to be running five to six seconds slower than his real pace once I was behind him. Obviously lifting on the straight like he did when I hit him is very dangerous. He has the experience to know that you do not slow down on a straight like that without giving any warning. So one could think he did it deliberately.'

The unstated implication, of course, was that Coulthard had in some devilish way done this to help Häkkinen's chase for the Championship. That made Coulthard angry enough to say any such accusation was 'paranoia in the extreme' and Schumacher needed 'to get some help for controlling his anger'.

To be entirely fair, when Schumacher had calmed down he accepted that he had 'over-reacted' but still insisted Coulthard made a mistake 'because it was clear he was going slower than normal and it was the wrong place at the wrong time to let someone through. No one could expect it there.'

The leaderboard lay undisturbed – Häkkinen 77, Schumacher 70, Coulthard 48 – with Monza, the Italian Grand Prix and the assumed annual communion next.

On the Saturday he took pole, his first of the season. 'We got everything right and picked the best moment to go out. I did my time on the first lap of my final run. I hadn't expected it to be good enough because my last lap should have been the quickest, but on that lap I made a mistake…'

The pole secured, the session completed, he stood on the pit lane wall facing the grandstands opposite and raised his arms, blew a kiss, waved with his left hand. Communion?

He made a poor start to the race and ran fifth, Häkkinen leading from Coulthard, Irvine third, Villeneuve fourth. Like Hungary, Schumacher seemed lost in captivity and the McLarens romping it already – except that Monza is neither rigid nor static. He moved inside Villeneuve at the second chicane, Irvine let him through and without warning Häkkinen waved Coulthard through – Häkkinen wasn't happy with the car.

On lap 17 Coulthard's engine failed and he swivelled the car off. Schumacher pressured Häkkinen at the second chicane and overtook him on the exit. Monza surrendered and the emotions were heightened when Irvine came home second. To complete the day Häkkinen had brake problems, spun late on and finished fourth. You could sense from the thousands gathering below the podium – *so* teeming that the track submerged beneath them for a hundred metres in either direction – a strong, living feeling. The Championship, denied them since that day when *Jo-dee* passed where they now stood, was *on*.

Häkkinen and Schumacher 80, Coulthard 48 and no longer a contender.

The Luxembourg Grand Prix was at the Nürburgring and he took pole, Irvine alongside. Irvine led then Schumacher then Häkkinen third. Irvine would let Schumacher through then block and baulk while Schumacher sailed off into the sunset. Schumacher went past Irvine on the opening lap but Häkkinen was phlegmatic, hustled Irvine and on lap 14 slipstreamed him into the chicane. Häkkinen remained phlegmatic and gradually increased his pace so that when Schumacher pitted on lap 24 the gap had fallen to five seconds. As Schumacher pitted Häkkinen sprinted and sustained that for the next three laps, set a new fastest lap and led by 17.037. He emerged from his stop directly in front of Schumacher, the decisive moment of the race and of enormous significance for the championship because only Suzuka remained.

Häkkinen 90, Schumacher 86.

If Häkkinen won the Japanese Grand Prix or came second he was champion. If he finished third, fourth, or fifth Schumacher had to win.

In qualifying they danced a desperate duet.

Häkkinen, out early, did a 1m 37.09s – a full second and a half quicker than anybody else. Schumacher wasn't surprised and said he'd foreseen something like it. Midway through the session he gave his response, an almost sensuous lap of power and poise: 1m 36.76. Häkkinen tried to respond but couldn't find the final fractions: 1m 36.85. Now Schumacher summoned a 1m 36.29. Häkkinen tried to respond to *that* but, moving under the weight gathering over him if he failed – pole might by crucial – went off onto grass, the lap destroyed.

On the grid Häkkinen went over and shook Schumacher's hand, reflecting the tone of the season. A dry afternoon at Suzuka, warm, sunny. They moved into the parade lap, that curious state of suspended animation. They settled but no red lights came, only three flashing yellows: *start aborted*. Trulli, on the seventh row, had stalled his Prost.

The mechanics poured onto the grid to do their work.

The second parade lap was six or seven minutes later. Schumacher led them away again and went round at a pace rather more than sprightly, then slowed. The crocodile broke up as the cars peeled off to their bays. The last of the 21 – Trulli, now at the rear – took his place. Then, from the pit lane wall, a yellow flag was being waved: *start aborted*.

Schumacher's right hand was up, the international signal for *I can't move*. He shook his head in disbelief. 'The engine stalled because the clutch didn't free itself and I don't know why.' The whole procedure would have to be gone through again and he'd be behind Trulli at the back. The Championship had saved this last twist until now.

Häkkinen took them round a third time, Schumacher a lonely vision at the rear. Finally the red lights blinked on and they accelerated away. Häkkinen led while in that other, lowly world at the far end of the grid Schumacher fed the power into the Ferrari and took it to mid-track, pointing it directly ahead like a missile. And it travelled like a missile, gathering speed. Along the straight towards the first corner it bisected Trulli and Esteban Tuero's Minardi; bisected Shinji Nakano's Minardi and Herbert's Sauber ('I'd stalled as well'). It powered clean round Toranosuke Takagi's Tyrrell.

Herbert said that Schumacher made a 'ridiculous start, I've never seen a start like that in my life. He just took off.'

Crossing the line to complete the opening lap Schumacher was 12th, 9.6 seconds from Häkkinen. On lap two he despatched Panis and Alesi – tenth. On lap three, on the long, long right curve after the hairpin, he outpowered Fisichella – ninth. On lap four he pressured Wurz then took a slingshot wide through the S curves – eighth. On lap five he caught and despatched his brother (who made him work to for it) – seventh.

He was in amongst the faster men and couldn't pick them off one a lap, something compounded by the fact that the full-attack he'd mounted would have to be paid for in tyre wear and he was beginning to pay. He spent long minutes behind Hill and Villeneuve, and at eight laps the gap was out to 18.680. On lap 14 Hill pitted – sixth. He despatched Villeneuve round the outside at the hairpin – fifth. On lap 16 he'd caught Coulthard but came in for his first pit stop. It cost him only one place – sixth.

Across the next four laps others pitted, too: Villeneuve, Frentzen, Coulthard. Each moved Schumacher up a place so that by lap 22 he was third, 26 seconds from Häkkinen. He ran third to lap 31.

The last twist had not been the stalling on the grid. It was now. He was taking the Ferrari into the corner after the pits, his speed reaching towards 170mph, when the right rear tyre disintegrated. He did not lose control of the car but managed to slow it, parking it on the grass. A great calmness descended on him. He clambered out of the cockpit and levered himself up on to a wall, spectated just like everybody else; lowered himself from the wall, stood, spectated again.

Why did Schumacher stall? Byrne explains that 'it wasn't a fault by Michael, it was something that happened with the hydraulic system.'

Why had the tyre punctured? Takagi and Tuero crashed, spreading debris everywhere, and Schumacher had run over it.

'We were *that* close to the Championship and we *could* actually have won it, yes, yes,' Byrne added.

The Horse remained untamed.

There was a nuance of regret mingled with a certain pride as Byrne reflected on 1998. 'It was a hell of a season! We and Goodyear definitely started off behind McLaren by a reasonable margin [McLaren on Bridgestones] but by the end of the year we were at least as quick, if not quicker. Take the last three races: we were on pole for each – and even if you take Häkkinen's qualifying and add Coulthard's, then take Michael and Eddie's qualifying, you'll find that as a team we outqualified McLaren over those races. We were running really quick, we'd come from way behind to be at least as quick. It was pleasing.

'We did a massive amount of development. I think the people here at Maranello were surprised at how much we did and how many new things we put on the car through the season. The reason we did that is we started the car relatively late – not because we wanted to but because we were still assembling the people. We really didn't have the depth of research to put into the car then. We were developing it rapidly through the season, and that's exactly what paid off at the end.'

The new Ferrari, the F399, was launched in late March but to an even harder tone than 1998. Todt stated unequivocally that the objective was no longer a few pole positions and a few wins scattered across another season of prelude, the objective was the title. The tone encompassed an imperative, too: *we have to be on the pace immediately, we can't afford another start like last year when the McLarens ran away from us.* Schumacher emphasised that. 'I cannot win the title if I am not able to be competitive in the first five Grands Prix.'

He tested the car at Fiorano, covering 57 laps and making Press Release noises, but when they went to Barcelona Häkkinen was half a second quicker in the new McLaren.

'What happened,' Byrne says, 'is that we got caught up in a massive race for the Championship in 1998 so we actually started the 1999 car too late. It's the perennial problem in that you have to concentrate both on the car you have and the car for next season, and you only have X number of resources, X number of hours in the day. It's a fine balance.'

The leading teams:

Benetton – Fisichella, Wurz.
Ferrari – Schumacher, Irvine.
Jordan – Hill, Frentzen.
McLaren – Häkkinen, Coulthard.
Williams – Zanardi, R. Schumacher.

On the parade lap at Melbourne Schumacher couldn't engage first gear and had to begin from the back. He rose robustly to fourth despite gear selection problems, went off and had a puncture, pitted and resumed last, pitted again to change the steering wheel because 'occasionally it caused the gearbox to slip into neutral'. He finished eighth (something lost under the weight of the celebrations for Irvine, victorious).

In Brazil 'I did not expect to be one second off the pole time.' Although he finished second to Häkkinen in the race that left him 'very satisfied. It was not what we expected after qualifying. I am not worried about the points situation because we are still at a very early stage in the season.'

For San Marino he'd been saying there'd be 'new developments' on the car which, finally, would enable it to run with the McLarens. No Ferrari had won at Imola for 16 years, since Patrick Tambay in the prehistoric days of turbocharged engines. In the untimed session Schumacher was third but now less than half a second from Coulthard and very, very close to Häkkinen; in qualifying closer still and 'this is a lot better than Brazil but I am a bit disappointed with my own performance. I did not manage a perfect lap. I could have gone better and pole position was within reach.'

Häkkinen led from Coulthard and Schumacher who briefly harried Coulthard but he drew away and, within a few laps, Häkkinen was clear of them both. Schumacher concentrated on 'keeping the gap to Coulthard under control'. At the end of lap 17, in the right-hander on to the start-finish straight, Häkkinen made a mistake, the car rode over the kerbing, spun and speared the barrier, so Coulthard led, Schumacher cutting the gap from 4.4 seconds to 3.9 to 3.7. As Coulthard and Schumacher hammered towards half distance Brawn began to explore flexibility.

Schumacher's on-board radio crackled. He accelerated, moving into qualifying mode. You could feel the intensity of the hunt, feel him wrenching the Ferrari through the corners. He pitted on lap 31, was stationary for 6.9 seconds, was given fresh tyres.

Schumacher sprinted. By lap 41 he'd extended the lead to 16.0s and now he set fastest lap. He pitted on lap 45 with a lead of 21.8, was stationary for 5.5 seconds and came out ahead. He'd say one of Ferrari's strengths was its 'tactical possibilities'.

Byrne feels 'there is no doubt that by the time the European part of the season started we'd got on the pace. It was very close, that's for sure.'

At Monaco in the untimed session Schumacher was quickest and described the driving as 'good fun although I hit the barrier after a track rod broke in the chicane. This was a bit frightening.' He qualified second (Häkkinen pole) and at the lights surged round the outside of Häkkinen into Ste Devote and, completing this opening lap, led by 1.3 seconds. He would lead every lap of the race. Schumacher 26 points, Irvine 18, Häkkinen 14.

What should have been the central core of the season proved straightforward. Spain, when he finished third, was a bore of a race and everyone agreed that. Häkkinen won.

In Canada Schumacher took his first pole of 1999 and led to lap 29 when 'I lost control of the car at the last chicane because I went off the racing line, got on the dirt and ended up in the wall. This was clearly my mistake. I apologise to the team.' He added: 'I usually make one mistake a year' and hoped this had been it. Häkkinen won, giving him the championship lead with 34 points, Schumacher 30, Irvine 25.

In France he qualified sixth in heavy rain after 'a chaotic session. Track conditions were very dangerous with a lot of aquaplaning and there was a risk of spinning even on the straights.' He described the race as 'chaotic' too. 'My radio stopped working early on so I tried to communicate with the pits with hand signals. My first problem was that I was having trouble changing gear and the reason I slowed a lot at one point was that I only had first and second. So I came in and changed the steering wheel but from this point on things did not really improve. The new set of tyres did not work. I am not sure why. At the end of the race I had a fight with my brother Ralf like in our old karting days...' He was fifth. Frentzen won, restricting Häkkinen to six points and that kept Schumacher in touch. Häkkinen 40, Schumacher 32, Irvine 26.

Britain was hot and sunny. The five red lights blinked off after three seconds, Häkkinen away fast, Coulthard behind, then Irvine, then Schumacher, but two cars stalled on the grid. Through Becketts Schumacher hustled Irvine and they moved onto Hangar Straight abreast. As they reached Stowe corner Irvine positioned his Ferrari over towards the left preparing to go round the right-hander, Schumacher inside him. At this moment the Stewards decided to stop the race because of the two stalled cars but, crucially, the drivers couldn't know that yet.

At racing speed Schumacher moved to mid-track, Irvine comfortably on the outside. Schumacher was doing 191mph (307kph) and it seemed Irvine was obeying the constrictions of his Ferrari contract by letting Schumacher through. Certainly, turning into Stowe, Schumacher was ahead – but locking wheels.

The brakes clawed the speed down. The FIA would describe what happened next graphically enough, once the Ferrari's black box had been downloaded. 'He first braked at 306kph and achieved an initial deceleration of 3.1G. This fell to 2.1G. At 204kph the front wheels locked.'

He shrieked across in front of Irvine and smoke billowed from the tyres.

'By the time he left the tarmac the deceleration had fallen to 1.3G.'

He was onto the run-off area, a broad arc of gravel. The Ferrari buck-bounded across that.

'The average deceleration in the gravel trap was 1.1G.'

Roger Chapman, sitting with his wife Amanda in the Jonathan Palmer stand on the inside of the corner, was a typical spectator. 'Effectively the cars came past us and as they did Schumacher obviously applied the brakes and just managed to miss the back end of Irvine. It happened right in front of us. Everyone stood up in the stand and cheered. That was the first thing. Everyone went *yeahhh*!'

The car buried itself deep in the tyre wall, speed at impact 67mph (107kph).

'When he hit the tyres the whole crowd just went deathly quiet,' Chapman said. 'You could tell what people were thinking. You didn't hear people saying it, although we said to each other *Christ, this looks bad…looks like the same thing that happened to Ayrton Senna*. It was amazing how the crowd went from being elated that Schumacher had gone off the track on the first lap to everyone thinking it could be serious: although we might not like the chap too much, we don't want to see him killed.'

Once the car was motionless he tried to lever himself out but he couldn't. 'It was not a nice experience,' he'd say. 'I was very soon aware of the problem but the worst moment was when I tried to get out of the car and couldn't because my leg was stuck inside. I couldn't really see what kind of injury it was.'

Chapman says that now the crowd was 'very subdued because they realised that although obviously he hadn't been killed outright there was still the possibility of serious injury – you saw him trying to lift himself out of the car and he clearly couldn't do it.'

Marshals were at the car and so was Professor Sid Watkins, Formula One's resident doctor, who'd give his arrival time as 85 seconds. Watkins found Schumacher 'completely rational and totally himself' and was impressed (as he described in *Autosport*) by what he described as Schumacher's 'whole demeanour and his politeness...he was very, very cool.'

'Hello Sid, it's just my leg,' Schumacher said, 'it's not a big problem.' He asked Watkins to telephone Corinna when he could and reassure her he'd suffered no more than a broken right leg – awkward since Watkins didn't know the number. He also asked that word be passed urgently to Todt to check Irvine's car because 'I've had brake failure'.

They removed him from the cockpit and laid him down. Watkins put a splint on the leg and a splint on his left knee – he said it hurt. He was carried on a stretcher to the ambulance with, for reasons of decency and privacy, marshals holding a large green sheet behind him so he couldn't be gawped at. As they bore him away he raised a hand and waved.

'They'd come along with this big sheet which they normally put up to screen the driver off,' Chapman says, 'but it meant nobody watching really knew what was going on. From the stand, although we had television monitors and the TV had more of a picture than we had, you couldn't really see. Everyone was still very concerned. As with Senna nobody knew at the time how serious the situation was. It wasn't until he was actually on the stretcher and then sat up – we saw him sit up – that everyone said, "Well, he seems to be OK." The atmosphere became much more normal.'

The request to ring home was resolved when Schumacher reached the track's medical centre, because someone handed him a mobile phone and he was able to do it himself. Within the hour his condition had been assessed and he was carried carefully to the helicopter which took him to Northampton General Hospital.

Late that afternoon, at the end of the restarted race (Coulthard won, Häkkinen out with a rear wheel problem), Ferrari issued a statement in which Todt said: 'Michael Schumacher had an accident on the opening lap because of a problem with the rear brakes. We are investigating the cause. Michael has broken the tibia [shin bone] and fibula [a smaller bone] of the right leg. He is currently undergoing an operation in Northampton General Hospital.'

Surgeons inserted a 300mm steel pin in the leg and no complications were envisaged.

Two days later Ferrari issued a statement explaining that they were 'conducting a full and urgent investigation. What has been established so far is that the accident was caused by a sudden loss of pressure of the rear brake circuit. This was due to the loosening of a brake bleed nipple on the left rear caliper. The reason for this loosening of the nipple has not yet been established. This component had been checked as part of the Saturday evening race preparation and there had been no subsequent servicing of that part. The data shows no problem either in the warm-up or indeed in the braking manoeuvres for the first half lap of the race. Ferrari will continue to try to establish the reasons for this failure.'

Schumacher was flown to Switzerland and as his recovery began in a clinic there the talk was of him being out for three months. Weber was circumspect. Speaking four days after the accident he said that 'the most important thing' for Schumacher was to 'become fully fit and recover properly. He doesn't want to come back too early and risk long-term consequences.'

There'd be endless shifting speculation but amidst it all a great truth emerged. Ferrari had sculptured the task of finding Scheckter's successor with exquisite care. They'd hired the best driver and paid him more than any driver had ever been paid. They already had Stepney, who's forgotten more about it than most people know. They'd hired Todt, a man of enormous and proven pedigree; and Brawn the clairvoyant; and Byrne who was as good as they come. They'd hired a number two for Schumacher – Irvine – whose contract was very constricting. His role was to cause no trouble, exhibit absolute obedience and garner points wherever he could. That is what he had done. He had the biggest yacht in the harbour at Monte Carlo and in the circumstances he'd earned it because no driver in the history of modern grand prix racing – *none* – had practised so much self-denial for so long.

To continue the dynasty which stopped with Scheckter, Ferrari must have spent, allowing for inflation, some $2 *billion* since 1979. Now, without warning or preparation, the dynasty was being entrusted to a broth of a boy from Conlig in County Down who'd won one race in his life, Melbourne, and that only because Schumacher couldn't win it. Irvine, second in the British Grand Prix, stood only eight points behind Häkkinen.

Schumacher's crash opened up a role reversal so outrageously improbable that thinking about it seemed a flight of fancy. It even seemed possible that somewhere in the final half of the season Schumacher might find himself under the constriction of team orders which demanded *help Irvine win the Championship*.

'By Silverstone we were on the pace, we were *there*, no doubt about that,' Byrne says. 'We were reasonably ahead in the Constructors' and contending strongly in the Drivers'. It was looking to be another exciting cliff-hanger of a season, us and McLaren virtually on par. Then of course we had the dreadful accident – and losing a key member of the team, who is also your number one driver, affects the overall performance.'

Had there been a feeling that this could be the year?

'Oh yes, very much so. It was a quiet feeling: this time we can do it. Certainly we felt we could.'

And the car?

'Once we got to Imola we'd sorted out how to set it up, we had a reasonable development programme and it was looking good. There was a feeling of quiet confidence. You should never *say* you're confident of winning a Championship, because McLaren are formidable. You can never be complacent with them around, never start thinking, "Oh we'll just win," but I felt we were competing on pretty equal terms.'

Stepney, speaking after the Italian Grand Prix in September, takes up the story. 'Eddie has been one of the closest drivers [in terms of performance] that Michael has had and that's been an important factor for us in continuing after the accident. OK, we haven't the same momentum that we had and McLaren have made a lot of mistakes, but everybody makes those.'

Stepney evaluates from the inside. 'If you look back over a season you have to see where your performances were. When you win races it's good, it's fantastic but at the end of the day you have to see what your performance would have been like *if McLaren had finished*. Look at most of the races. We'd probably have won about two on merit, Canada and Monte Carlo. The rest? We've been struggling and you have to put that into it although, OK, we're doing well and we've done well. We've done good races when McLaren have done bad races – and vice versa…'

Stepney explored the background, comparing Schumacher with Senna 'because that's the only comparison at that sort of level. I worked closely with Senna at Lotus, probably more closely than with Michael. The drivers seem to have gone further away, or I've gone further away, or they've been taken further away. I don't know which. Years ago you'd be a lot closer to them and spent a lot more time with them.

'Personally, I'd say Senna was a deeper thinker than Michael and a lot more aware of what was going on. That's not a criticism, it's just the way it is. Also this is a different era – no, not just a different era but with different technologies and that's the hardest thing to get into perspective.

'For example, these days everybody's talking about overtaking. Years ago you could overtake on skill and that's why Senna wanted electronic aids banned, because you wouldn't have the difference between top line drivers and the others. When you give someone full electronic aids he can drive the car just like anybody else. You don't get the gearchange mistakes like you used to – miss a gear and you'd be overtaken. With the electronic aids it's nearly impossible to miss a gearchange. The machine won't let you.

'It means you drive to the limit, you're always on the limit, so how do people overtake you? You're on the brakes, on the limit, and everything is so close. How much overtaking did you see at Monza? Only Barrichello, who overtook two. Look at Barcelona. We were stuck behind Villeneuve, we had a car a second faster and we couldn't get past him. You can't push the cars to go past any more but the drivers that are best always find a way past, always. You know immediately who can pass and who can't. The best think it through, throw the car – and they've done it. Senna was like that in the wet and so is Michael, both the same. They'd think ahead and place the car where they knew the other car won't be. They'd be on a different line and at a different point.'

And they'd done it.

That's what had been borne away forever on a stretcher at Imola, 1 May 1994, and what had been taken away on a stretcher at Silverstone, 11 July 1999.

The days, weeks and months which followed were a kaleidoscope of hard fact interwoven with hard fiction, and much else besides. Schumacher became a saga and there was something almost hypnotic about watching the episodes play themselves out. Subtly strong forces constantly – and unexpectedly – pulled at these episodes. That ultimately they pulled together and Schumacher created one of the most consummate drives of the generation in the Malaysian Grand Prix was climactic, with more to come in Japan. This, in strict chronological order, is the saga with all the twists and turns along the way and (as they say in the theatre) noises off too.

Tuesday 13 July. Ferrari statement. 'Ferrari announces that it has reached an agreement with driver Mika Salo for the current Championship, to drive Ferrari car n. 3 [sic] starting from the Austrian GP.'

Thursday 15 July. Willi Weber visited Schumacher in the Swiss clinic and estimated he'd be out for three months. 'The most important thing is for him to become fully fit and recover from his leg injury properly,' Weber said. 'For those reasons a pause of three months seems realistic. He will need that long for a full recovery.'

Monday 19 July. Schumacher left the clinic and went home to Geneva.

Tuesday 20 July. Schumacher gave his first interview since the crash, spoke of his feelings and actions as the Ferrari's brake locked, and said emphatically that talk of returning for the German Grand Prix on 1 August was 'complete nonsense'.

In Austria, Irvine drove a lovely tactical race to win, which prompted *Autosport* magazine to run a screamer across its front page: 'Who needs Schuey?'

Salo was ninth, admitting to a couple of mistakes. Irvine

accepted that this first race as team leader was 'very difficult because the expectations are so high.' Without Schumacher, he'd add, you lacked a point of reference for your own performance and 'I miss that comparison.'

Salo led Hockenheim after Häkkinen had problems and dutifully moved aside so Irvine could win it. Irvine 52 points, Häkkinen 44, and the church bells were rung in Maranello.

Monday 2 August. Schumacher was asked by German sports news agency SID whether he'd support Irvine when he did come back; whether by implication there really would be the astonishing role reversal. 'If that's the case' – Irvine going for the Championship – 'I will work for the team and drive for Irvine. I could live with this situation because Eddie has driven often enough for me. Why shouldn't one pay that back? Even if one might not want to do it, that's life.'

Tuesday 3 August. Weber said Schumacher might be driving again by the weekend if doctors gave him permission. The idea was that Schumacher would be examined by doctors at Fiorano then test there. Weber added that if Schumacher emerged from the driving 'fairly trouble-free' they'd have to think about Hungary on 15 August.

Wednesday 4 August. Schumacher's press officer, Heiner Buchinger, said: 'The heel is still swollen and at the moment he is not able to move it as freely as he should. When I left him on Sunday he was still on crutches but Ferrari have prepared the test for Saturday. I have to say it is very unlikely he will be able to make that.' The medical would now be on the Friday in Switzerland. 'Of course he must satisfy the regulation which insists that he is able to get out of the car in just five seconds, and there will be no special privileges for Michael.'

Friday 6 August. Ferrari statement. 'Today at 7 p.m. Michael Schumacher visited his doctors. The check-up was scheduled on the 19th of July when he left the Swiss clinic and returned home. The clinical evaluation is very good at this time, but it is too early for him to return to F1 racing in the coming weeks. In order to improve bone healing the consultant surgeons have decided to perform a partial hardware removal of the distal tibia. The rehabilitation programme will start again on the day after surgery. This might allow Michael Schumacher to make his comeback at Monza' – 12 September.

Monday 9 August. Di Montezemolo went a long way to confirming the role reversal by insisting that 'the day Schumacher gets back it will be to help Ferrari. There's no doubt about it. What we care about is Ferrari's victory.' Di Montezemolo reiterated that, by Monza, Schumacher would 'have no chance to contend for the title. Drivers must follow directives. Schumacher has said it and he will do it: he'll be at Ferrari's service.'

Irvine finished third in the Hungarian Grand Prix after losing control of the car on lap 63 and running wide. Salo, 12th and two laps down, had a 'terrible race'. Häkkinen won, making it Irvine 56, Häkkinen 54.

Thursday 19 August. Ferrari statement. 'Today at 7 p.m. Michael Schumacher underwent a further physical examination. This check-up had been planned at the time of his previous examination on 6th August. The outcome of the check-up showed that his physical conditions were positive and the next step will be to drive a few laps of the Mugello circuit at the wheel of an F399. This test will be carried out tomorrow.'

Friday 20 August. Schumacher was flown to Mugello by helicopter. Ferrari statement that evening:

Circuit:	Autodromo del Mugello, 5.20km
Driver:	Eddie Irvine, F399, chassis number 193
	Michael Schumacher, Mika Salo, F399, chassis number 194
Weather:	Air Temp. 22–30C, Track, 32–50C, sunny

Testing began on the dot at 09h30. Mika Salo did just one shake-down lap in car 194. Eddie Irvine continued his programme of working on set-up and adjustments in preparation for the forthcoming Belgian Grand Prix. Michael Schumacher's testing went smoothly with a series of runs of about five laps each, followed by one 20 lap run. Today was Ferrari's last day of testing at Mugello.

Michael Schumacher	1.28.379	65 laps
Eddie Irvine	1.28.648	59 laps

Jean Todt: 'It was great to have the whole group together, with Eddie and Mika when Michael arrived [sic]. I had expected Michael to only do a handful of laps but in the end he managed to do a whole day's testing. The two drivers worked on different programmes, with Eddie preparing for the Belgian Grand Prix and Michael reacquainting himself with the car in race trim. I had thought Michael could be back for Monza. We will see how he feels after this test and make a decision after a further medical examination. Tomorrow, at Fiorano, Mika Salo will shake down the three cars to be used in next week's Belgian Grand Prix.'

Eddie Irvine: 'I worked mainly in preparation for the race at Spa. Today I concentrated on brakes, which still give me a few problems to adjust correctly. I did all my laps today in race trim.'

Michael Schumacher: 'Above all I want to thank all the Ferrari fans. Today I was very happy with the reception I got from the team and it was great to see my friends again. It was like coming home after a too-long holiday. Almost straight away I felt comfortable with the car, although it took me a short while to adapt to the change of balance of the car. I did around sixty laps without any problems. Over the bumps my right leg hurt a bit but it had no effect on my performance. Over the next few days I will see how I feel and, after a further medical check, I will decide along with the team if I can make my comeback at Monza or earlier.'

Such statements are neat summaries but dry. Reading it you'd scarcely deduce that Schumacher had shaken Formula One with what was, and can legitimately be called, a sensational performance. Mugello is not the easiest of tracks, he had a pronounced limp, and yet his first proper lap was within a whisker of the best time Irvine had managed thus far in the day; and then Schumacher finished the day 0.3 of a second quicker.

Monday 23 August. Schumacher went cycling, a good test of his leg, and was in pain afterwards.

Tuesday 24 August. Ferrari statement. 'Eddie Irvine and Mika Salo will drive in the Belgian Grand Prix on 29th August. Michael Schumacher will drive the following week at Monza during tests for the Italian GP. At the test, which will run from the first to third September, he will carry out a race distance simulation as preparation for a possible participation in the Italian GP.'

In Belgium Coulthard won from Häkkinen, Irvine fourth and Salo seventh. Häkkinen 60, Irvine 59, Coulthard 46, Frentzen 40.

Wednesday 1 September. General testing at Monza. Ferrari statement. 'Testing began at 09h00. During the morning the drivers concentrated on setting up their cars. Irvine managed only a few laps before the lunch break, because of a problem with the hydraulic system. In the afternoon each driver worked on a different programme, all of them as part of the preparation for next week's Italian GP. Michael Schumacher's programme also ended prematurely, because of an hydraulic problem. Testing ended at 18h30.'

Several hundred of the *tifosi* were in the stand opposite the pits – where so long ago Scheckter had passed on his way to the finishing line – and they draped their banners, several in English.

SCHUMY YOU ARE MAGIC
WELCOME BACK SCHUMI
WE MISSED YOU MICHAEL

with one in Italian which requires no translation:

MAGICO SCHUMY!

Schumacher said: 'I made a test today and the problems in my leg are too big to do a proper job. It is basically impossible for me to run more than five laps at the moment and especially on this circuit. The bumps and curves are pretty severe. I had pain all the way through and you can't drive like that. I took painkillers but it didn't really help. I don't think I will compete in the next two races. After the surgery the doctor said I would not be back in the car for 12 to 16 weeks. Here I am after seven weeks. Maybe you can say it was too early, but we had to try. I will have a meeting with my doctors on Sunday.'

Saturday 4 September. Ferrari statement. 'Ferrari hereby announces that the driver Rubens Barrichello has been signed to drive for Scuderia Ferrari-Marlboro for the next two seasons alongside Michael Schumacher. Ferrari wishes to thank Eddie Irvine for his constructive and loyal collaboration with the team over the past four seasons. Both the team and the driver will put all their efforts and determination into tackling the decisive four remaining races of the championship.'

Monday 6 September. Buchinger said: 'The situation has not changed. The recovery process is taking place normally. Sadly, it is not going any quicker than expected.' This meant Schumacher would miss the European Grand Prix at the Nürburgring on 26 September.

Monday 20 September. Buchinger revealed that Schumacher would drive at Fiorano on 7 October. 'Michael will definitely be at Fiorano,' he said, adding that Schumacher wanted to compete in the last two races of the season.

Tuesday 21 September. The new Jaguar Formula One car (née Stewart) was unveiled at the Frankfurt Motor Show and Irvine confirmed as the man to partner Herbert.

Thursday 23 September. Schumacher gave an interview to German TV channel RTL. 'Ferrari will only win if McLaren keep making mistakes and give it away. For this race and for the championship McLaren have improved their car and they are in better shape than Ferrari. I think that it is not going to be Eddie's year. Only bad luck can stop Mika beating him and the only way Ferrari will finish with a championship is if McLaren give it to them.' This interview, variously described as an outburst and the perfect model of bad timing, exploded all around Irvine amid a riot of headlines.

WOUNDED IRVINE

SCHUMACHER DISMISSES IRVINE TITLE BID

and so on, in similar vein.

It gave ammunition to those who believed Schumacher didn't want Irvine to win the Championship and didn't intend to ride shotgun to help him do it. Schumacher could avoid any such dilemma by not racing, and his medical condition allowed that.

Deep in the background lurked a notion that Ferrari did not want Irvine to win it either. The supposed logic here was that having invested so totally in Schumacher they would look foolish if their humble and subservient No 2 achieved it instead. Ferrari vehemently denied this. The notion that Ferrari would have spent their annual $200 million in 1999 *not* to have a World Champion, *to deliberately deprive themselves of the Championship after 20 years of struggle for it,* seemed to me quite mad.

Friday 24 September. In practice for the European Grand Prix, Irvine was fourth and Salo second. That, of course, wasn't the story flooding out from the Nürburgring. Irvine, caught at the very heart of the fallout from the Schumacher-RTL explosion, insisted that 'what Michael says is not important. What matters is what happens on the track here on Sunday. All I can say is that he obviously has less faith in Ferrari than I do.'

Irvine finished the race seventh and Salo retired after 45 laps. Todt described it thus: 'The race was a series of problems enlivened with much drama.' Irvine arrived for a pit stop only to discover 'they could not find one of my tyres'. In fact Salo had just been in to change a damaged front wing and this confused everything. Häkkinen 62, Irvine 60, Frentzen 50.

The conspiracy theorists went to work like carnivores on the image of a mechanic by Irvine's rear wheel with no tyre in his hands, as if somehow here was proof that Ferrari didn't want Irvine to win. That was mad, too. There are many, many refined and invisible methods of nobbling a racing car, if that is what you want. One of those methods is *not* to do it in the most public and obvious way: a mechanic exactly framed on several hundred million television screens all over the world standing empty-handed.

Sunday 3 October. Ferrari statement. 'This afternoon Michael Schumacher underwent a medical examination in Paris. This showed that the bones have healed sufficiently for him to resume normal activities. Tomorrow, Schumacher will drive an F399 at the Mugello circuit for a series of shake-downs. Michael Schumacher has informed Ferrari of his decision not to take part in the remaining two Grands Prix of the season, as he feels he is not sufficiently fit to cope with the demands of a race.'

Monday 4 October. Schumacher tested at Mugello. He did 69 laps and had a spin, kissing a barrier and inflicting light damage on the car. He walked away unaided and continued in another car – but he did say he'd been frightened. 'My mind went back to certain bad things. It's not nice to be scared in that moment.'

Sections of the German press rounded on him for his decision not to race.

Bild Zeitung asked 'Doesn't he want to? Is he not able to? What's wrong?' and described it as the 'Schumi puzzle'.

Die Welt described his behaviour as 'a picture of an egomaniac' and added: 'There is no hint here of the sense of duty to his employer, which turned him into the best-paid driver in the history of motor racing.'

Thursday 7 October. Schumacher joined Irvine in testing at Fiorano.

Friday 8 October. The Fiorano testing continued, Schumacher producing a lap of 1m 00.9s, and that was fast.

Some hours later…

'Ferrari announces that Michael Schumacher will take part in the Malaysian and Japanese Grands Prix. After three days of intensive testing at Mugello and Fiorano, Michael saw that there had been a big improvement in his physical condition and therefore he has decided to take part in the two final and very important races of the season, to give the maximum support to Ferrari in the fight for the championships [Drivers' and Constructors'] and to fulfil the wishes of the team and all the fans.'

Saturday 9 October. 'The belief that I'd be able to make it has grown bit by bit over the last few days,' Schumacher said. 'What was important was seeing how much the team wanted me to be there. I'm not at 100% but I've realised that I have to be there. Obviously I too wanted to make this comeback but I had to convince myself – and these practice sessions, first at Mugello then at Fiorano, gave me the confirmation. And then there was also the desire to help the team and to help Eddie.'

Before the final test Corinna expressed 'strong reservations' about his coming back. However, Schumacher said 'When she saw me come back home after the last test at Mugello she reacted intelligently. For the first time in a long time she saw a smile on my face.'

Di Montezemolo insisted he had ordered Schumacher back and recounted how he'd telephoned him but his daughter,

Gina-Maria, had answered and said 'daddy was getting out his football boots'. Di Montezemolo concluded, not unnaturally, that if Schumacher could play football he could drive the Ferrari; and would.

Schumacher explained he'd met di Montezemolo although 'I think I'm independent enough to make my own decisions. I discussed my feelings and reservations. I explained why I said no and why I said yes.'

What he would or would not do in Malaysia might have fascinated those who follow racing but the Ferrari insiders entertained no doubts. Long *before* Malaysia, Stepney said: 'Personally I think that when Michael comes back he's going to be stronger – stronger mentally because drivers get tired and they don't realise it. Sometimes it's like you, me, anybody, it's better to walk away and leave it for a couple of weeks. When you come back you feel better and you work better. At the point of the Silverstone accident he had reached – how can I say it? – saturation. He was very tired and started to get very nervous, which is not like him, but he wanted the Championship this year, you could *see* he *wanted* it. OK, he'd got close in 1997 and 1998 but close is still a long way away.'

Nor was Byrne remotely surprised that Schumacher could reach real racing pace immediately. 'A typical example was the test he did at Mugello after his accident when he hadn't driven a car for a couple of months or whatever it was. We'd had Mika Salo and Eddie testing for two days – or Mika for two and Eddie for one, anyway – and Michael got in. Nothing special done to the car, proper fuel load, standard tyres, no tricks, and on his very first run of the day he put in a faster lap than either Mika or Eddie had done in the last two. Straight away, just *bomp*, just like that. In my view that is natural ability.'

Stepney's judgement went beyond just driving. 'Nobody can handle the overall situation at Ferrari better than him. I don't think there is another driver in Formula One at the moment who could. Senna had such a big following and people loved him but it wasn't just for his driving – he was just a person who pulled people along. People came to see *him* because they knew he was magic and there was always going to be something happening, something special. That's true of Schumacher as well although it's a different following because South American people are a lot warmer than the following of Schumacher.'

In Malaysia he had to prove he was fit enough to get out of the cockpit in less than five seconds, an essential precaution in case of accidents. He did. Professor Watkins said 'he is in perfect and sound health. He did a little hop for us' – a cryptic reference to one of Watkins' tests for complete recovery of a leg injury: prove to us you can jump up and down on it. The master could do that.

Schumacher said he thought he could win the race but 'my fitness is not as it was before. Hot weather and a hot race can affect you and you are not able to predict how in advance.' Of Irvine he said: 'I must make it clear that I am first of all driving for the team and not in the interests of Eddie. The only way I can help him is to be in front and let him past. If that is not the case he will have to manage on his own.'

On the Saturday he took pole and he was stunning. 'I expected we would be strong here but to be one second ahead is surprising. As for the race, I plan to go flat out to the finish, then we will see what the positions are. Of course if I am in front at the end with Eddie behind me I will let him through.'

In the race Schumacher proved beyond any doubt that he was the best driver in the world. He led, waved Irvine through and although Coulthard overtook him – 'that was not part of the plan' – he kept Häkkinen behind. Towards the end, when Coulthard was out with a fuel pressure problem, Schumacher led again and let Irvine through again. An impression of Schumacher: controlling cars in front *and* behind, shaping the whole race, deciding who was doing what. Brundle, commentating on television, caught that nicely: 'Schumacher has spent the afternoon going as slowly as possible and he's still had to give the lead away twice…'

A question to Brawn: *What did you make of Schumacher's race in Malaysia?*

'It was astonishing.'

Even to you?

'Yes, a bit. I'd started to see it in testing because Jean [Todt] and I decided the best way to convince Michael to come back was to give him a good car and let him enjoy himself. So, in the testing at Fiorano and Mugello, our approach was to not put pressure on him – he was the only one who could make the decision whether he was ready to come back – but to make sure we gave him the maximum opportunity to enjoy himself.'

Which he did and said he did.

'We must always remember that these guys are doing it – or at least they began to do it – because they love motor racing.'

I think he still does.

'They all still do, absolutely. They get the fame and the fortune, and sometimes people forget that deep down they are racing drivers, they love racing, they love beating their competitors, they love making the car work. All those things are their real passion. People say, and it's true, that they earn all this money but certainly Michael's objective is to win with Ferrari, that's his number one ambition. So when we were able to put him in a car that was working very well – we'd been able to have a bit of a development programme on a couple of things that were very interesting – you could see his enthusiasm was enormous. By the end of that week, when we said, "Look, Michael, it would really help us if you could join us for the last couple of races," it didn't take [small laugh] much to convince him. We knew he was in a really strong frame of mind.'

Everything about him suggested he was strong.

'Yes, he was A1.'

Watching that race, he was controlling what was happening in front of him, he was controlling what was happening behind him: it was like somebody conducting an orchestra and everyone had to play when he waved the baton at them. We are back to going fast with plenty in hand if you need it.

'He always has spare mental capacity when he's driving a car. When some of the drivers are at the limit they've got nothing left mentally or physically. Michael, you always feel, has a margin – not to make the car go faster but to think about other things, and in a race like Malaysia he's perfect because he's taking everything into consideration.'

Are you born with that?

'I think a large percentage, yes. I mean, he is a very bright person and he has realised that he needs to maintain his physical fitness to a level where that's not even a consideration during a race. That was probably the only reason for his reluctance to come back too early: he knows the level he can perform at and he was very concerned that his physical fitness would distract from the way he knows he can race. It wasn't just a question of coming back and driving a car – because he knew he could do that – but competing and being at the front, where he wants to be. He needed to have that margin of physical fitness back at the level where it didn't encroach on his ability to drive a race or control a race. And it didn't. At that stage he had overcome his difficulties to the point where he could handle it.'

There remained a controversy over the Ferrari's bargeboards – aerodynamic 'fins' on the flanks of the cars aiding air-flow and stability – which were found to be 10mm too small on their bottom edges. This led to the exclusion of the cars and made Häkkinen Champion pending Ferrari's appeal, heard in Paris the week after the race. It was upheld and it opened up the Championship again.

Had Malaysia finally led to communion?

For many, many years Pino Allievi has been the motor racing correspondent of the Italian daily *La Gazzetta dello Sport*. He is inevitably steeped in Ferrari lore and is an absolute authority on the team. He said at the time: 'Schumacher is like a cyber-pilot. Italians respect him but they love people who have something to transmit from the heart – he speaks in Press Releases.

'Italians are indifferent to him. Ferrari is important to him because he is racing for Ferrari – it could just as easily be a team from Luxembourg or anywhere. Italians are not anti-German or anti-anybody. We've had German footballers like Haller, Muller and Bierhoff, speaking very good Italian, and that was no problem. Look at Berger, a German speaker. Look at Niki Lauda, if you want to talk about Anglo-Saxons, and remember how much people felt for him. And Jody Scheckter – he was loved.'

All weekend at Suzuka, Schumacher wore his different faces. On the Thursday it was the boy next door, relaxed and a little naughty. He made his way to the Media Centre for a set-piece Press Conference and there espied Brundle, came over and feigned tweaking Brundle's ear before they fell to affectionate banter spiced with occasional naughtiness. Schumacher wielded his broad, warm smile and at such moments he can look something more than the boy next door. He becomes the most ordinary bloke in the world. He wore blue jeans and sneakers. Corinna, in casual slacks and jumper, was outside the Ferrari office chatting and looking exactly like the girl next door.

He handled the Press Conference effortlessly and gave a secondary conference in German. He was hemmed so tightly he vanished within the journalists. Microphones and tape recorders were pressed virtually into his mouth but he talked quite naturally. Cameramen held their cameras over the heads of the journalists and the flash bulbs went off like explosions of lightning. They did not make him blink once.

Towards the end he was enjoying himself, making jokes and creating laughter although – inevitably – one serious topic could not be avoided. Would he, on the Sunday, help Irvine to the Championship? He seemed ambivalent: 'I have said right from the start that I won't have to be a support to Eddie, but I will have to win the race to ensure the Constructors' Championship [for Ferrari], and in doing that I will be helping Eddie as much as possible.'

To take the title Häkkinen needed to win the race and if he didn't fourth place would suffice for Irvine so if Schumacher came first Häkkinen might well be in trouble.

The German-speaking Press Conference broke up and as Schumacher wandered slowly towards the door someone presented him with a flower, I assume as a joke. If it was designed to embarrass him it failed because he held the flower quite naturally and kept holding it. As he reached the door he saw a Swiss reporter sitting on the floor with his back to the wall. This reporter is famed for the enormous cigars he always smokes, and he was smoking one now. Schumacher took it from him and examined it. 'Romeo and Juliet,' he murmured as a non-smoker would – unaware of its cost, quality and rarity – when he read the label wrapped round it. He returned it and they chatted, unhurried, unpressured: the normal bloke having a normal conversation.

The grey of the day was melting into twilight and still the spectators sat in the concrete grandstand, holding their mini-binoculars, locked into their eternal patience. They smiled a lot but gesticulated hardly at all. They just waited.

On the Friday, the face was that of a racer again as he moved to third fastest in the practice session behind Häkkinen and Coulthard. Then at 4.20 he went to the office of the FIA, the sport's governing body: Room 208 on the top floor. Schumacher prepared to be interviewed by Hill for *F1 Racing* magazine. It had been arranged by Matt Bishop, Group Editor of Haymarket Motorsport Magazines because Hill was to guest-edit *F1 Racing* for one issue after his retirement.

Bishop had been astonished to learn that apart from obligatory politeness the longest conversation Hill and Schumacher had had was after the birth of Schumacher's first child. Hill went up to him, shook his hand and said, 'You're a dad now same as me.'

Schumacher: 'Yes, yes, that's right.'

Hill: 'How's the baby, how's your wife?'

Schumacher: 'Fine, fine.'

However, Bishop adds: 'I believe Damon was one of only three drivers to visit Schumacher in hospital after the accident at Silverstone. His brother Ralf and Jean Alesi were the other two.'

A great deal of what Schumacher had to say carried authentic insights and although I'm only quoting a small portion (with kind permission) the extracts are striking. The interview began in exactly the right tone: irreverence.

Schumacher: 'How long before you knew you were going to stop?'

Hill: 'Er, I'm supposed to be asking the questions here, Michael!'

In fact Hill probed perceptively, including an exploration of Schumacher's confidence, which was, Hill said, 'very apparent from the outside', to which he replied 'I don't have the kind of confidence you think I might have. Not at all. Actually, I question myself very often. When things don't go well, I always question myself first. And I try very hard – I will never give up trying. So, you know, personally I don't believe I have as much self-belief as people think from the outside. But then in relation to my competitors, I don't know. I don't know what their level of self-belief is. I can't say that.'

Hill mentioned that Schumacher had shown emotion on the podium: 'You'd jump up, stick your fist in the air – even if you were second.'

Schumacher: 'In my view I'm a very stable person. I don't have many ups and downs. That's why my emotions are not often seen as dramatic, certainly not as dramatic as maybe people want to see. And it really takes a lot to make that happen. You have seen me very often – like you say, it's my trademark – being excited. You have seen me very rarely being depressed and showing those kind of other emotions. I don't need the kind of thing you see with some pop stars or movie stars, you know, extremes of emotion.'

The interview ended in the same tone of irreverence.

Hill: 'Are you worth the money?'

[Laughter]

Schumacher: 'That's the big question, isn't it?'

[More laughter]

Hill: 'You can't answer that, can you?! I think we'll have to decide that one for ourselves.'

Schumacher: 'No, Damon, you'll answer that one for me!'

Hill: 'OK, yeah. I'll work on it. Thanks for the chat.'

Schumacher: 'Pleasure.'

Bishop feels sure that Hill's visit to Schumacher in hospital in Northampton helped sway the decision to give the interview and 'I think there was a feeling – this wasn't said to me, this was something I gathered from the atmosphere – that their careers had been entwined and sometimes that had caused friction. There'd been words in the Press and they'd never really buried the hatchet, if you like. Now it was Damon's last race, Damon was no longer a threat and Schumacher was pleased to have a proper, open and pleasant conversation which put a natural and civilised lid on it.'

On the Saturday the face was as we had known it, greyhound-lean and utterly concentrated. He summoned a stunning lap of 1:37.47 which was not to be beaten. Afterwards, pressed about the Irvine situation (Irvine had qualified fifth), he said: 'I don't think my tactics will change. It is very clear that the best thing which can happen for us is if I win the race. I will give the most help I can for Eddie and the team. That will be the strategy.'

Will you be helping overnight to sort out the set-up on Irvine's car?

'Certainly. We are a team and we will be working with each other very deeply in terms of set-up. Whatever information he wants he will have available. Obviously he has the Number 1 package, which is normal. All number one parts go to him and I am driving the second class... if you can call it that, because to be honest we only have number one parts.'

Nightfall, and still the spectators sat in the concrete stand, illuminations from the fairground which nestled against the circuit falling across them, creating patterns of light and darkness. At the other side of the track mechanics toiled under lamplight and the fraternity ebbed and flowed along the alley. It is where strangers with their common destiny quite literally rub shoulders and exchange the obligatory politenesses, because it is a place of movement and hustle and scurry. Invariably Schumacher moves calmly through this, and he did now.

On the Sunday he put his different faces on again. Fifty minutes to go before the race and brother Ralf was chatting to someone behind the pits. Schumacher – earplugs in, overalls hanging from his waist like a peeled banana – was moving past him and took a good-natured swipe above his head. Ralf turned, thought *it's only him,* turned back. Schumacher strode on, the leg stiff again, turned into the Ferrari garage and disappeared among the huge metal containers.

On the grid he spoke briefly to Brawn while he drank liquid from a red canister. He nodded, flipped the lid of the canister shut and put it in a little buggy; took from the buggy his balaclava and drew that on, Brawn still talking to him. He put his helmet on and adjusted it, the face lost within. He was ready. He sat in the car and flipped the visor up. He shut his eyes for a long moment composing himself, opened his eyes again.

The start went wrong because Häkkinen was away fast, Schumacher slewing full across the track towards him. By then Häkkinen was clearly in the lead, the race decided. At no stage could Schumacher threaten him and it continued like that lap after lap in a sort of suspended animation. More than halfway through the race Coulthard went off and destroyed the McLaren's nosecone. He pitted and emerged in front of Schumacher but a lap down. The rules insist that Coulthard was entitled to hold Schumacher up (and thus help Häkkinen) but on sight of waved blue flags had to get out of the way. Coulthard was in no particular hurry to do that, which made Schumacher very angry. In fact when Coulthard did move over Schumacher made the *Ferrari* seem angry as he pitched it past.

A question to Brawn:

Does he get excited in the race? Senna used to come on the radio and give them a hell of a time with the language and all the rest of it: part of his brain was shouting 'What's going on?' and the other part of his brain was very cold.

'Michael doesn't do that at all. The other remarkable thing about Michael is when we talk on the radio it's like you and I having this conversation, it's a perfectly normal discussion. He gets upset with other things that can happen in the race, like the incidents with Coulthard. Then you hear a different side of Michael on the radio that you never hear during the ordinary running of a race. What I like about Michael is that even the most aggressive tactics from other drivers in normal racing never solicit a comment from him – so if somebody does something to him in a race that I, from the outside, would think was a pretty audacious move he will just treat it as normal racing, nothing to be complaining about.'

...whereas with Coulthard in Suzuka he didn't feel it was normal racing, it was a deliberate attempt to obstruct him.

'In both Spa and Suzuka Coulthard was being lapped, and I think that's what upset Michael. Any comparisons with the tactical decisions that we made in Malaysia weren't valid because that was two drivers on the same lap racing for position.'

Häkkinen won the race and the Championship comfortably

enough and while he toured on his lap of honour Schumacher was back in the pit lane. Ron Dennis, the man running McLaren, slapped him on the back.

Dennis: 'Michael, you're a great driver!'

Schumacher: 'Don't think I wasn't trying.'

Todt's telephone rang. He heard the voice of di Montezemolo saying he was very happy and proud of the team.

But the Horse had not been tamed.

The ceremony on the podium was as it should have been, a shower in the champagne for the first three – Häkkinen, Schumacher, Irvine – and Schumacher with his best smiling face on: not elation but a proper smile. Then they trooped off to the televised question-and-answer session. Häkkinen answered first as Champion, was clearly drawn between several emotions and finding words more elusive than usual.

In the McLaren pit the personnel were watching this on several television monitors.

Nearby Stepney beamed. Ferrari had won the Constructors' Championship, so highly prized by all teams, for the first time since 1983.

Up there, in the tele-conference room literally above the McLaren pit, it was Schumacher's turn to speak, starting with the start.

'I am not quite sure yet what actually happened. I had a problem when I went off the grid at the green light – things weren't working normally and I don't want to get into details, but we obviously have to analyse what was going on. Despite that I just went into wheelspin and Mika caught a very good start without making the mistake. It's something we have to work hard on to get to their level: things going very consistently for them and that's something we have to improve.'

Going through the race, you began to get quite close to Mika but you got held up by David Coulthard. You seemed very annoyed when you went past him.

Schumacher's face moved to somewhere between the stern and the severe.

'Yes. I mean Mika is definitely a great Champion today, he made the Championship by winning the race so there is no reason why he shouldn't celebrate that 100% but the team should wonder why they ask the drivers to do things like they have done – because it was a different thing in Malaysia when I was racing actually for position and not being lapped. You can play tactics. But if you are lapped...'

(Ron Dennis, in the McLaren pit and watching a monitor, said: 'Here it is – having a go at David.')

'...you should give space and David passed many blue flags. He had a kind of problem but he was really driving zig-zagging...'

(A ripple of anger spread through the McLaren pit and someone shouted 'Bullshit' towards a monitor.)

'...and actually I'm not sure whether I should believe whether Spa [1998] wasn't really done purposely, the way he behaved today – because I didn't expect him doing such a thing when it was clear he was out of the race, he was lapped. I am very disappointed seeing a manoeuvre from a guy which nobody expected to see – because I was really challenging Mika... I think this situation cost me about ten seconds so I'm very disappointed.'

Later Schumacher amplified this by claiming Coulthard held him up from turns 2 to 11.

Coulthard reacted with anger of his own, claiming that Schumacher had made it clear to 'two key people' in the McLaren team 'that he would not be upset if Mika won the Championship and not Eddie.' Coulthard, hemmed by journalists on the upper walkway, spoke crisply and clearly. 'So, despite his public image of being out there to give Eddie a hand, and the admirable work he did in Malaysia, he will be quite happy. He's chucked this in as a smokescreen to deflect from the outcome of the race.'

Coulthard threatened legal action over Schumacher's assertion that the Spa crash was done on purpose, although he withdrew this after the two had spoken. They felt towards a measure of reconciliation. Schumacher said that overall his criticism of Coulthard may have sounded harsher than he had intended, and Coulthard said they had agreed to differ.

On the walkway stood Häkkinen's manager – Rosberg.

You've beaten the unbeatable Schumacher two seasons running. How?

'Today you have the answer and it was done in the best possible way, it was sporting, it was man against man and I take my hat off to a phenomenal performance from Mika.'

Last season was the first time anyone had gone head-to-head with Schumacher and it didn't end in tears, it didn't end in fighting in the pit lane.

'And it was very sporting today as well, except I thought Michael's comments in the Press Conference were let's say a bit... [Rosberg didn't finish the sentence, so add your own word]. But one has to take your hat off and say Eddie was a great second in the Championship today, very sporting, congratulated Mika – *well done* – and that's the way it should be. Michael couldn't bring it over his lips. He just couldn't, no.'

Do you think that's the sort of man he is?

'Seems to be, yes. Seems to be.'

Into the evening Schumacher returned to being the boy next door. Around the pits, offices and the alley he played out high jinks here, there and everywhere. Later he went to the Log Cabin, a place in the grounds of the circuit's hotel, and, wearing a sticker across his head – *Goodbye, Damon* – evidently indulged in more high jinks.

One press agency report said he'd been with McLaren and 'newspapers ran photographs of Schumacher which they said were taken at the party. They showed the German looking relaxed and wearing a bandana. Some reports claimed the former World Champion was drunk.'

Di Montezemolo had to clear up this potential 'incident' and did so with delightful elegance by dismissing it for the trivia it was. 'Schumacher was at his "last day at school". He was with the Italians, Germans and British. He had been with the Ferrari team from eight in the evening until midnight.' Di Montezemolo added: 'I would rather have a Schumacher who gets drunk sometimes and jokes and laughs. If he was too serious it would be a problem. It's fine as long as he only gets drunk once a year.'

There was a time when the news story would have been leading drivers *not* having had a drink or two, but that was before the media multiplied and went mad, before the Press Relations industry descended upon the paddock and sanitised everything with surgical gloves, and before the ethos of sport was overwhelmed by manicured corporate imagery in every damned direction you looked. There was a time when drivers were only human beings being human, and cheers.

The irony, of course, remained that Michael Schumacher was too big, too powerful and too talented to be completely sanitised.

That Sunday evening at Suzuka another Championship had been won and lost, and still Ferrari were without a Champion since 1979, since the human days. Soon enough there'd be another launch of another new Ferrari amidst the annual pomp and circumstance, another season beckoning, another chance to ride the Horse.

Almost quietly, and as far away from headlines as you can get, Schumacher said: 'Next year will be my time.'

Even he cannot have had any notion of the extent to which he would be right.

Chapter 9

CREATING HIS OWN ERA

Between the dry, warm late afternoon of 12 March 2000 at Albert Park, Melbourne, and the dry, sunny late afternoon of 10 October 2004 at Suzuka, Michael Schumacher and Ferrari imposed their will on Formula One so completely that nothing like it had ever been seen before. In retrospect – when, as we have seen, everything is clear – this had been coming from the day he joined Ferrari, and that going in to 2000 a rare conjunction had been reached: a team with resources to do whatever it considered necessary, a great driver now matured and at the height of his powers, key personnel at the height of their powers.

Through it all walked the craggy figure of Schumacher himself, seemingly a mystery within a mystery because in the way he conducted himself he appeared so ordinary, mostly trapped within political correctness in every utterance and seemingly forever content to be a prisoner there. No doubt it was easier that way, but even so…

The domination, now a permanent masterclass, meant danger to Grand Prix racing, dividing the televiewing audience into two tiers, a smaller one understanding all the nuances and sipping Schumacher's races like complex wine, the larger one poised with a can of lager and the remote control buttons demanding excitement.

Sometimes he was able to satisfy both audiences but, as the domination grew, more and more rarely. Grand Prix racing existed, as it had always done, on uncertainty enacted at high speed, and once certainty replaced that there were problems. Too many people had too much invested for remote control buttons round the world being pressed *off* regularly to be anything but alarming. It is fanciful to say that something so solid and entrenched as Grand Prix racing could be threatened by one man and one team, but, equally, it could be damaged.

Here, first, is the historical perspective from the season after Scheckter won. The figures in brackets after the drivers' names are their Championship positions, and the figure in brackets after the season's points total is where Ferrari finished in the Constructors' Championship.

1980: Scheckter (19), Gilles Villeneuve (10) 8 points (10)
1981: Villeneuve (7), Pironi (13) 34 points (5)
1982: Villeneuve (15), Pironi (2), Tambay (7),
      Andretti (19) 74 points (1)
1983: Tambay (4), Arnoux (3) 89 points (1)
1984: Alboreto (4), Arnoux (6) 57.5 points (2)
1985: Alboreto (2), Arnoux (17), Johansson (7) 82 points (2)
1986: Alboreto (8), Johansson (5) 37 points (4)
1987: Alboreto (7), Berger (5) 53 points (4)
1988: Alboreto (5), Berger (3) 65 points (2)
1989: Mansell (4), Berger (7) 59 points (3)
1990: Prost (2), Mansell (5) 110 points (2)
1991: Prost (5), Alesi (7), Morbidelli (24) 55.5 points (3)
1992: Alesi (7), Capelli (12), Larini (−) 21 points (4)
1993: Alesi (6), Berger (8) 28 points (4)
1994: Alesi (5), Berger (3), Larini (14) 71 points (3)
1995: Alesi (5), Berger (6) 73 points (3)
1996: Schumacher (3), Irvine (10) 70 points (2)
1997: Schumacher (2*), Irvine (7) 102 points (2)
1998: Schumacher (2), Irvine (4) 133 points (2)
1999: Schumacher (5), Irvine (2), Salo (10) 128 points (1)
(*Subsequently excluded for crashing Jacques Villeneuve)

The Constructor's positions, season by season, are surprisingly good after the disaster of 1980 and stand contrary to the mythology of Ferrari wandering in the wilderness. The drivers are a rich array, and five – Pironi in 1982, Arnoux the following year, Alboreto in 1985, Prost in 1990, Irvine in 1999 – might have been Champions. Prost *would* if Senna hadn't taken him out at Suzuka in the deciding race.

By then, however, the whole question of Ferrari generated an invitation to mythology: could *any* driver take on the temperament at Maranello, the politics at Maranello, the entrenched positions at Maranello, the resources of Maranello, and ride the Horse into the sunset? Berger had accepted, tried, failed, and would try and fail again. Mansell had tried and failed. Prost had tried and failed. These three were among the leading drivers of their time. If the Horse unseated them, who could ride it?

Until the dry, warm late afternoon of 12 March 2000 at Albert Park, Melbourne, it was not at all clear that anybody could. Schumacher's tries since 1996 had so far brought a couple of second places, joining him to Pironi, Arnoux, and Prost. He would surely have won it in 1999 if he hadn't broken his leg, just as Pironi surely would have won it if he hadn't mangled his legs.

One of the basic tenets of motor racing insists that second place is nowhere. This is perhaps inevitable in an activity dispensing dollars by the million in order to win. It certainly loaded pressure, sometimes intolerably – Capelli was almost broken by it – on to any driver confronting the challenge at Ferrari. The simple, brutal truth was that, so far, Schumacher had failed. The broader implications of this will be explored in Chapter 12.

In February the new car was unveiled. By now Irvine had gone to the lucrative pastureland of Jaguar (formerly Stewart) and Barrichello come from Stewart.

Customary pomp and circumstance accompanied the unveiling. Schumacher and Barrichello drew back the covering like a cloak to reveal the F1-2000 while Todt stood nearby, microphone in hand. Di Montezemolo said: 'We all know what the goal is. I don't want to talk about it too much – the track will provide the final answers. Our competitors are strong and highly sophisticated, but we will face them with determination and humility.'

The drivers in the leading teams:

Benetton – Fisichella, Wurz.
Ferrari – Schumacher, Barrichello.
Jordan – Frentzen, Jarno Trulli.
McLaren – Häkkinen, Coulthard.
Williams – R. Schumacher, Jenson Button.

McLaren seemed the team to beat, Häkkinen and Coulthard settled there and Häkkinen, of course, going for a straight hat-trick of World Championships, something which had only been done once before (Fangio, four, 1954–7). Immediately Häkkinen announced his intentions, taking pole at Melbourne from Coulthard, Schumacher third, but in the race both the McLarens' Mercedes engines failed so that Schumacher moved from third to the lead and didn't lose it except for pit stops.

'I'm delighted. This is the fifth time we have tried to win the race and be competitive at the start of the season. When I got into my new car for testing in February I immediately felt that this is the car I'm going to do it with. I believe I proved today that I was right. The car was reliable and just so bloody fast.'

Häkkinen took pole again in Brazil but McLaren decided on a one-stop strategy, Ferrari two. Schumacher hustled into the lead on lap 2 and built a gap, but Häkkinen went after lap 30 (oil pressure) and although Coulthard finished second he was disqualified: an illegal front wing. Schumacher had 20 points,

McLaren 0, but more than that the Ferrari team had changed. We've already heard Prost say that when they won they suffered 'a crisis of optimism'. No chance of that now with pragmatic Todt and Brawn in charge and pragmatic Schumacher in the car.

A current was running, a strong current.

At Imola, Häkkinen took pole again and led, but suffered a variety of problems. When he pitted a second time Schumacher had three clear laps to gain enough time to pit himself and emerge in front. He started hammering in fastest laps and beat Häkkinen by 1.1 seconds.

Britain at Silverstone – astonishingly in April for, as it was said, reasons of fixture congestion (17 races; 1998 and 1999 had been 16) – sank in a sea of mud off the track while on it Barrichello, pole, led to lap 35 when the hydraulics failed. That let the McLarens in and Schumacher slogged to a useful third place. He had 34 points, Coulthard 14, and Häkkinen 12.

Pole in Spain but a difficult race: at his first pit stop he was waved away too soon and knocked over Stepney, breaking his ankle. At his second there was a rig problem, making him fifth at the end – Häkkinen won.

On lap 10 of the European at the Nürburgring he was following Häkkinen when rain fell. Into the chicane he sliced through and vanished into the murk, winning it by 13.8 seconds. The current bore him forward because, after six rounds, he led Häkkinen 46–28 and each race where Häkkinen did not cut into that shifted the Championship another notch towards Schumacher.

As if to emphasise that, he led Monaco from pole until a pushrod broke after 55 laps, letting in Coulthard, but Häkkinen was sixth. He dominated Canada absolutely, pole and leading every lap except after his first pit stop, Häkkinen a distant fourth. He had 56 points, Coulthard 34, Häkkinen 32.

Häkkinen did cut into the lead in France, where Schumacher led from pole before the engine failed after 58 laps, but

Coulthard won that and in his calm, precise way now looked the strongest challenger.

The current was diverted in Austria where Schumacher became involved in a crash at the first corner after the start with Ricardo Zonta's BAR, Häkkinen winning from Coulthard; was diverted at Hockenheim where he crashed with Fisichella at the start and Häkkinen finished second to Barrichello. Schumacher 56, Coulthard and Häkkinen 54, Barrichello 46.

Six races remained and when Häkkinen won Hungary, beating Schumacher by 7.9 seconds, he led the Championship for the first time in the season. Inevitably, the mythology stalked the landscape. Was the great effort disintegrating as so many before it had? Was there, somehow, always to be the final component – whatever that might be – missing?

'There is no crisis,' Schumacher said. 'I was knocked off the road in Austria, before that I had an engine failure and a suspension failure. I don't know if it is justified to talk about a crisis when I win races in between. We do, however, believe we have lost ground a little bit towards McLaren Mercedes and that we have to work harder to catch up again. But we are not in a crisis.'

At Spa, in obligatory wet-dry conditions, he led but Häkkinen hunted him down and, at Les Combes on lap 40, Schumacher chopped him to keep him back – and did it so late that Häkkinen thought they might have touched, damaging the McLaren.

Mika Häkkinen, most mild mannered of men, did not care for any of this.

After slowing to check the McLaren remained in full working order he caught Schumacher again. Into Les Combes they came upon Zonta, holding mid-track and minding his own business. Zonta saw Schumacher but had no idea Häkkinen was coming like the wind immediately behind the Ferrari. In the instant that Schumacher flicked out to the left, going round Zonta, Häkkinen flicked out to the right, slicing past both of them.

We are talking 190mph and a tight, corkscrew of a right-hander; we are talking eye blinks; and we are talking something Schumacher wasn't expecting at all.

It was gorgeous.

On the podium Schumacher looked sombre. Häkkinen led 74–68, all 17 rounds counting and no need for any permutations except one: who, at some definitive moment between now and the final round in Malaysia, would have a total which the other could not overtake? Coulthard, on 61, might have something to say about that, too.

Schumacher created a tremendous response at Monza – a response so personally intense, accompanied by great tragedy, that afterwards he broke down in tears. He took pole from Barrichello although Häkkinen got his McLaren into the 1:23s as well. Schumacher moved into the lead but extensive crashing behind him claimed the life of a marshal when debris hit him.

Coulthard was among those who crashed and his Championship hopes ended. When the Safety Car pulled off Schumacher moved away from Häkkinen and it remained like that except for three laps deep into the race when Schumacher made his pit stop. By then he had created enough of a lead that Häkkinen couldn't negate it in those three laps. He pitted, passing the lead back to Schumacher who won it by 3.8 seconds. 'I think it is obvious why I am emotional,' he said.

It was.

Häkkinen 80, Schumacher 78.

Formula One returned to the United States and a new track to it, Indianapolis, home of the Indy 500. The Formula One cars would go round in the opposite direction to the IndyCars and use a special new infield section because the 500 configuration, a straightforward high speed oval, was against the traditions, ethos and philosophies of Formula One.

Schumacher took pole, Coulthard – alongside on the front

row – took the lead on a drying track. On lap 7, Häkkinen close behind, Schumacher went past Coulthard, who received a 10 second stop'n'go penalty for jumping the start. Häkkinen pitted early for dry tyres and Schumacher stayed out another nine laps. The race was decided nine laps further on – lap 25 – when Häkkinen's engine failed. Schumacher led to the end, Barrichello following him home. During the race Schumacher and Coulthard rubbed wheels when Schumacher muscled through. 'Immediately after, I was angry,' Schumacher would say, because Coulthard appeared to move over on him. However, 'after seeing the television pictures I had to change my opinion.' That apology cleared the debris of the season away – Schumacher and Coulthard had been squabbling for months. Suzuka, with half the planet watching, could now be a clean fight.

The Formula One community gathered, as it does, on the Thursday. In the concrete grandstand opposite the pits thousands of Japanese sat in silence. They would see, this day, no car going round. They wanted a glimpse of a driver, a feeling of proximity but, out of their sight, Schumacher and Häkkinen shook hands then faced the Media. The two men had a genuine mutual respect which they didn't talk about in public.

Question to Häkkinen: *Will you be doing anything different?* 'No. Nothing really. Just that I will be braking a couple of metres later for every corner.'

Schumacher: 'I'll have to brake five metres later, I guess.'

Häkkinen: 'But then you'll be in the gravel.'

Schumacher: 'We'll be together...' [laughter]

Coulthard applied some double-edged comments. 'I have a lot of respect for Michael. He has earned that because he is hard, aggressive and hungry in every condition, wet or dry. There are, however, enough indications that when Michael is desperate he is prepared to do something that people are likely to question as unsporting. He should push it to the limit but not beyond. I will do what I can to help the team, but I will do so within the rules and they would not ask me to go beyond that.'

There was a (real) earthquake in Japan on the Friday. Its epicentre was some 150km away and measured 7.1 on the Richter Scale, reducing to 3.9 when it reached Suzuka at 1.30 but still strong enough to shake the pits and offices for 30 seconds and make people run outside. Schumacher was driving but 'out on the track I did not feel a thing'. He finished this practice 0.611 seconds faster than Häkkinen.

The second practice was tighter, Häkkinen 0.139 seconds up, but, the sense of theatre mounting, everything concentrated onto Saturday's qualifying. This, too, Schumacher felt would be very tight. Winter sunlight fell across his face, the peak of his cap casting a shadow across his eyes, as he said, 'We feel optimistic because we know that we have a very good car and if we get the maximum out of this car we know we can do it but then that's the point: do we always get the maximum or not? And what about the other side?'

He strode purposefully to his pit with his overall top folded down over his waist revealing the white tee shirt underneath. His face looked sombre, preoccupied. He vanished into the bosom of the pit still striding. The sun was weaker now, fashioning a narrow wedge of shadow from the pit lane wall. Within the bosom he sat, hands clasped, and made a joke to a team member. He held the smile and seemed in no hurry. 'In my view, the circuit wasn't in good condition in the early stage [of the session]. There was no point in going out early and just wasting a set of tyres.' He and Brawn began to concentrate on what would happen later.

Of the front-runners, Coulthard went out first – the sun dipped behind cloud – and did 1m 36.633s. Some 25 minutes in, Schumacher emerged, pulling his visor down, twisting the car rightwards down the pit lane. He seemed to strike the visor with his forearm, flipping it up. He pulled it down again. As he circled towards the hot lap Häkkinen emerged. Schumacher attacked: smooth and very near the limit. As he was going faster than Coulthard had in the third sector, Häkkinen was going faster than he had in the first sector. Schumacher crossed the line at 1:36.094 and Häkkinen at 1:36.168.

Schumacher quickest by 0.074.

With 21 minutes to go Häkkinen was out, in the second sector went 0.098 faster and crossed the line at 1:36.017.

Häkkinen quickest by 0.077.

Schumacher was out with 17 minutes to go, soothed the Ferrari round, built towards the lap and attacked again. The car looked sensuous now, a beautiful, predatory animal. He crossed the line at 1:35.908.

Schumacher quickest by 0.109.

Häkkinen, in the cockpit in the McLaren pit, gazed at a television monitor and briefly shook his head. Eleven minutes to go and he made his response, Schumacher now watching the monitor. Häkkinen was slower by 0.043 in the first sector – Schumacher's expression didn't react to that – and slower by 0.025 in the second sector. But not the third. He crossed the line at 1:35.834.

Häkkinen quickest by 0.074.

Schumacher smiled, fleeting, wistful; and he responded. Brawn had chosen this moment with exquisite timing – a minimum of traffic. Three and a half minutes to go and Schumacher forced the Ferrari through the sweepers beyond turn one, forced it through the first sector but was 0.039 slower. In the second sector he rattled the kerbs, the sun drawing shadows from the wheels, and he went 0.012 quicker. As he moved into the third sector Häkkinen emerged in a flurry of movement. Schumacher crossed the line at 1:35.825.

Schumacher quickest by 0.009.

Häkkinen began his final lap. Schumacher saw 'the first two sectors, then I was a little more quiet' – Häkkinen 0.002 up in the first, 0.088 down in the second. 'I knew it could have been a tight qualifying situation [now] and if he had got the lap together either of us could have been on pole.' Häkkinen crossed the line at 1:36.018. Schumacher had pole by that 0.009 – centimetres hewn from Suzuka's 5.8 kilometres. The Ferrari pit surrendered to broad grinning and back-slapping. Schumacher drank from a bottle, examined the times on a monitor, strode up the pit lane and – as Häkkinen's McLaren was being pushed into the *parc fermé* garage – stopped. He gazed intently at it, dissecting it.

He went to the Press Conference and someone said, 'You seem much quieter, and more reflective on getting the job done here this weekend than you usually are. How much pressure are you under?'

He dissected that. 'Naturally this is not a race like any other. We can finish the Championship here, but there is no point in celebrating this pole position big time. It's nice, but it isn't the end result. We will have to fight for that very hard tomorrow. We are ready.'

The Sunday morning warm-up is a curious creature, given almost no publicity but arguably of more significance than qualifying because here cars run in race trim. Qualifying's reticence, where a session could be ten minutes old before you saw a car, was reversed by an immediate cavalcade; and there was one here, Schumacher among it. Under a leaden sky, he did a 1:38.005 – Häkkinen 1:38.526 – and that was a real gap.

The weather forecast suggested rain during the race.

Half a world away, in Maranello, it rained in the darkness and the Ferrari faithful sheltered under umbrellas as they prepared to watch the race on a giant screen. Ferrari flags fluttered, saddened in the rain but defiant too. Young men jumped up and down in front of a television camera while others staged a mock funeral, carrying a coffin with Mercedes (whose engines McLaren had) on it to a local church and then the Ferrari headquarters. In Kerpen some 3,000 people prepared to watch, most of them wearing blood-red clothing and waving Ferrari flags confidently. Young men jumped up and down in front of a television camera.

Di Montezemolo telephoned Schumacher. He 'listened to Schumi, then I only said "I thank you. I am doing it now because in an hour's time I will be drunk" – with delight.'

At Suzuka the cars came to the grid. A young Japanese lady in a kimono stood by Schumacher's bay holding a placard on a pole. Schumacher nosed the Ferrari into the bay and the team surrounded it. He got out and surveyed the car, chatted to Brawn: slightly bearded, bespectacled, his earphones with their antennae resembling a Viking helmet. The mood was calm, *Anglo-Saxon*. Schumacher gazed at the sky searching for signs of the rain, gave a brief TV interview – if this side of the track or that bestowed an initial advantage – and chatted to Brawn again.

The grid cleared like a sudden migration, leaving the twin column of cars alone. They covered the formation lap, Schumacher taking them round at a respectable pace. They settled on the grid facing 53 laps. Häkkinen was away fast, Schumacher slewing full across towards him – wheelspin, he'd explain. Häkkinen veered clear but didn't back off and, into turn one, led. 'Mika was very quick and there was nothing I could do.' The race might have been settled already. They drew away from the others and waltzed lap after lap, the gap expanding to 2.5 seconds, contracting to less than 1.0; waltzed to the first pit stops. Häkkinen made his on lap 22: stationary 6.8 seconds, taking on fuel for 13 laps. Already Brawn was bringing Schumacher in next lap: stationary 7.4 seconds, fuel for 15 laps. When Häkkinen made his second stop Schumacher would have those two laps to do what he'd always done – create.

At lap 30 drizzle fell from a dark sky and wind raked the circuit but they waltzed on, the gap expanding and contracting again until, in this drizzle, Schumacher closed up. Then, into the chicane, Zonta let Häkkinen through but almost brushed against Schumacher's rear wheel. Nightmare: if Zonta had been centimetres further over the history of motor racing might have been altered forever.

On lap 37 Häkkinen did stop again (stationary 7.4 seconds) and Schumacher had the two laps for creation. He had to gain enough time to pit himself and hold the lead – 'this was the crucial time' – but both Jaguars lay in front of him. Irvine, in one of them, scampered clear but Schumacher didn't pass Herbert in the other until they began the next lap. 'The traffic cost me a little bit of time.' Rain fell, Brawn on the pit lane scanning it. As Schumacher flowed out of the chicane on his 'in' lap Wurz spun but there was just enough room to get through. Nightmare: 'It was moving backwards in front of me and I didn't know where he was going to go'.

Schumacher pitted. 'I didn't think I had done enough. It was spitting with rain and I thought I hadn't gone as fast as I should have done.' Wrong. He'd gained half a second – the creation – and was stationary for only 6.0 seconds. While Schumacher travelled with agonising slowness down the pit lane, a prisoner of the speed limit, Brawn watched for Häkkinen to come from the chicane and seize the lead.

'It's looking good,' Brawn said on the radio. Schumacher wasn't sure about that.

'It's looking good,' Brawn updated in a running commentary. Still Schumacher wasn't sure about that.

'It's looking good,' Brawn continued.

Schumacher waited to hear the fateful words *sorry, it's not looking good enough*. With the pit lane wall between him and the track, he could see absolutely nothing of where Häkkinen was.

'It's looking bloody good!' Brawn said.

Schumacher would remember this as an amazing moment and, as he regained the track, Häkkinen was far, far back in the distance. Twelve laps remained, history beckoning. Schumacher 'just hoped nothing broke' on the car, survived a wobble in the wet, withstood late Häkkinen pressure, and Ferrari dreams came true.

When he had brought the car to rest he sat for a long moment with his head bowed in supplication before the fact, a private moment. Behind barriers a gaggle of Ferrari team-members in their blood-red uniforms had abandoned themselves: their faces were consumed. Some cried, some clapped wildly, some waved their arms, some brandished clenched fists. Some looked suddenly exhausted in their exultancy as if, after so long, the moment was too much.

Todt, small, almost birdlike, had dipped into the cockpit and clasped Schumacher's gloved hands. Irvine, who'd helped him towards this at Ferrari and left before the consummation, stretched down and shook the gloved hands. Todt patted the side of Irvine's forehead – affection – and then Irvine melted away. Schumacher removed the steering wheel and pumped a fist. Todt, meticulous, set the steering wheel lightly down on the nosecone and he melted away.

Schumacher was alone. He levered himself up in the cockpit, raised his head, clenched both fists and worked them to and fro like pistons. He clasped the helmet and bowed his head in supplication again. He was shedding the weight and when he got out of the car he walked like a free man. The rest was lost in the pull and push of emotion: his wife Corinna weeping with joy, everyone embracing everyone, two Ferrari mechanics shaving their heads. Schumacher conducted the Italian national anthem on the rostrum; Todt was so soaked in champagne he tried to wring it from his shirt; Brawn explained that, unemotional by nature, he was trying to control his emotions; and Häkkinen was utterly gracious in defeat.

In Maranello, Father Alberto Bernardoni apologised for not ringing the bells as Schumacher crossed the line. He'd been saying Mass at that moment.

Di Montezemolo touched on history. 'It is the first victory since the passing away of the Company's founder, Enzo Ferrari, in 1988, and Gianni Agnelli of the Fiat dynasty [who own Ferrari] said his first thought was how happy the old boy would be today.'

Italy's President, Carlo Azeglio Ciampi, joined in. 'Finally, after 21 years, we earned it.' Gerhard Schroder, the *Bundeskanzler*, sent a message of congratulations which arrived so swiftly it surprised Schumacher as well touching him.

The celebrations at the track that night had to be improvised because Schumacher insisted nothing be planned in advance 'as I felt it would be unlucky'. Heavy rain was falling but that didn't matter. The party really did begin. It was, we are assured, of historical proportions.

He'd tamed the bronco.

Schumacher had the two Championships with Benetton and now a third, already enough to place him with Jack Brabham, Stewart, Lauda, Piquet and Senna. Ahead lay only Prost on four and Fangio on five – and Schumacher fully intended to win more. He was in his early 30s, when many drivers reach a specific kind of maturity, balancing ambition with experience; and everything about Ferrari looked mighty.

The 2001 season began with the unveiling of the new car, at Maranello in late January. As Schumacher arrived for the launch several hundred supporters chanted 'Champions, Champions,' and they might have been speaking for the whole of Italy. He insisted that his motivation remained undiluted. 'I am a natural,' he would say. 'I want to be at the limit and there is still a lot of joy for me in driving. I can't say I am more motivated because that is impossible, but the weight is off our shoulders and the motivation now is to improve constantly.' He looked in a powerful mood, crisp and concentrated. He had good reason.

'I am not a movie star. Either things come naturally to you or they don't. You cannot learn emotions.' Schumacher was speaking in Italian, itself a news item. He and the Italian public were growing towards each other, and had been since before he won the Championship for himself and for them. Now he was reaching towards beautiful phrases in their own language, rather than in English, to touch *their* emotions. Finally, communion.

They did not know – nobody knew – that we were in the Schumacher era. They did not know – nobody knew – that it would exist on two levels: the masterstrokes flowing into the masterclass to make a competitive massacre. It became so complete that, as I have said, it threatened to damage the well-being of Formula One itself because the millions of tele-viewers who had only a casual interest simply turned off. There was no point in staying. Some behaved tactically, watching the start and the finish only. Some stopped altogether.

To the connoisseur, however, Schumacher was now operating at a level where the expression of his art – its purity, its certainty, its intellectual ability to mould movement – was fascinating.

As Schumacher celebrated a decade of Grand Prix racing all manner of records were coming steadily into view, the natural consequence of sustained success. You can have ambivalent feelings about the relevance of records themselves, and how accurate they are as a gauge, but when many of the major all-time records are at a man's mercy you cannot ignore them. Beginning 2001, this was the situation:

Prost had most points (798.5), Schumacher next (678). With 17 races in 2001, Prost's total was potentially vulnerable.

Senna had most poles (65), Clark and Prost 33, Schumacher and Mansell 32. Senna's total would be completely out of reach for at least three seasons.

Prost had most wins (51), Schumacher 44, Senna 41. Prost's total was very vulnerable.

Prost and Schumacher shared the number of fastest laps (41) from Mansell, 30. That would go very quickly, probably at the first race.

Schumacher moved into the season on 23 January at Barcelona. 'I feel well. I had a good rest and I am in top form.' The new car, the F-2001, was launched at the Fiorano circuit on 29 January, Schumacher making all the right noises.

Villeneuve and Schumacher had had a sharp relationship for years and round about now Villeneuve said he had qualms about racing Schumacher because 'you don't know if the track will be wide enough, you don't know if he has seen you and it is very difficult to judge, whereas with Mika [Häkkinen], he thinks like a normal human being.'

It is true that Schumacher often adopted robust tactics at the start of a race, ruthlessly protecting his lead from the lights to the first corner, but apart from that, what Villeneuve implied seemed largely to have disappeared: the crashes with Hill, Villeneuve and even Coulthard, and the anger they had brought, were years ago. In Formula One terms, Schumacher was now into comfortable middle age and supervising the young drivers rather than barging and bumping a path through them.

He drove the new car at Fiorano on 1 February, and rather solemnly Ferrari pointed out that it 'carried the Number 1 for the first time' since 1980.

'The first impression is very good. The car is very competitive.' He hadn't slept well before the test: 'I was a little bit nervous.' But he wasn't nervous after it.

The drivers in the leading teams:

BAR – Olivier Panis, Villeneuve.

Benetton – Fisichella, Button.

Ferrari – Schumacher, Barrichello.

Jordan – Frentzen, Trulli.

McLaren – Häkkinen, Coulthard.

Williams – R. Schumacher, Juan Pablo Montoya.

The first race – Melbourne in 2001 – is invariably an accurate guide to the rest of the season. The fast cars are already fast, the slower cars will have enormous difficulty making up the difference.

Schumacher crashed heavily on the Friday. Under yellow flags 'I was really on the limit. I touched the brakes a little bit harder to slow down enough for the situation and that's why I lost the back end. It was not actually a heavy impact because I did not hit the wall, so it was just a gentle roll and I am fine.' The pictures of this roll looked very spectacular indeed.

Next day he put the F-2001 on pole, from Barrichello, and he led throughout the race except for the pit stops. Schumacher had now matured to the point where he could pace himself as if the others weren't there, drive comparatively slowly when he wished and still win. Oh, and did set fastest lap, going past Prost's 41.

During the race a marshal was killed when a wheel from Villeneuve's car struck him. Schumacher, shocked like everybody else, said, 'We must see what can be done to improve their working conditions from a safety point of view.' People convinced that Schumacher was a cold and calculating man had somehow to reconcile this view with the way he betrayed the most human emotions – including tears at the death of a marshal at Monza the previous season – and invariably found the right words to cover the sombre moments.

He took pole in Malaysia and made a powerful start to the race, Barrichello behind him, but on the third lap rain fell and both Ferraris skated off like synchronised swimmers. They resumed with Barrichello third, Schumacher seventh and the rain becoming a tempest. Cars were going off everywhere and the Safety Car came out.

The Ferraris pitted on lap 4 but by now the confusion of the race had reached into the team. Brawn saw Barrichello skate off a second time and assumed, incorrectly, that Schumacher was now in front of him again. The mechanics assumed Schumacher would be pitting first and were ready for him – and Barrichello arrived. In this confusion they fitted Schumacher's tyres to Barrichello's car and had to take them off again. Barrichello was stationary for 72 seconds, Schumacher patiently waiting his turn parked behind him. Schumacher's pit stop took 8.0 seconds but, cumulatively, lasted 80 seconds plus the time it had taken him to slow and would now take getting back to the track.

It is at such moments that Schumacher presents his willpower, his breadth of vision and his ability to apply genius to race-craft. Where so many drivers would accept that the race had gone from them, he saw only advantages to be exploited.

He had intermediate tyres on and the circuit was a monsoon on one side, dry on the other. That was one method of exploitation, sailing safely through the monsoon, accelerating into the dry.

The Safety Car circled so that he and Barrichello would catch up the snake of cars following it and, when the restart came, they would have regained most of the time lost in the pits – something else to be exploited (no matter that, as Schumacher joined the tail of the snake, 'the conditions were atrocious and undrivable, and at times the Safety Car was quicker than us').

At that restart, on lap 11, Barrichello ran tenth and Schumacher eleventh. Completing that lap Barrichello was up to eighth, Schumacher ninth, at 10.06 seconds from the leader, Coulthard. In the rolling spray the sleek-nosed Ferraris were moving like a pair of sharks. Schumacher overtook Barrichello and they hunted down Jarno Trulli in the Jordan: Schumacher sixth, at 8.91 from Coulthard. They hunted down Frentzen in the other Jordan, Schumacher describing a great arc of power outside him. Schumacher drew up to Ralf and dealt with him almost immediately. And, describing another great arc, went outside Häkkinen. On lap 13 Schumacher was third, at 6.27

from Coulthard. He caught Jos Verstappen (Arrows) and pressured him, placed the Ferrari inside as they approached a right-hander, and he was second.

Coulthard was within reach and for once Schumacher pushed so hard that the Ferrari shivered. The gap to Coulthard was down to 1.96. He tried the arc of power but Coulthard resisted. On the start-finish straight he squeezed up behind Coulthard, came out and went round the outside. The race was decided and the records were coming now. This was Schumacher's sixth Grand Prix victory in succession, taking him past the five of Brabham (1960), Jim Clark (1965) and Mansell (1992). Ahead lay Alberto Ascari with nine (1952–53).

He didn't reach that – second in Brazil to Coulthard – and he retired at Imola with a mechanical problem. That did not prevent him expressing delight that Ralf won. 'This is the first time that two brothers have won Formula One Grands Prix.'

He won Spain, although that was inherited because Häkkinen broke down at the end, was second in Austria (to Coulthard) despite a brush with Montoya. 'The fight had been fair until the incident,' Schumacher said. 'Then he tried to take me out at the corner and I had to go onto the grass because I could not turn in. He was not looking where he was going, he was looking where I was going.'

On 22 May, Ferrari announced that Schumacher and Barrichello had extended their contracts, Schumacher to the end of 2004 and Barrichello to the end of 2002.

Schumacher described Monaco as 'in some ways an easy and straightforward race because I was out in front on my own, but at the same time it was quite hard as we still had to do fast lap times. The traction control made the race rougher physically as we are going quicker. I love the circuit – it is always a challenge. Today I just had to think about reliability and make sure I didn't make a mistake. I asked Ross Brawn what some other drivers were doing and he told me to concentrate.'

This was the seventh race and made the Championship Schumacher 52, Coulthard 40. Schumacher now put a strong run together which virtually settled the title: second in Canada to Ralf – who beat him in a straight fight – then winning the European at the Nürburgring after squeezing Ralf very, very hard at the start. The pit lane wall was not far away.

'The start was a kind of key to the race and I had to do anything I could to keep Ralf behind me. I left him room and it was hard, I know that, but it was necessary for me because I knew I was on two stops and I didn't know what Ralf was on.'

After the race Ralf was so enraged he did not trust himself to speak.

Schumacher won in France and was second in Britain (to Häkkinen) so that he had 84 points, Coulthard 47. The Championship had become when, not if – although not at Hockenheim, where he had a gear selection problem from the grid and Luciano Burti (Prost) helplessly ran into the back of him. Since Coulthard didn't finish – a mechanical problem – the points remained the same.

A race and a Championship were compressed into a few seconds one August afternoon and, when it was done, Schumacher found this compression of words to describe it: 'A beautiful weekend.'

In those first few seconds he thrust his Ferrari from pole position to the first corner of the Hungaroring. This was more than taking the lead in the Hungarian Grand Prix, it was the decisive moment of the race and it would bring the World Championship with it. For the next hour and 41 minutes Schumacher circled essentially alone, at his own pace and in his own time. This was a master at the height of his art, smoothing the ferocity of a racing car into a great simplicity, soothing the turbulence of a Grand Prix into a processional thing, and utterly under his control. L'Equipe compressed that into a headline across their front page next day:

SCHUMI ALONE IN THE WORLD.

He was.

You cannot pretend that the Hungarian Grand Prix was a gripping race in any meaningful sense because Schumacher and Ferrari were now too good to permit anything like that.

They came to the Hungaroring, the 13th of the 17 rounds, with Schumacher on 84 points and Coulthard on 47, a differential so enormous that the Championship was no longer gripping in any meaningful sense either. Schumacher was going to win it somewhere, sometime. Here? Brawn – most shrewd reader of men, machines and moments – surveyed Schumacher and judged him to be in 'great shape'. The Championship pressure, Brawn concluded, had been passed from him to the others who have to try and catch him.

Schumacher confirmed how relaxed he felt, saying this 'wasn't a tactic to stop putting too much pressure on myself. It was just like that, not deliberate at all.' He even told Todt 'You know, I haven't got a very good feeling, I'm not sure that this is the weekend we'll do it.'

He chanced to meet Prost, now running his own team, the day before the race and Prost told him to win. Prost had held the record number of victories, 51, since 1993 and was 'bored' having to talk endlessly about it. Schumacher, having to talk endlessly about beating it, replied 'I feel exactly the same.' Schumacher had 50. This was really what the Hungaroring was about: not just a World Championship but helping to establish Schumacher's place in history.

Jo Ramirez, McLaren's team co-ordinator and fiercely proud of the team, pointed out that 'Alain had, I think, 30 wins when he was with us.' Out of loyalty to what Prost achieved at McLaren, Ramirez told him 'Michael is very close to breaking your record and we are going to do everything in our power to stop him doing it this year...'

Schumacher established a mood by going fastest on the

Friday. Coulthard was tenth: 'I hit the kerb at an unfortunate angle, damaging the chassis' in the first of the two sessions, he said, so couldn't drive in the second.

On the Saturday, Schumacher required only two runs. Moving towards the half hour, Häkkinen held provisional pole with 1m 15.41. Schumacher forced that to 1m 14.41 and it stayed there until, with 20 minutes to go, he forced it to 1m 14.05. This was itself a compression of a lap, to which he brought so much balance and so much speed that, as someone observed, it appeared to defy physics. Coulthard produced a forceful lap to join him on the front row but 0.801 seconds slower. This is what such a gap really represented set against the preceding five years:

1996 (Schumacher from Hill)	0.05
1997 (Schumacher from Villeneuve)	0.1
1998 (Häkkinen from Coulthard)	0.1
1999 (Häkkinen from Coulthard)	0.1
2000 (Schumacher from Coulthard)	0.3
Now...	0.8

'It's the result of a perfect lap,' Schumacher said, 'and a car that was already 100% in the morning. I only did six laps' – out lap, fast lap, in lap, twice – 'but not to save tyres. I just felt I had got the maximum out of myself and the car so it was better to sit rather than waste effort.'

Brawn judged this 'an exceptional performance from Michael. The fact that he won the Championship last year has made this season less stressful for him. I have seen no signs of pressure.'

He'd had the car through a gravel trap on the warm-up lap – at Turn 12, the right-hander before the left-loop and the pits – and that stirred a flurry of activity from the mechanics when he'd settled it on the bay for pole.

He led them round on the parade lap knowing that historically he who reaches Turn 1 in the lead can commandeer and then command the race from there. At the instant the five red lights blinked off Schumacher was away, Barrichello working a path in behind him and going over to the right, masking Turn 1 from Coulthard. Schumacher, ahead, fled – free.

Barrichello rode shotgun behind, masking Coulthard from the whole maddening point-and-squirt circuit. Completing the opening lap Schumacher siphoned a lead of 1.3 seconds, next lap 1.3 then 1.3, 1.2, 1.4. On lap 7 it was 1.3, Coulthard hammering out fastest lap after fastest lap but still Barrichello stayed ahead of him. On lap 9 Barrichello cut the gap to Schumacher to 0.9 seconds.

The received wisdom – born, nurtured and confirmed during Schumacher's decade of Grand Prix racing – was that if you gave him the lead you didn't see him again, never mind cut gaps. Here at the Hungaroring he was happy to go round and round preserving his tyres, as he would say, 'for later', and when he was satisfied that he was doing that he simply accelerated. The fractions are important to underscore how it happened.

On lap 11 he set fastest lap and made the lead 2.7 (Coulthard at 3.4), on lap 12 it was 3.4 – fastest lap again – and out it went, to 4.1, 4.4, 5.3 (fastest lap). On lap 16 he broke Mansell's track record set in 1992. By the posture of the Ferrari on the track you would never have known Schumacher had just done such a thing, because this was the control of a master: to settle himself and the car down and, when he was ready, to increase his pace to the point where nobody else could stay with it while never looking faster.

The rest passed into history itself, Schumacher pitting and regaining the lead, repeating this at the second pit stops then cantering it. He'd say that 'later in the race' Barrichello 'gave me a lot of pressure'. He'd add that 'towards the end I was worried about making a mistake because one car was leaving oil on the track.' He needn't have worried. He did not permit himself to think he would take the Championship until three laps from the end when 'now this has the feeling of it being here, truly!' He won it by four seconds and on the slowing down lap said on the radio to the team it was 'amazing. It is so lovely to work with you guys.'

Coulthard finished third.

'I might be a good driver but I am not good at finding the right words to describe this,' Schumacher said. He paid due tribute to the team. 'They are wonderful guys and we have stuck together through the good and the bad times and I am really in love with all of them.'

He was now level with Prost in Championships and only Ascari had ever won back-to-back Championships with Ferrari, in 1952–3. Several factors helped Ascari, apart from the fact that he was a superb driver. The Ferrari proved to be the dominant car in both seasons and Fangio was absent in 1952. Ascari, moreover, was competing against small fields and many of the drivers were known for competence rather than conquest. Arguably, Schumacher had had it tougher against Häkkinen and Coulthard at McLaren, and brother Ralf and Juan-Pablo Montoya at resurgent Williams.

The Hungaroring represented a compression within a compression because, in a very real sense, the whole of 2001 had been that.

There remained Belgium, Italy, the USA, and Japan.

At Spa he won a bizarre race when both Williamses ahead had problems at the start (and restart) but the next two races were pitched into shadows and personal questioning. The terrorist attack on the twin towers in New York was on 11 September, Monza on 16 September. Schumacher felt in no mood to celebrate the World Championship. He questioned aloud the wisdom of going to the United States Grand Prix – Indianapolis on 30 September – and, just before the race at

Monza, tried to persuade the drivers to go in grid order through the first two chicanes after the red lights as a safety precaution. He finished the race fourth and went quietly away. Evidently he had even considered retirement from Formula One.

They all did go to Indianapolis and he finished second. It scarcely seemed to interest him and mentally he was somewhere else. That didn't apply to Suzuka in mid-October where he lifted willpower and race-craft to a new level in qualifying. He made three qualifying runs and each of them would have been ample for pole. The third run – which of course he had no need to make and appeared a gesture of personal satisfaction – became a mesmeric thing. He danced the Ferrari through Suzuka's 18 curves, corners and chicane, danced it for 3.6 miles. This wasn't rock'n'roll, wasn't disco, it had the elegance of a ballroom quickstep, each precise movement flowing into the next. It lasted 1m 32.48 – Montoya next, 1m 33.18.

Breathless, the team announced: 'Eleventh pole position of the season for Ferrari and Michael Schumacher, a season record for both the team and driver. This is Michael's 43rd career pole, his sixth at Suzuka. It is the team's 148th pole, the fifth at this event.' In strictly Ferrari terms, the 11 beat the nine of Schumacher in 2000, Lauda in 1974 and again in 1975. The 11 was still short of Mansell (14, 1992), Senna (13, 1988 and 1989), and Prost (13, 1993). It equalled Häkkinen's 11 in 1999.

At the start of the race he moved diagonally across, blocking Montoya, and took the racing line through Turn One. Schumacher shed Montoya and…well, you know the story.

He had now scored more Grand Prix points – 801 – than Prost's 798.5. He had 123 points in the season, beating the record of 108 he held with Mansell. It was all 'the perfect end to the season'.

By nature, Rory Byrne is a quiet man who rarely goes to the races. Like many genuine artists (and a Formula One designer is certainly that) he prefers to let what he creates speak for itself. This, however, is his summary of the 2001 season, exquisite in its brevity and simplicity.

'Michael was under real pressure when he came second in the Championship in 1997, second in 1998 and then had the crash at Silverstone in 1999. It meant that the pressure went on to 2000. Since then, when that particular pressure came off, he's been driving even better. The 2001 Championship wasn't as easy as it might have looked. What helped us was our reliability, which the opposition lacked. They could perhaps match us for speed but not reliability. I think what has happened at Ferrari is important for Formula One. I was in South Africa recently [at the end of the 2001 season] and the interest and enthusiasm was genuinely unbelievable. That's when you realise.'

Ferrari hadn't gone global because they had always been that.

What they were now was a bigger global presence than they had ever been.

Chapter 10

TOTAL DOMINATION

On the evening of 21 July 2002, the compression on the season was more intense even than 2001. In another way it was – forgive me – absurd. The French Grand Prix had been the 11th round of the 17. When Schumacher won it he took the World Championship not just with the six races but three months to spare.

He stood level with Fangio's five.

From Australia at the beginning of March he'd put together this sequence: victory, third and pole, victory, victory and pole, victory and pole, victory, second, victory, second, victory, victory. Consider three aspects. On the way to France he had won all but three races and his lowest place was third in Malaysia where, after a crash with Montoya on the opening lap, he had been 23rd. He had only the three poles while in Austria, Monaco, the European and British he hadn't even been on the front row. He and the Ferrari F-2002 had reached the point where they were massacring even the importance of grid positions. He set only three fastest laps and clearly would have had more if he'd cared to but – why risk that if it is no more than a luxury?

Confining ourselves to recent years, here are the number of rounds that drivers took to win the Championship:

1990 and 1991	Senna	15/16
1992	Mansell	11/16

1993	Prost	14/16
1994	Schumacher	16/16
1995	Schumacher	15/17
1996	Hill	16/16
1997	Villeneuve	17/17
1998 and 1999	Häkkinen	16/16
2000	Schumacher	16/17
2001	Schumacher	13/17
2002	Schumacher	11/17

The season began quietly enough, with Luca Badoer and Luciano Burti, the test drivers, lapping Barcelona on 8 January. Schumacher first drove at Fiorano on 14 January. The traditional build-up had begun. Schumacher first drove the new car, the F2002, at Fiorano in early February and said it was 'very promising.'

The drivers in the leading teams:

BAR – Villeneuve, Panis.
Ferrari – Schumacher, Barrichello.
McLaren – Coulthard, Kimi Räikkönen.
Renault – Trulli, Button.
Williams – R. Schumacher, Montoya.

They took the old car to Melbourne and on the first day Schumacher and Barrichello were the only ones in the 1.27s, which prompted Brawn to say, 'Of course, the other teams are running new cars which might have more potential than ours, but I think we will be competitive.' Barrichello took pole from Schumacher, who said 'the lap that counted for my grid position could have been better because I went off onto the grass' and added, with a nice line of humour and understatement, that funnily enough there wasn't much grip there.

A chaotic start to the race, with much crashing at the first corner. 'I didn't see everything,' Schumacher said, 'except that cars were flying everywhere.' The afternoon settled, Schumacher versus debutant Montoya in the Williams, and it finished like that.

Australia: Front row, First, 10 points: Next, Montoya, 6 points

Ferrari did not take the new car to Malaysia, where on the Friday Schumacher was third and on the Saturday took pole and said 'maybe I could have gone quicker if I had waited to the very end of the session, but we chose to start my last run at the time we did because it seemed the best moment to avoid the traffic.' Montoya was alongside. Schumacher finished the race third, although that was not without controversy because at the first corner he and Montoya bumped. 'Maybe Juan could have given me more room but he chose not to and we just touched. That's racing.'

Malaysia: Pole, Third, 14 points: Next, Montoya, 12 points

Schumacher was understood to be pushing hard for the new car for Brazil. Two days after Malaysia, Barrichello drove it for the first time, covering 78 laps round Barcelona. Two days after that Schumacher did 70 laps, next day a full race distance of 85 laps. Nobody doubted the F2002's speed nor, now, its reliability. They'd take it to Sao Paulo. On the Friday there he was fifth – 'we are learning all the time' – and next day put it on the front row (Montoya pole). He won the race although Montoya claimed he chopped him. Montoya was attacking and Schumacher did move across to defend. Montoya had to pit and was very unhappy afterwards, particularly since Schumacher wasn't punished. Montoya made dark noises about the future, Brawn appealed for calm, and Schumacher said 'I went for the inside line to leave him the outside.'

Brazil: Row 1, First, 24 points: Next, R. Schumacher, 16 points

Imola was as straightforward as it gets, Schumacher fastest on the wet Friday from Barrichello and pole from Barrichello, who 'really pushed me. When I start the race, I will have competed in more races for Ferrari than any other driver. That means a lot to me because it shows the mutual confidence we have.' He led every lap except two – refuelling – and beat Barrichello by 17.90 seconds. 'There are many reasons to be proud today. We failed here last year and now we have given something back to the *tifosi*. It was a special Grand Prix for me and I'm proud of the way it went. It was right that Rory Byrne should be on the podium. He is unique, very motivated and a great person. We did not expect to be so dominant. Bridgestone has produced a tyre that is more consistent and although the win was down to the whole package it was mainly due to the tyres. We will enjoy a glass of champagne to celebrate but at this early stage in the season we are already thinking about the next race in Spain and we start testing again on Tuesday.'

San Marino: Pole, First, 34 points: Next, R. Schumacher, 20 points

Spain was straightforward, too. He went quickest on the Friday and Saturday, from Barrichello, and he 'enjoyed this session and the fight with Rubens. It was a challenge, especially as he was quicker on the first two runs. I looked at his sector and corner times to see where I could improve. Sometimes you think you are going flat out and your team-mate shows you that you are not.' He raced the spare (his had a hydraulic problem) and said, 'Although I was out in front I was not bored.' This was because, near the end, he had come up behind Frentzen and watched him battle with Felipe Massa (Sauber) for fifth place. Schumacher led every one of the 65 laps – meaning he didn't lose the lead even during his two pit stops.

Spain: Pole, First, 44 points: Next, Montoya, 23 points

Austria convulsed Formula One. To dispense with the preliminaries: Barrichello, from pole, drove a magnificent race, Schumacher following him home. As they approached the finishing line Barrichello suddenly slowed, as he had been ordered to do on the radio, gifting it to Schumacher. The margin, 0.182 seconds, had no meaning.

The aftermath was ugly. Howls of protest mingled with cat calls greeted Schumacher on the podium while the crowd, the media, and no doubt a hundred million tele-viewers prepared to vilify Ferrari. That Schumacher refused to mount the top step of the podium, vacating it for Barrichello, seemed a gesture of contrition or a recognition of natural justice.

'I take no joy from this victory,' he said. 'I enjoyed the race but not the last hundred metres. Only at the end was I called on the radio and told Rubens would move over. I know the decision is not popular but imagine if we had lost the Championship by this number of points at the end of the season. The team would look stupid in that situation.'

Going into Austria, Schumacher had 44 points then Montoya 23, Ralf 20, Barrichello (sixth) 6. If Barrichello had been allowed to keep the Austrian win the Championship would have been Schumacher 52, Montoya 27, Ralf 23.

Team orders deciding a race was nothing new and you can postulate that, since many teams have had official No 1 and No 2 drivers, they intended to decide in which order their drivers finished. Inevitably it brought controversy as well as condemnation from those who, gazing into a sport they did not understand, assumed it betrayed some pure sporting ethos. Perhaps Frank Williams expressed this conflict best when he said that Grand Prix racing is sport for an hour and a half on a Sunday and business the rest of the time. It is more than multinationals at play, however. As I've said, Grand Prix racing is uniquely about winning, finishing second *really is* failure, and – even though some purists disagree – the Championship *really is* what it's all about (Drivers' and Constructors'). So the teams control their drivers to protect the team's chances of winning, and since the drivers are their employees, legally bound, the teams are fully entitled to do that.

The criticism against Ferrari in Austria was that they had no need to protect their chances so early in the season and, even if they felt they did, it might have been executed with finesse rather than so blatantly – and bluntly – that the crowd expressed fury and the tele-viewers bafflement before reaching for their remote control buttons.

If these team orders are not exactly in the Olympic spirit, well, the teams will say, we are not competing in the Olympic Games…

Ferrari had long been owned by multinational Fiat and, however tempted you are to see Italy as a glorious fairground of emotions, some very sharp-eyed and numerate people at Fiat watched, even though di Montezemolo would claim that the team was 'self-financed' (through sponsorship and road car sales).

This same summer of 2002, Fiat were in financial difficulties and sold 34% of their Ferrari holding to an investment bank for £500 million, and that bank sold 10% on to another bank for £147m. We are talking big business, and who can doubt that Schumacher's Championships in the Ferrari were not a significant part of it?

Brawn summed it up when he said that, early in the season, 'we told the drivers we didn't want them racing. That's the nature of Formula One.'

On 12 May 2003, Schumacher had to face it out at the Press Conference afterwards. Normally these are so mechanical that you'd swear it was a puppet show. Now, the Press Conference alive, Schumacher could be nothing but defensive and refused to answer the final three questions, which were: *Isn't this a sport? Do you want to win because you are the best driver or have the best contract? If it's a team sport, why have individual champions?*

I think Schumacher conducted himself with admirable tact, restraint and dignity, because *he* didn't ask for team orders, he was informed of the corporate decision and by implication *he* was ordered to go by when Barrichello pulled over. Should he have said *no*? Which employee thinks like that when a vast team effort of $200m (or whatever) and all those people is in play, the Fiat bean counters are counting, and what if you do lose the Championship by a point? How would disobedience play then?

'Rubens,' he said, 'did a superb job and he outpaced me all weekend.' There were many other things Schumacher could have said. Silence was better.

Austria: Row 2, First, 54 points: Next, Montoya, 27 points

At Monaco, he qualified third and finished second behind Coulthard. 'I kept pushing right to the end because in Monaco you never know what can happen, but David drove well and never gave me a chance.'

Monaco: Row 2, Second, 60 points: Next, R. Schumacher, Montoya, 27 points

Montoya took pole in Canada, Schumacher next to him. Schumacher was on a one-stop strategy – Barrichello and Montoya two – and ran third behind them until the stops. Montoya retook the lead when Schumacher finally pitted (lap 38) and led to his second stop. After that he hunted Schumacher and was beginning to catch him when, on lap 57, the engine let go. 'I kept a good pace because we knew Montoya was on a two-stop but I could not ease up until I knew I would be in front of him after his second stop.'

It was Ferrari's 150th win, and Schumacher – with Fangio's five firmly in view – uncharacteristically moved into history. He described Fangio's feat as 'incomparable. I have a lot of respect for what he did, and I think that what we are doing now doesn't even come close to it.'

Canada: Row 1, First, 70 points: Next, R. Schumacher, Montoya, 27 points

By something approaching irony, Barrichello had a very good European Grand Prix at the Nürburgring, leading every lap with

Schumacher behind him virtually the whole way. 'Why was Rubens not asked to let me by? The situation was very different to Austria. Now we are in a much stronger position.' Both Todt and Brawn confirmed that this was the team's thinking although, on the eve of Ferrari appearing before the FIA's World Council over Austria, Brawn added that they would continue to apply team orders if they felt it desirable.

Europe: Row 2, Second, 76 points: Next, R. Schumacher, 30 points

The World Council met in Paris, heard evidence and could not find a way of punishing Ferrari except for the podium offence of Barrichello being on the top step. They were fined £320,000 for this.

Schumacher qualified third at Silverstone, Montoya pole and leading the race until rain fell. The drivers pitted and, of the two tyre companies, Bridgestone was the one to have – Brawn decided on intermediates. With them Schumacher was several seconds a lap quicker than Montoya and overtook him on lap 16. The race was over (although Barrichello, starting from the back of the grid after a problem on the warm-up lap, finished second). France was next.

Britain: Row 2, First, 86 points: Next, Barrichello, 32 points

Between Silverstone and Magny-Cours he tested improvements to the Ferrari at Fiorano. On one day he did 107 laps with a best time of 57.47s, some 0.8 of a second faster than his own lap record. He said he wanted to 'get the title off our backs as soon as possible.' To do that he needed to win France with Montoya and Barrichello no higher than third.

He qualified on the front row (Montoya pole) and spoke in guarded terms about the race. 'I think it will be much closer than the last ones.'

Every race which can decide a Championship bears within it an inherent element of drama. Small moments have big consequences. As the cars moved off on the formation lap Barrichello – second row – sat immobile, his Ferrari up on its jacks. The mechanics had been unable to fire the engine up and Barrichello was out.

As the red lights went off Montoya made the better start, carving across to keep Schumacher behind him and they moved out into the country like that, Räikkönen third. Schumacher laid heavy pressure on Montoya and they duelled, Räikkönen trying to search out an opening as they did. Montoya stretched away and, as was the way in modern Grand Prix racing, the three ran equidistant towards the first pit stops.

Montoya pitted on lap 24 and the stop took 8.4 seconds stationary. Schumacher attacked the circuit for two laps and 1m 15.3, 1m 15.4 – Montoya 1m 15.9 on his lap exiting the pits. Schumacher pitted, 8.4 seconds stationary. As he emerged, Montoya was bearing down on him at ferocious speed. To get onto the track faster, Schumacher cut fractionally across the end of the white tramlines from the pits. He did hold Montoya, stretched away from him. Ten laps later Schumacher was given a 'drive-through' penalty for crossing the line. After it he emerged third behind Montoya and Räikkönen.

Schumacher thought *it's all over for here*. The Championship would have to wait until the next race, Germany.

He attacked Räikkönen because, thinking tactically, he needed Räikkönen behind him so that the second pit stops would be like the first: Schumacher gaining enough time on a clear track to regain the lead when the stops were done. Räikkönen resisted.

Montoya pitted, 11.6 seconds stationary. Five laps later Schumacher pitted, 8.8 seconds stationary. Räikkönen pitted, 8.7 seconds stationary, and emerged just in front of Schumacher, who swarmed all over him. Räikkönen, most phlegmatic of men, was unmoved. Montoya, meanwhile, struggled with the balance of the Williams and ran fourth, drifting back.

Schumacher 'took it a bit easy and then started to push with ten laps to go.' On lap 68 of 72 he was close and at the Adelaide hairpin Räikkönen turned in very deep – he'd slithered on oil left by the Toyota of McNish, which had just expired. Räikkönen got the McLaren back on but by then Schumacher was through.

'Seeing him in trouble helped to warn me,' Schumacher would say. 'That's why I was able to change my line.' He had a moment or two of alarm when he realised he'd overtaken Räikkönen under a yellow flag and *before* he reached a green flag. He would not be punished for this.

The final laps were 'the worst of my life because I realised the Championship was again in my pocket. I had a weight on my shoulders and felt enormous pressure not to make a mistake.'

He didn't.

'As I took the flag I felt an outburst of emotion and realised how much it means and how I love the sport.'

France: Row 1, First, 96 points: Next, Montoya, 34 points

He faced all the microphones in the paddock and confessed, his face betraying bemusement, that he felt so emotional he wasn't quite sure what to say.

L'Equipe compressed that perfectly with a headline across their front page above a photograph of Schumacher, arms raised, mouth seeming to bay in triumph.

ALONE WITH FANGIO.

'I don't want to get into comparisons,' Schumacher said when somebody mentioned Fangio, but Lauda was quite prepared to get into them and did. Schumacher, Lauda insisted, was the greatest of all.

Schumacher could have regarded the rest of 2002 as anti-climactic, gone through the motions and gathered strength for 2003, but that wasn't his level. This was: victory in Germany, second in Hungary, victory in Belgium, second in Italy, second in the USA, and victory in Japan. No other driver had ever been on the podium after every race of a season. His 11 victories were a record, beating his own nine (1995, 2000, 2001), a record he'd shared with Mansell (1992). His points total of 144 beat his own record, 123, set the season before. His winning margin – 67 – over the next man, Barrichello, beat his own record of 58 set the season before.

He had 64 wins, Prost next on 51. He had 945 points, Prost next on 798.5. He had 50 pole positions, only 15 behind Senna's absolute record. More than all that, he'd said when he won in France that 'it is not records that challenge me, it is the races. I do not feel I have achieved everything I want in my life and I will carry on treating each race as a new challenge.'

He would take that philosophy, undiluted, into 2003.

Extensive rule changes were introduced to shake the whole thing up and that made Schumacher's attempt on Fangio's monument much more interesting. Qualifying became a one-run shoot-out, and the cars had on board the fuel they'd start the race with. The points were extended and bunched (10-8-6-5-4-3-2-1), the 2 points from first to second making it more difficult for Schumacher to romp into the distance. Team orders were banned and electronic aids due to be phased out by Silverstone. Brawn would say, discussing the rule changes, that 'nothing... favoured Ferrari one jot. There wasn't one decision in our interests. We were dominating Formula One, we had everything together, a good way of working and it all got turned upside down.'

Even so, when the new Ferrari – the F2003-GA – was launched it seemed to be the next step forward.

Spring comes earlier to the Emilia Romagna district than it does to more northerly outposts, and a welcoming sun warmed Maranello for the launch soon before the season began. Maranello looks typical Italian but you can *feel* Ferrari's presence and half the shops seem to have – or be selling – memorabilia, while the other half would like to be. One garden even has tyres for ornaments.

Imagine a broad, grassy area with a cluster of older buildings to the left (where Ferrari had his office) and the test track (and

Shell petrol station) unfolding beyond; to the right an enormous, modern building: a kind of adaptable conference centre. It has a couple of Ferrari Enzos parked outside, casually, and for a moment you understand that however rare these prehensile cars (think $1m each) are anywhere else in the world, here they make them and...well, there are probably lots about.

That sets a tone.

Everything for the next two hours was organised precisely, choreographed, timed, and when you reached the Enzos they weren't parked casually but equidistant and in line – and (of course) both red. There was, however, an undercurrent of sadness, because Agnelli, who ran Fiat and was a motor racing enthusiast, died in January.

Inside the conference centre the unveiling is literally theatre: there's a stage with the car camouflaged by a red canopy, and there are the actors, each dressed in the uniform of Ferrari lounge-suit semi-casual, Todt and Brawn (who makes a speech in Italian) and Byrne and Martinelli. Todt makes a brief speech and the veiled car begins to rotate slowly. As it does, spotlights in the ceiling come on, projecting onto the stage two prancing horses which rotate at exactly the same speed as the car.

Schumacher and Barrichello perform the unveiling to applause and there, suddenly, is the car. Byrne would say: 'Last year I predicted that the F2002 would prove to be the best Ferrari F1 car ever and it proved to be the most successful. We have not yet run the F2003 but so far all our performance objectives have been reached or exceeded, so I am confident the F2003-GA will be the best Ferrari F1 car ever.'

Afterwards the media are divided by language into mini-conference rooms and the key personnel visit each in rotation so that everyone gets a chance to question everyone.

The Brits have Todt first, and people familiar with political Press Conferences will recognise the way it went.

Is it in your mind that Schumacher's going to get past Fangio and maybe past Ayrton's poles and set records we have never seen before?

'We love the driver, we love him, we love the team and it's a good combination. I think he will never drive for any other team and as long as he wants to drive for Ferrari we will be proud to have him at Ferrari.'

But do you see him beating Fangio?

'Well...'

The subject of whether the new rules would favour Schumacher was raised.

'We inhabit our little world which is Formula One,' Todt says, and adds: 'When more is being expected of the driver, the one driver you'd think would be able to give more is Michael Schumacher. I think it will not have a direct effect because if you drive in Formula One I am sure you will be able to manage with less driver aids. When I see Michael with the steering wheel like this [full lock] I am always terrified because I know he is going to the limit of the car ...'

Then Brawn, in good form. 'Did you,' he inquires, 'understand my Italian?'

To which someone says, 'Did you?'

'No!'

That got a roar of laughter.

'We can't predict what is going to happen this year, we can only work hard. It's a little frustrating for the rules to be changed five weeks before the season because engineers like certainty, but if it's good for Formula One we welcome it. We know that at the moment it is a new challenge. With regard to driver gizmos, then certainly Michael is not complaining.'

Then Barrichello, sparkling, eyes wide open with pleasure whenever he discusses the car. He only saw it for the first time the night before and speaks of the moment in the sort of language lovers use.

Then Schumacher: the familiar presence, familiar face,

familiar intonations and familiar caution. He wears racing overalls zipped up to his neck, each decal present and correct.

You were excited by last year's car but this one is something special isn't it?

'Yes. Very special, yes.'

Are you surprised the team has been able to make such a big step over last year, which everyone thought was close to perfection?

'The question of whether the step is big or not is to be proved right now. I am surprised that they have been able to make so many changes – which, actually, they do for the better – and have made it so nice. I mean for me it is something very, very special, although last year it was special already.'

Michael, Luca [di Montezemolo] spoke of the emotion of the Ferrari launch. You've been here for a few years now. What is for you the emotion of seeing the Ferrari?

'Obviously I had the pleasure of seeing the car last night and it's something unique and you will not experience it anywhere else. Today though there was a completely different emotion around because of the death of Gianni Agnelli and you could feel that everywhere: not over-emotional and excited, rather everything a little bit down by showing respect. It's something I'm very proud of, to have known Gianni Agnelli as closely as I did. We worked together with him and got his support.'

You've seen the car. Is it realistic to think of the Championship?

'It's never realistic to think like that upfront but I feel – because we have to start with the old car, and we have a good old car – it should give us important points at the beginning of the season. Then the new car, hopefully, gives us another step forward. You have seen with the [pre-season] testing it has been much closer than people may have expected after last year. You have to anticipate that McLaren is coming with Mercedes with their new car in whatever time, so it's going to be very important that we do a good job to be able to fight for it again.'

You're on the verge of beating Fangio. Jean Todt was very diplomatic about it. You can break all sorts of records. Sometimes you say these are not important to you, sometimes they seem important. What do you really think about that?

'For me it's not a goal now that I feel I am going to beat this particular record. For me it's much more important to show the respect and get the results for the hard work that everybody is doing in the team.'

Don't you really think about that at all in your private moments?

'I am proud of the achievement in terms of what we have been able to do, but to compare it in the way you think I may – no.'

Those were my questions and they were certainly not intended to trick him. I was curious to know because he had dedicated his life to Grand Prix racing and was now within reach of becoming the most successful driver – using the World Championship as the measure – of all time. And, although presumably he spent every minute of every working day thinking about the car, the team, the races and the Grand Prix world generally, he said he did not think about becoming the most successful.

I was so charged with astonishment and scepticism that we played who-will-blink-first, and it only ended when someone asked:

What do you think about qualifying?

'The qualifying thing is going to be an entertaining situation and, I think, for the betterment of the show. We are going to have a few surprises because here and there people will make mistakes. The rules from Silverstone onwards – well, I'm not a big fan of it because I like the electronic challenge you have. It simply allows you to get the car much closer to perfection and not have to move around with all the compromises which you have to without the electronic systems. In this respect I am not going to look forward to it but on the other side everybody has it and I don't mind if everybody is the same. I see it as much

ABOVE: *Walking on water. Schumacher's first win for Ferrari, in Spain in 1996. He goes past Gerhard Berger.*

BELOW: *Mayhem on the first lap of the 1997 Argentine Grand Prix, with Schumacher among the victims.*

LEFT: *The other side of Schumacher, discreet charity work worldwide – here with young landmine victims in Sarajevo* (Willi Schneider/Rex Features).

BELOW LEFT: *Jerez, the loneliest place in the world after he'd crashed into Villeneuve in 1997. It brought him widespread condemnation and cost him the Championship.*

BELOW: *Axis of strength: Schumacher and Jean Todt, the mastermind behind the rejuvenation of Ferrari. They showed solidarity in all circumstances including this, the FIA inquiry over the 1997 crash with Villeneuve.*

ABOVE: *Japan 1998. He stalled on pole, started from the back of the grid and locked up making his way through the field. It was another title lost.*

BELOW: *Schumacher crashed at Stowe corner at the start of the 1999 British Grand Prix and broke his leg.*

ABOVE: *The third championship, Suzuka, 8 October 2000, with one race to go. He beat Mika Häkkinen by 19 points.*

BELOW: *Brothers in arms: Ralf and Michael.*

RIGHT: *Defying gravity on the podium after clinching his fourth drivers' title and Ferrari's third consecutive constructors' championship.*

ABOVE: *The fourth championship, the Hungaroring, 19 August 2001, taken with four races to spare. He'd beaten David Coulthard by an extraordinary 58 points.*

BELOW: *The fifth championship, Magny-Cours, 21 July 2002, won with six races still in hand. Fangio's record of five world titles, which was going to stand unequalled forever, didn't.*

Home in Vufflens-le-Chateau, Switzerland – far from the madding crowds.

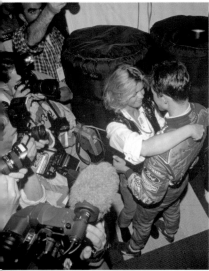

ABOVE: *The seventh championship, Spa, 29 August 2004. He was now so dominant that it threatened the wellbeing of Grand Prix racing. People were getting bored. He beat team-mate Rubens Barrichello by 34 points – and by contract Barrichello wasn't allowed to beat him!*

BELOW: *Farewell, 2004 – with a practice crash at the final race, Brazil.*

LEFT: *The body language of anger after crashing with Takuma Sato of BAR early in the 2005 Belgian Grand Prix. It was a barren season. He finished only third in the championship, with 62 points to Fernando Alonso's 133 and Kimi Räikkönen's 112.*

BELOW: *Monza, 10 September 2006, announcing the retirement – much anticipated but still somehow sombre. The Schumacher era was ending. But the driver who had in turns horrified and inspired Grand Prix enthusiasts so many times over the years would not be going quietly.*

better for the smaller teams to have possibilities to score points rather than to change anything up front.'

This answer compounded my astonishment, because he felt free to be eloquent about a safe topic – offering his judgement about qualifying – in exactly the opposite way to offering anything much at all about the Championships.

After Silverstone will the rule changes sort the men from the boys in terms of seeing which are the good drivers and which are the not so good drivers? Do you feel that strengthens your ability to win the Championship?

'No. Certainly not. Because I don't agree with this sort of saying – it will simply not change as much. The only area it will change is for young, inexperienced drivers who at the moment seem not to have many troubles jumping in to a Formula One car and driving at least at a certain pace. You now have the possibility of making a very safe car because you can set the traction control to a very safe target and then you go around – not very fast, but without problems and people think they are fast. I feel without the traction control you increase again some sort of danger as well, because in rain the traction control can be very helpful in keeping the car on the road, especially with the one-tyre rule this year.'

Would you like a season which was a little closer than last year or are you tired of winning the races as you do?

'No, I am not tired. There have been a couple of races which haven't been the biggest challenge but I am quite happy to take them. It's my 12th year and I've had one season out of 12 like last year so why not have a little bit more of it?'

What is it like to hear other drivers being told that they've got to be more like Michael Schumacher, put in the hours, ring the factory, be more dedicated, fitter and so on?

'Well I think it creates problems for people who have said this because they'll probably be disturbed every night! Whether it helps we'll find out…' [Laughter.]

What do you think of radio communication being broadcast, like in America?

'We are not America and we are not Champ car racing and therefore you will not have, I think, as much use of it as you think. You see Ralf, he hardly talks on the radio. He takes off his helmet and he only talks to his engineer because he doesn't want to be listened to. Naturally everybody doesn't want to be listened to either for important information.'

Has Ralf given any indications about what he feels about the new Williams yet?

'You know, he keeps his mouth as closed as concrete. [Gives little laugh] No, he doesn't say anything.'

Do you still see Rubens being your main challenger this year or do you see this year really is going to be more mixed up?

'It depends very much where McLaren will end up. If they end up very close to us then we're going to have the McLaren drivers *and* Rubens. Rubens will certainly be a big challenge. We have seen in winter testing and last year that he is a bloody fast racing driver. To me it's big challenge to keep the upper hand.'

How conscious are you that Formula One needs to put on a good show? People want to see competition, a race.

'You have maybe in some countries a reduction of interest in Formula One. Whether that's to do with the so-called not-so-good show – which I feel isn't sometimes so different to what it was in '98 and other seasons – I don't know. You have other countries where there is an increase in interest. It is clear that certain changes have been made to improve the show and I think they will achieve their goal. Whether that is achieved consistently or not depends on the competition coming from the other teams. If they do their job we are going to have interesting races all the time. If not then it will be only several times.'

But your priority remains to win it as easily as possible?

'That's what I aim to do.'

Is your motivation as high now as it was when you came in to the sport?

'No! [Laughter] It's very hot here.'

Can I ask you one quick question?

'You don't have to wear overalls!'

…with logos on…

'Exactly' [laughing].

Will there at all be any sense of disappointment if you don't match what you did this last year?

'No, I don't expect to match what we did last year. It would be too much to think we could do it again.'

So there won't be a sense of disappointment?

[Softly] 'No.'

But you'll still have achieved a lot.

'For me it's important to achieve the Championship and if it is in the last race or it is in the middle of the season – well, it's more comfortable to do it earlier but it's the same goal.'

Schumacher drove the car for the first time at Fiorano on 11 February, covered 78 laps and pronounced himself happy. It was due to make its Grand Prix debut at Imola, fourth race of the season.

The drivers in the leading teams:

BAR – Villeneuve, Button.
Ferrari – Schumacher, Barrichello.
McLaren – Coulthard, Räikkönen.
Renault – Trulli, Fernando Alonso.
Williams – Montoya, R. Schumacher.

Australia went wrong although Schumacher took pole. As it seems, Ferrari didn't make the right tyre choice – the weather distinctly mixed – and he hit a kerb hard enough to damage the car. He finished fourth. The question reared whether to bring the new car to Malaysia. Brawn rejected that, saying that what happened during the Melbourne race would have happened regardless of which car they had.

Schumacher qualified third in Malaysia and finished the race sixth, a lap down. 'It was a tough race with an unfortunate start. I made a mistake and hit Jarno [Trulli] and I have apologised to him. That was the decisive moment.' This happened on the second corner and 'it came as a big surprise that I was still able to drive for points after the drive-through penalty, so I am happy enough in the circumstances.'

He qualified seventh in Brazil but, a wet race, aquaplaned into a crash. Significantly he said: 'The gap to the Championship leader' – Räikkönen 26 points, Schumacher 8 – 'is not so big, given there are still 13 races, so there is no need to be concerned about it.' For perspective he pointed out that 'this is my first non-finish since Hockenheim in 2001.' That, of course, was due to the reliability of the car as much as Schumacher's ability to keep it out of trouble.

The F-2003 did not go to Imola...

Instead, his mother critically ill in Germany, he flew to her bedside after taking pole for the San Marino Grand Prix. Ralf went with him. Their mother died.

They raced, and Schumacher won. Todt said, 'This was a special victory. Michael proved yet again, even to those who do not seem to accept it, that he is a special man. Despite being in mourning, he wanted to take part in this race for the sake of the team and went on to win it. Then, going on to the podium, he wanted to acknowledge all the team and our fans who love him as much as we do. We have gone through some very stressful moments and Michael appreciated the way the team supported him. It is at moments like these that the values we hold dear and cultivate in the team come to the fore.'

At this time the public broadcast television channel ZDF were preparing to set up (with BBC Worldwide) a series on the greatest German – the BBC had already done this with Britons.

Hitler and the Nazis proved a problem for ZDF, and viewers weren't allowed to vote for them. East German communists proved another problem because of the shoot-to-kill policy along the West German border and the Berlin Wall. One British newspaper, *The Daily Telegraph*, felt that sporting stars like Franz Beckenbauer, Boris Becker, Steffi Graf and Schumacher might 'out-poll the politicians' while no self-respecting newspaper overlooked the chance to carry a photograph of supermodel Claudia Schiffer while falling short of suggesting she had made a greater contribution than Einstein or Marx except visually. The results were due in November.

Schumacher did take the F-2003 to Spain, took pole and the race; took pole in Austria and won despite a cockpit fire at a pit stop. 'I could see the fire. Maybe the mechanics thought I was cold and wanted to warm me up! But the team did a good job to control the situation, reacting quickly with the extinguishers.'

Räikkönen still led the Championship with 40 points, Schumacher next on 38, Barrichello 26. Grand Prix racing was alive again, and more so after Monaco, where he qualified fifth and finished third. Montoya won, the fifth winner in seven races.

On 9 June, between Monaco and Canada, Ferrari announced that the senior executives in their team – Todt, Brawn, Martinelli, Byrne, head of engine design Gilles Simon, and Schumacher – would be staying until the end of the 2006 season. The assumption was that Schumacher would drive until then (rather than be an ambassador for the company, a technical adviser or whatever) and that put every leading Grand Prix record at his mercy.

He qualified third in Canada and won the race despite concerns about his brakes. 'I had to be careful to look after them so I did not push too hard at first. I only really pushed hard in the period around the pit stops.' Todt murmured that it had been an 'incredible race.'

He qualified second at the European Grand Prix at the Nürburgring (Räikkönen pole) and finished fifth after a 'moment' when Montoya took him at the hairpin on lap 43. He described the 'collision' as a 'straightforward racing incident. He was faster than me, tried to pass, and gave me just enough room to survive. Maybe I could have wished for a little bit more space but I have no problems with Juan Pablo over this.' Ralf won: Schumacher 58, Räikkönen 51, Ralf 43, Montoya and Alonso 39.

The new rules and the improvement of McLaren and Williams changed everything. Only the season before, Schumacher had gone to France leading Barrichello 86–32 and taken the Championship.

To emphasise the change, Ralf took France (Schumacher third) and Barrichello took Silverstone (Schumacher fourth) so that with five races left he had 69 points, Räikkönen 62, Montoya 55, Ralf 53, Barrichello 49. Schumacher was running second in Germany when a left rear tyre punctured with five laps to go. Montoya won and was now in prime form.

To further emphasise the change, Schumacher qualified eighth in Hungary and was beset by all manner of problems while Alonso won by commanding the race from the front. Schumacher finished eighth, a lap down. He'd spent 'a lot of time stuck behind a slower car.' Hungary was being viewed as a debacle within Ferrari because, too, Barrichello's left rear wheel suddenly came off.

The Championship had become Schumacher 72, Montoya 71, Räikkönen 70, Ralf 58. Schumacher said 'I love fighting', and said he still 'believed in our possibilities.' That could not disguise the fact that a sense of uncertainty – perhaps even a sense of self-doubt – was permeating Ferrari while such as Montoya and Räikkönen circled for the kill.

There were three weeks to the Italian Grand Prix and a major test session at Monza before it. Schumacher tested from 2

September (30 laps, setting the best time of the day at 1m 22.524s). Ralf crashed so heavily in the Williams that he was taken to hospital and, as it proved, that destroyed any lingering chance of the Championship he held.

Meanwhile the test session heated up. On 3 September Schumacher did 60 laps (best 1m 22.131s), next day 79 laps (1m 21.286s), the day after that 61 laps. Here are the final times (Marc Gene deputising for Ralf):

Schumacher	1m 20.730s
Barrichello	1m 20.850s
Montoya	1m 21.054s
Gene	1m 21.488s
Coulthard	1m 21.546s
Räikkönen	1m 21.710s

Schumacher drew, as he was entitled to do, confidence from the week at Monza. In his perceptive way he pointed out that up until the British Grand Prix, only three races back, the Ferrari had been 'the car to beat' so its intrinsic qualities were not in doubt. However 'we' – by implication the team as well as himself – didn't 'get everything' out of it in Germany or Hungary. He fully intended to do that in the Monza race, which might well be the fastest Grand Prix ever run.

Montoya was quickest on the Friday, from Barrichello and Schumacher. Qualifying on the Saturday distilled the season.

Räikkönen went fifth last and constructed a neat, self-contained lap which belied its speed.

The timing devices froze: 1m 21.466.

Cristiano da Matta (Toyota) provided something approaching light relief with 1m 22.914 before Schumacher took it on. He constructed a lap tightly held between precision and throwing the car. His first sector time (25.995s) was decisively ahead of Räikkönen's (26.202) and the Italian crowd adored that. Schumacher carried that speed through the second sector

343

(27.793, Räikkönen 28.021) and he pumped that up on the run for home.

The timing devices froze: 1m 20.963.

Barrichello went next and thought his brakes might not have 'been up to temperature'.

The timing devices froze: 1m 21.242.

Now Montoya, armed with the mighty BMW engine – and hadn't he set the fastest lap ever driven here last year? He forced the Williams to 25.992 on the first sector, and that was .003 quicker. He forced it to 27.720 on the second sector, and that was .073 quicker, but slight imprecision on his run for home cost him pole.

The timing devices froze: 1m 21.014.

To spare you the mental arithmetic, Schumacher had it by 0.051 over 3.6 miles (5.7km). 'We have turned the situation around,' he said, 'thanks to the hard work of everyone in the team and at the factory. Our President [di Montezemolo] has helped us to focus on the problems we experienced in the last two races, but we have not been put under any extra pressure here. We have made improvements to all areas of the car and Bridgestone has given us a very good tyre.'

The start at Monza is always unusually pressured because the surge from the grid to the first chicane is so long and wide, and the chicane itself so tight, despite reshaping and refining over the years. As the red lights blinked off Schumacher moved straight ahead and clear, Montoya on his right and pulling in behind as they reached the funnel. Schumacher went in too deep – 'I made a mistake' – and, even at this speed and with all this pressure, coldly weighed the option of short-cutting the chicane.

They went round the Rivazza horse-shoe like that, but into the second chicane – a left-right – Schumacher moved over to protect the racing line. He found Montoya outside him. Montoya squeezed *into* the corner so that Schumacher rode the kerbing, and Montoya moved ahead by half a car's length.

Montoya clipped a kerb and was pitched over towards Schumacher, squeezing him again, but the clip had given the impetus back to Schumacher. Coming out, Schumacher held mid-track and Montoya searched for a way back at him.

Schumacher described this as a 'good fight, hard and fair'.

Montoya would speak of making a good start, seeing the chance to try and pass 'but he had better acceleration than me. We competed cleanly – neither of us could afford not to finish.' Schumacher won it by five seconds.

It was, Schumacher judged (atypically), 'the greatest day of my career. It was a beautiful and emotional feeling on the podium. The result is also a relief. *We* believed in ourselves and we knew *we* could fight back. The Championship' – Schumacher 82, Montoya 79, Räikkönen 75 – 'is still very open. *We* have improved and *we* keep on improving. The engine guys have done a tremendous job and that should help us in the last two races.'

He and Corinna stopped off at Las Vegas on the way to the next race, the American at Indianapolis. 'We were invited to a show and it fitted in with things well. No one recognised me, except for a few European holidaymakers.' He took on the slot machines but only with small change, and even he didn't win.

Indianapolis ought to have favoured Montoya, who won the Indy 500 there in 2000, said the place felt like home and would have vociferous support from a large Colombian contingent in the crowd.

In first qualifying Schumacher was only eighth. He'd had to go first, the running order decided of course by the finishing positions at Monza. He judged this a disadvantage, 'especially after the rain which fell in the morning, which meant the track was a bit dirty and lacked grip.' Next day he qualified seventh and wasn't sure what had gone wrong or why it had gone wrong. Räikkönen had pole, Montoya fourth. This is how Schumacher rationalised it: 'At least seventh place is on the clean side of the track, which is better than being on the dirty inside line. In terms of the championship, my closest rival is only three places ahead of me, so this is not a disaster and with Kimi on pole the race is a bit more open now.'

The race was described by Todt as 'incredibly intense' and that's almost an understatement. Schumacher made a confident start and took fourth, ahead of Montoya. Räikkönen led. It was all deceptively normal – and then Montoya and Barrichello collided. Barrichello went off and couldn't get back on. 'We were running side by side. I thought I had left him enough space but he touched me and I spun.' At that moment rain began, bringing uncertainty with it.

On lap 4, Schumacher was still fourth and 3.8 seconds behind Räikkönen. Schumacher cut past Panis and Montoya charged. The rain was heavier and initially that favoured the cars with Michelin because their dry tyres were better in the wet than Bridgestone. Coulthard sailed past Schumacher, swiftly followed by Montoya and Alonso. The rain eased and stopped, and Montoya was under investigation by the Stewards for the Barrichello collision.

On lap 9, Schumacher was in sixth place and more than 11 seconds behind Räikkönen. He set fastest lap, Montoya's pit stop went wrong – a fuel rig failed – and rain fell again. By now the pit stops were coming in a flurry. Schumacher led briefly then pitted himself. 'We decided to stay with dry tyres but the rain got stronger as I came into the pit lane and I did suggest changing the choice. But it would have been too much of a mess so I came straight back in [next lap].'

Montoya got a drive-through penalty, and from that moment his Championship was over.

Schumacher was now on Bridgestone intermediates and they were absolutely superior to anything Michelin had. The conditions forced Räikkönen and Alonso in to change tyres and Schumacher prepared to seize the race. He was seventh, and that became sixth when he moved past Coulthard. He was 11 seconds away from the lead. He moved past Alonso and Justin Wilson (Jaguar) on the same lap. He caught Räikkönen and took him on the inside. He lapped Montoya, moved on Frentzen – but the rain was stopping. Schumacher swept inside Frentzen and was only four seconds from Button. He cut into that, tracked Button down the start-finish straight towards the right-hander, went out onto the *wet* part of the track and went by.

Button's car broke down so that when Räikkönen overtook Frentzen it was for second place, 18 seconds behind Schumacher. The Championship was still alive, although it had been reduced to a great simplicity. Räikkönen had to win the Japanese Grand Prix and Schumacher get no points.

At Suzuka in first qualifying he was third, Räikkönen fifth. Schumacher had to go first (again) because of the win at Indianapolis and judged that 'a slight disadvantage', so he was 'quite happy with my lap and my time.' Second qualifying proved a roulette wheel.

Montoya did 1:32.412 and Barrichello, next, did 1:31.713. That was fastest of the session and Alonso couldn't get near it. He did 1:33.044 – fifth. Drizzle fell, and Räikkönen took it on but the change in track conditions slowed him to 1:33.272 – seventh. Schumacher, impassive, watched a monitor from the cockpit deep within the Ferrari garage. Coulthard, next, took that seventh place from Räikkönen while Schumacher circled, preparing for his run. Everybody knew that the Bridgestone tyres did not like a track altering from dry to wet.

At the first split, just over half a minute in, Schumacher was 1.008 seconds off Barrichello's provisional pole time, an enormous difference in context; and 2.034 off at the second split, again enormous in context. He crossed the line in 1:34.302 – 14th. He hadn't been this far down a grid since Spa 1995. Räikkönen was eighth and said that at least Schumacher wasn't in front of him. Schumacher described the conditions as 'inconsistent' and the session as 'interesting. Everybody knows I love a challenge but [smile] it's an unpredictable challenge. We have to see the whole picture and having one car – Rubens – on the front row is ideal for us.'

From the lights the grid broke up on the long run towards turn one, Barrichello in the lead but Schumacher – over to the right – lost in the pack. As Barrichello turned in Schumacher was 13th, 12th out of turn one.

The race would be run in two distinct dimensions, far apart but constantly affecting each other. In one Räikkönen had to get up into the lead; in the other Schumacher had to get up into eighth.

Montoya attacked Barrichello and streamed past, streamed into the distance. At lap 2 he was 3.4 seconds ahead of Barrichello, Räikkönen sixth at 6.0.

Schumacher was still 12th but he had Wilson, Takumo Sato (BAR) and Mark Webber (Jaguar) within reach. Immediately he moved inside Wilson and advanced towards Sato. On lap 7 he made a hesitant attempt to squeeze past Sato into the final chicane and was never near to doing it. Sato turned in and Schumacher clipped the BAR's rear. He pitted for a new nosecone and was stationary for 18.1. The Championship had been brutally wrenched open. He rejoined 19th.

Räikkönen was some 15 seconds away from Montoya with Barrichello, Alonso and da Matta in between, but Montoya's hydraulics failed so that Barrichello inherited the lead and everybody moved up a place. Da Matta pitted and that made Räikkönen third.

Schumacher, 18th, set fastest lap but, without taking into account all the cars in between, he was more than 40 seconds behind Sato in eighth.

At lap 11 Räikkönen was 14.641 seconds behind Barrichello, Alonso still between them. Barrichello and Alonso pitted together and so, fleetingly, Räikkönen led.

Schumacher was 16th.

Räikkönen had to pit and that returned the lead to Barrichello – Räikkönen stationary for 9.2, which seemed to indicate only two stops. Barrichello would be making three...

At lap 16 Schumacher was 14th, Heidfeld (Sauber) immediately ahead, then Ralf. He hunted Heidfeld down and at the final chicane eased through. *Thirteenth*.

Räikkönen ran fourth and Alonso stopped out on the circuit with an engine problem so everybody moved up a place. Räikkönen, heavy with fuel, was 20.107 seconds behind Barrichello, with – now – Coulthard in between. Clearly Coulthard would cede the position to his team-mate whenever necessary.

Schumacher was 11th and Webber pitted. *Tenth*. Sato and Ralf were wrestling and Schumacher hunted Ralf down *but* then the brothers pitted and emerged in the same order – Ralf still ahead.

Barrichello pitted, emerged 8.0 in front of Räikkönen.

Schumacher tried to mount an attack on Ralf but Ralf passed Panis (Toyota) and Schumacher did, too, at the final chicane, just as he'd done Heidfeld.

Barrichello was widening the gap to Räikkönen, who pitted, as did Button.

Amidst all this, Schumacher ran sixth but he had to pit again, was stationary for 7.6 and rejoined tenth. Da Matta and Ralf pitted and, as they emerged, Schumacher slotted the Ferrari between them. Ralf attacked so vehemently that down the start-finish straight Schumacher had to veer across to keep him at bay.

Barrichello pitted a last time.

On lap 41, at the final chicane, da Matta braked and Schumacher – probing the inside – locked brakes, the wheels churning white smoke. He lurched to the left, into Ralf's path. Under his own braking, Ralf lurched to the left too and touched the Ferrari's rear wheel. Ralf's front wing broke and

Schumacher had to plough a furrow across the grass beyond the chicane to get back on the track. He'd damaged his tyres and the vibration from them was 'so bad I had vision problems down the straight. I was also worried about a puncture and I was just trying to get the car to the flag.'

Schumacher, eighth, attacked da Matta.

Barrichello led Räikkönen by 16.4 seconds.

With five laps to go, the Barrichello-Räikkönen gap was 16.3, but Barrichello kept 'pushing' because rain had been forecast and even at three laps from the end, Barrichello thought, that could spoil everything.

Schumacher let da Matta go and eased off. On the final lap he was out at the back of the circuit when Barrichello crossed the line to win the race and deprive Räikkönen.

Schumacher approached the line, dipped the car across to the Ferrari mechanics on the pit wall, continued down the straight. Usually he'd fling the car towards the mechanics and punch the air with both fists as if an explosion was happening within him and, maybe, make the car wriggle violently left–right, left–right. At Suzuka, it all felt strange – his word. Eventually, somewhere past turn one, he raised his right arm from the cockpit and waved it then shook his head in a sort of wonder.

He had a champagne fight in the Ferrari pit. He sat, faced the camera and described his emotional confusion. He retraced the race, describing how he felt anything could happen at the front and so he had to make sure of it himself. 'You have to think about the worst to be safe. I'm empty and exhausted and just proud of what we all have achieved.'

Outside, Corinna almost bubbled over. She wore a hat with six times World Champion on it but said Michael didn't know anything about that. He'd have been annoyed at any tempting of providence.

She thought it would take him a few days to really grasp what he had achieved.

Fangio, you see, was history – if you take my meaning.

Speaking of which, in late November ZDF announced the result of their Greatest German poll. The top three:

Konrad Adenauer
Martin Luther
Karl Marx

Schumacher was 26th. As he might have said himself, you can't win them all. Some of his races seemed to defy Einstein's Theory of Relativity (nothing can go faster than the speed of light) but that notion would have made the old boy chuckle – he came tenth.

Steffi Graf? 32nd. Becker? 35th. Oh, and personable, polite, popular Heinz-Harald Frentzen – 59th.

Chapter 11

THE SINGULARITY

A fter five races in 2004 the many fascinating facets of Formula One racing had narrowed to a singularity. Schumacher. Everything apart from Schumacher seemed curiously detached, as if it was all being enacted in a lesser formula by drivers who were only near him through some inexplicable geographical accident. They found themselves in his presence at precise intervals, which was when warning flags were being waved so that they moved to one side as he lapped them.

In Australia, five other cars finished on the same lap; in Malaysia, six; in Bahrain, six; at Imola, six; in Spain, six. There is an unconscious symmetry about this and a deceptive one. In each of these Grands Prix Schumacher had been barely extended so that nobody had the remotest idea what he might do if he was, or what the symmetry might look like. From time to time his former team-mate Brundle said in a sigh, 'And we haven't even seen him pushed yet.'

Shorthand will cover it.

Australia	Pole	Fastest lap	First
Malaysia	Pole		First
Bahrain	Pole	Fastest lap	First
San Marino		Fastest lap	First
Spain	Pole	Fastest lap	First

Even the little eddies of controversy which swirl endlessly round Formula One to enliven it – Montoya has a plan to beat Schumacher, Montoya accuses Schumacher, and so forth – lost all their currency. He took pole and won, and if he didn't take pole he hustled whoever had had the temerity to take it and, if he couldn't force an error from them, he tracked them to the initial pit stops. They peeled off and he did one or two more laps. At will, and without the unaccustomed obstruction of another car actually in front of him, he'd set a murderous pace – enough to let him pit and emerge in the lead.

In our story we have seen the masterstrokes many times before and it still worked, because to counter it a driver had to be able to summon and execute thunderous laps at will. Few could.

The rest of the race was like suspended animation at 200mph, as if all uncertainty had been removed from a fraught, delicate, maddeningly complex and dangerous human activity. A great inevitability hung over it and somewhere around ten laps from the end he'd smooth his pace down, guide the beautiful blood red Ferrari safely into port, emerge entirely fresh – and where do we go from here?

Those middle laps which he cruised, you really did wonder if he had a transistor radio in there so he could listen to some music while he arranged sandwiches on his lap – afternoon tea – and poured himself a coffee from a thermos flask.

I am being flippant, but only just.

Since the World Championship began in 1950, other drivers had known a conjunction of circumstances which permitted dominance: Clark in 1965 with the Lotus, Senna in 1991 with the McLaren Honda, Mansell in 1992 with the Williams Renault, Prost with the Williams Renault in 1993. None except Schumacher had been able to sustain it season after season.

Of the 72 Grands Prix between 2000 and the spring of 2004, he failed to win only 32. Nothing like this had ever been imagined before, never mind witnessed. He had scattered records to the point where they seemed as curiously detached as the other drivers. Only one of any real significance remained, the 65 poles of Senna, and that would take him to the opening race of 2006 to equal.

Schumacher had reached the point where he was driving for himself, by himself and against himself.

If you were a thrill seeker, it was not thrilling. If you were an aesthete, and you had the imagination to comprehend how Schumacher had reduced all the complexities to the singularity, it was deeply rewarding – and absurdly wonderful because it said human beings do not have to be enslaved by the technology around them, they can make it obey them. Each lap which Schumacher covered he was showing it could be done and how it could be done.

And yet he remained a familiar stranger, even after all these years, speaking entirely predictable sentences as if someone had written a master-script and he had learned it by rote.

For example: 'The hero status is unpleasant for me. I do not want that at all so I have a problem with the hysteria which surrounds me.'

Or: 'We are a very united team. We talk a lot. Over the years, the team has never taken a decision which I reckon was bad for the team and the team has never felt that I have made a poor decision. We nearly always have the same opinion. The team is run by Jean Todt and Luca di Montezemolo and neither of them has ever asked me to take a decision for them. They are doing a great job.'

The drivers in the leading teams:

BAR – Button, Takuma Sato.
Ferrari – Schumacher, Barrichello.
McLaren – Coulthard, Räikkönen.
Renault – Jarno Trulli, Alonso.
Williams – Montoya, R. Schumacher.

The familiarity of the stranger became more and more pointed because he was everywhere and nowhere: after Spain he led Monaco but Montoya crashed into him in the tunnel under the Safety Car, romped the Grand Prix of Europe at the Nürburgring from pole (seven cars on the same lap), romped Canada (three cars on the same lap), romped the USA (five cars on the same lap), romped France (ten cars on the same lap). That was the tenth race of the season and he now had 90 points, Barrichello 68, Button 48.

Barrichello's predicament – or situation, or whatever you want to call it – as Schumacher's team-mate prompted Brawn to say in the middle of 2003 (the London *Observer* 11 July): 'The problem for Rubens is that he is trying to beat him in the same equipment. He knows he can't blame his car or anything else. Rubens has the toughest job in Formula One and he copes admirably.'

The new rule from 2003, 10 points for a win and 8 for second, prolonged the Championship in the sense that establishing a definitive lead was more difficult than when it had been 10–6; and the 10 for a win prolonged it, too, because in theory if Schumacher didn't finish the next three races and Barrichello won them, Barrichello would be leading 98–90. It was a very artificial prolongation and the points Schumacher had won did not reflect the reality of what he had imposed on the season.

To emphasise this, Schumacher now won Britain, Germany and Hungary so that, fantastically, he had won all 13 rounds except Monaco and the crash.

He went to Spa, the Championship at hand. On the Saturday after he'd qualified second to Trulli he explained that the changeable weather hadn't made the session an easy one. 'As for my lap, I struggled a bit at the top of the hill, going sideways into turn five. I think I lost the majority of the time at the last chicane because I did not have enough traction on the way out, but I have no complaints.'

You would scarcely be able to guess from these staid, stolid and ordinary words that the Championship really was at hand; or that anything other than an ordinary race meeting was in progress. Perhaps to him that was what it was.

Young Räikkönen won the race, Schumacher 3.13 seconds behind him. It was enough. Fangio lay far behind now, and everybody else who'd ever stepped into a Grand Prix car since 1950 much further behind than that.

Schumacher said: 'Every title has felt different and has given me different emotions. This one is very special coming here in Spa, which means so much to me, and to do it for the seventh time at Ferrari's 700th Grand Prix is also something special. I am very proud to have done it with such an exceptional team, who have done an amazing job – look at the way they got Rubens back on track [he'd been involved in a crash at the start and had to pit]. In fact Rubens drove a great race today. This is what makes our team so strong. Of course, I would have preferred to have taken the title with a win but it was not possible. The better man won today, but I am quite happy with what I have achieved. All three of us on the podium today have reason to celebrate. On the track I struggled to get my tyres up to the right temperature and pressure when we were behind the Safety Car, but it was not a surprise for us, especially as it was quite cool today.'

Quite cool today? That might be a description of Schumacher himself. And if you read carefully the words he's just spoken you see they are arranged to cover what business people call Matters Arising. They are an exquisite example of the modern man in control of his world and in control of himself. They are born of imagery, or rather the importance of talking to the image. They reveal almost nothing at all beyond that.

And somewhere behind it all sat the familiar stranger.

Because the season stretched over 18 races the most-points-in-a-season record was at his mercy, ironically his own, the 144 in 2002. Departing Spa, Schumacher had 128 and four races to run. He came second at Monza but had a bizarre and humbling race at Shanghai, the Chinese Grand Prix new to the calendar. He made a mistake in qualifying and went into a gravel trap. Starting from the back of the grid he reached as high as sixth but that masks the fact that he had a collision, then a spin, then a puncture. He finished 12th and a lap down.

He won Japan and was seventh in Brazil after another excursion during qualifying which put him on the fourth row of the grid. He completed the season with 148 points and, as if to demonstrate just how good the Ferrari really was, Barrichello finished on 114.

You can wander the highways and byways of motor sport records for as long as you want because, just like anything involving – simultaneously – teams, individual drivers, points, circuits, engines and the rest there are endless possibilities. However, only a very few major records, particularly for drivers over their careers, really matter. The most important is the number of World Championships, then the number of wins, then the number of points – and I am placing that third because the first two are unchanging whereas the distribution of points has changed five times since 1950. That makes direct comparisons very difficult unless you are to make all manner of adjustments.

The number of poles is fourth, the number of fastest laps is fifth, the number of laps led is sixth, and that's about it. Completing 2004, Schumacher was massively ahead of all comers except in the number of poles, 63 to Senna's 65.

How do you quantify five successive Championships? Where do you go to find their real context? These are controversial questions, as Chapter 12 will reveal. In sheer weight of statistics, the only person who could stand comparison with Michael Schumacher was – Michael Schumacher. All this led to further questions. Would his, and Ferrari's, stranglehold continue through 2005? If they did, would they be strangling the basic appeal of the races? As it was, a whole generation of Grand Prix drivers – among them Alonso, Räikkönen, Montoya,

Button, Webber – had never known another World Champion, and never been in a race where they hadn't had to confront him and that sleek Ferrari. The Schumacher era was so complete that, most unusually, in all the races of 2004 except the last three he was the only World Champion on the grid. All those before him (except Jacques Villeneuve, who came in for those last three) had retired long before.

Try this context:

1974 – three champions on the grid, Fittipaldi (1972), Denny Hulme (1967), and Graham Hill (1962 and 1968).

1984 – Lauda (1975, 1977), Piquet (1981, 1983), Rosberg (1982).

1994 – Senna (1988, 1990, 1991), Mansell (1992).

It made 2005 all the more amazing because what happened during it 'really hurt and it forced us to react'. The car had aerodynamic problems and the Bridgestone tyres proved to be another problem because Ferrari were the only major team using them and as a consequence there was no 'cross-reference point', in Brawn's phrase. It was something Michelin – with input from Renault, McLaren, Williams, Toyota and BAR – did not face. Nobody could mistake, however, how hard Schumacher pushed himself or the car.

He began testing at Barcelona on 18 January, driving the F-2004 and covering 104 laps (the Spanish Grand Prix is only 66), following that with 126 the following day. He'd be back later in the month, working constantly on developing the Bridgestone tyres, and continue that work at Valencia and Jerez moving into February before the launch of the F-2005 on the 29th.

The drivers in the leading teams:

BAR – Button, Sato.
Ferrari – Schumacher, Barrichello.
McLaren – Räikkönen, Montoya.
Renault – Alonso, Fisichella.
Williams – Mark Webber, Heidfeld.

Ferrari took the old car to Australia but changing weather made qualifying a matter of luck – and Schumacher was unlucky. The team just got him onto rain tyres before he made his run. He'd start 19th and get as high as seventh before Heidfeld (now Williams) ran into the back of him. Schumacher said, 'I made it clear I was defending my position.' Fisichella won it from Barrichello, Alonso in the other Renault third – so the Renaults were fast and reliable.

Alonso confirmed that when he won Malaysia (Schumacher seventh: 'We are simply not strong enough in several areas at the moment') and Bahrain (Schumacher retired, hydraulics, in the F-2005). Alonso had 26 points, Schumacher 2. Whatever happened from here on, the stranglehold had been broken and would be difficult to reimpose.

At Imola on the first day Schumacher said, 'We are looking competitive compared to the others.' He'd been fourth in the first session and sixth in the second – but qualified only 14th when, in the second session, he made a mistake at Rivazza. 'I braked on a bump with a full fuel load and locked up a wheel.' After the initial qualifying session he thought he could 'fight for the win' in the Grand Prix. Alonso led but Schumacher worked his way up and finished 0.215 of a second behind.

'I am happy in one way and excited after such a race. If not for the mistake in qualifying this would have been the perfect day for us. But I have second place and it is due to a stunning effort from everyone, the engineers, the test team, Luca Badoer, Marc Gene [the test drivers] and everyone else who worked so hard since the last race. And big, big thanks to Bridgestone whose performance today is just a first step and there is more to come from them. There is more to come from us, too, and we are still in the fight.'

They weren't, and Barcelona proved that: eighth in qualifying ('reasonable') and he judged third place within the art of the possible in the race but he had two punctures. He 'felt the car becoming unbalanced, then suddenly the tyre pressure was gone. Then, after the rear tyre was changed, the same thing happened again. It is strange they were both on the same side and the other tyres were fine. We have a lot of work to do across the entire package before Monaco.'

You might have thought Monaco would welcome him and the car because, there, driver precision and tactical skill can compensate. In free practice the car developed a vibration and in qualifying it was simply not on the pace. He spoke again of the need for hard work to improve the situation. In the race he ran midfield and finished seventh despite, at the end, giving Barrichello a very heavy overtaking move and then repeating that to Ralf. It drew strong words afterwards and just for a moment we were back in The Bad Old Days of the tramp across the Place de la Concorde and Grand Prix racing living on a diet of an eruption a day.

The Barrichello overtaking happened at the traditional place, the chicane down from the tunnel. Barrichello insisted he did not let Schumacher through although, to be fair, Barrichello did leave the inside untenanted and Schumacher, in full racing mood, put the Ferrari there. At the mouth of the chicane Barrichello did not turn in – and turn into Schumacher – but stayed on the outside. Schumacher said he didn't think the move represented much of a risk and anyway 'we are all here to race.'

That dismissed any notions about his motivation or that he was going through the motions.

Barrichello said: 'He overtook me at a place where he should not have. I had to move my car out of the way. If I had not, we would certainly have crashed. If I had been behind him and tried that move we would have crashed. I have spoken to Michael and Jean Todt about this but it won't change anything. A few years ago I would have said nothing, but…'

On the rush to the line Schumacher went inside Ralf who

clearly wasn't expecting him and twitched the Toyota out of the way. Ralf said: 'One millimetre more and one of us could have been dead. He's crazy. He should have switched on his brain before he tried that move at the end. I had to avoid him.'

Now consider that Schumacher took seventh place from Barrichello and would have taken sixth from Ralf. Räikkönen had crossed the line 37 seconds before to win it but that had no relevance for Schumacher. In this sense he was Senna's direct successor: you control the races from the front, you fight a mighty battle to get to the front or you maximise whatever you can wherever you happen to be. Perhaps the true definition of a *racer* is his physical and mental ambitions running eighth on the last lap of a race with, by definition, no remote hope of winning.

The surprise is that Barrichello and Ralf were surprised.

Räikkönen ought to have won the European at the Nürburgring but he took a chance on getting to the end with a vibrating wheel and crashed, letting Alonso in. Schumacher had by now accepted that the Ferrari couldn't compete in qualifying but he did not accept it couldn't compete in the races. He finished fifth and said that before the start he might have predicted finishing there. 'My race pace was not as good as usual. We know what we have to do, which is to keep on working hard on all areas of the car.'

Canada offered a measure of hope, which was curious because after free practice he said 'we are not looking too competitive here'. However, he qualified second, between Button and Alonso, and ran strongly throughout the race, getting to within 1.137 seconds of winner Räikkönen at the end, Barrichello third after starting from the pit lane. 'We can be happy with this result.'

Nobody could be happy at Indianapolis where the United States Grand Prix descended into farce after Ralf crashed on the Friday afternoon in the banked Turn 13, where the tyres were subjected to maximum loading. Ralf's tyre let go and Michelin couldn't guarantee the safety of their tyres. This is no place to revisit the many-headed monster which the situation became except to say that only the three teams with Bridgestone tyres took part, reducing the field to six cars. Schumacher 'won' from Barrichello with both Jordans a lap behind and both Minardis a lap behind that.

It was Schumacher's lone victory of the season and it made him third in the Championship: Alonso 59, Räikkönen 37, Schumacher 34.

Curiously, France finished in exactly that order ('the best I could have done') but Silverstone is, by its nature, no place you can hide. He wasn't happy with his qualifying lap and, from tenth on the grid, wasn't happy with his sixth place. 'Clearly we are simply not fast enough at the moment.'

He was fifth in Germany from fifth on the grid so, as he pointed out, he hadn't gone very far; but second to Räikkönen in Hungary after taking his only pole of the season, which brought him to 64, one behind Senna's record. He described the lap as good and expressed 'delight' to be on pole again 'after suffering for so long'. He was happy with the race performance.

After that, Ferrari announced that Barrichello would be leaving for 2006 and Felipe Massa was replacing him – Schumacher's tenth team-mate (De Cesaris, Piquet, Brundle, Patrese, Lehto, Verstappen, Herbert and Irvine the others).

Räikkönen won Turkey and Schumacher retired when Webber hit him. He seemed almost fatalistic, explaining that the car hadn't been competitive all weekend.

He tried so hard at Monza in free practice that he spun. He qualified seventh, finished tenth. He was hit by Sato (BAR) at Spa after 13 laps. 'Every accident is unnecessary but this one seemed more unnecessary than usual. Obviously I am not happy about it.'

Alonso became the youngest champion when he came third in Brazil, making him uncatchable whatever happened in Japan and China.

	Years	Months	Days
Alonso	24	1	27
Fittipaldi	25	8	29
Schumacher	26	10	10
Lauda	26	6	16

Schumacher, fourth in the race, said: 'First of all I want to congratulate Fernando and his team on winning the title. They have done a great job and from a personal point of view it is nice to see some of the guys I worked with at Benetton looking so happy. I look forward to fighting them again next season.'

At Suzuka he qualified 14th, finished seventh. Listen. 'The best thing to come out of today is that we have secured third place in the Constructors' Championship. Considering the performance of our package this season and the tough time we have had this is not such a bad result, especially when you consider that in the ten years I have been with Ferrari this will have been our worst season. As for the race, unlike in Brazil, I was disappointed I was unable to keep pace with the Renaults.'

Shanghai was a 'weird' end which, he felt, reflected the tenor of the season. He qualified sixth and on the installation lap before the race wandered into the path of Christijan Albers (Minardi). 'I was just warming up my tyres when suddenly I felt a big bang.' Both cars suffered damage and the Stewards were not happy. He spun off after 22 laps of the race under the Safety Car. 'I simply spun because my tyres were completely worn and they were very cold, so when someone braked ahead of me and I had to brake I went off the track. The only positive thing is that I am third in the Championship. Now let's look ahead to putting things right next season.'

It is what people say and obviously he could contemplate that when he'd had a nice long rest. He'd earned it, all right, especially over 19 races stretching from Australia at the beginning of March to China in mid-October. They all had. So off he'd go to the soothing heat of the Middle East, the cleansing air of Norway or perhaps an extended stay at a ski resort.

Hmm.

On 15 December he went to Jerez and covered 68 laps in the F-2004 working, and I quote the official report, 'on the development of the V8 engine, in collaboration with Shell.' The next day he did 30 laps with the F-2004 and 84 with the F-2005. 'I am happy to be back driving again and I am very pleased with these two days of testing at Jerez which went off without any particular problems. It shows the team has worked well over the past few weeks, as has Bridgestone on the tyre front. I can't wait to be back when testing resumes. I wish everyone a good Christmas and a happy 2006!'

He meant it – all of it.

Chapter 12

ALL TIME HIGH

Schumacher did go skiing in the Alps, to the favourite haunt of Madonna di Campiglio. He was 37 now. He spoke about his future with these words: 'It does not mean we have to win the Championship but we have to be in a position to do so. The joy comes from competitiveness. If all the effort has no meaning then it is just frustrating. I need time for myself to find out if I want to go on or not. Corinna very often helps me to make a decision. Her advice is very important to me.'

The six races before the 2006 Monaco Grand Prix were, with the benefit of hindsight, good, combative fare between Schumacher and Alonso, generation against generation, but not quite yet between the past against the future.

Alonso beat him by 1.2 seconds in Bahrain, a result he called 'excellent' because 'if someone would have told us during the winter months that this is the way we would finish the first race of the season, I wouldn't have believed them.' The context for that was the disappointment of 2005, Schumacher only third in the Drivers' Championship and Ferrari third in the Constructors' points.

Fisichella won Malaysia from Alonso, reinforcing the opinion that both Renaults were strong. Schumacher started from the second row, penalised by having an engine change. He finished sixth, the best result he could draw from the car, and went on holiday with Corinna before Melbourne.

There, he qualified eleventh and, while Alonso won the race from Räikkönen, he crashed off. He was following Button. 'I tucked in behind him and unexpectedly I got some heavy understeer. I finished on the grass. I had to push because that's the part of the track where it's possible to pass.'

He won Imola, beating Alonso by 2.0 seconds, and rationed out his thinking. 'The key moment was staying ahead after the second pit stop. Overtaking at this track is almost impossible unless the guy in front makes a mistake. With all my years of experience I knew that what I wanted to do was keep Alonso behind me, but at my pace – not pushing flat out – and that's what I did.' From now on, he added, the team would be competitive.

He emphasised that in the European Grand Prix at the Nürburgring, beating Alonso by 3.7 seconds. 'We are back, with car, engine, tyres and fuel all working superbly.'

In Spain, Alonso beat him by 18.5 seconds. It was decided 'in the first stint. Fernando was able to pull out quite a gap because I simply did not have the pace to stay with him.'

Alonso had 54 points, Schumacher 39 but, of more importance, Alonso seemed able to match Schumacher in mental strength, tactical acumen, certainty of car control and *cool*. In one memorable exchange at a race (caught by television) the pits radioed Alonso that they were pretty relaxed and he said, deadpan, he was pretty relaxed himself. *Chilling out,* something like that. Oh, and he was leading ...

Schumacher had known two full generations of drivers, but arguably Alonso was the first to take him on when both had good cars and, more than survive the experience, to prosper. Perhaps that contributed to what happened next.

At Monaco, in the two free practice sessions Schumacher came fourth and fifteenth. 'The situation is not looking good.' In Saturday qualifying he had a run good enough for provisional pole and, with seconds to go, was out again. Webber was somewhere behind on a hot lap and Alonso was somewhere behind too, on a hotter lap. Schumacher's time became suddenly vulnerable and, whatever reality proves, the mythology remains that you need pole at Monaco: pole assumes the *mental* status of an absolute imperative.

Schumacher did a fast first sector, a slow middle sector – 0.8 seconds down – and any chance of improving his time had gone. As he approached the *Rascasse* corner, the hard-right taking the cars away from the seafront, everything appeared normal. Since this is not an overtaking place, any Formula 1 driver threads the car through the eye of a needle and continues on the little spurt to the next right, feeding into the start-finish straight. An eye of the needle is no great problem for these drivers and these cars because it's what they were both born to do and, down the years, almost nothing has happened at *Rascasse* except cars turning right and continuing.

That compounded the next few seconds.

As Schumacher approached *Rascasse* he had to run round gently curving Armco on his right and he positioned the Ferrari quite normally to do that. Deep into the braking zone he needed to turn into the apex of *Rascasse* – right – but instead, at the mouth of *Rascasse*, he momentarily turned the steering wheel slightly left and away from the corner.

This was an extraordinary moment. Pictures from a helicopter showed that at no stage was he in a position to take the corner as he had done so many times since 1992.

He corrected that by turning hard right and braked hard enough to draw smoke from his front right tyre. The car appeared to be travelling straight ahead into the barrier at the far side and he hauled it away from that. It came to rest facing up the little spurt, with the left front wheel next to the barrier. In other words he parked it. As one of the Stewards, Joaquin Verdegay, remarked in *F1 Racing*, if Schumacher had 'damaged his car, we'd probably have filed the incident as an error. As it was, to park it like that, well, you can only do that deliberately.'

Alonso's lap was compromised because of the position of the Ferrari – yellow flags came out – and a great furore broke, although Schumacher claimed 'I did not know where his car was because I had been told nothing over the radio.' Some, like Keke Rosberg, said quite openly that Schumacher had done it deliberately and therefore blatantly cheated. Others said it was simply a disgrace.

Martin Brundle wrote a lengthy and powerful article of admonition in the *Sunday Times*, which moulded itself into a *cri-de-coeur*. Here is a flavour.

'We know he braked around 50 per cent harder at one point than on his pole position lap. The problem is that his car has a number of systems focused on keeping itself glued to the track. He had to introduce a pathetic left sweep of the wheel in order to have an "incident". Then the car stalled after a few half-hearted hand gestures that would have had you thrown out of a bad panto for poor acting. Then, can you believe it, it was stuck in gear? "I'm sorry I spoiled Alonso's lap, I didn't know he was out on track," he said.'

And:

'The pity is that Schumacher is so good that he doesn't need to pull these strokes. I am in awe of his skill at the wheel, his achievements, his driving style, his technical mastery, his bravery and his ability to galvanise an entire team of 1,000 people around him.

'Please, Michael, my old mate, just stand up and say: "I'm really sorry, it was the wrong thing to do, I regret it, please forgive me, I accept the Stewards' decision and it won't happen again."'

The Stewards did not announce their verdict until 10.42 that night, after they'd had a chance to examine telemetry, video footage and so on. Schumacher was relegated to the back of the grid – lucky, perhaps, not to be kicked out of the whole thing.

Schumacher said that 'to a certain point I am used to living with criticism, but nobody else but me was sitting in the car, and without all the information which we had, and in terms of what feeling I had in the car, you cannot make a proper judgement. I have to admit that some of it looks quite strange from the outside but there are reasons for all of this. For those who are thinking I tried to destroy Fernando's lap on purpose, I have to disappoint them.'

Jean Todt issued a regal press release, which was hardly calculated to soothe frayed nerves or indignant pundits:

'Ferrari notes with great displeasure the decision of the race Stewards, which is to delete the times set by Michael Schumacher in qualifying for the Monaco Grand Prix. We totally disagree with it. Such a decision creates a very serious precedent, ruling out the possibility of driver error. Michael was on his final timed lap and he was trying to put his first place beyond doubt, as could be seen from the fact that the first split time was the best and could have seen him do another very good lap. With no real evidence, the Stewards have assumed he is guilty.'

Jackie Stewart, clinical thinker and perceptive observer, came, I believe, closest to the explanation which Schumacher and Ferrari would not give. It was this: Schumacher got *Rascasse* wrong without intending to and, once he'd done that, thought with a racer's brain *how can I turn this to my own benefit?* He had no time to work through the ramifications of doing that, he just reacted to the situation – and that was why he parked the car rather than crashing it to make the error authentic.

After that, the incident assumed a logic of its own. Schumacher continued to plead innocence and Ferrari, of necessity, backed him while almost universal derision rose all around them to the point where, when Schumacher announced his retirement at Monza four months later, people still felt that *Rascasse* – the latest of many controversies – precluded him from being considered the greatest driver.

I don't suppose Schumacher minded, either way.

In the race he worked his way up to fifth and said 'everyone could see today that I am not the sort to give up.'

Alonso took pole at Silverstone, Schumacher third quickest, and he finished 13.9 seconds behind Alonso. 'We were simply not quick enough to win,' he said. When the finishing order was repeated in Canada two weeks later a great paradox revealed itself. The scoring system introduced in 2003 had had the effect of preventing Schumacher and Ferrari from paralysing a season by seizing the Championship with many races left. Now it worked against Alonso. The 10 points for a win, balanced against the eight for second place, meant that Alonso was only pulling away at two points per race and that, in turn, kept Schumacher's chances of an eighth world title alive. Alonso had 84 points, Schumacher 59.

This placed a premium on reliability. If you didn't finish a couple of races then that might change everything, and Ferrari had a reputation for finishing.

At Indianapolis Schumacher took pole and won, while Alonso couldn't get the Renault on the pace and finished fifth, 28.4 seconds away. As Schumacher pointed out, 'we have made up six points'. Alonso countered by saying he still had a healthy lead.

The season was getting more and more interesting as it tightened onto the two men – and it tightened further when Schumacher beat Alonso by 10.1 seconds in France. 'I got a good start and from then on I could run my own race. The Championship is far from over and these two points are very important.'

Alonso 96, Schumacher 79: seven races left.

It was tighter still after Germany, where Renault had to run without a 'mass damper' system, suddenly considered illegal, and costing them an estimated 0.3 seconds a lap. Alonso finished fifth, 23.7 seconds behind Schumacher, who had no problems all weekend and expressed particular delight to have won at home. He said: 'the fight for both titles' – Drivers' and Constructors' – 'is now very open.'

Alonso 100, Schumacher 89: six races left.

Button won Hungary and neither Alonso (who had a wheel nut problem) nor Schumacher (who chose not to pit for dry tyres towards the end and collided with Heidfeld) finished. Schumacher was classified ninth, however, and that became eighth when the BMW Sauber of young Polish rookie Robert Kubica was disqualified for being underweight. That single point might prove to be wonderful. 'Did we take a risk staying out on track with intermediate tyres in the fight with my rivals? That's the way I am. I always want to fight for the top, which is why I have won so often.'

Alonso 100, Schumacher 90: five races left.

Massa took pole in Turkey, Schumacher alongside him on the grid, Alonso next. In the race, Schumacher lost second place to Alonso when he was 'stacked' as Massa pitted under the Safety Car. Schumacher felt the car was 'nervous', lost time on his second stint and even went briefly off.

Alonso 108, Schumacher 96: four races left.

Schumacher announced his retirement at Monza, won the race, and Alonso's engine blew up. Kubica finished third, his first podium finish, in the BMW Sauber, and said: 'I can tell you it was an honour for me' to stand next to him.

Alonso 108, Schumacher 106: three races left.

He shed no tears in announcing the retirement. Somehow it wasn't his style. A long time before, he'd said 'the problem is that I'm obviously not a person who likes to show too many emotions. I control myself as much as I can, because there is too much that can be made out of it. I mean, I cry in front of the television when there's a good movie. It just happens. I am an emotional person to a degree.'

Perhaps it had all been a movie, an action movie: the most successful Grand Prix racing career of all time, played out on a global stage with some violence, a hero who seemed one-dimensional, and no script.

The podium ceremony at Monza *was* from the movies. The star and his supporting cast – Jean Todt – embraced and fired champagne and brandished trophies while, below them, like some gigantic slow-moving scenery, many thousands of Ferrari adorers howled and cheered and whistled and carved the air with their flags. One carried a message about eternal love for Schumacher – *amore eterno*. Firecrackers released a thin, ethereal mist above them. The colours were red, of course, red for Ferrari.

Schumacher had drawn up to within two points of Alonso. There were three races still remaining and an eighth title was now possible.

Schumacher had invariably seemed lucky and he was about to get luckier still in China. A watery weekend at Shanghai produced a grid able to strangle him, because Alonso took pole and Fisichella lined up alongside him. Schumacher, indulging in damage limitation (his phrase), qualified sixth and in the race – even if he managed to get past Räikkönen, Button and Barrichello immediately ahead – Fisichella could ride shotgun, allowing Alonso to cruise over the horizon. A wet track created tactical chaos because the Michelin and Bridgestone tyres exchanged superiority as the surface dried. Räikkönen retired with a mechanical problem and Schumacher advanced towards the Renaults, but Alonso *had* cruised over the horizon.

Alonso made two pit stops. After the first he couldn't get his tyres up to working temperature for an age – Fisichella passed him, Schumacher passed him – and a later 19-second pit stop, because a rear wheel misbehaved, essentially presented the race to Schumacher. Alonso put together a tremendous assault over the last ten laps but couldn't regain the lost distance and Schumacher won by just over three seconds, easing back.

When he emerged from the car he rushed to the Ferrari team – there must have been 50 of them – and went wonderfully crazy, embracing, slapping hands, vaulting into the air, embracing again. He, and they, had set up a real chance of winning the Championship, and not just because of the points. They had struck a psychological blow at Renault and Alonso.

Todt, moved, spoke of an 'incredibly tense race in which Michael's genius, the team's talent and the exceptional Bridgestone tyres all made this extraordinary result possible.'

The truth of it was that Schumacher crafted a race worthy of any of his masterclasses: *this* is how you win from sixth place on the grid. Even he, however, could not have achieved it if Renault hadn't lost the functional smoothness they had, we thought, perfected to the same degree as Ferrari. In other words, Old Schuey's luck held and that can only have impacted on the fall-out at Renault.

Alonso 116, Schumacher 116, but Schumacher leading because, if it came to a tie-break, he had more wins, 7–6: two races left, Japan and Brazil.

During the week before Suzuka, the psychological blow reached full into the Renault team, with Alonso allegedly complaining on Spanish radio he wasn't getting all the support he needed and hinting that, since he was leaving for McLaren, Renault were more interested in the Constructors' title. At Suzuka he'd say *don't believe what you get from the media*, but by then he looked edgy, not the chirpy chappie he'd always been. In the most direct sense, the merciless weight of comparison had now come to him, despite his Championship the year before.

More than that, a Formula 1 team constantly strives for internal harmony and external unity, because it is composed of fiercely competitive individuals who all have their own ideas and work under real, remorseless pressure. When the harmony starts to break up it can be the devil's own job putting all the pieces back together again. Clearly, Renault were not breaking up, but you could hear cracks appearing. A spokesman (unnamed) said: 'I don't know what he [Alonso] means' and put it down to frustration after China. That is what spokesmen say.

Qualifying heightened the difficult mood because Massa put the Ferrari on pole from Schumacher, the Toyotas filling the row behind, and all of them on Bridgestone tyres. Alonso, on Michelins of course, hauled the Renault to fifth.

Schumacher radiated something approaching delight. 'In the dry, our performance has proved to be very consistent, thanks also to the valuable support of our friends at Bridgestone, and that means we can be confident. Driving on this track, in the way the performance of our car has allowed us to do, is really marvellous. I am having so much fun, especially in the Esses – part of the track I am particularly keen on.'

Massa led the race for a couple of laps and then Schumacher went by, as he was always going to do. Alonso dealt with Trulli clinically enough and, after the initial pit stops, ran second. He tried to force his way up to Schumacher but Schumacher kept the gap between them more or less constant. As much as you can ever say such a thing, the remainder of the race – we are on lap 37 of the 53 – stretched away into a Schumacher victory and a strong second place for Alonso, meaning that Schumacher would travel to Brazil as the clear favourite for the Championship.

Approaching the Degner curve – named, by a savage irony, for the East German motorbike rider Ernst Degner, who managed to flee to West Germany in 1961 to find freedom – Schumacher was about to find the impotency of captivity. A wisp of smoke from the engine became a billow.

Alonso imagined it wasn't Schumacher but someone else. 'I was concentrating so hard on watching for oil on the track that it was not until I was alongside that I realised it was Michael. I punched the air…'

Schumacher had not suffered an engine failure since mid-season 2000.

The mathematics now moved against him: he needed to win Brazil and Alonso to take no points. For most of a decade Schumacher had been in control and now, just when he most needed control, it had gone.

He got a lift back to the pits and made a point of shaking a lot of Ferrari hands, slapping a lot of Ferrari shoulders. 'We are,' he would say, 'a great team. Our guys are the best and I have a great affection for everyone at Ferrari. Incidents like today's can happen and they are part of racing. You win together but you also lose together.' He said the Drivers' Championship 'is lost. I don't want to head off for a race hoping that my rival has to retire.'

Schumacher's plane had an engine problem so he switched to a Frankfurt flight. Keke Rosberg happened to be on it and, as he says, 'China–Japan is a long trip [the races just one week apart]. I was completely exhausted. I just wanted to crawl home.'

Three days later Schumacher was testing at Jerez where, the team said, he 'concentrated mainly on evaluating Bridgestone tyres' for Brazil. He did 118 laps and I wonder if, during any of them, he remembered another October, in 1997, and the crash with Villeneuve – and what might have been. If he'd won that title he would, this October day in 2006, already be an eight times World Champion.

Did he wonder? I bet he didn't. He's not like that.

This Jerez test strikes me as something quite remarkable, almost symbolic, and Rosberg agrees. 'You could understand, after the engine failure at Suzuka, that he'd be a bit peed off but no, he goes to Jerez and so soon after Suzuka. Now *that* is impressive.'

Because he'd announced his retirement, on those grounds alone the team might have excused him from pounding round Jerez. He had just been to China and Japan, with all that this involved, including the red-eye commercial flight home. To ask a man to fly to southern Spain for tyre 'evaluation' three days later, when his chances in Brazil appeared to be very long indeed, was revealing.

Next day he 'continued evaluating' the tyres 'as well as finding the best set-up for the 248 F1.' He did 104 laps and, as Ferrari said, his fastest [1:15.684] was the best by a 2006 car. It was also 'just a few hundredths off the record of 1:15.629 he set on the 30th of September 2004'.

This is how ordinary teams become great teams, by doing what they feel they must do, regardless of circumstances. You work at that level, no compromise. This is also how Michael Schumacher became a great driver. He worked at that level and hadn't compromised – from Spa 1991 to here. He was not about to start now.

'I'll tell you what he brought, right from the start,' Rosberg says. 'A completely new level of fitness – of stamina – and he's maintained it. That's how he could go to Jerez and do 118 laps on the Wednesday. And then to get near his own record the next day…'

A week later in Sao Paulo – on the Thursday, contemplating only three more days as a competitive Formula 1 driver – Schumacher gave a Press Conference. Shell are a major sponsor and it was at their behest: this was the sort of thing he'd had to do for a decade. The fact that this was the last of them, in a great, forgotten vista stretching so far back, did not move him to lower his guard. He was on familiar territory and the assembled Media, surveying it, were on familiar territory too: *him*. He was still the familiar stranger, rationing out answers that always seemed to reveal a bit and conceal a bit.

On the Monday morning it would never be like that again.

He spoke of how he had come here with no thoughts of the eighth Championship and repeated the mantra that he didn't want to win it because somebody else – Alonso – had had to drop out of the race. There was little else he could add and the conundrum continued. Now he could be accused of insincerity –

surely he'd take the eighth title any way it came – but if he hadn't said that then he became the unsporting German again. He was still, moving towards the final moments of his career, powerless to prevent people moulding his words into whatever meaning they wanted. So he said what he said, and he left it alone.

He did however offer something genuinely striking. 'What's going to be my life afterwards I don't know. I've thought many times that I don't feel like I should know because I'm in the fortunate position that I can retire and don't have to have a reason for my life afterwards. I have plenty of time to make my vision and to live life.'

As we now know, for Schumacher the Brazilian Grand Prix of 22 October 2006 went wrong from the third qualifying session, through the fifth row of the grid, to the puncture which made him last. An air of inevitability hung over the weekend because Alonso was such a good driver and the Renault such a good car. Schumacher might have the beating of it but even he could not win the race and simultaneously beat it into ninth place. Eighth gave Alonso the title, of course.

A measure of Schumacher is that, following the puncture, he got to fourth and after the extraordinary, extended turbulence of his career, who would have bet against Alonso, comfy in second place, breaking down, Schumacher storming past Button, and Massa obediently slowing, ceding rites of passage as Schumacher came up to him? Todt summed it all up. 'Destiny had other plans.'

Let's be candid. As Schumacher put his charge together after the puncture, some of the drivers did cede rites of passage rather than defend their positions vigorously and, given the weight and poignancy of the occasion, you can understand why. Maybe they were demonstrating the difference between themselves and him: because, as he came up behind, they were all racing for position – he wasn't lapping them, obliging them to move aside.

Reversing the situation, if they had come up behind him, racing for position, he would not have done any ceding, thank you.

This is why the move on Räikkönen – when Schumacher challenged him down the start-finish straight into the left-hander at the end – was a moment constructed for memory. Schumacher the racer had to be true to himself, had to set down the challenge, had to execute it even if, by then, it was no more than gesturing. *There is a car in front and I will overtake it if I can, because that is what I do and what I have always done.*

Once upon a time, Niki Lauda went to the final race of the season – Estoril, 1984 – with the Championship to win. The background is familiar: face seared after a dreadful crash and fire at the Nürburgring eight years earlier, given the Last Rites, retirement, return and now he qualified far down the Estoril grid. Several drivers said they would not be the ones to hamper him as he came up to them. They almost wanted to help him to the title. One driver – in his first season, as it happened – said he had no intention of getting out of Lauda's way.

That was Senna, who had gone to Estoril to try to win: all the others could take care of themselves, just as he would be taking care of himself.

Now you know why Senna was mourned, just as the great unwritten chapter of Grand Prix racing – Senna versus Schumacher across the mid and late 1990s – remains mourned. Now you know why Schumacher once went quietly and privately to Senna's grave at the Morumbi Cemetery, in Sao Paulo, and wept. And now you know why, with all possible respect to the other 21 drivers at Interlagos on 22 October 2006, Schumacher was not compared to any of them, only to Senna.

How to find the true context of Michael Schumacher and his career?

First, the context of talent. Marc Goossens, the Belgian driver who raced him in karts, says: 'Who gets which seat is very often controlled by money. In Michael's case it was very easy. He was racing go-karts like many of us did, basically as a privateer. He never had any works support and his dad didn't have any money, no family money involved.

'OK, because of his talent, at one stage with limited equipment he actually managed to be running in third place in the European Championship – which would have been a great result – and then, near the end, the first two clashed and ran into each other and went off. Because I hadn't qualified for the final, I was sitting in the grandstand and I thought *how lucky is this German!* The two Italians had been miles ahead – and he came across the finish line first.

'That's what happened to Schumacher. He won the European Championship and all of a sudden it drew the attention of a businessman in Germany and I remember he had something to do with gambling machines in pubs, and that's the guy that supported Michael when he went into Formula Ford. And then he gets the chance to show the talent, which he did, and then he went to test in Formula 3 with WTS and Willi Weber said "Oh, this guy's got real talent, I'm going to support him" – and he moved on to sell the whole project to Mercedes. So that's how his career came about.'

When it's put like that, everything seems smooth, easy, inevitable and almost predetermined. That's one of the strangest aspects of motor racing, because it is *not* a meritocracy in any ordinary sense. Money buys better equipment, and better equipment begets a better chance to win – so it ought to be smooth, easy, inevitable and almost predetermined for the rich and an impossibility for the poor.

In this sense motor racing reflects life itself, because real talent does not accept constraints but forever emerges from them. The one thing you never hear about drivers is their social background. It is irrelevant, so nobody cares. Motor racing is mercilessly objective. *How good is he?* That's the constant question, not *what strata of society does he come from, or what nationality is he?* During the 2006 season, a Pole came in and a Colombian went out.

The consequence of fierce competition is that everyone is searching for talent and there are enough people around who know it when they sense it, never mind see it. Their own commercial survival depends on finding it, signing it, nurturing it and exploiting it, just as the talent will be exploiting them.

This runs like a theme throughout Schumacher's career. His talent forced all manner of karts and cars to perform, and racing people sensed it straight away – usually a glimpse or two was enough.

Jordan at Spa in 1991 begat Benetton and two Championships, and that begat Ferrari.

Along the way it begat a minor mansion near Lausanne, via an apartment in Monaco. The mansion, down a little lane and heavily fortified, nestles in a sleepy village. The regulars in the pub say *we don't pry into other people's lives here. Peter Ustinov lived up the road and nobody bothered him. A Hollywood actress lived just over there and nobody bothered her. If Schumacher came in here he'd be left alone, just like everybody else.*

In this ambience Schumacher lives a normal family life, nicely remote from Formula 1's eternal storms and calms. With his money he could, of course, live wherever he wanted and behave like a potentate when he got there. Instead, he says the finest value you can give your children is honesty, and there are rumours he plays for a local third division football team. I bet he doesn't give the ball away easily.

The second context is social and difficult because German history requires delicate discussion. Professor Dr. Ralph Jessen of the Cologne University history department says: 'I am not sure whether national stereotypes are so important. The idea of what a German is or what an Italian is has changed in the last decades. Why? We are living in a Europe with open borders and a lot of contact, a lot of travel, a lot of exchanges between people, a lot of ideas. It's part of the "Europeanisation" of Europe – the development of coming into closer contact at the everyday level, helped by communication in many different forms: internet, telephone, travelling.'

I'm thinking of people like Boris Becker and Steffi Graf – one doesn't really think of them as Germans, only as terrific tennis players.

'We shouldn't over-emphasise this. The German public sees them as Germans – they are interested in their success because they are Germans, but it's not the old story to see them only as Germans. We see them also as professional sportsmen or sportswomen.'

We must also remember that Schumacher was born in 1969. What that means is that all his life he has known what you're talking about, and all that happened before is a very distant place to him. For example he regarded Spa in Belgium as his home circuit because it was closer to Kerpen than any in Germany.

'He grew up in a region which itself is the border between Belgium, the Netherlands and Luxembourg. It's the heartland. So he grew up very close to Europe and not so close to the traditions of German nationalism. For example and by contrast, Bavaria is very proud of its special traditions.'

It is very difficult for anybody who wasn't in Germany in 1945 to realise the extent of the destruction and German shame. How did it get from there to the point where Germans like Schumacher were happy to celebrate being German?

'It's not easy to give one answer. In 1945 we have this situation of destruction and humiliation and the feeling that so much was wrong in German history in the 20th century. During the 1950s and early 1960s you had a situation of silence and a kind of ignorance of history while people concentrated on economic success. The 1950s have been called the Decade of Silence.

'The 1960s was the decade of change in political culture but not in the form of a revival of nationalism. It was of westernisation and cultural opening to the west, looking more to America than France or Britain. Becoming a western culture is a phenomenon of that time, so the form of national identity changed from very German-ness and pride in Germany – with those arrogant, chauvinistic views of the first half of the 20th century. It changed under the impact of shame and silence and then these contacts with western Europe and North America.

'In 1969, the year Schumacher was born, I'll give you an anecdote about the redefinition of the emotional view of the nation. The President of the Republic was elected that year and asked 'do you love Germany?' He answered 'I love my wife but I do not love this country.' Even this high-ranking politician – the President – formulated a kind of emotional distance to the idea of a nation.

'It's very interesting that as far as I can see the use of the national flag changed and was not very important for political symbolism. When you're looking at the election campaigns in the 1960s you will not find very often these symbols. Only in the beginning of the 1970s it was used again as a symbol of political identity.

'In the 1970s it began in a moderate form, closely connected to the ideal of a model liberal Germany enjoying economic success: a new connotation of national priorities.

'In the 1960s and 1970s, when Schumacher was growing up, we have a critical debate about what it means to be German and what a nation means. The Americans and Britons haven't had this because you have no problem with your national identity. We came to the idea of the patriotism of political values, meaning republican constitution, guarantee of human rights and so on. The idea was that the phrase "the German nation" does *not* mean a strong nation, a dominant, military power but does mean democractic constitution. They tried in a way to reinvent the nation.

'And he grew up in a situation where the more traditional idea of a nation was not important for him. When he was a schoolboy in the 1970s, here in North Rhine Westfalia, he had teachers who were to some degree influenced by the student movements of the late 1960s – maybe they were left-wing in their ideas, left-wing liberal. This spirit of the times was very sceptical concerning national symbols. I don't, however, want to argue that there is no nationalism at all.'

Was there a time when you felt it became respectable to be nationalistic about the football team or success on the international scene in terms of other sport, arts, films?

'In 2004 we had the fiftieth anniversary of the German victory in the 1954 soccer World Cup. In 2003 we had the *The Miracle of Berne*, a German movie celebrating that.'

Schumacher can be seen as continuing that success. But I wonder: Does a German deep down – especially when he's abroad or doing something in public – feel that he must be seen to be correct and fair and proper because of the reputation Germans have? Schumacher, for instance, is always very fair and he praises people, even his opponents.

'I do not think that every German has it in mind when say he goes on holiday to Spain but maybe a lot of Germans. This generation of Germans grew up in a system of education which did not put much emphasis on these national emotions – they put emphasis on values like tolerance, democracy, human rights and so on. That was the political culture in which Schumacher grew up.'

You heard Schumacher speak many times, the slightly chiselled face speaking, usually firmly but softly, into the thicket of microphones or tape recorders – or both. Now you know why he always chose the words so carefully, and where they came from, and perhaps why.

The third context, stemming from the first two, is where Schumacher fits in the history of Grand Prix racing and, on the bigger scale, in the history of all sport.

To make definitive judgements about the latter is impossible because too many variables come into play at once, but very few competitors in *any* sport have exercised dominion over it for a full decade, and even fewer to the extent Schumacher did.

Who shall we cite? Oarsman Steve Redgrave with five Olympic gold medals (1984–2000) … Carl Lewis, arguably the greatest track and field competitor of all time, with his four Olympic gold medals (1984–1996) … athlete Jesse Owens, with four gold medals at the 1936 Berlin Olympics, all in one week? Bill Shoemaker won 8,833 horse races between 1949 and 1990; Gordon Richards won 4,000 between 1921 and 1954, Lester Piggott 5,300 between 1948 and 1995. The Tour de France is arguably the most gruelling event of all, which elevates Lance Armstrong and his seven consecutive victories to something utterly exceptional.

You can talk of Rod Laver, Borg and McEnroe and Federer bestriding the tennis courts … Tiger Woods moving inexorably on the 18 Masters of Jack Nicklaus. You can tremble at distant memories of Joe Louis felling one whole generation of toughs and Ali weaving spells round another. You can *still* struggle to accommodate how many runs Donald Bradman made between 1928 and 1948.

You can mix in Pele and Eusebio and George Best from football, the world game … take to the water with Jim Thorpe and Mark Spitz who made Olympic swimming pools their dominion. You have to look at Wayne Gretzky in ice hockey … Babe Ruth, Joe DiMaggio, Hank Aaron and Pete Rose in baseball. Bike racing followers point to Giacomo Agostini, Mike Hailwood and Valentino Rossi.

And so it goes. It's a game anyone can play and in any combination.

But whoever plays it and whenever they play it for the next 50 years, they will have to include Michael Schumacher.

That leaves the history of Grand Prix racing. When Schumacher announced his retirement, many F1 notables pronounced on whether or not he was the greatest driver ever. This is another game anyone can play, but again there are so many variables. What you cannot argue about is who has been the most successful. Schumacher's seven World Championships seal that argument immediately, before you even get to the victories or the points.

Sir Jackie Stewart had already said long before (2004): 'Motor racing in my day was very dangerous – and sex was safe. Michael Schumacher makes more mistakes every Grand Prix weekend than any Grand Prix multiple World Champion I have ever known. The number of times I went off in my entire Grand Prix career I could count on the fingers of one hand, because if you went off the road there was a very good chance you were going to hit something hard and hurt yourself, never mind the car.'

Here is a fundamental difference between everything up to the mid-1980s and everything after. Before it, cars were too fragile in their construction to allow bumping and barging. The drivers were more gentlemanly, not least because the alternative was much, much worse. They were also more prudent in what they tried to make the car do because circuits offered minimal protection and, out in the country at a place like Spa, no protection at all.

Let's be specific. Riccardo Paletti was killed at Montreal in 1982 and, mercifully, there were no other circuit deaths until Elio de Angelis, testing at Paul Ricard in 1986. Death became a stranger again until the dark weekend of Imola in 1994. In that span – 1982 to 1994 – hundreds of thousands of laps were driven and many cars crashed, some heavily. Advances in technology meant that drivers sustained minor injuries, if any injuries at all. Certain drivers, especially Senna, were able to drive on muscle. In one notorious incident (Japan, 1990) Senna, enraged because he couldn't have pole position on the side of the track he wanted, made a premeditated decision to drive flat out into turn one and let the consequences be whatever they would be.

Nobody before the mid-1980s *dreamed* of such a thing. It would have been lethal, madness.

So, the etiquette broke down as the cars got safer. When Schumacher crashed into Hill at Adelaide and into Villeneuve at Jerez, none of the drivers even sprained an ankle. He thundered into the wall at Silverstone and only broke his leg. He flipped the Ferrari in Australia and made jokes about it immediately after.

There is another difference. The modern racing car is much more reliable than its predecessors, which allows leading cars to rack up mountains of points. If Schumacher had driven in the 1980s his mountain would have been much smaller because the car would have broken down many times.

It is no use mourning the lost innocence of days long gone, and it is very difficult to judge one generation against the standards of any others. Every era in Formula 1 is hard: all you can say is that Michael Schumacher drove at a time when F1 was hard in a way it hadn't ever been before.

I happened to be on a radio discussion with Gary Anderson after Schumacher's retirement and asked why Schumacher had done some of the things he had done. *It's easy,* Anderson said, *these are super-competitive people in super-competitive situations and occasionally it will go wrong or they'll go too far.*

As someone said about Senna, *you can want it too much.*

Those were the too-hard moments and they were ugly things, however you care to rationalise the rights and wrongs. The 1994 Hill incident was (being diplomatic) highly suspicious; the on-board camera showed Schumacher turned full into Villeneuve in

1997; and the on-board camera showed he positioned the Ferrari to take *Rascasse* broadside on in 2006. It was these moments which many of the F1 notables wielded as a counter-balance to the weight of Schumacher's achievement.

After the Monza retirement weekend, Alonso said on Spanish radio: 'Michael is the most unsporting driver with the largest number of sanctions in the history of Formula 1, but that doesn't take away from the fact he has been the best driver...'

You can't put the dilemma more adroitly than that.

Nor had Ferrari made themselves easy to love in their, and Schumacher's, pomp. They could play hard too, and did, on all fronts – and shamelessly distorted the Austrian Grand Prix that time when Barrichello was ordered to move over at the end. Everyone shrieked *foul!* except those already wolf-whistling and jeering from the grandstands. Ferrari were unmoved and unrepentant.

It was a corporate decision, involving points for the Championship and consequently of great interest to the mother company, the multi-national Fiat. You simply cannot use the cottage industry ethics of the 1950s, 1960s and 1970s to judge this. Schumacher lived daily with pressures that Moss, Fangio, Clark and Stewart never experienced. Of course they had other pressures that Schumacher never knew, which is why making a comparison is so problematical.

I believe Schumacher's claim to greatness rests on several factors.

As Rosberg says, he brought to Grand Prix racing a unique level of mental and physical preparation, and he allied that to total attention to detail. As Chairman Mao said, *when they advance, we retreat, when they get tired, we advance*. It may have worked at the geo-political level but not with Schumacher because he advanced and didn't get tired, he just kept on advancing.

387

He was able to bring races under his control in an almost hypnotic way, he was able to exploit any openings and he drew positives from every negative. Rain's begun to fall? *Suits me better than the others.* Sixteenth on the grid at Spa? *Let's work out how I win from there.* Boxed in at the Hungaroring? *You change the tactics, Ross, I implement them and win.* Only one gear left on the Benetton? *OK, I drive it like a sports car.*

This leads to a staggering conclusion, and it is one endorsed by those who have worked with him: except at rare moments, Schumacher was driving within himself, able to tap the reserve – mental and physical – at will. Only the great have the reserve and know when and how to use it. Hence the masterstrokes and the masterclasses.

He understood the internal dynamics of a team and, because he could translate the communal effort into victories, the team worked for him. He repaid them by *always* equating their contribution with his own, and did so with absolute sincerity. In a turbulent, torrid and triumphal decade at Ferrari – once a nest of intriguers, back-stabbers and would-be assassins on a scale reminiscent of the coliseum in ancient Rome – I do not remember a single word of criticism from anybody about anybody. That was partly corporate discipline, no doubt, but partly the internal harmony that Schumacher, and continuing success, fostered. It stands in fantastic contrast to the nest that had gone immediately before. More than that, he was able to either choose or approve the key personnel as Jean Todt built the team so he belonged to it as it belonged to him.

No other driver had been able to do this and before 1996 it was unthinkable.

Todt even said (in a *Guardian* interview with Alan Henry): 'It's obvious I love Michael. I love him. Not I *like* him. I *love* him, like my boy.

'In life you must always understand why you fail and why you have success. We are humble here. Everybody has a respected position in the company and all respect each other's position.'

And Ross Brawn once told me, long before Schumacher's announced retirement: 'Championships are won by groups of people, not by an individual, and we have a very good group of people here – with Michael driving the car, obviously, Todt in charge. Todt's done an outstanding job and not been given the praise. It's a very unfortunate situation in that people don't understand what Todt does.'

Brawn, expanding, gave the view from the inside.

I say *I remember what it was like before he got there*.

'Others have very short memories, wherefore I think it's a tragedy that Jean is not given the credit for what he's done here and what he continues to do. It is a very unfortunate side of the media – they don't really understand. They draw opinion from outside and that opinion escalates like a snowball and sometimes there's no stopping it. He has been very instrumental in putting everything together.'

What sort of a chap is Schumacher? This is a particularly English question because, whatever he does, some will see him as the archetypal German and I guess he has accepted that and said 'well, there's nothing I can do.'

'I think people who know him have, at the very least, a great deal of respect for him and most of the people who know him like him a great deal. If you talk to any of the people at Benetton they love Michael. They thought he was a great driver and he was great for the team and they all do have a huge respect. The people who work closely with him have a great deal of passion for Michael.'

Maybe it's those who've only seen him from a distance.

'I had an instance a couple of years ago. My accountant comes to the British Grand Prix on a Saturday and that Saturday evening he was in the garage with his wife and his son. The son was a huge Michael fan but his wife was one of the ones who perhaps believed the media image of him. I introduced them and Michael was his normal charming self. I had a letter from her a few days later: she was completely bowled over. She'd had the image of Michael being this vicious Kraut, she met him and it was totally the opposite. She confessed she was completely taken with him and that's the contrast: there's the media image and there's the real opinions of people who work with him.

'I find him a very genuine person. I mean, he's very ambitious and very strong and sometimes we disagree on things but it's never in a personal way. We have a professional disagreement about how something should be done or how it should be run but he's never Machiavellian, he deals with things straight up in front. He's just very, very straight.'

Both of you think the same way.

'Yes, the majority of times, yes.'

You're not telepathic or anything, are you? I've called you clairvoyant but telepathy on top of that would be too much.

'No!'

When you get on the phone and say 'right, we're going to Plan B', does he say 'I knew you were going to say that, I've been waiting for you to ring'?

'No, he doesn't quite do that but there is, I guess, an empathy. I know he's going to do a job and hopefully he knows I am going to do a job: you know that together is the only way to go forward.'

If you can find a better definition of team-work, I can't.

While I was writing this chapter, a documentary appeared on a cable television channel about Toyota and their enormous effort to become a leading Formula 1 team. Many of the senior personnel were interviewed and they all said that they were there to win, the winning was the important thing, *that's what we are constantly working towards,* and, beyond that, to win regularly.

It is what all personnel in all teams say all the time.

If you have an appetite for history you can quickly find drivers who had more flair than Schumacher, took more risks, had more raw pace, used a more exciting style, were more popular, gave more pleasure, seemed to enjoy themselves more, communicated better, drove more fairly, behaved on the track with more decorum. Funny. Ferrari never mentioned going to the races to get any of that, and neither did all those Toyota people.

Sir Stirling Moss, interviewed by *The Times* after Schumacher's retirement, said: 'From my point of view he is one of the best drivers around, but he has blotted his copybook. There is no way he can be considered the greatest – you must be kidding. I must say he's in the second batch, and very near the top, but he's certainly not the greatest in my mind. I was a great fan of Michael. I think he's done a tremendous amount for Ferrari and for motorsport, but to me he negated the whole lot at Monaco this year ... when a guy's got the credits he has, then all he's done for people like myself is that no longer do I consider him a great person.'

To relegate the only driver with seven Championships, 91 wins and 1,369 points to less than the top of the second batch is a truly astonishing statement, and more astonishing still when set against the slavish culture of winning-is-all.

The day after the Japanese Grand Prix I happened to fall into conversation with Moss and he said yes, he had been quoted accurately. He defended his views by saying, 'Schumacher makes too many mistakes and you can't compare him with Fangio or Jim Clark, who didn't'. I pointed out that Schumacher could make mistakes because the cars were so safe, in the same way that Fangio and Clark simply couldn't. He accepted that but I don't think he found it a very convincing argument...

The Monaco 'crash' at *Rascasse* still rankled. Moss could have understood if Schumacher had hurled the Ferrari into the barrier, creating a real crash, and then limped away clutching his back: understood, but not forgiven. In the Moss creed, to be truly great you have to behave as a truly great.

Stewart, while accepting that inevitably there can be no question that Schumacher is statistically supreme, points to the psychological flaws which produced Adelaide, Jerez and – yes – Monaco; and is troubled by them. They are heavy evidence for the prosecution, and Schumacher only narrowly escaped charges of GBH a time or two.

It's up to you to decide how to strike a balance between Schumacher's hardness, Schumacher's flaws and Schumacher's mountain. One part of the fascination of his career was that he seemed to leave nobody indifferent. They railed against him or they defended him ferociously. Another part of the fascination was that the balance between good guy and bad guy constantly swung to and fro, unpredictably, and usually at racing speed.

I think in time the memories of the incidents will soften and the success will remain, and generations of young drivers, some still unborn, will have to measure themselves against him.

These generations will gaze back and murmur *that guy had to be a hell of a driver.*

He was.

Appendix

THE RACES

DISQ = disqualified; DNF = did not finish; DNR = did not run; DNS = did not start; FL = fastest lap; NC = non-Championship; P = pole; Qual = qualifying; R = retired; SWC = Sportscar World Championship.

THE KARTING YEARS

1984	German Junior Championship	1
1985	German Junior Championship	1
	Junior World Championship (Le Mans)	2
1986	German Senior Championship	
	(9th, Garching; 4th, Odenwald; 1st Utersen;	
	2nd Hagen)	3
	Munkolm 79 pts, Rabe 49, Schumacher 47	
	European Championship North Zone (Gothenburg)	2
	European Championship Final (Oppenrod)	3
1987	German Senior Championship	
	(1st Kerpen; 3rd Geesthacht; 1st Fassberg;	
	1st Wittenborn; 3rd Fulda; 1st Oppenrod;	
	1st Burg-Brueggen; 2nd Walldorf)	1
	Schumacher 127 pts, Hantscher 112, Gruhn 68	
	European Championship North Zone (Genk)	2
	European Championship Final (Gothenburg)	1
	South African Grand Prix (Kyalami)	2

THE JUNIOR FORMULAE

1988

(FK = Formula Koenig; EF = Formula Ford 1600 Euroseries;
GF = German Formula Ford 1600)

24 Apr	FK	Hockenheim	Fiat	1
8 May	FK	Nürburgring	Fiat	1
	GF		Van Diemen	5
22 May	FK	Zolder	Fiat	2
29 May	GF	Berlin	Van Diemen	2
5 June	GF	Mainz	Van Diemen	1
				DNF
12 June	FK	Hamburg	Fiat	1
23 July	GF	Nürburgring	Van Diemen	5
24 July	FK	Luxemburg	Fiat	1
31 July	EF	Osterreichring	Van Diemen	2
7 Aug	EF	Knutstorp	Van Diemen	2
14 Aug	GF	Zandvoort	Van Diemen	2
21 Aug	FK	Siegerland	Fiat	1
28 Aug	GF	Salzburg	Van Diemen	1
11 Sept	FK	Zolder	Fiat	1
	EF		Van Diemen	P/R
	GF		Van Diemen	1
18 Sept	EF	Zandvoort	Van Diemen	1
2 Oct	FK	Hockenheim	Fiat	1/FL
16 Oct	FK	Hockenheim	Fiat	1
23 Oct	FK	Nürburgring	Fiat	1/P
30 Oct	FF1600			
	Festival	Brands	Van Diemen	R

FK: Schumacher 192 points, G. Hutter 131.5, H. Schwitalla 122.5; EF: M. Salo 80, Schumacher 50, M. Wagner 45; GF: M. Wagner 177, J. Kosceniak 156, F. Kreutzpointe 146, Schumacher sixth, 124.

1989

German Formula 3

18 Mar	NC	Hockenheim	Reynard 893 VW	2/FL
2 Apr	NC	Hockenheim	Reynard 893 VW	1
16 Apr		Hockenheim	Reynard 893 VW	3
30 Apr		Nürburgring	Reynard 893 VW	3
28 May		Avus	Reynard 893 VW	3
11 June		Brunn	Reynard 893 VW	5
18 June		Zeltweg	Reynard 893 VW	1/P
2 July		Hockenheim	Reynard 893 VW	3
9 July		Wunstorf	Reynard 893 VW	12
29 July		Hockenheim	Reynard 893 VW	DNF
6 August		Diepholz	Reynard 893 VW	4
9 Sept		Nürburgring	Reynard 893 VW	5
24 Sept		Nürburgring	Reynard 893 VW	1/P
30 Sept		Hockenheim	Reynard 893 VW	3
26 Nov	F3 GP	Macau	Reynard-Speiss VW	R

Wendlinger 164 points, Frentzen 163, Schumacher 163.

1990

German Formula 3 (SWC = Sportscar World Championship)

Date	Class	Circuit	Car	Result
25 Mar	NC	Hockenheim	Reynard 390 VW	1
31 Mar		Zolder	Reynard 390 VW	DNF/P
7 Apr		Hockenheim	Reynard 390 VW	19/P
21 Apr		Nürburgring	Reynard 390 VW	5
5 May		Avus	Reynard 390 VW	1/FL
20 May	SWC	Silverstone	Mercedes C11	DNS
2 June		Wunstorf	Reynard 390 VW	1/P
30 June		Norisring	Reynard 390 VW	2
14 July		Zeltweg	Reynard 390 VW	1/P/FL
22 July	SWC	Dijon	Mercedes C11	2
4 Aug		Diepholz	Reynard 390 VW	1/FL
18 Aug		Nürburgring	Reynard 390 VW	1/P/FL
19 Aug	SWC	Nürburgring	Mercedes C11	2
1 Sept		Nürburgring	Reynard 390 Opel	4/P
7 Oct	SWC	Mexico	Mercedes C11	1/FL
13 Oct		Hockenheim	Reynard 390 VW	2
25 Nov	Int F3	Macau	Reynard-Spiess	1
2 Dec	Int F3	Fuji	Reynard-Spiess	1

German F3: Schumacher 148 points, Rensing 117, Kaufmann 81;
SWC: joint 5th, 21 pts.

1991

Sportscar World Championship

Date	Class	Circuit	Car	Result
14 Apr		Suzuka	Mercedes C291	R
5 May		Monza	Mercedes C291	R
19 May		Silverstone	Mercedes C291	2
22/23 June		Le Mans	Mercedes C11	5/FL
28 July	F3000	Sugo All-Japan	Ralt-Mugen	2
18 Aug		Nürburgring	Mercedes C11	R

THE GRAND PRIX YEARS

Key: Country, circuit, date; car; 1st qualifying time (position), 2nd qualifying time (position), Row he started on (R); Pole if not Schumacher, and time. Sunday warm-up time (position); Weather; Race.

1991

Belgium, Spa, 25 Aug; Jordan 191; Qual 1:53.290 (8), 1:51.212 (7), R4; Pole Senna 1:47.811; Warm-up 1:56.986 (4); Dry, warm; R, 0 laps, clutch.

The most astonishing debut of modern times. Schumacher did a few laps in the Jordan the week before, his first time in a Formula One car. He'd never raced at Spa. Qual: he outperformed team-mate Andrea de Cesaris (debut 1980) and in the Sunday warm-up was faster than Prost and Piquet. Race: at the start he burnt the clutch.

Italy, Monza, 8 Sept; Benetton B191; Qual 1:22.471 (7), 1:22.553 (7), R4; Pole Senna 1:21.114; Warm-up 1:27.435 (7); Dry, warm; 5.

The convoluted and bizarre departure from Jordan and arrival at Benetton did not affect him. Qual: outperformed Piquet in the other Benetton. Race: because the car was balanced so well he ran through without a tyre stop, was never out of the first seven and finished 34.4s behind winner Mansell.

World Sportscar Championship, Magny-Cours, 15 Sept; Mercedes C291; Qual 1:22.784 (3); Pole Yannick Dalmas (Peugeot) 1:21.821; Warm, sunny; R, 23 laps, water leak.

Schumacher partnered Wendlinger and made a strong start, staying with the two Peugeots in front. On lap 9 he collided with a Porsche, pitted for repairs, and worked his way back up through the field, but a water clip hose broke and the car stopped wreathed in smoke.

Portugal, Estoril, 22 Sept; Benetton B191; Qual 1:16.477 (12), 1:15.578 (8), R5; Pole Patrese 1:13.001; Warm-up 1:20.477 (15); Hot, dry; 6.

A solid race, although he needed to stop twice for tyres, finishing 1:16.5s behind winner Patrese.

Spain, Barcelona, 29 Sept; Benetton B191; Qual 1:19.733 (5), 1:20.779 (12), R3; Pole Berger 1:18.751; Warm-up 1:47.088 (11); Damp, warm; 6.

Race: the Benetton well-balanced again, but he spun and made a mistake signalling for a pit stop, finishing 1:19.4s behind winner Mansell.

World Sportscar Championship, Mexico City, 6 Oct; Mercedes C291; Qual 1:20.332 (2); Pole Philippe Alliot (Peugeot) 1:19.229.

Schumacher was stunning in qualifying but rain fell during the race and an oil pump failed.

Japan, Suzuka, 20 Oct; Benetton B191; Qual 1:39.742 (9), 1:38.363 (9), R5; Pole Berger 1:34.700; Warm-up 1:44.319 (9); Dry, warm; R, 34 laps, engine.

Race: ran as high as fifth, dropped back a place after his pit stop.

World Sportscar Championship, Autopolis, Japan, 27 Oct; Mercedes C291; Qual 1:30.261 (6); Pole Teo Fabi (Jaguar) 1:27.188; Overcast, fog; 1.

Schumacher and Wendlinger worked well as a team, and when Dalmas dropped out with an engine problem after 20 laps they brought the Mercedes safely home – which surprised Schumacher because 'in practice we killed so many engines.'

Australia, Adelaide, 3 Nov; Benetton B191; Qual 1:15.840 (5), 1:15.508 (5), R3; Pole Senna 1:14.041; Warm-up 1:20.010 (5); Wet; R, 5 laps, crash.

Qual: on his quick lap he missed a gear. Race: ran fourth in a deluge, went back to fifth, spun trying to overtake Piquet and went into Alesi's Ferrari.

SWC: joint 9th, 43 points. Formula One: joint 12th, 4 points.

1992

South Africa, Kyalami, 1 Mar; Benetton B191B; Qual 1:18.251 (5), 1:17.635 (6), R3; Pole Mansell (Williams) 1:15.486; Warm-up 1:19.775 (2); Dry, warm; 4.

He began his first full Grand Prix season partnered by Martin Brundle. Qual: spun and over-revved the engine. Race: oil over his visor from a Ferrari, tore three 'tear-off' visors off by mistake and when the fourth had gone he used his hand, finishing 47.8s behind winner Mansell.

Mexico, Mexico City, 22 Mar; Benetton B191B; Qual 1:17.554 (2), 1:17.292 (3), R2; Pole Mansell 1:16.346; Warm-up 1:19.280 (4); Hot, dry; 3.

Qual: used the spare car in second qualifying. Race: still in the spare. Brundle let him through to attack Senna and when Senna went on lap 11 (transmission) he ran third to the end, 21.4s behind winner Mansell.

Brazil, Interlagos, 5 Apr; Benetton B191B; Qual 1:18.541 (3), 1:18.582 (5), R3; Pole Mansell 1:15.703; Warm-up 1:20.204 (3); Dry, hot; 3.

Qual: an over-rev forced him into the spare. Race: he could not hold the Williamses and finished a lap behind winner Mansell.

Spain, Barcelona, 3 May; Benetton B192; Qual 1:21.195 (2), DNR (wet), R1; Pole Mansell 1:20.190; Warm-up 1:44.692 (9); Cool, wet; 2.

Qual: the rain in Spain did fall on second qualifying. Before that Schumacher got on the front row, driving so hard he spun off. Race: he took Senna early, took Alesi, and when Patrese spun brought the new Benetton home 23.9s behind Mansell.

San Marino, Imola, 17 May; Benetton B192; Qual 1:23.701 (4), 1:24.177 (6), R3; Pole Mansell 1:21.842; Warm-up 1:26.555 (3); Hot, dry; R, spin and suspension.

He had an engine failure in qualifying and, lying sixth, he tried again and again to take Brundle then spun off at Rivazza. He pitted but the car was too badly damaged.

Monaco, Monte Carlo, 31 May; Benetton B192; Qual 1:23.150 (6), 1:21.831 (6), R3; Pole Mansell 1:19.495; Warm-up 1:25.162 (6); Warm, dry; 4.

He had not been to Monaco before and learnt fast, despite a spin and kissing the barrier. In the race he and Alesi kissed, Alesi dropped out and he ran fourth to the end 39.2s behind the winner, Senna.

Canada, Montreal, 14 June; Benetton B192; Qual 1:20.456 (5), 1:21.045 (4), R3; Pole Senna 1:19.775; Warm-up 1:23.460 (4); Hot, dry; 2.

The usual (!) over-rev in qualifying and Brundle led him in the race until a mechanical problem. Mansell had spun off, Senna had an electrical problem and Berger (McLaren) won it from Schumacher by 12.4s.

France, Magny-Cours, 5 July; Benetton B192; Qual 1:16.969 (5), 1:15.569 (5), R3; Pole Mansell 1:13.864; Warm-up 1:32.690 (8); Dry, turning wet; R, accident, 17 laps.

Gearbox problems forced him into the spare on Friday and he couldn't improve position next day. On the opening lap he rammed Senna at the Adelaide hairpin but the race was stopped. Shortly after the restart Schumacher and Stefano Modena (Jordan) collided.

Britain, Silverstone, 12 July; Benetton B192; Qual 1:22.066 (4), 1:41.227 (7), R2; Pole Mansell 1:18.965; Warm-up 1:26.259 (3); Hot, dry; 4.

His confidence growing, he spoke of exploiting the car's potential. Brundle, Senna and Schumacher scrapped, Senna had transmission problems and Brundle was third, Schumacher fourth 53.2s behind the winner, Mansell.

Germany, Hockenheim, 26 July; Benetton B192; Qual 1:42.183 (5), 1: 41.132 (6), R3; Pole Mansell 1:37.960; Warm-up 1:45.106 (7); Hot, dry; 3.

In second qualifying he went off and couldn't improve. Late in the race Patrese, who'd taken him, spun – and that was third place, 34.4s behind the winner, Mansell.

Hungary, Hungaroring, 16 Aug; Benetton B192; Qual 1:17.070 (4), 1:16.524 (4), R2; Pole Patrese 1:15.476; Warm-up 1:20.154 (5); Hot, dry; R, rear wing, 63 laps.

He reached towards pole on Saturday but spun twice. Running third deep in to the race, after an encounter with Brundle his rear wing snapped going into the fast turn one and the Benetton flew into the sand trap.

Belgium, Spa, 30 Aug; Benetton B192; Qual 1:53.221 (3), 2:11.770 (4), R2; Pole Mansell 1:50.545; Warm-up 1:56.571 (2); Warm, dry-wet-dry; FL, 1.

Saturday rain kept Schumacher on the second row but the weather favoured his sensitivity and car control – and he was lucky. He spun, Brundle went by, he saw Brundle's tyres were blistered and pitted for slicks at, crucially, the right moment. He beat Mansell by 36.5s and wept at his first win.

Italy, Monza, 13 Sept; Benetton B192; Qual 1:24.143 (6), 1:23.629 (4), R3; Pole Mansell 1:22.221; Warm-up 1:27.377 (5); Dry, hot; 3.

The usual spin (!!), in second qualifying, but from the flag he bumped into Thierry Boutsen's Ligier, pitted for a new nose cone and – from last – worked his way solidly up: 16th after ten laps, seventh after 20, fifth after 30. Four laps from the finish he took Patrese and that was third, 24.3s behind the winner, Senna.

Portugal, Estoril, 27 Sept; Benetton B192; Qual 1:15.356 (5), 1:15.890 (5), R3; Pole Mansell 1:13.041; Warm-up 1:24.861 (25); Warm, dry; 7.

An ordinary qualifying but on the parade lap his engine cut and he started from the rear of the grid. Then he had to pit for a puncture. He kept on but was two laps down on the winner, Mansell.

Japan, Suzuka, 25 Oct; Benetton B192; Qual 1:40.922 (5), DNR (wet), R3; Pole Mansell 1:37.360; Warm-up 1:44.778 (6); Dry, warm; R, gearbox, 13 laps.

In qualifying he felt he'd exploited the Benetton to the maximum. He was running third when the gearbox failed.

Australia, Adelaide, 8 Nov; Benetton B192; Qual 1:15.210 (5), 1:16.613 (5), R3; Pole Mansell 1:13.732; Warm-up 1:18.550 (5); Dry, warm; FL, 2.

Yes, a spin.... then in the race worked his way up to second by lap 35 and stayed there to be 0.7 behind Berger at the end – Berger easing off.

Mansell 108 points, Patrese 56, Schumacher 53, Senna 50.

1993

South Africa, Kyalami, 14 Mar; Benetton B192A; Qual 1:17.507 (3), 1:17.261 (3), R2; Pole Prost (Williams) 1:15.696; Warm-up 1:19.961 (3); Hot, cloudy; R, crash, 39 laps.

The pattern of the season established already: Prost with the superior Williams, Senna and now Schumacher (partnered by Patrese) the challengers. Prost went off into the distance, Senna held Schumacher until the latter tried a move down the inside and they touched. Schumacher spun and halted.

Brazil, Interlagos, 28 Mar; Benetton B192A; Qual 1:19.061 (4), 1:17.821 (4), R2; Pole Prost 1:15.866; Warm-up 1:21.781 (6); Dry-wet; FL, 3.

Senna v Schumacher for third quickest, but Schumacher spun. He reached second in the race, then the heavy rain came and he fought back from a stop'n'go (overtaking under yellow flags), took Johnny Herbert (Lotus) and finished 45.3s behind the winner, Senna.

European, Donington, 11 Apr; Benetton B193B; Qual 1:26.264 (7), 1:12.008 (3), R2; Pole Prost 1:10.458; Warm-up 1:31.302 (6); Wet; R, accident, 22 laps.

Schumacher ended qualifying believing there was more to come from the car but, in slip-slither conditions, he couldn't prove that. He ran fifth and spun off.

San Marino, Imola, 25 Apr; Benetton B193B; Qual 1:23.988 (3), 1:23.919 (3), R2; Pole Prost 1:22.070; Warm-up 1:27.166 (4); Wet, dry; 2.

Strong qualifying and a strong race from fourth on lap 1 but Prost was not to be caught and won it by 32.4s.

Spain, Barcelona, 9 May; Benetton B193B; Qual 1:21.148 (4), 1:20.520 (4), R2; Pole Prost 1:17.809; Warm-up 1:24.229 (4); Hot, dry; FL, 3.

He got something in his eye which didn't help qualifying and ran fourth from lap 1 to lap 41, including his pit stop. Damon Hill's Williams engine let go, opening up third but he finished 27.1s behind the winner, Prost.

Monaco, Monte Carlo, 23 May; Benetton B193B; Qual 1:40.780 (3), 1:21.190 (2), R1; Pole Prost 1:20.557; Warm-up 1:24.220 (2); Hot, dry; R, active suspension failure, 32 laps.

Schumacher expressed delight after qualifying: he had only been on the front row once before, Spain, 1992. Prost led but got a stop'n'go penalty (for jumping the start) and Schumacher led...until a hydraulics failure halted him in clouds of smoke.

Canada, Montreal, 13 June; Benetton B193B; Qual 1:20.808 (3), 1:20.945 (3), R2; Pole Prost 1:18.987; Warm-up 1:23.454 (2); Hot, dry; FL, 2.

Schumacher liked the way the Benetton felt here. After a bad start he worked his way up and ran third until Senna's alternator failed. Prost finished 14.5 seconds ahead.

France, Magny-Cours, 4 July; Benetton B193B; Qual 1:16.720 (3), 1:16.745 (7), R4; Pole Hill 1:14.382; Warm-up 1:20.181 (5); Warm, dry; FL, 3.

Qual: on Saturday Benetton used harder compound tyres which lacked grip. Race: from the fourth row Schumacher made a long thrust and by lap 48 ran fourth behind Senna. He pitted twice for tyres, Senna only once – a mistake. Schumacher went by and finished 21.2s behind winner Prost.

Britain, Silverstone, 11 July; Benetton B193B; Qual 1:37.264 (4, wet), 1:20.401 (3), R2; Pole Prost 1:19.006; Warm-up 1:26.106 (3); Dry, cool; 2.

Qual: on Saturday he went off at Copse, got into Patrese's car and went 1.9 faster than the Italian, and 1.5 faster than Senna. Race: deep in, Hill's engine failed, Schumacher finishing 7.6s behind winner Prost.

Germany, Hockenheim, 25 July; Benetton B193B; Qual 1:39.640 (2), 1:39.580 (3), R2; Pole Prost 1:38.748; Warm-up 1:59.951 (4); Dry, warm; FL, 2.

Qual: the circuit ought to have made the Williamses impregnable and it did. Race: running for home Hill, leading Prost, had a puncture and Schumacher was through – 16.6s behind at the end.

Hungary, Hungaroring, 15 Aug; Benetton B193B; Qual 1:16.003 (2), 1:15.228 (3), R2; Pole Prost 1:14.631; Warm-up 1:19.217 (2); Hot, dry; R, fuel pump, 26 laps.

Qual: a good run and no disappointment when Hill went faster on the Saturday, pushing him to the second row. Race: he ran third.

Belgium, Spa, 29 Aug; Benetton B193B; Qual 1:50.305 (3), 1:49.075 (3), R2; Pole Prost 1:47.571; Warm-up 1:53.557 (2); Hot, dry; 2.

Qual: fine tuning in qualifying to take Eau Rouge flat. Race: he tracked the Williamses and, car and driver feisty, went past Prost at Les Combes on lap 31. He finished 3.6s behind winner Hill.

Italy, Monza, 12 Sept; Benetton B193B; Qual 1:23.888 (6), 1:22.910 (5), R3; Pole Prost 1:21.179; Warm-up 1:25.038 (3); Hot, dry; R, engine, 21 laps.

Qual: the right set-up proved elusive. Race: he ran second to Prost until the engine failed in a billowing of smoke.

Portugal, Estoril, 26 Sept; Benetton B193B; Qual 1:13.403 (5), 1:14.135 (8), R3; Pole Hill 1:11.494; Warm-up 1:17.750 (12); Dry, sunny; 1.

Qual: third row. Race: he led by lap 30 – he changed tyres nine laps earlier, planning a second stop later. Prost, behind and going for the championship, tracked and attacked and Schumacher never did risk the second stop: he held Prost by a mixture of brilliant car control, merciless movement through traffic and some blocking.

Japan, Suzuka, 24 Oct; Benetton B193B; Qual 1:38.589 (2), 1:37.530 (4), R2; Pole Prost 1:37.154; Warm-up 1:43.561 (3); Dry-wet; R, accident, 10 laps.

Qual: did as much as could be done. Race: tried to take Hill, who was mixing it with Berger's Ferrari. The Williams and Benetton collided – Schumacher's suspension broken.

Australia, Adelaide, 7 Nov; Benetton B193B; Qual 1:14.098 (3), 1:14.494 (2), R2; Pole Senna 1:13.371; Warm-up 1:16.675 (2); Warm, dry; R, engine, 19 laps.

Qual: second row. Race: he ran fourth from the start despite an early, tactical pit stop. He was fast and might have dealt with the Williamses.

Prost 99 points, Senna 73, Hill 69, Schumacher 52.

1994

Brazil, Interlagos, 27 Mar; Benetton B194; Qual 1:16.575 (2), 1:16.290 (2), R1; Pole Senna 1:15.962; Warm-up 1:20.035 (10); Warm, dry; FL, 1.

Senna to Williams, Schumacher strong enough to challenge him directly – certainly in the races. (He had a cold in qualifying and was still on row 1.) Schumacher took the lead at the first pit stop – for refuelling, something new – and, chasing him, Senna spun off.

Pacific, Aida, 17 Apr; Benetton B194; Qual 1:10.440 (2), DNR, R1; Pole Senna 1:10.218; Warm-up 1:14.023 (1); Warm, dry; FL, 1.

The weather became hotter and Schumacher didn't run in second qualifying to save tyres (7 sets per weekend, but maybe two stops in the races). Schumacher made a crisp start and, trying to get level, Senna was hit by Mika Häkkinen (McLaren). Schumacher led every lap and won from Berger by 1m 15.3s.

San Marino, Imola 1 May; Benetton B194; Qual 1:22.015 (2), 1:21.885 (1), R1; Pole Senna 1:21.548; Warm-up 1:24.978 (11); Hot, dry; 1.

The race that changed everything: Senna leading, Schumacher hustling, the Safety Car out after a startline crash and, when the race restarted, Schumacher watching Senna's car 'bottoming' and next lap going into the wall at the curving left-handed Tamburello. At that instant, from the gathering darkness, Senna's mantle passed to Schumacher.

Monaco, Monte Carlo, 15 May; Benetton B194; Qual 1:20.230 (1), 1:18.560 (1/P); Warm-up 1:21.294 (1); Dry, warm; FL, 1.

The first pole of Schumacher's career, but the front row left empty in memory of Senna. By second qualifying Schumacher was going consistently fast and commanded the race so completely that it represented a glimpse of the future. He beat Brundle (McLaren) by 37.2s.

Spain, Barcelona, 29 May; Benetton B194; Qual 1:23.426 (1), 1:21.908 (1/P); Warm-up 1:23.925 (2); Dry, warm; FL, 2.

Formula One still wrestled with the implications of life after Senna but Schumacher was already beginning to fill the void on a consistent basis. Qualifying, he said, was perfect. He produced an astonishing race. Leading on lap 24, the car stuck in fifth gear: he was still able to make a pit stop and finished 24.1s behind the winner, Hill.

Canada, Montreal, 12 June; Benetton B194; Qual 1:26.820 (2), 1:26.178 (1/P); Warm-up 1:29.079 (10); Cloudy, showery; FL, 1.

An experimental qualifying and then he led every lap of the race, beating Hill by 39.6s. If anybody doubted it after Monte Carlo and Barcelona, this now *was* the Schumacher era.

France, Magny-Cours, 3 July; Benetton B194; Qual 1:17.085 (1), 1:16.707 (3), R2; Pole Hill 1:16.282; Warm-up 1:18.743 (1); Hot, dry; 1.

Dominant in first qualifying, he spun it away on the second day – Mansell now in the mix with Williams. From the second row Schumacher went between the Williamses and led every lap again, Hill at 12.6s at the end, Berger next at 52.7, the rest a lap away.

Britain, Silverstone, 10 July; Benetton B194; Qual 1:26.323 (1), 1:24.963 (2), R1; Pole Hill 1:24.960; Warm-up 1:26.298 (2); Hot, dry; 2, DISQ.

A small mistake in second qualifying cost Schumacher pole. The race developed into the black flag saga (see chapter 5) – a parade lap offence, a dispute over the rules – which resulted in disqualification.

Germany, Hockenheim, 31 July; Benetton B194; Qual 1:44.875 (3), 1:44.268 (4), R2; Pole Berger 1:43.582; Warm-up 1:46.642 (1); Overcast, warm; R, engine, 20 laps.

Hockenheim's long straights didn't suit the Benetton and he was satisfied to qualify fourth. The warm-up offered promise and he ran second to Berger until the engine went. It might not have mattered: Berger stopping only once, Schumacher intending to stop twice.

Hungary, Hungaroring, 14 Aug; Benetton B194; Qual 1:19.479 (1), 1:18.258 (1/P); Warm-up 1:20.502; Hot, dry; FL, 1.

The first authentic example of total Schumacher: quickest in all three sessions, leading every lap except for a pit stop, setting fastest lap, doing three pit stops comfortably, beating Hill by 20.8s.

Belgium, Spa, 28 Aug; Benetton B194; Qual 2:21.494 (2, wet), 2.25.501 (2, wet), R1; Pole Barrichello (Jordan) 2:21.163; Overcast, dry; 1, DISQ.

Barrichello nipped out at the end of the Friday session and took pole on a drying track. Schumacher led throughout but was disqualified because part of the Benetton's undertray was held illegal.

(Suspended from Italy and Portugal for the Silverstone black flag saga.)

Europe, Jerez, 16 Oct; Benetton B194; Qual 1:24.207 (3), 1:22.762 (1/P); Warm-up 1:24.402 (2); Warm, overcast; FL, 1.

Disappointed after first qualifying, he duelled with Hill in the second session – and won. Hill led but into lap 18 Schumacher made the first of three stops and when Hill (planning two) pitted Schumacher took the lead. He never lost it and won by 24.6s.

Japan, Suzuka, 6 Nov; Benetton B194; Qual 1:37.209 (1/P), 1:57.128 (3, wet); Warm-up 1:59.431 (7); Wet; 2.

Schumacher confident in first qualifying, running less and using fewer tyres than Hill – but rain engulfed the race, stopping it after 13 laps, Schumacher leading by 6.8s from Hill. It restarted, to be decided on aggregate, and the Benetton strategy of two pits stops proved a pit stop too long. Hill won it by 3.3s.

Australia, Adelaide, 13 Nov; Benetton B194; Qual 1:16.197 (2), 1:32.627 (1, wet), R1; Pole Mansell 1:16.179; Warm-up 1:17.153 (3); Warm, dry; FL, R.

The championship shoot-out and how decisive would Mansell's pole be? He didn't figure: Schumacher in the lead, Hill following, searching for a chance to attack. On lap 36 Schumacher went off into a wall – unseen by Hill – and came back on again as Hill arrived. They collided amidst controversy and acrimony but Schumacher had the championship.

Schumacher 92 points, Hill 91, Berger 41.

1995

Brazil, Interlagos, 26 Mar; Benetton B195; Qual 1:22.131 (6), 1:20.382 (1), R1; Pole Hill 1:20.081; Warm-up 1:22.124 (3); Cloudy, warm; FL, 1.

Changes to the Benetton put Schumacher near Hill's pace in second qualifying. He led early but was stopping three times, Hill twice. Hill took the lead at the first of them but his suspension failed. Coulthard (Williams) took over but lost it to Schumacher when he pitted and Schumacher brought it home 8.0s ahead. He was then disqualified for a Benetton fuel irregularity – and later reinstated.

Argentina, Buenos Aires, 9 Apr; Benetton B195; Qual 1:57.056 (10), 1:54.272 (3), R2; Pole Coulthard 1:53.241; Warm-up 1:32.176 (4); Cloudy, warm; FL, 3.

After a spin in second qualifying Schumacher went faster and faster, and might have had pole. He stopped three times again and finished third, 33.3s behind the winner, Hill.

San Marino, Imola, 30 Apr; Benetton B195; Qual 1:27.274 (1/P), 1:27.413 (1); Warm-up 2:02.359 (3, wet); Overcast; R.

Happy after qualifying, he led to his first pit stop on lap 10 but, on cold tyres, hit water and went off.

Spain, Barcelona, 14 May; Benetton B195; Qual 1:23.535 (4), 1:21.452 (1/P); Warm-up 1:23.432 (1); Dry, warm; 1.

An overnight set-up change enabled Schumacher to plunder pole and he led every lap of the race, not even losing it during his two pit stops. He beat Herbert in the other Benetton by 51.9s.

Monaco, Monte Carlo, 28 May; Benetton B195; Qual 1:24.146 (2), 1:22.742 (2), R1; Pole Hill 1:21.952; Warm-up 1: 25.230 (3); Dry, warm; 1.

A mini-crash in the morning of second qualifying disturbed Schumacher's car and he couldn't take pole from Hill. Hill led to his pit stop on lap 24 and Schumacher took it up: he was only stopping once. When he did, Alesi (Ferrari) led but pitted after a lap and Schumacher sailed home 34.8s ahead of Hill.

Canada, Montreal, 11 June; Benetton B195; Qual 1:27.661 (1/P), 1:27.708 (1); Warm-up 1:51.844 (4); Warm, overcast; FL, 5.

Dominant in qualifying, he led until his second stop on lap 57 – unscheduled because the Benetton developed a gearbox problem. He emerged seventh and drove hard to fifth 44.6s behind the winner, Alesi.

France, Magny-Cours, 2 July; Benetton B195; Qual 1:18.893 (3), 1:17.512 (2), R1; Pole Hill 1:17.225; Warm-up 1:37.695 (4); Hot, dry; FL, 1.

Schumacher made a late run for pole but was baulked by a slower car. Hill led, Schumacher applying pressure, Schumacher pitted and went fast, Hill – himself baulked – came out from his stop in second place: the race was decided. Schumacher beat him by 31.3s.

Britain, Silverstone, 16 July; Benetton B195; Qual 1:28.397 (2), 1:48.204 (2), R1; Pole Hill 1:28.124; Warm-up 1:30.665 (6); Dry, warm; R, crash, 45 laps.

A tense struggle for pole with Hill, who led the race until the first pit stops when Schumacher took it from him. Hill took it back when Schumacher pitted, returned it after his second stop. Hill attacked into the Complex and they collided: Hill ambitious, Schumacher unyielding.

Germany, Hockenheim, 30 July; Benetton B195; Qual 1:45.505 (3), 1:44.465 (2), R1; Pole Hill 1:44.385; Warm-up 1:47.452 (1); Dry, warm; FL, 1.

He was happy to be on the pace of the Williams. Hill made a strong start, Schumacher behind, but spun at the first corner in the second lap. Schumacher, uncatchable, beat Coulthard by 5.9s.

Hungary, Hungaroring, 13 Aug; Benetton B195; Qual 1:19.490 (4), 1:17.558 (3), R2; Pole Hill 1:16.982; Warm-up 1:18.838 (1); Hot, dry; 11, fuel pump.

He was having to push the Benetton so hard he spun in

qualifying. From third he overtook Coulthard on lap 13 but had fuel rig problems and towards the end, running safely in second, the mechanical fuel pump failed. He was classified eleventh.

Belgium, Spa, 27 Aug; Benetton B195; Qual 2:14.962 (2), wet, 1:59.079 (16), R8; Pole Berger 1:54.392; Warm-up 2:16.710 (3, wet); Dry-wet; 1.

In changing conditions qualifying was about timing and luck. Schumacher was unlucky. From this he constructed a great race: after 10 laps, fifth, after 20 second to Hill – when Hill had wet tyres and Schumacher didn't – and defended his lead robustly. After a brief waltz of pit stops Schumacher settled in the lead and beat Hill by 19.4s.

Italy, Monza, 10 Sept; Benetton B195; Qual 1:26.098 (4), 1:25.026 (2), R1; Pole Coulthard 1:24.462; Warm-up 1:27.021 (4); Dry, warm; R, crash, 23 laps.

In qualifying Schumacher could not hold Coulthard, who was more than half a second quicker. After 14 laps Berger moved into the lead from Schumacher and Hill, who grappled. Into the second chicane Hill ran into the back of Schumacher: they were both angry and they were both out.

Portugal, Estoril, 24 Sept; Benetton B195; Qual 1:21.885 (3), 1:21.301 (3), R2; Pole Coulthard 1:20.537; Warm-up 1:24.941 (9); Dry, warm; 2.

He couldn't find grip in qualifying and couldn't catch Coulthard in the race, although after the second pit stops found himself behind Hill. He took him cleanly, Hill playing the gentleman, and finished 7.2s behind Coulthard.

Europe, Nürburgring, 1 Oct; Benetton B195; Qual 1:19.470 (3), 1:19.150 (1), R2; Pole Coulthard 1:18.738; Warm-up 1:38.960 (4); Damp; FL, 1.

Slippery conditions, the Williams just quicker but from the third row Alesi had the lead by lap 13 and still had it with three to go. Schumacher thrust the Benetton into the tight chicane and somehow threaded through to win by 2.6s, the championship all but decided.

Pacific, Aida, 22 Oct; Benetton B195; Qual 1:14.524 (3), 1:14.284 (3), R2; Pole Coulthard 1:14.013; Warm-up 1:18.181 (8); Dry, warm; FL, 1.

He almost outqualified Hill because the Benetton handled so well – he was using fewer sets of tyres. He ran fifth early on, worked up to second behind Coulthard and when Coulthard pitted on lap 49 went through, going so fast he could make a pit stop and retain the lead. He beat Coulthard comfortably, by 14.2s, the championship safely his.

Japan, Suzuka, 29 Oct; Benetton B195; Qual 1:38.428 (1), 1:38.023 (1/P); Warm-up 2:00.414 (2, wet); Cloudy, dry; FL, 1.

Pole from Alesi by 0.865 of a second – a lifetime in Formula One. Schumacher led and, when Alesi's differential failed after 24 laps, Hill advanced, led at the pit stops – and slithered off. Schumacher beat Häkkinen (McLaren) by 18.3s, his ninth win of the season equalling Mansell's record in 1992.

Australia, Adelaide, 12 Nov. Benetton B195; Q: 1:16.039 (4); 1:15.839 (2), R2; Pole: Hill 1:15.505. Warm-up: 1:18.199 (3). Dry, Warm. R, crash, 25 laps.

A defective shock absorber held him back in second qualifying and, briefly leading the race, he emerged from a pit stop determined to exploit his new tyres. He went to overtake Alesi and Alesi wasn't having that. They collided, and although Schumacher limped on for a couple of laps his race was over, and so was his season.

Schumacher 102 points, Hill 69, Coulthard 49.

1996

Australia, Melbourne, 10 Mar; Ferrari F310; Qual 1:33.125 (4), R2; Pole Villeneuve 1:32.371; Warm-up 1:34.176 (4); Warm, sunny; R, brakes, 32 laps.

A new era with Ferrari and a new era in Formula One with a single, Saturday qualifying. Schumacher had the spare (his race car suffered gearbox problems in the morning 'free' session) and couldn't get it on the pace. He got to third by overtaking team-mate Irvine on the second lap and ran there behind the Williamses of Villeneuve and Hill – deceptive because he ran with a light fuel load for two stops. Then the brakes failed.

Brazil, Interlagos, 31 Mar; Ferrari F310; Qual 1:19.474 (4), R4; Pole Hill 1:18.111; Warm-up 1:20.310 (5); Wet-dry; 3.

Chassis problems in qualifying meant Schumacher had to *force* the car. He ran a careful race, holding off a challenge from Barrichello (Jordan) but was lapped by the winner, Hill.

Argentina, Buenos Aires, 7 Apr; Ferrari F310; Qual 1:30.598 (2), R1; Pole Hill 1:30.346; Warm-up 1:29.318 (3); Warm, dry; R, rear wing, 46 laps.

He had pole until three minutes before the end of the session and ran second behind Hill but that disguised a truth. Schumacher had to run light – planning three fuel stops – to stay with Hill and even then he couldn't. Some debris hit his rear wing and it broke up.

Europe, Nürburgring, 28 Apr; Ferrari F310; Qual 1:20.149 (3), R2; Pole Hill 1:18.941; Warm-up 1:21.785 (5); Warm, dry; 2.

Couldn't find grip in qualifying and, from fourth, was down to fifth by lap 6. At the first pit stops he charged and vaulted up to second place behind Villeneuve, finishing 0.7 of a second behind him.

San Marino, Imola, 5 May; Ferrari F310; Qual 1:26.890 (P); Warm-up 1:29.033 (4); Warm, dry; 2.

He took his first Ferrari pole with a daunting lap minutes before the end and then spun in Tamburello. A long run to second place, first behind Coulthard then Hill, but the margin at the end – 16.4s – showed how far Ferrari had to go.

Monaco, Monte Carlo, 19 May; Ferrari F310; Qual 1:20.356 (P); Warm-up 1:24.289 (3); Wet-dry; R, accident, 0 laps.

Pole after a tug-of-war struggle with Hill, then, on the opening lap of the race, the slippery track claimed Schumacher. At Portier he floated helplessly in to the wall.

Spain, Barcelona, 2 June; Ferrari F310; Qual 1:21.587 (3), R2; Pole Hill 1:20.650; Warm-up 1:44.219 (2); Heavy rain; FL, 1.

Hill against Schumacher in qualifying but Villeneuve in there and on the front row. Then it rained and Schumacher completed the opening lap sixth. Into the second lap six cars had gone off. By lap 11 Schumacher was second, next lap in the lead: the rainmaster was at work, lapping four seconds faster than the others. His first Ferrari win was simply overwhelming – Alesi (Benetton) 45.3s behind him.

Canada, Montreal, 16 June; Ferrari F310; Qual 1:21.198 (3), R2; Pole Hill 1:21.059; Warm-up 1:23.364 (13); Warm, dry; R, 41 laps, driveshaft.

In qualifying an engine problem put Schumacher in the spare and at the parade lap he couldn't get away – fuel pressure. He started from the back and cut a path upwards: lap 1, 17th; 2, 15th; 4, 14th; 11, 13th; 20, 12th; 22, 11th; 24, tenth; 36, ninth; 37, eighth – and a driveshaft was blown back off the car.

France, Magny-Cours, 30 June; Ferrari F310; Qual 1:15.989 (P); Warm-up 1:18.689 (5); Warm, dry; DNS.

He was satisfied with his qualifying lap but felt it could have been better. On the parade lap an engine failure halted him.

Britain, Silverstone, 14 July; Ferrari F310; Qual 1:27.707 (3), R2; Pole Hill 1:26.875; Warm-up 1:29.889 (4); Warm, dry; R, hydraulic leak, 3 laps.

Third on the grid was what the Ferrari could be made to do, then, running fourth, a hydraulic leak locked the car in sixth gear.

Germany, Hockenheim, 28 July; Ferrari F310; Qual 1:44.477 (3), R2; Pole Hill 1:43.912; Warm-up 1:47.412 (6); Warm, dry; 4.

The art of the possible: Schumacher squeezing the car in qualifying, accepted third philosophically. In the race he was as low as sixth (from laps 23 to 32), rose to fourth when Berger (Benetton) – leading – went out (engine) and finished 41.5s behind the winner, Hill.

Hungary, Hungaroring, 11 Aug; Ferrari F310; Qual 1:17.129 (P); Warm-up 1:18.971 (1); Hot, dry; Classified 9, throttle, 70 laps.

Stunning confidence and car control in qualifying. He led the race and when the first pit stops played themselves out ran second to Villeneuve. He went to third after his third stop when the gearbox began to misbehave and eventually he stopped out on the circuit.

Belgium, Spa, 25 Aug; Ferrari F310; Qual 1:51.778 (3), R2; Pole Villeneuve 1:50.574; Warm-up 1:55.928 (12); Damp-dry; 1.

He crashed heavily in the free session on Friday and could do nothing about the Williamses on the Saturday. He tracked Villeneuve at the start but the pit stops shook everything up and he led, dropping to second when he pitted again. He got the race when Villeneuve pitted and came out fractionally behind him. The margin: 5.6s.

Italy, Monza, 8 Sept; Ferrari F310; Qual 1:24.781 (3), R2; Pole Hill 1:24.204; Warm-up 1:25.765 (3); Hot, dry; FL, 1.

He settled for second row of the grid again philosophically. Hill led and spun off, Alesi led but when he pitted Schumacher conjured a lap of such speed that it covered the lead when he made his own stop a couple of laps later. Alesi finished 18.2s behind.

Portugal, Estoril, 22 Sept; Ferrari F310; Qual 1:21.236 (4), R2; Pole Hill 1:20.330; Warm-up 1:22.666 (1); Warm, dry; 3.

A messy qualifying marked by late rain and a race from the art of the possible, distantly chasing the Williamses. He finished 53.7s behind the winner, Villeneuve.

Japan, Suzuka, 13 Oct; Ferrari F310; Qual 1:40.071 (3), R2; Pole Villeneuve 1:38.909; Warm-up 1:53.677 (7); Warm, dry; 2.

No holding the Williamses in qualifying again and no holding Hill in the race. He led every lap and, exploiting the first round of pit stops, Schumacher got into second place and, from lap 19, stayed there to the end, finishing 1.8s behind. He had, as he said, 'done everything I could' to get past Hill.

Hill 97 points, Villeneuve 78, Schumacher 59.

1997

Australia, Melbourne, 9 Mar; Ferrari F310B; Qual 1:31.472 (3), R2; Pole Villeneuve 1:29.369; Warm-up 1:32.704 (9); Warm, dry; 2.

Satisfied in qualifying, he felt the new car handled better than 1996's. He ran third early on, behind Frentzen (Williams) and Coulthard, and made three stops, the third unscheduled because of a fuel cell problem. Frentzen's brakes failed, enabling Schumacher to finish 20.0s behind Coulthard.

Brazil, Sao Paulo, 30 Mar; Ferrari F310B; Qual 1:16.594 (2), R1; Pole Villeneuve 1:16.004; Warm-up 1:18.316 (9); Cloudy, humid; 5.

He was 'surprised' to be so close to his main competitors in qualifying but in the race couldn't find grip and had a tyre problem, leaving him 33.7s behind the winner, Villeneuve.

Argentina, Buenos Aires, 13 Apr; Ferrari F310B; Qual 1:25.773 (4), R2; Pole Villeneuve 1:24.472; Warm-up 1:27.957 (7); Warm, dry; R, collision, 0 laps.

He set his time early and couldn't improve on it. There was chaos at the first corner, and Schumacher and Barrichello met there. Schumacher set off for the spare car but the race was not stopped.

San Marino, Imola, 27 Apr; Ferrari F310B; Qual 1:23.955 (3), R2; Pole Villeneuve 1:23.303; Warm-up 1:49.160 (5); Warm, dry; 2.

Understeer in qualifying. Villeneuve led but eventually had a gear selection problem, leaving Schumacher and Frentzen – the old Formula 3 rivals – to duel and indulge in a little blocking. Frentzen won it by 1.2s.

Monaco, Monte Carlo, 11 May; Ferrari F310B; Qual 1:18.235 (2), R1; Pole Frentzen 1:18.216; Warm-up 1:21.843 (5); Wet, cloudy; FL, 1.

Understeer again but a wet race and Schumacher seized the lead, seized the race in the course of the first lap, leading Fisichella (Jordan) by 6.6s. At that point he could only beat himself and didn't, beating Barrichello by 53.3s.

Spain, Barcelona, 25 May; Ferrari F310B; Qual 1:18.313 (7), R4; Pole Villeneuve 1:16.525; Warm-up 1:21.302 (10); Warm, dry; 4.

Qualified in the spare after the race car chassis failed. A nondescript race, constantly re-arranged by pit stops. He finished 17.9s behind the winner, Villeneuve.

Canada, Montreal, 15 June; Ferrari F310B; Qual 1:18.095 (P); Warm-up 1:20.489 (9); Hot, dry; 1.

He snaffled pole at the very end of the session, the Ferrari better balanced. He led from Fisichella but when the first pit stops unscrambled Coulthard led – from Schumacher. They both stopped twice more – the last unscheduled, for tyres. Coulthard stalled. Panis crashed and the race finished under the Safety Car, giving it to Schumacher.

France, Magny-Cours, 29 June; Ferrari F310B; Qual 1:14.548 (P); Warm-up 1: 31.613 (2); Wet-dry; FL, 1.

A touch of understeer, a surprising time even for him (because 1s faster than when testing here) and a majestic, masterful race, leading every lap except two, at his pit stops. Even in heavy rain towards the end he made only one mini-mistake, slithering off – and back on.

Britain, Silverstone, 13 July; Ferrari F310B; Qual 1:21.977 (4), R2; Pole Villeneuve 1:21.598; Warm-up 1:38.670 (4); Warm, dry; FL, R, wheel bearing, 38 laps.

The Williamses (and Häkkinen's McLaren) were just too strong in qualifying. Villeneuve led to his pit stop on lap 22 but was stationary for more than half a minute – a handling problem. A turbulent mid-race: from laps 23 to 37 Schumacher, leading now, had four different cars behind him; then a bearing failed on the left rear wheel.

Germany, Hockenheim, 27 July; Ferrari F310B; Qual 1:42.181 (4), R2; Pole Berger 1:41.873; Warm-up 1:46.662 (14); Warm, dry; 2.

A different pattern to qualifying, Berger, Fisichella and Häkkinen in front of him – Schumacher was fine-tuning the car. Berger led throughout the race except for his first pit stop, Schumacher running third behind Fisichella until, at lap 40, the Jordan's oil cooler failed. Berger beat Schumacher by 17.5s.

Hungary, Hungaroring, 10 Aug; Ferrari F310B; Qual 1:14.672 (P); Warm-up 1:16.996 (1); Warm, dry; 4.

He confessed to a 'slight mistake' in qualifying on what otherwise was a devastating lap. He led but couldn't find grip and had to stop for tyres on lap 14, emerging 12th. From there it was a long struggle up to fourth, 30.7s behind the winner, Villeneuve.

Belgium, Spa, 24 Aug; Ferrari F310B; Qual 1:50.293 (3), R2; Pole Villeneuve 1:49.450; Warm-up 1:54.593 (15); Wet-dry; 1.

Balance problems forced him into the spare in qualifying. Villeneuve led but, the circuit drying, Schumacher – who had risked intermediate tyres – took Alesi for second at La Source and Villeneuve after Les Combes. He controlled the race from there, beating Fisichella by 26.7s.

Italy, Monza, 7 Sept; Ferrari F310B; Qual 1:23.624 (9), R5; Pole Alesi 1:22.990; Warm-up 1:26.228 (14); Warm, dry; 6.

He had so little grip he qualified in the spare car. He ran seventh to lap 27 when the pit stops began – leading for a lap before he made his own, resumed seventh, and went to sixth when Häkkinen had tyre problems. He finished 11.4s behind the winner, Coulthard.

Austria, A1 Ring, 21 Sept; Ferrari F310B; Qual 1:11.056 (9), R5; Pole Villeneuve 1:10.304; Warm-up 1:13.173 (3); Warm, dry; 6.

Schumacher went for hard tyres and Irvine (softer

compound) outqualified him. A race hauntingly similar to Monza: running seventh to lap 26, leading during the first pit stops, resuming ninth, working his way up to sixth and finishing 33.4s behind the winner, Villeneuve.

Luxemburg, Nürburgring, 28 Sept; Ferrari F310B; Qual 1:17.385 (5), R3; Pole Häkkinen 1:16.602; Warm-up 1:19.512 (5); Warm, dry; R, accident, 2 laps.

Qual: he thought he'd extracted the maximum from the car. Race: at the first corner, always a tourniquet, cars went all over the place. Schumacher took to the gravel trap and Ralf ran into him.

Japan, Suzuka, 12 Oct; Ferrari F310B; Qual 1:36.133 (2), R1; Pole Villeneuve 1:36.071; Warm-up 1:39.163 (4); Hot, dry; 1.

With the Championship very much alive, the front row was fine. A complicated race, Villeneuve leading and keeping the rest in a bunch – hoping someone would take Schumacher off? Schumacher pitted first and had two hot laps before Villeneuve did – emerging just behind him. He beat Frentzen by 1.3s.

Europe, Jerez, 26 Oct; Ferrari F310B; Qual 1:21.072 (2), R1; Pole Villeneuve 1:21.072; Warm-up 1:24.063 (7); Warm, dry; R, crash, 47 laps.

Yes, they did have the same qualifying times (and so did Frentzen) – an astonishing statistical coincidence. The race became notorious when Villeneuve tried to overtake Schumacher on the inside and the Ferrari turned into him: Schumacher out, Villeneuve going on to third place and the Championship.

Villeneuve 81 points, Schumacher 78,* Frentzen 42.
(*Because of the incident with Villeneuve, Schumacher was excluded from the final classification).

1998

Australia, Melbourne, 8 Mar; Ferrari F300; Qual 1:30.767 (3), R2; Pole Häkkinen 1:30.010; Warm-up 1:34.364 (3); Warm, dry; R, engine, 5 laps.

The two McLarens ominously swift in qualifying as grooved tyres were introduced. They pulled away from him and completing the fifth lap his engine gave way.

Brazil, Sao Paulo, 29 Mar; Ferrari F300; Qual 1:18.250 (4), R2; Pole Häkkinen 1:17.092; Warm-up 1:20.578 (4); Cloudy, humid; 3.

In qualifying he couldn't find the right set-up and by lap 46, when he'd settled into third place, the McLarens could not be approached. He finished a minute behind the winner, Häkkinen, and said frankly it was the best he could do.

Argentina, Buenos Aires, 12 Apr; Ferrari F300; Qual 1:26.251 (2), R1; Pole Coulthard 1:25.852; Warm-up 1:48.501 (3); Cool, dry; 1.

To get between the McLarens in qualifying seemed significant, especially since Irvine was only just behind Häkkinen. Coulthard led from Häkkinen but Schumacher took the Finn on lap 2 and collided with Coulthard as he took him. The first pit stop (lap 28) passed the lead to Häkkinen but when the Finn stopped (lap 42) Schumacher went into the distance and won it by 22.8s.

San Marino, Imola, 26 Apr; Ferrari F300; Qual 1:26.473 (3), R2; Pole Coulthard 1:25.973; Warm-up 1:29.434 (3); Warm, dry; FL, 2.

He said he might have gone slightly quicker in qualifying, but not get near the McLarens. Same in the race, Coulthard leading every lap and Häkkinen running second to lap 16 when his gearbox failed. Schumacher was 4.5s behind Coulthard at the finish.

Spain, Barcelona, 10 May; Ferrari F300; Qual 1:21.785 (3), R2; Pole Häkkinen 1:20.262; Warm-up 1:24.852 (5); Warm, dry; 3.

The season's theme established, the McLarens not to be caught in qualifying or the race. Schumacher finished 47.0s behind the winner, Häkkinen.

Monaco, Monte Carlo, 24 May; Ferrari F300; Qual 1:20.702 (4), R2; Pole Häkkinen 1:19.798; Warm-up 1:24.107; Warm, dry; 10.

A difficult qualifying because in the Saturday morning session a broken driveshaft prevented him running at all. He worked his way up to third by lap 31 but collided with Wurz (Benetton) and pitted for repairs. That made him last and he finished two laps behind the winner, Häkkinen.

Canada, Montreal, 7 June; Ferrari F300; Qual 1:18.497 (3), R2; Pole Coulthard 1:18.213; Warm-up 1:22.360 (5); Cool, cloudy; FL, 1.

He qualified behind the McLarens but in the race Häkkinen was gone immediately (gearbox) and he tracked Coulthard until he too went on lap 18 (throttle). Schumacher pitted and as he came out he muscled Frentzen across the track and off. Schumacher served a stop'n'go for that and ran behind Fisichella, who went to lap 44 for his stop. Schumacher thrust in fast laps, made another stop and kept the lead, beating Fisichella by 16.6s.

France, Magny-Cours, 28 June; Ferrari F300; Qual 1:15.159 (2), R1; Pole Häkkinen 1:14.929; Warm-up 1:17.189 (3); Warm, dry; 1.

He felt the Ferrari was reaching the point where it could take the McLarens on. He led every lap except one (pit stop) and Irvine finished second, covering him.

Britain, Silverstone, 12 July; Ferrari F300; Qual 1:23.720 (2), R1; Pole Häkkinen 1:23.271; Warm-up 1:40.296 (5); Dry-wet; FL, 1.

He made a mistake on his last flying lap, and with it went pole. The race was surreal: when the rain fell – a storm – Schumacher supposedly overtook Wurz with the Safety Car out. The Ferrari team were informed he must serve a stop'n'go and, chaotically, he did on lap 60 – after he'd crossed the line.

Austria, A1 Ring, 26 July; Ferrari F300; Qual 1:30.5551 (4), R2; Pole Fisichella 1:29.598; Warm-up 1:14.307 (3); Warm, dry; 3.

A wet-dry qualifying and he didn't get intermediates on in time for a serious improvement. On lap 17 he went off and limped back to the pits for repairs, rejoining last.

Germany, Hockenheim, 2 Aug; Ferrari F300; Qual 1:43.459 (9), R5; Pole Häkkinen 1:41.838; Warm-up 1:46.002 (5); Hot, dry; 5.

Punished by lack of grip in qualifying, it persisted in to the race where he got as high as third during the pit stops and eventually finished 12.6s behind the winner, Häkkinen.

Hungary, Hungaroring, 16 Aug; Ferrari F300; Qual 1:17.366 (3), R2; Pole Häkkinen 1:16.973; Warm-up 1:20.325 (4); Hot, dry; FL, 1.

He wrestled the car to the second row behind, inevitably, the McLarens. Häkkinen led to lap 45, Schumacher having got past Coulthard for second place. He'd stop three times, giving him a fast second stint. Häkkinen had handling problems and Schumacher crossed the line 9.4s before Coulthard.

Belgium, Spa, 30 Aug; Ferrari F300; Qual 1:50.027 (4), R2; Pole Häkkinen 1:48.682; Warm-up 2:07.839 (1, wet); Wet; FL, R, collision, 25 laps.

No catching the McLarens in qualifying, or Hill (Jordan), who led the race until Schumacher went past him on lap 8. Coulthard was running a lap down and couldn't see Schumacher coming up to him in the spray, and Schumacher clouted the back of him.

Italy, Monza, 13 Sept; Ferrari F300; Qual 1:25.289 (P); Warm-up 1:26.924 (3); Warm, dry; 1.

A drying qualifying, timing everything, and at the end Schumacher got his right. Häkkinen led from Coulthard (of course), Schumacher third. On lap 16 Coulthard – now leading – had an engine failure and in the billowing smoke Schumacher edged past Häkkinen, Monza in tumult. He beat Irvine by 37.9s.

Luxemburg Nürburgring, 27 Sept; Ferrari F300; Qual 1:18.561 (P); Warm-up 1:21.515 (4); Cool, cloudy; 2.

He did his time on his third run, decisively quicker than everybody else. He led to his pit stop on lap 24, passing the lead to Häkkinen who used Schumacher's own ploy – fast laps to protect your own stop – and settled the race, Schumacher 2.2s behind him.

Japan, Suzuka, 1 Nov; Ferrari F300; Qual 1:36.293 (P); Warm-up 1:40.431 (1); FL, R, puncture, 31 laps.

A thrilling qualifying with Häkkinen. He stalled on the grid and started from the back, flung the Ferrari at the circuit and by lap 5 was seventh. He kept on coming and by lap 20 was fourth, two laps later third, but when debris punctured his right rear tyre his race was over and Häkkinen World Champion.

Häkkinen 100 points, Schumacher 86, Coulthard 56.

1999

Australia, Melbourne, 7 Mar; Ferrari F399; Qual 1:31.781 (3), R2; Pole Häkkinen 1:30.462; Warm-up 1:33.638 (3); Warm, dry; FL, 8.

Qualifying suggested the McLarens were continuing 1998 and Schumacher expressed disappointment. The race was ragged and rude: an electrical problem made him start from the back but by lap 22 he was up to fourth but having a gearbox problem. A pit stop put him to the back again and he finished a lap behind the winner, Irvine.

Brazil, Sao Paulo, 11 Apr; Ferrari F399; Qual 1:17.578 (4), R2; Pole Häkkinen 1:16.568; Warm-up 1:18.295 (3); Warm, dry; 2.

The qualifying struggle was with Barrichello (Stewart) – the McLarens uncatchable. The race was a tale of three drivers, Häkkinen, Barrichello and Schumacher. All led but Barrichello's engine failed, Schumacher's pit stop (on lap 38) let Häkkinen in and he won it by 4.9s.

San Marino, Imola, 2 May; Ferrari F399; Qual 1:26.538 (3), R2; Pole Häkkinen 1:26.362; Warm-up 1:29.084 (4); Warm, dry; FL, 1.

The familiar qualifying position. Häkkinen led to lap 17 when he crashed, Coulthard inheriting. Schumacher pitted on lap 31, came out and took it on. When Coulthard stopped and emerged, Schumacher had gone. He won it by 4.2s.

Monaco, Monte Carlo, 16 May; Ferrari F399; Qual 1:20.611 (2), R1; Pole Häkkinen 1:20.547; Warm-up 1:23.792 (1); Warm, dry; 1.

Schumacher seemed to have pole before Häkkinen responded, not an eyeblink between them. McLaren gambled on Häkkinen taking the lead but Schumacher won the race to Ste Devote, led every lap and beat Irvine by 30.4s.

Spain, Barcelona, 30 May; Ferrari F399; Qual 1:22.277 (4), R2; Pole Häkkinen 1:22.088; Warm-up 1:24.431 (3); Warm, dry; FL, 3.
A frustrating qualifying: whatever he tried, the car didn't improve. He ran fourth to the first pit stops, third after them from lap 27 to the end, 10.8s after the winner, Häkkinen.

Canada, Montreal, 13 June; Ferrari F399; Qual 1:19.298 (P); Warm-up 1:21.560 (7); Hot, dry; R, accident, 29 laps.
A new engine might have been decisive (0.029 over Häkkinen). He led comfortably from Häkkinen until he made a mistake and crashed.

France, Magny-Cours, 27 June; Ferrari F399; Qual 1:41.127 (6), R3; Pole Barrichello (Stewart) 1:38.441; Warm-up 1:32.449 (3); Dry-wet; 5.
A downpour drowned qualifying and drowned the race too. Häkkinen spun on lap 38 and Schumacher moved past Barrichello for the lead but pitted for a new steering wheel – trying to cure a gear selection problem. He finished 47.8s behind the winner, Frentzen (Jordan).

Britain, Silverstone, 11 July; Ferrari F399; Qual 1:25.223 (2), R1; Pole Häkkinen 1:24.804; Warm-up 1:27.497 (3); Hot, dry; R, accident, 0 laps.
He set his time on his first run and, at the start of the race, tried to take Irvine into Stowe corner. He went off at great speed and struck the tyre wall hard enough to break his leg. The Championship was gone.

Malaysia, Sepang, 17 Oct; Ferrari F399; Qual 1:39.688 (P); Warm-up 1:42.563 (5); Hot, dry; FL, 2.

The return – to help Irvine to the Championship? Immediately he reasserted himself with a stunning lap almost a second quicker than Irvine, next. A stunning race too, leading three times and passing that lead to Irvine *twice*. He covered Irvine at the end from Häkkinen, finishing 1.0s behind him.

Japan, Suzuka, 31 Oct; Ferrari F399; Qual 1:37.470 (P); Warm-up 1:40.761 (2); Warm, dry; FL, 2.

A thunderous lap in qualifying, markedly quicker than the McLarens. In the race Irvine couldn't get on the pace and Schumacher, running second to Häkkinen, could do nothing about that. He finished 5.0s behind Häkkinen, who retained the title.

Häkkinen 76 points, Irvine 74, Frentzen 54 (Schumacher fifth, 44).

2000

Australia, Melbourne, 12 Mar; Ferrari F1-2000; Qual 1:31.075 (3), R2; Pole Häkkinen 1:30.556; Warm-up 1:33.557 (8); Hot, dry; 1.

He crashed on the Friday and in qualifying the car didn't look perfectly stable. Häkkinen led to lap 18 when the engine failed, opening it to Schumacher. He beat new team-mate Barrichello by 11.4s.

Brazil, Interlagos, 26 Mar; Ferrari F1-2000; Qual 1:14.508 (3), R2; Pole Häkkinen 1:14.111; Warm-up 1:16.348 (2); Hot, dry; FL, 1.

He went off in qualifying and switched to the spare, but still no catching the McLarens. He took Häkkinen into lap 2 and would pit stop twice, the McLarens once. It worked. He lost the lead only after his first stop and beast Fisichella (Benetton) by 39.8s.

San Marino, Imola, 9 Apr; Ferrari F1-2000; Qual 1:24.805 (2), R1; Pole Häkkinen 1:24.714; Warm-up 1:27.620 (3); Warm, dry; 1.

He made a mistake on his third run and blamed himself. From the start he tracked Häkkinen, leading, to lap 44 when Häkkinen made his second pit stop. Schumacher had four laps to gain enough time to make his own and keep the lead. He did, and won it by 1.1s.

Britain, Silverstone, 23 Apr; Ferrari F1-2000; Qual 1:26.161 (5), R3; Pole Barrichello 1:25.703; Warm-up 1:27.134 (5); Warm, dry; 3.

Uncertain weather and Schumacher went out fractionally too late to get a final lap. He ran eighth early on, working a path to the lead (on lap 36) during the first pit stops. His own stop made him sixth, rising to third 19.9s behind winner Coulthard.

Spain, Barcelona, 7 May; Ferrari F1-2000; Qual 1:20.974 (P); Warm-up 1:22.855 (1); Warm, dry; 5.

He judged he could take pole and he was right (from Häkkinen, 1:21.052 – 0.197 difference). He led to lap 41 and his second pit stop, had a controversial moment when Coulthard tried to overtake him – 'he moved over on me,' Coulthard said – and drifted back with a slow puncture, finishing 47.9s behind winner Häkkinen.

Europe, Nürburgring, 21 May; Ferrari F1-2000; Qual 1:17.667 (2), R1; Pole Coulthard 1:17.529; Warm-up 1:20.251 (1); Wet-dry; FL, 1.

Changeable weather in qualifying and the race, which Häkkinen led until, on lap 11, Schumacher dived by into the final chicane. He led to lap 35, his second pit stop, giving it back to Häkkinen for ten laps – then Häkkinen pitted. Schumacher beat him by13.8s.

Monaco, Monte Carlo, 4 June; Ferrari F1-2000; Qual 1:19.475 (P); Warm-up 1:22.307 (2); Hot, dry; R, pushrod, 55 laps.

He danced the Ferrari round Monaco and took pole from Trulli's Jordan. He led every lap until the mechanical failure.

Canada, Montreal, 18 June; Ferrari F1-2000; Qual 1:18.439 (P); Warm-up 1:18.932 (1); Dry-wet; 1.

He took pole at the end of qualifying after a hectic session against the McLarens – and Barrichello. Coulthard, second quickest, stalled his engine giving Schumacher a clear run. Apart from his pit stop he led throughout, beating Barrichello by 0.1s.

France, Magny-Cours, 2 July; Ferrari F1-2000; Qual 1:15.632 (P); Warm-up 1:19.960 (3); Warm, dry; R, engine, 58 laps.

He took pole with his first run and led every lap to 40 – except a pit stop – when Coulthard, strong and in the mood, squeezed by. Schumacher's tyres were going off – and the engine went off too.

Austria, A1-Ring, 16 July; Ferrari F1-2000; Qual 1:11.046 (4), R2; Pole Häkkinen 1:10.410; Warm-up 1:13.281 (5); Hot, dry; R, accident, 0 laps.

Häkkinen, who'd had a complete rest since France, seized qualifying: any of his three fast laps would have been pole. In the compression of the first corner Zonta's BAR punted Schumacher off, amidst much other crashing and bashing.

Germany, Hockenheim, 30 July; Ferrari F1-2000; Qual 1:47.063 (2), R1; Pole Coulthard 1:45.697; Warm-up 1:44.782 (4); Dry-wet; R, accident, 0 laps.

After a crash on Saturday morning, he used the spare in qualifying and set his time at the end of the session. From the grid he and Fisichella collided. It meant in two Grands Prix he hadn't covered a lap.

Hungary, Hungaroring, 13 Aug; Ferrari F1-2000; Qual 1:17.514 (P); Warm-up 1:19.381 (2); Hot, dry; 2.

He conjured a tremendous lap for his 28th pole, equalling Fangio but, pit stops aside, Häkkinen led every lap, Schumacher always behind him and losing it by 7.9s.

Belgium, Spa, 27 Aug; Ferrari F1-2000; Qual 1:51.552 (4), R2; Pole Häkkinen 1:50.646; Warm-up 2:03.562 (2, wet); Wet-dry; 2.

He met traffic on one run, yellow flags on another. He had a race-long duel with Häkkinen – exchanging the lead four times – until on lap 41 Häkkinen went down the inside of Zonta at Les Combes, Schumacher outside Zonta and outfoxed. Häkkinen won it by 1.1s.

Italy, Monza, 10 Sept; Ferrari F1-2000; Qual 1:23.770 (P); Warm-up 1:26.593 (3); Hot, dry; 1.

He maintained an advantage over the McLarens throughout qualifying and stormed the race, leading every lap except three (his pit stop). He beat Häkkinen by 3.8s.

USA, Indianapolis, 24 Sept; Ferrari F1-2000; Qual 1:14.266 (P); Warm-up 1:23.922 (3); Overcast, cool; 1.

He got pole by slipstreaming Barrichello on the straight into his fast lap. Coulthard led to lap 7 when Schumacher went by, dominating the remainder of the race. He beat Barrichello by 12.1s.

Japan, Suzuka, 8 Oct; Ferrari F1-2000; Qual 1:35.825 (P); Warm-up 1:38.005 (1); Dry, shower at end; 1.

The Grand Prix where Schumacher could become Ferrari's first World Champion since 1979. A gripping qualifying struggle between Schumacher and Häkkinen (0.009 of a second between them). Häkkinen into the lead, Schumacher after him full across 36 of the 53 laps and stole it at the second pit stops.

Although Häkkinen pressed him – 1.8s at the line – Italy had their World Champion at last.

Malaysia, Sepang, 22 Oct; Ferrari F1-2000; Qual 1:37.397 (P); Warm-up 1:40.246 (3); Hot, dry; 1.

He went implacably on, experimenting with rear wing settings and going comfortably quicker than Häkkinen who led the race, then Coulthard. At the first pit stops Schumacher stayed out for six crucial laps and blasted the Ferrari round so he could lead to the end. He beat Coulthard by 0.7s.

Schumacher 108 points, Häkkinen 89, Coulthard 73.

2001

Australia, Melbourne, 4 Mar; Ferrari F2001; Qual 1:26.892 (P); Warm-up 1:30.839 (6); Hot, dry; FL, 1.

On the Friday he crashed and overturned; made light of it afterwards. Then something changed. Schumacher was no longer a driver trying to retain his title: he and Ferrari opened a new era – their own. His pole was the only lap in the 1:26s – Barrichello next, 1:27.263. He led every lap (except four after his pit stop) and beat Coulthard by 1.7s.

Malaysia, Sepang, 18 Mar; Ferrari F2001; Qual 1:35.220 (P); Warm-up 1:52.316 (7); Dry-wet; 1.

Brother Ralf (Williams) went fastest in mid-session, forcing Schumacher to dig deep for pole. Schumacher led but rain suddenly lashed down and both Ferraris went off, came back on. From 12th on lap 10 he showed his force and finesse, led six laps later and never lost it, beating Barrichello by 23.6s.

Brazil, Interlagos, 1 Apr; Ferrari F2001; Qual 1:13.780 (P); Warm-up 1:15.971 (1); Dry-wet; 2.

A Schumacher front row, Ralf alongside (1:14.090). Schumacher led but into lap 3 Montoya (Williams) ripped down the inside, banged wheels and was through. On lap 39 he had a crash, letting Coulthard in for the win from Schumacher by 16.1s.

San Marino, Imola, 15 Apr; Ferrari F2001; Qual 1:23.593 (4), R2; Pole Coulthard 1:23.054; Warm-up 1:26.948 (6); Warm, dry; R, brakes, 24 laps.

He had a slow final sector on his fast lap. Ralf led every lap of the race, Schumacher seventh when the brake problem claimed him.

Spain, Barcelona, 29 Apr; Ferrari F2001; Qual 1:18.201 (P); Warm-up 1:21.211 (4); Warm, dry; FL, 1.

Tight in qualifying, Häkkinen at 0.085. Schumacher led to lap 22 and the pit stops, led again to the second stops – Häkkinen did six fierce laps, pitted and emerged in the lead. Schumacher had a tyre vibration but on the last lap Häkkinen's clutch failed. Schumacher beat Montoya by 40.7s.

Austria, A-1 Ring, 13 May; Ferrari F2001; Qual 1:09.562 (P); Warm-up 1:12.790 (5); Warm, dry; 2.

Delicate getting the set-up right, he said, but he did. A tough race, an incident overtaking Montoya and at the end Barrichello moved aside to give him second place, 2.1s behind Coulthard.

Monaco, Monte Carlo, 27 May; Ferrari F2001; Qual 1:17.631 (2), R1; Pole Coulthard 1:17.430; Warm-up 1:21.650 (3); Hot, dry; 1.

He brushed a barrier, probably costing him pole. He led every lap except five after his pit stop and beat Barrichello by 0.4s.

Canada, Montreal, 10 June; Ferrari F2001; Qual 1:15.782 (P);
Warm-up 1:18.663 (6); Hot, dry; 2.

Schumacher not under qualifying pressure (Ralf, next, at
0.515), and an historic race, Schumacher leading from Ralf to
lap 45 (pit stop) and Ralf leading to the end, 20.2s ahead.

Europe, Nürburgring, 24 June; Ferrari F2001; Qual 1:14.960
(P); Warm-up 1:18.371 (2); Hot, dry; 1.

Straightforward Schumacher. The only man in the 1:14s
(Ralf 1:15.22), he led every lap except 29, his first pit stop, and
beat Montoya by 4.2s.

France, Magny-Cours, 1 July; Ferrari F2001; Qual 1:12.999
(2), R1; Pole Ralf Schumacher 1:12.989; Warm-up 1:15.429
(2); Hot, dry; 1.

He had to force the Ferrari very hard in qualifying, and it
showed. Ralf led to lap 23 and the pit stops. Schumacher made
a swifter stop and had the lead which he only lost at his second
stop – to Montoya. When he pitted Schumacher ran for home,
Ralf 10.3s behind.

Britain, Silverstone, 15 July; Ferrari F2001; Qual 1:20.447 (P);
Warm-up 1:24.407 (5); Dry, warm; 2.

Häkkinen the only threat in qualifying (at 0.082), and strong
in the race after Schumacher led to lap 5. Häkkinen took him
into Becketts and was not to be caught on a two-stop strategy,
Schumacher (on a one) finishing 33.6s behind.

Germany, Hockenheim, 29 July; Ferrari F2001; Qual 1:38.941
(4), R2; Pole Montoya 1:38.117; Warm-up 1:42.747 (4); Hot,
sunny; R, fuel pressure, 23 laps.

A difficult qualifying trying to get the car right. He ran third
behind the Williamses, dropped to fourth when Barrichello went
by, was up to third again when he parked at the side of the track.

Hungary, Hungaroring, 19 Aug; Ferrari F2001; Qual 1:14.059 (P); Warm-up 1:17.338 (2); Hot, sunny; 1.

He used only half his 12 laps to get pole and led every lap of the race except six at his two pit stops. He beat Barrichello by 3.3s and retained the Championship. Mansell had won the Championship here in 1992 when it was the 11th race – it was the 13th race of 2001.

Belgium, Spa, 2 Sept; Ferrari F2001; Qual 1:54.685 (3), R2; Pole Montoya 1:52.072; Warm-up 1:49.495 (1); Warm, dry; FL, 1.

He had a crash on the Friday (hitting de la Rosa's Jaguar) and in qualifying the Bridgestones didn't seem to like the damp, drying conditions. He led to lap 5 when the race was stopped after Burti (Prost) crashed at great speed. He led every lap from the restart, beating Coulthard by 10.0s. It was his 52nd win, beating Prost's record.

Italy, Monza, 16 Sept; Ferrari F2001; Qual 1:22.624 (3), R2; Pole Montoya 1:22.216; Warm-up 1:26.029 (1); Warm, dry; 4.

Run deep in the shadow of 9/11 in America. Schumacher found concentration elusive in qualifying and a terrible accident to Zanardi in Germany deepened the shadows. He was never higher than third, finished 24.9s behind winner Montoya and was happy nothing had happened.

USA, Indianapolis, 30 Sept; Ferrari F2001; Qual 1:11.708 (P); Warm-up 1:14.029 (4); Dry, warm; 2.

Formula One's gesture to bringing normality to America. In qualifying Schumacher didn't need his last run. A lively race, leading, letting Barrichello into the lead, being overtaken by Montoya and finishing 11.0s behind winner Häkkinen.

Japan, Suzuka, 14 Oct; Ferrari F2001; Qual 1:32.484 (P); Warm-up 1:36.231 (1); Warm, dry; 1.

Plenty of grip and his 11th pole (the record being held by Mansell, 14) and a commanding race – beating Montoya by 3.1s. He now had 801 points, beating Prost's record 798.5. This was his ninth win in the season, equalling the record set by Mansell in 1992 and equalled by himself in 1995 and 2000.

Schumacher 123 points, Coulthard 65, Barrichello 56.

2002
(Ferrari F2001 to Malaysia, then F2002)

Australia, Melbourne, 3 Mar; Ferrari F2001; Qual 1:25.848 (2), R1; Pole Barrichello 1:25.843; Warm-up 1:41.509 (1); Warm, dry; 1.

Last year's car was still good enough to fill the front row. Coulthard made a strong start from Trulli (Renault) but Schumacher worked his way into the lead by lap 11. Montoya attacked and took him on the outside, Schumacher counter-attacked for five laps and took *him* on the outside. He won by 18.6s.

Malaysia, Sepang, 17 Mar; Ferrari F2001; Qual 1:35.266 (P); Warm-up 1:39.748 (2); Hot, dry; 3.

Last year's car *still* good enough, a rasping pole from Montoya (at 0.231). A collision with Montoya at the first corner, and a pit stop for a new nosecone, made Schumacher last. The rest of the race was a long recovery: 13th at lap 10, 12th after a pit stop at lap 20, sixth by lap 30, fourth by lap 41, and finally third 1:01.7 behind winner Ralf.

Brazil, Interlagos, 31 Mar; Ferrari F2002; Qual 1:13.241 (2), R1; Pole Montoya 1:13.114; Warm-up 1:15.866 (1); Hot, dry; 1.

The new car, but Schumacher had to take it to the edge for his time. He duelled with Ralf throughout the race and in the final frantic laps held him off, crossing the line 0.5s ahead.

San Marino, Imola, 14 Apr; Ferrari F2002; Qual 1:21.091 (P); Warm-up 1:25.906 (2); Warm, dry; 1.

An intense struggle with Barrichello for pole, replicated in the race once Ralf went to third place at the first pit stops. Schumacher won by 17.9s.

Spain, Barcelona, 28 Apr; Ferrari F2002; Qual 1:16.364 (P); Warm-up 1:20.884 (3); Hot, dry; FL, 1.

Even small mistakes couldn't keep Schumacher from pole and he led every lap of the race, including both pit stops, to beat Montoya by 35.6s.

Austria, A1-Ring, 12 May; Ferrari F2002; Qual 1:08.704 (3), R2; Pole Barrichello 1:08.082; Warm-up 1:10.895 (2); Warm, dry; FL, 1.

Wasn't happy with the race car in qualifying and switched to the spare. A notorious race: Barrichello led the rush to the chequered flag, when he was ordered to move over and let Schumacher by. Nobody was happy, especially Barrichello and Schumacher.

Monaco, Monte Carlo, 26 May; Ferrari F2002; Qual 1:17.118 (3), R2; Pole Montoya 1:16.676; Warm-up 1:20.972 (2); Warm, dry; 2.

A difficult qualifying finding a clear lap. He ran third behind Coulthard and Montoya to lap 44 when he pitted. Montoya's engine let go, and he ran second to the end, 1.0s behind Coulthard.

Canada, Montreal, 9 June; Ferrari F2002; Qual 1:13.018 (2), R1; Pole Montoya 1:12.836; Warm-up 1:16.780 (1); Warm, dry; 1.

A duel with Montoya in qualifying but Barrichello led from Montoya, Schumacher third: second when Montoya pitted, leading when Barrichello pitted. After the second round of stops he led again and beat Coulthard by 1.1s.

Europe, Nürburgring, 23 June; Ferrari F2002; Qual 1:30.035 (3), R2; Pole Montoya 1:29.906; Warm-up 1:32.987 (2); Warm, dry; FL 2.

He had to switch to the spare after a transmission problem. Barrichello led throughout and Schumacher followed him from lap 3 – when he overtook Ralf. No team orders were applied and Barrichello won it by 0.2s.

Britain, Silverstone, 7 July; Ferrari F2002; Qual 1:19.042 (3), R2; Pole Montoya 1:18.998; Warm-up 1:22.815 (2); Cloudy, some rain; 1.

Montoya and Barrichello outqualified him. Barrichello started from the rear of the grid after an electrical problem, Montoya leading from Schumacher. They both pitted on the same lap (13) – for wet tyres – and resumed in the same order but two laps later Schumacher took him and moved majestically away, mastering the shifting weather and slippery track to beat heroic Barrichello by 14.5s.

France, Magny-Cours, 21 July; Ferrari F2002; Qual 1:12.008 (2), R1; Pole Montoya 1:11.985; Warm-up 1:14.174 (1); Warm, dry; 1.

On his first qualifying run his time didn't count because he went straight through a gravel trap. Montoya led, Schumacher tracking, but a complicated race: successively Schumacher, Montoya, Räikkönen (McLaren), Coulthard, Räikkönen and, with five laps left, Schumacher when Räikkönen slithered on oil. He had retained the Championship in this the 11th race – equalling Mansell.

Germany, Hockenheim, 28 July; Ferrari F2002; Qual 1:14.389 (P); Warm-up 1:16.726 (1); Hot-dry; FL, 1.

As near absolute domination as you can get: he was quickest in the Friday and Saturday free session as well as qualifying and the Sunday morning warm-up. He led every lap except five, when he made his pit stops, and beat Montoya by 10.5s.

Hungary, Hungaroring, 18 Aug; Ferrari F2002; Qual 1:13.392 (2), R1; Pole Barrichello 1:13.333; Warm-up 1:16.864 (1); Hot, dry; FL, 2.

Barrichello was having a good season, Schumacher's first partner to stretch him in qualifying. They waltzed the race, first and second apart from one lap during the first pit stops, and Barrichello won it by 0.4s.

Belgium, Spa, 1 Sept; Ferrari F2002; Qual 1:43.726 (P); Warm-up 1:48.044 (1); Overcast, dry; FL, 1.

Amazingly, he hadn't been on pole here before and Räikkönen might have had it from him but met traffic. He bestrode the race, mighty and sure, beating Barrichello by 1.9s, the rest scattered far back. He had now won ten races in a season, beating his own and Mansell's record of 9.

Italy, Monza, 15 Sept; Ferrari F2002; Qual 1:20.521 (5), R1; Pole Montoya 1:20.264; Warm-up 1:25.137 (4); Warm, dry; 2.

Qual: happy on the front row. Race: led for nine laps in mid-race when Barrichello pitted, followed him home 0.2s behind.

USA, Indianapolis, 29 Sept; Ferrari F2002; Qual 1:10.790 (P); Warm-up 1:13.183 (1); Warm, dry; 2.

Qual: best run baulked by yellow flags. Race: he and Barrichello dominated and at the end tried to stage a dead heat. After the fiasco in Austria, comment is superfluous – and F1 was trying to sink roots in the USA. Barrichello 'won' it by 0.011s.

Japan, Suzuka, 13 Oct; Ferrari F2002; Qual 1:31.317 (P); Warm-up 1:36.249 (1); Warm, dry; FL, 1.

Qual: liked the car, which translated means pole. Race: led every lap except one (first pit stop) and Barrichello ran second (apart from his stops). They finished 0.5 apart. That gave him 11 wins.

Schumacher 144 points, Barrichello 77, Montoya 50.

2003

Australia, Melbourne, 9 Mar; Ferrari F2002; Qual 1:27.173 (P); Warm-up 1:27.844 (2); Wet-dry; 4.

In the new one-shot qualifying he went fourth from last and was decisively quickest. Led, pitted at lap 8 for dry tyres – but a wheel-nut stuck. Resumed eighth, vaulted to second when others pitted, even led when Montoya pitted a second time. Pitted himself and fourth was the best he could salvage.

Malaysia, Sepang, 23 Mar; Ferrari F2002; Qual 1:37.393 (3), R2; Pole Alonso (Renault) 1:37.044; Warm-up 1:39.483 (16); Hot, dry; FL, 6.

Qual: 'Third was the best I could do.' Race: he hit Trulli at the start (and later apologised). He faced a long climb and by lap 42 ran fifth, dropping a place in the last pit stops.

Brazil, Interlagos, 6 Apr; Ferrari F2002; Qual 1:14.130 (7), R4; Pole Barrichello 1:13.807; Warm-up 1:14.166 (3); Wet-dry; R, accident, 26 laps.

Qual: one small mistake cost him many places. Race: he was up to third by lap 16, ran there and spun off. 'I was aquaplaning… you are just a passenger.'

San Marino, Imola, 20 Apr; Ferrari F2002; Qual 1:22.327 (P);
Warm-up 1:23.452 (2); Warm, dry; FL, 1.

The difficult race: his mother died not long before the start.
Qual: he felt comfortable. Race: Ralf into the lead but when the
first pit stops were played out he led and beat Räikkönen by
1.8s.

Spain, Barcelona, 4 May; Ferrari F2003; Qual 1:17.762 (P);
Warm-up 1:19.260 (4); Hot, dry; 1.

Qual: the new car was fine and 'faster'. Race: a perfect day,
leading every lap except the pit stops and beating Alonso by 5.7s.

Austria, A-1 Ring, 18 May; Ferrari F2003; Qual 1:09.150 (P);
Warm-up 1:09.639 (3); Showers; FL, 1.

Qual: a wobble, but a good run. Race: he led to the first pit
stop but the rig malfunctioned, the car covered in fire. They
sent him back out and afterwards he made a little joke about it.
He beat Räikkönen by 3.3s.

Monaco, Monte Carlo, 1 June; Ferrari F2003; Qual 1:15.644
(5), R3; Pole Ralf Schumacher 1:15.259; Warm-up 1:16.127
(5); Warm, dry; 3.

Qual: not competitive in the second and third sectors. Race:
because of the grid position he fuelled long, which meant
following Trulli, who was fourth. Finishing third (1.7 behind
winner Montoya) was 'quite good'.

Canada, Montreal, 15 June; Ferrari F2003; Qual 1:16.047 (3),
R2; Pole Ralf Schumacher 1:15.529; Warm-up 1:18.845 (17);
Dry, windy; 1.

Qual: not 'one of my better laps'. Race: a tough, tight race.
Ralf led but Schumacher went a lap further before pitting, just
keeping the lead when he emerged. He won it from there,
beating Ralf by 0.7s.

Europe, Nürburgring, 29 June; Ferrari F2003; Qual 1:31.555 (2), R1; Pole Räikkönen 1:31.523; Warm-up 1:31.981 (1); Warm, dry; 5.

Qual: locked a front wheel and got away with it. Race: he ran third but Montoya went by and he spun, drove for points. He finished 1:06.1 behind winner Ralf.

France, Magny-Cours, 6 July; Ferrari F2003; Qual 1:15.480 (3), R2; Pole Ralf Schumacher 1:15.019; Warm-up 1:15.879 (5); Hot, dry; 3.

Qual: he thought the circuit would suit the car better. Race: he knew the Ferrari would not be competitive here. Ran fourth early and was satisfied with third, 19.5s behind winner Ralf.

Britain, Silverstone, 20 July; Ferrari F2003; Qual 1:21.867 (5), R3; Pole Barrichello 1:21.209; Warm-up 1:22.074 (3); Overcast; 4.

Qual: made a mistake at Abbey, running wide. Race: ran fifth. A maniac ran onto the track and under the Safety Car everybody pitted – Schumacher waiting for Barrichello to be done, and emerging 14th. 'Fourth is not too bad.'

Germany, Hockenheim, 3 Aug; Ferrari F2003; Qual 1:15.898 (6), R3; Pole Montoya 1:15.167; Warm-up 1:16.532 (9); Hot, dry; 7.

Qual: the handling not exactly right. Race: a long thrust from fifth on lap 1 to second by lap 59, but with four to go he had a puncture and finished a lap behind winner Montoya.

Hungary, Hungaroring, 24 Aug; Ferrari F2003; Qual 1:22.755 (8), R4; Pole Alonso 1:21.688; Warm-up 1:22.210 (1); Hot, dry; 8.

Qual: 'a bit disappointed'. Race: 'a lot of things did not go the way we wanted' – trapped for a long time behind Coulthard, a slow second pit stop, and finished a lap behind winner Alonso.

Italy, Monza, 14 Sept; Ferrari F2003; Qual 1:20.963 (P); Warm-up 1:27.906 (19); Hot, dry; FL, 1.

Qual: back on the pace, as he said. Race: he led every lap except one (his first pit stop), beat Montoya by 5.2s and said 'I think this is the greatest day in my career'.

USA, Indianapolis, 28 Sept; Ferrari F2003; Qual 1:12.194 (7), R4; Pole Räikkönen 1:11.670; Warm-up 1:12.688 (6); Dry-wet; FL, 1.

Qual: the car slid too much. Race: quickly up to third (lap 5), back to sixth and after the first pit stops 12th, then a remorseless rise to the lead, beating Räikkönen by 18.2s. They went to Suzuka with Schumacher leading 92 points to 83.

Japan, Suzuka, 12 Oct; Ferrari F2003; Qual 1:34.302 (14), R7; Pole Barrichello 1:31.713; Warm-up (no time); Overcast, rain; 8.

The decider, Räikkönen needing to win. Qual: 'an interesting session' – rain fell when his turn came. Race: taut, drawn into several dimensions – Schumacher running down the field and after a collision with Sato (BAR) he pitted, emerging last. Up front Räikkönen and Coulthard exchanged second place under pit stops but Barrichello was not to be caught, enough to make Schumacher champion despite Ralf hitting him.

Schumacher 93 points, Räikkönen 91, Montoya 82.

2004

Australia, Melbourne, 7 Mar; Ferrari F2004; Qual 1:24.408 (P); Warm, dry; FL, 1.

New qualifying: two practice sessions on Friday, two on Saturday then qualifying. No Sunday warm-up. Schumacher immediately dominant – not surprised to be on pole (from

Barrichello) and leading every lap, including three pit stops. A 'perfect race'. He beat Barrichello by 13.6s.

Malaysia, Sepang, 21 Mar; Ferrari F2004; Qual 1:33.074 (P); Hot, dry; 1.

Qual: a 'mindblowing lap', although Webber (Jaguar) separated the Ferraris. Race: led despite a prolonged struggle ('tough') with Montoya in second, Schumacher beating him by 5.0s.

Bahrain, Sakhir, 4 Apr; Ferrari F2004; Qual 1:30.139 (P); Overcast, rainy; FL, 1.

Qual: 'cannot say I got a perfect lap'. Race: led every lap except the pit stops, beating Barrichello by 1.3s. 'A dream result' – and a nightmare for the rest of F1.

San Marino, Imola, 25 Apr; Ferrari F2004; Qual 1:20.011 (2), R1; Pole Button (BAR) 1:19.753; Warm, dry; FL, 1.

Qual: 'Our competitors have picked up their pace.' Race: Button led to the first pit stops, Schumacher very robust, keeping Montoya behind at the start. When Button pitted Schumacher produced two thunderous laps, pitted and emerged in the lead – race settled. He beat Button by 9.7s.

Spain, Barcelona, 9 May; Ferrari F2004; Qual 1:15.022 (P); Warm, dry; FL, 1.

Qual: so fast in the first two sectors he played safe in the third. Race: Trulli (Renault) powered into the lead from the second row but when the first pit stops were done Schumacher led from Barrichello, and beat him by 13.2s. 'I opted to let the strategy do the work.'

Monaco, Monte Carlo, 23 May; Ferrari F2004; Qual 1:14.516 (5), R2; Pole Trulli 1:13.985; Warm, dry; FL, R, accident, 45 laps.

Qual: disappointing – his word. Race: sixth on the opening lap, steadily up to the lead by lap 43 when Trulli pitted. The Safety Car was out (Alonso crashed) and Schumacher braked, accelerated to warm his tyres. Montoya ran into the back of him.

Europe, Nürburgring, 30 May; Ferrari F2004; Qual 1:28.351 (P); Warm, dry; FL, 1.

Qual: 'The perfect lap.' Race: 'It was fantastic to see how I could pull away.' He led every lap except the pit stops and beat Barrichello by 17.9s.

Canada, Montreal, 13 June; Ferrari F2004; Qual 1:13.355 (6), R3; Pole Ralf Schumacher 1:12.275; Warm, dry; 1.

Qual: difficult – his word – but running fuel heavy to make two stops, not three. Race: the car allowed him to run consistently fast and, from fifth on the opening lap, he led by lap 18: the first pit stops. He worked back into the lead by lap 33 and beat Barrichello by 5.1s. (Ralf, second, was disqualified – illegal brake cooling ducts.)

USA, Indianapolis, 20 June; Ferrari F2004; Qual 1:10.400 (2), R1; Pole Barrichello 1:10.233; Warm, dry; 1.

Qual: 'I expected to be further back.' Race: Barrichello led but the Safety Car came out after four cars crashed. When the Safety Car pulled off Schumacher powered past Barrichello and stayed there, finishing 2.9s ahead.

France, Magny-Cours, 4 July; Ferrari F2004; Qual 1:13.971 (2), R1; Pole Alonso 1:13.698; Warm, dry; FL, 1.

Qual: 'Just not quick enough in the third sector.' Race: Alonso led to the second pit stops – but Schumacher came in three laps before he did, then went fast enough to lead. Ferrari had moved to a four-stop strategy and Schumacher was not to be caught, beating Alonso by 8.3.

Britain, Silverstone, 11 July; Ferrari F2004; Qual 1:18.710 (4), R2; Pole Räikkönen 1:18.233; Overcast; FL, 1.

Qual: 'I had a good lap.' Race: Räikkönen led to the first pit stops, Schumacher staying out and going fast, pitting and keeping a lead he did not lose. Räikkönen kept after him and was only 2.1s behind at the end.

Germany, Hockenheim, 25 July; Ferrari F2004; Qual 1:13.306 (P); Hot, dry; 1.

Qual: not surprised to be on pole. Race: he led throughout except the pit stops, although it was a 'tough' race with successively Räikkönen, Alonso and Button. He beat Button by 8.3s.

Hungary, Hungaroring, 15 Aug; Ferrari F2004; Qual 1:19.146 (P); Hot, dry; FL, 1.

Qual: 'a good lap' – Barrichello on the pace too (at 0.177). Race: led every lap to beat Barrichello by 4.6s.

Belgium, Spa, 29 Aug; Ferrari F2004; Qual 1:56.304 (2), R1; Pole Trulli 1:56.232; Dry, cloudy; 2.

Qual: unlucky to go out in a shower. Race: happy to run second to Räikkönen for the second half, finishing 3.1s behind – but giving him his seventh Championship.

Italy, Monza, 12 Sept; Ferrari F2004; Qual 1:20.637 (3), R2; Pole Barrichello 1:20.089; Wet-dry; 2.

Qual: a mistake, running wide, at Parabolica. Race: a nudge and a spin at the second chicane put him back to 15th completing the opening lap. He worked his way up – the Ferrari ferociously fast – and was within 1.3s of Barrichello at the end.

China, Shanghai, 26 Sept; Ferrari F2004; Qual (no time), R10; Pole Barrichello 1:34.012; Warm, dry; FL, 12.

Qual: spun into the gravel trap and had no idea why. Race: starting from the back he forced his way to sixth by lap 19, then sank back, but as he said, all his bad luck came in this race – a crash with Klein (Jaguar), a spin, and a puncture. He finished a lap down on winner Barrichello.

Japan, Suzuka, 10 Oct; Ferrari F2004; Qual 1:33.542 (P); Warm, dry; 1.
Qual: moved to Sunday morning – a typhoon threatened on the Saturday. This gave Schumacher an historic opportunity to take pole and a race on the same day, and he did, leading every lap and beating Ralf by 14.0s.

Brazil, Interlagos, 24 Oct; Ferrari F2004; Qual 1:11.386 (8), R9; Pole Barrichello 1:10.646; Wet-dry; 7.
Qual: he crashed in the morning and the car 'picked up some understeer'. Race: he wanted more than light rain to gain an advantage and didn't get it. He finished 50.6s behind winner Montoya, said he didn't feel tired but was looking forward to a break.

Schumacher 148 points, Barrichello 114, Button 85.

2005

Australia, Melbourne, 6 Mar; Ferrari F2004M; Qual 1:57.931 (18), R10; Pole Fisichella 1:33.171; Dry, overcast; R, accident, 42 laps.
Qual: a downpour flooded the track as Schumacher was out. Race: He got as high as tenth by lap 22, fell back, was up to seventh by lap 40 and crashed into Heidfeld (Williams). 'It is impossible to blame either of us.'

Malaysia, Sepang, 20 Mar; Ferrari F2004M; Qual 1:34.072 (13), R7; Pole Alonso 1:32.582; Warm, dry; 7.

Qual: 'It's clear that on a quick lap with new tyres our performance is not at the same level as our rivals.' Race: he rose steadily, reaching sixth by lap 42, made a pit stop and lost a place. 'I did the best I could.' That was 1m 19.9s behind winner Alonso.

Bahrain, Sahkir, 3 Apr; Ferrari F2005; Qual 1:30.237 (2), R1; Pole Alonso 1:29.848; Hot, dry; R, hydraulics, 12 laps.

Qual: the new car and 'all the work has paid off'. Race: he stayed with Alonso, fell back a little and spun when the hydraulics failed. 'The car was very competitive.'

San Marino, Imola, 24 Apr; Ferrari F2005; Qual 1:20.260 (14), R7; Pole Räikkönen 1:19.886; Dry, cloudy; FL, 2.

Qual: a mistake at Rivazza pushed him back down the grid. Race: he was 'happy' and 'excited' after rising to third by lap 25 and second by lap 43, finishing 0.21s behind winner Alonso.

Spain, Barcelona, 8 May; Ferrari F2005; Qual 1:15.398 (8), R4; Pole Räikkönen 1:14.891; Warm, dry; R, puncture, 46 laps.

Qual: 'A reasonable performance' – losing time in the last two sectors. Race: the story of the season so far, a steady rise – to second by lap 30 – before two punctures hobbled him. 'It is strange that both were on the same side.'

Monaco, Monte Carlo, 22 May; Ferrari F2005; Qual 1:16.186 (8), R4; Pole Räikkönen 1:13.644; Warm, dry; FL, 7.

Qual: 'Not a good session' – and going early the track was slippery. Race: not good either. Stuck behind Coulthard and needed a new nosecone, effectively taking him out of contention. He finished 37.2s behind winner Räikkönen.

Europe, Nürburgring, 29 May; Ferrari F2005; Qual 1:31.585 (10), R5; Pole Heidfeld 1:30.081; Warm, dry; 5.

Qual: understeer slowed him. Race: another long recovery – 'race pace not as good as usual' – and went off once, understeer. He finished 50.4s behind winner Alonso.

Canada, Montreal, 12 June; Ferrari F2005; Qual 1:15.475 (2), R1; Pole Button 1:15.217; Warm, dry; 2.

Qual: there were worries about the gearbox. Race: a bad start – no grip – and at the end he hadn't enough extra pace to get past the winner, Räikkönen. The margin: 1.1s.

USA, Indianapolis, 19 June; Ferrari F2005; Qual 1:11.369 (5), R3; Pole Trulli (Toyota) 1:10.625; Overcast, dry; FL, 1.

The notorious race. Qual: he judged the car competitive but Ralf had crashed – a tyre failure – and Michelin advised their runners to withdraw. Race: just six cars took the start and Schumacher beat Barrichello by 1.5s.

France, Magny-Cours, 3 July; Ferrari F2005; Qual 1:14.572 (4), R2; Pole Alonso 1:14.412; Warm, dry; 3.

Qual: he hoped realistically for pole and felt the car was more competitive than for some time. Race: a solid run to third – 'the best I could have done' – finishing 1:21.9s behind winner Alonso.

Britain, Silverstone, 10 July; Ferrari F2005; Qual 1:21.275 (10), R5; Pole Alonso 1:19.905; Warm, dry; 6.

Qual: unhappy with his third sector – 'excessive sliding'. Race: another solid run but 'we are simply not fast enough'. He finished 1m 15.3s behind winner Montoya.

Germany, Hockenheim, 24 July; Ferrari F2005; Qual 1:15.006 (5), R3; Pole Räikkönen 1:14.320; Overcast, dry; 5.

Qual: a clean lap, making the most of the car. Race: 'I struggled a lot with my tyres.' He finished 52.2s behind winner Alonso.

Hungary, Hungaroring, 31 July; Ferrari F2005; Qual 1:19.882 (P); Hot, dry; 2.
Qual: a good lap which made him very happy. Race: leading, then running second to Räikkönen after the second pit stops and finishing 35.3s behind him. He was slowed by his tyres.

Turkey, Istanbul, 21 Aug; Ferrari F2005; Qual (no time), R10; Pole Räikkönen 1:26.797; Hot, dry; R, collision, 32 laps.
Qual: he went off – 'we expected Turn 9 to be difficult because the wind had picked up and I thought I had taken this into account, but obviously not enough.' Race: a collision with Webber. 'He moved to the right. As I began to brake I could no longer see him and when I was in mid-corner I felt a bang at the back.'

Italy, Monza, 4 Sept; Ferrari F2005; Qual 1:21.721 (7), R4; Pole Räikkönen 1:20.878; Warm, dry; 10.
Qual: running a light fuel load. Race: ran down the field and, skirmishing with Button, went off on lap 50, finishing 1:36.0s behind winner Montoya.

Belgium, Spa, 11 Sept; Ferrari F2005; Qual 1:47.476 (7), R4; Pole Montoya 1:46.391; Overcast, dry; R, collision, 13 laps.
Qual: 'The bumpy and slippery nature of the track makes the car quite uncomfortable to drive.' Race: ran fifth early, braked for La Source and Sato (BAR) rammed him. 'I don't know what sort of therapy might help him.'

Brazil, Interlagos, 25 Sept; Ferrari F2005; Qual 1:12.976 (7), R4; Pole Alonso 1:11.988; Changeable; 4.

Qual: the lap started well then he lost grip. Race: 'reasonable' – the Bridgestone tyres worked and Schumacher exploited that, finishing 35.6s behind winner Montoya. Alonso, third, took the Championship.

Japan, Suzuka, 9 Oct; Ferrari F2005; Qual 1:52.676 (14), R7; Pole Ralf Schumacher 1:46.106; Warm, dry; 7.

Qual: rain as he started his run. Race: 'disappointed'. He couldn't stay with the Renaults, and finished 33.8s behind winner Räikkönen.

China, Shanghai, 16 Oct; Ferrari F2005; Qual 1:35.301 (6), R3; Pole Alonso 1:34.080; Warm, dry; R, spin, 22 laps.

Qual: a small mistake, going wide at Turn 2. Race: a 'weird ending' to the season – he was hit on the warm-up lap and later, when the Safety Car was out, 'I spun simply because my tyres were completely worn.'

Alonso 133 points, Räikkönen 112, Schumacher 62.

2006

Bahrain, Sakhir, 12 Mar; Ferrari 248F1; Qual 1:31.431 (P); Dry, windy; 2.

Qual: 'I wasn't expecting to be on pole.' He was proud to equal Senna's 65 poles. Race: if he'd had one more lap before his second stop he might have beaten winner Alonso.

Malaysia, Sepang, 19 Mar; Ferrari 248F1; Qual 1:34.668 (14, dropping 10 places, engine change), R2; Pole Fisichella 1:33.840; Hot, dry; 6.

Qual: he was satisfied because Alonso and Räikkönen 'aren't too far ahead on the grid'. Race: 'I don't think we could have achieved much more.' He finished behind team-mate Massa (fifth) and 43 seconds behind winner Fisichella.

Australia, Melbourne, 2 Apr; Ferrari 248F1; Qual 1:26.718 (11), R6; Pole Button 1:25.229; Dry; R, accident, 32 laps.
Qual: failed to make the top ten cut – rain. Race: he got the Ferrari up to sixth when, going over a bump, he hit the wall. 'I was pushing to the maximum.'

San Marino, Imola, 23 Apr; Ferrari 248F1; Qual 1:22.795 (P); Dry; 1.
Qual: a clean, almost clinical lap gave him his 66th pole – one more than the Senna record set at this same track 12 years before. Race: he led every lap except for his two pit stops, beating Alonso by 2 seconds.

Europe, Nürburgring, 7 May; Ferrari 248F1; Qual 1:30.028 (2), R1; Pole Alonso 1:29.819; Dry, fine; FL, 1.
Qual: Alonso produced a stunning lap leaving Schumacher 'happy to be on the front row'. Race: he set four fastest laps before his second stop and emerged in front of Alonso. 'A great race, great strategy and a great performance from the whole team.'

Spain, Barcelona, 14 May; Ferrari 248F1; Qual 1:14.970 (3), R2; Pole Alonso 1:14.648; Dry, fine; 2.
Qual: 'We based our decision about tyres more on how they would perform in the race.' Race: 'The result was decided in the first stint because Fernando was able to pull out quite a gap – simply because I did not have the pace to stay with him.' Alonso beat him by almost 19s.

Monaco, Monte Carlo, 28 May; Ferrari 248F1; Qual (no time – stripped of pole), R11; Pole Alonso 1:13.962; Dry; FL, 5.

The great Rascasse controversy when he punted the barrier and Alonso had to back off on a hot lap. Race: Schumacher, relegated from pole to the back of the grid, hauled the car up to fifth, expressing pleasure at that but disappointment about the Stewards' decision over qualifying.

Britain, Silverstone, 11 June; Ferrari 248F1; Qual 1:20.574 (3), R2; Pole Alonso 1:20.253; Hot, dry; 2.

Qual: 'Track conditions mean it's been difficult to find the right balance and the wind added to the difficulties.' Race: the Ferrari still lacked the pace of the Renault and couldn't catch Alonso, although he got past Räikkönen in the second pit stops.

Canada, Montreal, 25 June; Ferrari 248F1; Qual 1:15.986 (5), R3; Pole Alonso 1:14.942; Hot, dry; 2.

Qual: 'We are still suffering from a lack of grip.' Race: it was about 'damage limitation' – getting as near to Alonso as he could. Alonso, backing off, won it by 2s and now had 84 points, Schumacher 59.

USA, Indianapolis, 2 July; Ferrari 248F1; Qual 1:10.832 (P); Hot, dry; FL, 1.

Qual: 'I am a bit surprised at the gap to the others' – Massa 1:11.435, Fisichella 1:11.920. The car was well balanced, the tyres consistent. Race: he led every lap from Massa except the first pit stop, Alonso finishing fifth. 'We have been strong since the start of free practice on Friday.'

France, Magny-Cours, 16 July; Ferrari 248F1; Qual 1:15.493 (P); Hot, dry; FL, 1.

Qual: pole surprised him, especially as it was three-tenths quicker than Alonso, third. Race: victory was 'in all honesty unexpected. I got a good start and then could run my own race.' He beat Alonso by 10s.

Germany, Hockenheim, 30 July; Ferrari 248F1; Qual 1:14.205 (2), R1; Pole Räikkönen 1:14.070; Hot, dry; FL, 1.

Qual: Räikkönen produced a stunning lap for pole but Schumacher was running more fuel. It made him confident. Race: Räikkönen had to pit after ten laps, opening Hockenheim to Schumacher. Massa followed him home, Alonso fifth. Schumacher had, he said, no problems over the whole weekend. Alonso 100, Schumacher 89.

Hungary, Hungaroring, 6 Aug; Ferrari 248F1; Qual 1:20.875 (2 second penalty for overtaking under red flag), R6; Pole Räikkönen 1:19.599; Wet; 8.

Qual: he preferred 'not to go into a long explanation of what happened'. Race: a very Schumacher thing. He reached *fourth* on the opening lap, went back to ninth after his pit stop on lap 17, worked up to second behind winner Button but didn't pit for dry tyres and tangled with Heidfeld. He was classified ninth – up to eighth (and a precious point) when BMW's Robert Kubica was disqualified.

Turkey, Istanbul, 27 Aug; Ferrari 248F1; Qual 1:27.284 (2), R1; Pole Massa 1:26.907; Hot, dry; FL, 3.

Qual: 'I did not deliver a great performance, failing to get all the potential out of the car.' Race: the car felt 'nervous' and in the pit stop rush under a Safety Car he lost second place to Alonso. Massa won it. Alonso 108, Schumacher 96.

Italy, Monza, 10 Sept; Ferrari 248F1; Qual 1:21.486 (2), R1; Pole Räikkönen 1:21.484; Warm, dry; 1.

Qual: He seemed to have pole but Räikkönen conjured a fraction. 'Obviously two thousandths of a second is a tight battle.' Race: Räikkönen was running a light fuel load and when he pitted Monza lay at Schumacher's mercy. Alonso's engine expired in a vast plume of smoke and a roar from the crowd. On his slowing-down lap Schumacher told the team he was retiring. Alonso 108, Schumacher 106.

China, Shanghai, 1 Oct; Ferrari 248F1; Qual 1:45.775 (6), R3; Pole Alonso 1:44.360; Wet–dry; 1.

Qual: 'We did the best we could in these conditions as our chances were damaged by the rain. You could call it a damage limitation operation.' Race: Alonso established a commanding lead but had a slow pit stop and Renault made a mistaken tyre choice. Schumacher went past him ('the crucial moment') and then Fisichella. Alonso made a late charge but Schumacher won it by 3.1s.

Japan, Suzuka, 8 Oct; Ferrari 248F1; Qual 1:29.711 (2), R1. Pole: Massa 1:29.599. Dry. R

Qual: 'Two Ferraris on the front row is the perfect position for the start, given that our rivals are on row three. There was a lot of wind and even when you're trying to push hard there is always the thought that you mustn't go over the limit.' Race: He was in control even as Alonso came up towards him from the fifth row – but the engine blew in a cloud of smoke on lap 37.

Brazil, Sao Paulo, 22 Oct; Ferrari 248F1; Qual no time (10), R5. Pole: Massa 1:10.680. Dry. FL/4.

Qual: a disaster when, before the crucial third session, the Ferrari developed a fuel pressure problem and he couldn't do a single fast lap. He faced a seemingly impossible task from the fifth row. 'Of course I am disappointed but these things happen.' Race: a genuinely heroic charge to fifth, a puncture, another heroic charge from twentieth to fourth, 24 seconds behind the winner, his team-mate Massa. Schumacher was gracious about this and about Alonso, who had retained the Championship.

Alonso 134, Schumacher 121, Massa 80.

INDEX

Figures in italics refer to illustrations

Aaron, Hank 384
Active differential 204
Active suspension 104
Adelaide *132, 135,* 151-153, 177, 386, 392
Adenauer, Konrad 351
Agnelli, Gianni 173, 301, 325, 327
Agostini, Giacomo 384
Aichinger, Werner 36, 38
Aida 116, 118, 159, 177
Albers, Christijan 363
Alboreto, Michele 24, 28-29, 36, 138,
    288-289
Alesi, Jean 51, 66, 83, 85-87, 89-90, 96-97,
    100, 103-104, 112, 114, 116-118, 123-
    124, 138-139, 145, 160-161, 165, 167,
    169, 173-174, 176-177, 179-180, 183,
    185, 189-190, 193, 195, 197-200, 206,
    216-217, 248, 253, 279, 288
Ali, Muhammad 384
Allen, James 240
Allievi, Pino 175, 178, 277
Alliott, Philippe 115
Alonso, Fernando 7-8, 10, *336,* 339, 342,
    346-349, 354, 357-359, 361-363, 365-366,
    368-372-377, 387
Amon, Chris 18-19
Anderson, Gary 70-71, 386
Andretti, Mario 175, 288
Argentine GP 1981 165; 1995 162, 166;
    1996 185, 188; 1997 207, *329;* 1998 231
Armstrong, Lance 384
Arnoux, René 24, 175-176, 288-289
Arrows 176, 200, 222, 306
Ascanelli, Giorgio 194, 204
Ascari, Alberto 306, 311
Audi 39
Aumonier, Pierre 128
Australian GP 386; 1979 206; 1991 80;
    1992 96, 99; 1993 115; 1994 *134,* 158,

161; 1996 183, 1997 206; 2002 314, 316,
    321; 2003 339; 2004 352; 2005 359, 363
Austrian GP 387; 1997 217; 1998 240;
    1999 264; 2000 292; 2002 314, 317,
    319-320; 2003 341
Autopolis, Japan 80
Autosport magazine 41, 45, 47-49, 55, 57,
    62, 64, 66, 68, 119, 259, 264
Avus circuit 45, 56

Badoer, Luca 185, 315, 359
Bahrain GP 2004 352; 2005 359;
    2006 12, 365
Baier, Andreas 38, 42
Bailey, Julian 50-51
Baldi, Mauro 51-52, 57, 59, 64-65, 68
Banzai laps 245
BAR 292, 303, 315, *336,* 339, 348, 354,
    358, 362
Barcelona 12-13, 88, 117, 121, 123, 145,
    229, 232, 255, 263, 303, 315-316,
    358-359
Barnard, John 29, 51, 103, 160, 172-173,
    178, 180-182, 185-187, 190, 194, 200-
    203, 226-229-230, 236, 244, 247
Barrichello, Rubens 10, 128, 139, 161, 183,
    188, 207, 212-214, 263, 269, 289-291,
    293, 303-306, 310, 315-318, 320-322,
    324-326, *335,* 338-339, 341-344, 346-350,
    354-360, 362, 372, 387
Bartels, Michael 44-45, 47-49
BBC 13, 340
Beckenbauer, Franz 341
Becker, Boris 23, 341, 351, 381
Beggio, Gianluca 25
Belgian GP 1982 24; 1991 68, 70, 75-76;
    1992 96; 1993 113; 1994 149; 1996 196-
    197; 1997 216; 1998 248; 1999 267-268;
    2001 311; 2002 323; 2005 *336*
Bellof, Stefan 74
Beltoise, J-P. 194

Benetton 76, 78-80, 82, 85-87, 93, 97, 100,
102, 104-105, 108, 116, 119, 121, 123,
125-127, *132, 135-136*, 138, 140-143, 145-
147, 150-151, 154-155, 157, 161, 163,
166, 168-171, 173-174, 176, 179, 183,
189, 199-201, 203-204, 206-207, 216, 230,
232, 255, 290, 300, 303, 380, 388-389
disqualifications, fines and appeals 127,
137, 146, 149, 163, 166
B194 116
Bennetts, Dick 59-63
Berger, Gerhard 29, 36, 43, 74, 82-84, 86,
91, 95-96, 99, 104, 108, 113, 115-116,
118-121, 126, 138-139, 158, 160-161,
164, 167-168, 173-174, 176, 179-180,
183, 192-193, 195, 199-200, 204, 207,
218, 245, 247-248, 277, 288-289, *329*
Bernardoni, Father Alberto 300
Best, George 384
Bickinger, Heiner 163
Biela, Frank 41-42
Bierhoff, Oliver 277
Bild Zeitung newspaper 272
Bishop, Matt 278-280
Blair, PM Tony 12
Blundell, Mark 120, 139, 161
BMW 8-9
BMW Sauber 371
Bogle, Graham 59
Bollingtoft, Rene 30-32
Bonnet, Michel 164
Borg, Björn 384
Boullion, Jean-Christophe 176
Boutsen, Thierry 73, 98, 178
Brabham 18, 81, 175
Brabham, David 50
Brabham, Jack 301, 306
Bradman, Don 384
Brands Hatch 36, 41, 49, 100
Brawn, Ross 11, *132*, 143, 146, 191, 200-
201, 203-204, 221-222, 229, 239-242,
244-247, 256, 261, 275, 281-282, 291,
295, 298-300, 304, 306, 308-309, 315-
316, 319, 321, 324-325-326, 339, 341,
355, 358, 388-389
Brazilian GP 1989 43; 1991 68; 1992 84, 94,
105; 1993 105; 1994 117-118, 137, 159;
1995 162, 164-165, 169; 1996 184; 1997
207; 1998 231; 1999 255-256; 2000 290;
2001 306; 2002 316; 2003 340; 2004 *335*,
357; 2005 362-363; 2006 6-7, 11, 373-377
Briatore, Flavio 78, 121, 127, *135*, 140, 147,
162, 200
Bridgestone tyres 11, 28, 40, 254, 317, 321,
346, 358-359, 362, 364, 372-375
British GP 389; 1992 93; 1993 111; 1994
128; 1995 171; 1996 196; 1998 237; 1999
11, 257, 261, *331*; 2000 291; 2001 307;
2002 314; 2003 343; 2004 355

BRM 18
Brundle, Martin 81-84, 87, 91, 93, 95, 97,
99-100, 102-104, 111, 118, 121, 158, 183,
274, 277, 362, 368
Brunn 46
Buchinger, Heiner 265, 269
Buenos Aires 165, 185
Burgess, Alan 22
Burti, Luciano 307, 315
Button, Jenson 10, 290, 303, 315, 339, 347,
349, 354-355, 358, 361, 366, 371-372, 377
Byrne, Rory 203, 206, 208, 214, 229, 235,
237, 244, 254-256, 261-262, 273, 312,
317, 325, 341

Camel Germany 52
Canadian GP 1978 100; 1993 109-110;
1994 123, 125; 1996 196; 1997 214; 1998
234, 236; 1999 257, 262; 2000 291; 2001
307; 2002 320; 2003 341; 2004 355; 2005
361; 2006 370
Canon Williams Renault 96
Capelli, Ivan 22, 103, 288-289
Catalunya 121
Chapman, Roger and Amanda 258-259
Cheever, Ross 67
Chinese GP 2004 357; 2005 362-363; 2006
372, 374-375
Ciampi, Carlo Azeglio 301
Citation 2 plane 178
Clark, Jim 123, 302, 306, 353, 387, 391
Constructors' Championship 262, 272, 278,
283, 288-289, 318, *332*, 363, 365, 371-372
Coulthard, David 125-126, 139, 148-149,
161-163, 166, 168, 177, 183, 188, 190,
196-197, 206-208, 214-215, 223-225, 230-
232, 235, 238, 240-244, 248-251, 253-254,
256-257, 259, 268, 274, 278, 282-285,
290-292, 294-296, 303, 305-307, 309-311,
320, *333*, 339, 343, 346, 349, 354

Daily Telegraph, The 341
Dallara 44-46
da Matta, Cristiano 343, 348, 350
Danielsson, Thomas 67
de Angelis, Elio 385
de Cesaris, Andrea 72, 138, 362
Degner, Ernst 374
Dennis, Ron 43, 249, 283-284
Diepholz 47, 57, 67
Die Welt newspaper 272
Dijon 57, 59, *130*
Dilke, Jurgen 39
DiMaggio, Joe 384
di Montezemolo, Luca 103, 160, 172, 178,
183, 185-186, 196, 199, 201, 229, 266,
272-273, 283, 286, 290, 298, 301, 319,
327, 343, 354
Diniz, Pedro 185, 192, 235

Donington 107, 194
Drivers' Association 215
Drivers' Championship 262, 272, 318, *332*, 365, 371, 375
Dunlop tyres 28
Dutch GP 1992 88

Ecclestone, Bernie 15
Einstein, Albert 341, 351
Electronic aids 324
Elf fuel 163-164, 166
Engines
    Alfa 41
    BMW 344
    Cosworth 70-71, 76, 123
    Ferrari V8 364
    Fiat 37
    Ford 104, 127, 145, 147; Series VII 108; Zetec-R 116, 123
    Honda 41, 67, 74, 353
    Mercedes 205, 290, 292, 297, 327
    Mugen 59, 67
    Mugen-Honda 50
    Opel 49
    Renault 96, 116, 125, 145, 157, 166, 180, 353
Engstler, Frank 41
Eriksson, Conny 30
Estoril 99, 148, 161, 180-181, 378
EUFRA team 35-36, 39
European Commission 225
European GP 1985 100; 1993 107, 194; 1994 150; 1995 177; 1996 186; 1997 219; 1999 269-270; 2000 291; 2001 307; 2002 314, 320; 2003 342; 2004 355; 2005 361; 2006 366
Eurosport 123
Eusebio 384

F1 Racing magazine 278, 367
Fabi, Teo 66
Fangio, Juan Manuel 290, 301, 311, 314, 320, 323-324, 326-327, *333*, 351, 356, 387, 391
Federer, Roger 384
Ferrari 7-8, 10-14, 18-21, 29, 43, 51, 66, 88-89, 100, 103-104, 108-109, 113, 116, 118, 124, 138-139, 160, 164, 166, 170, 172-175, 178 et seq. 150th win 320 ; 700th GP 356
    F1-2000 290
    F300 229
    F310 183, 186, 196; F310B 201-202
    F399 254, 266, 271
    F-2001 303
    F-2002 314-316, 325
    F-2003 325, 340-341; F-2003-GA 324-325
    F-2004 358-359, 364
    F-2005 358-359. 364

248 F1 376
    Enzo 325
Ferrari, Enzo 18, 24, 29, 301
FIA 121, 128, 137, 140-143, 146-147, 163, 166-167, 219, 225-226, 258, 278, 321, *330*; Appeals Committee 166; International Court of Appeal 137
Fiat 173, 301, 319-320, 387
Fiorano test track 179, 184, 202, 214, 229, 255, 265, 267, 269-270, 272, 275, 303, 315, 321, 339
FISA 79, 107, 121
Fisichella, Giancarlo 9-10, 206, 210-213, 216, 218, 230, 232, 235, 253, 255, 290, 292, 303, 358-359, 365, 372
Fittipaldi, Christian 25, 358, 363
Ford 116, 123
Formula Ford 35-36, 41-42, 379
Formula Ford 1600 35, 39, 42, 64, 80
    EFDA Euroseries 36, 39-40
    Festival 36, 41, 49
    German Championship 36, 39, 43
Formula Koenig 35-37, 42-43, 50, 64, 80, *130*
Formula Opel 37
Formula Panda 36-37
Formula Renault 37
Formula 3 27, 40, 42, 44, 50-51, 54, 61, 64-66, 68-69, 80, *130*, 205, 212, 379
    British Championship 59-60
    French Championship 59
    German Championship 41, 42, 50, 52-60, 63-64
    Italian Championship 59
Formula 3000 27-28, 51-52, 67, 69, 80; All-Japan 67, 205
Forti 185
Foster, Trevor 69-72, 75
Foulds, Ian 126
Frankfurt Motor Show 1999 270
French GP 1981 100; 1993 110; 1994 124, 137; 1995 171; 1996 196; 1998 237; 2000 291; 2001 307; 2002 314, 321, 323-324; 2003 342; 2005 362
Frentzen, Heinz-Harald 35, 43-54, 64, 206-208, 212, 215-217, 220, 222-223, 230, 234-235, 253, 255, 257, 268, 290, 303, 305, 317, 347, 351
Fullerton, Terry 28

Gachot, Bertrand 68, 174
Geesthacht kart track 33
Gellerman, Thomas 43
Gemmo, Frederico 30-31
Gene, Marc 343, 359
Genk kart track 30
German GP 1982 24; 1992 93-94; 1993 112; 1994 137, 141; 1996 196; 1997 216; 1999 264; 2002 323; 2003 343; 2004 355; 2005 362; 2006 370

Gewinnus, Kurt 43
Giadone, Roger 178
Gilardi, Andrea 25-26
Goodyear tyres 107, 231, 254
Goossens, Marc 378
Gothenburg 28, 30
Graf, Steffi 23, 341, 351, 381
Gretzky, Wayne 384
Grisham, John 109
Group C Sportscars 45, 51-52, 54, 65-66, 75, 101, 122
Guardian, The newspaper 388
Guy-Johnson, Andrew 41

Häkkinen, Mika 59-63, 96, 101, 118, 120-122, 128, 139, 153, 161, 167, 183, 188, 196-197, 206, 208, 218, 223, 225, 229-232, 234-235, 237-241, 243, 245, 250-253, 255-257, 261, 268, 271, 274, 276, 278, 281-282, 285, 290-291, 293-297, 299-300, 303, 306-307, 309, 311-312, 315, *332*
Hailwood, Mike 384
Haller, Helmut 277
Hamilton, Maurice 144-145
Hamper, Albert 39, 49
Hantscher, Peter 33-34
Hawkela, Harry 164
Haymarket Motorsport Magazines 278
Head, Patrick 152, 163
Heidfeld, Nick 349, 358-359, 371
Hellberg, Lotta 30
Henry, Alan 388
Herbert, Johnny 97, 106, 122, 151, 161, 171-172, 177, 212-213, 232, 248, 253, 270, 299, 362
Hill, Damon 104, 107-108, 111-117, 120-122, 125-127, *135*, 137-140, 143-145, 148-149, 151-158, 161-163, 165, 167, 169-174, 176, 183, 188, 190-192, 197, 199, 216, 222, 230, 235, 248-249, 253, 255, 279, 285, 303, 309, 315, 386; death threats 172; guest editor 278-280
Hill, Graham 358
Hitler, Adolf 341
Hockenheim 35-36, 38, 42, 44-45, 47-48, 56, 59-61, 93-94, 98, 105, 112-113, 128, 137-138, 140, 142, 146-147, 172, 241, 265, 292, 307, 340; club circuit 49
Hoecker, Gustav 35, 37
Hoffmann, Elmar 27
Hofmann, Markus 43
Honda 10, 99, 187
Horrem 18
  kart track 20-21
Hulme, Denny 358
Hungarian GP 1992 95; 1993 112; 1994 143; 1995 173; 1996 196; 1997 216; 1998 241, 244, 246-247, 250; 1999 266; 2000 292; 2001 307-308; 2002 323; 2003 342-343; 2004 355; 2005 362; 2006 371
Hungaroring 242, 307-308, 310-311, *333*, 388
Hunt, James 127, 228
Hutter, Georg 43

Ickx, Jacky 19, 194
IMG 76-77
Imola 12, 22, 24, 59, 86-89, 107-108, 116-117, 139, 159, 167-168, 189, 208, 255, 262, 264, 291, 306, 339-340, 352, 359, 366, 385
Indianapolis 293, 311-312, 345, 361, 370
Indy 500 race 293, 345
IndyCars 81, 99, 148, 166, 175, 293
Inoue, Taki 176
Interlagos 6-7, 10-12, 162, 378
Intertechnique refuelling equipment 140
Irvine, Eddie 50, 137, 161, 178-179, 183, 191-192, 201-203, 206, 215, 218-220, 230, 235, 237, 241, 248, 250-251, 254-255, 257-259, 261-262, 264-267, 269-274, 278, 280-281, 283-284, 288-289, 300, 362
Italian GP 1980 22; 1982 175; 1991 75, 78; 1992 96, 98; 1993 114; 1994 146-147; 1995 176; 1996 197; 1998 250; 1999 262, 268; 2001 311; 2002 323; 2003 342
ITV 240

Jaguar 67, 270, 289 299, 347-348
Jakobi, Julian 77
Japanese GP 391; 1988 1989 41; 1990 51, 386; 1991 80; 1992 96, 99; 1993 115; 1994 161; 1995 177; 1996 198-199; 1997 218; 1998 251, *331*; 1999 264, 272; 2000 294; 2001 311; 2002 323; 2003 347; 2004 357; 2005 362; 2006 7, 373, 375
Jenkinson, Denis 103
Jerez 65, 121, 148-149, 202-204, 219, 221, 225-226, 229, *330*, 358, 364, 375-376, 386, 392
Jessen, Prof. Dr Ralph 380
Johansson, Stefan 28, 68-70, 199, 288
Jordan 68, 70-71, 75-76, 78-79, 92, 128, *131*, 137, 145, 161, 183, 205-206, 210, 218, 230, 255, 290, 303, 305, 362, 380
Jordan, Eddie 68-69, 72, 74-79

Karting 36, 75
  European Championships 27-28, 30-32, 379; Northern Zone 29-30; Southern Zone 30
  German Juniors 24, 44, 205
  German Seniors 28, 33
  Italian Championships 26
  World Junior Championships 24-27
Karting magazine 25-26, 28-31
Katayama, Ukyo 67, 139

Kaufmann, Josef 40-41, 44, 46, 55, 63, 67
Kaufmann, Wolfgang 46-47, 49, 55, 58
Kehm, Sabine 11, 13
Kelleners, Ralf 29
Kerpen 17-22, 32, 298, 381
    kart track 23, 27, 33, 39, 43-44, 98-99,
    182, 220-221
Koene, Martijn 30
Koenig, Richard 36
Koester, R. 38
Kolner Stadt-Anzeiger newspaper 80
Kracht, Thomas
Kramer, Frank 46, 49, 58
Kramer, Gert 68
Kremer, Frank 43
Kubica, Robert 371
Kyalami 18, 81, 105

La Gazzetta dello Sport newspaper 277
Lamborghini 35
Lamy, Pedro 119
Larini, Nicola 103, 116, 118, 120, 288
Larrousse 115
Lauda, Niki 19-20, 119, 127, 166, 175, 182,
    277, 301, 312, 323, 358, 363, 378
Laver, Rod 384
Lehto, J. J. 116-117, 119, 125, 147-148; 362
Le Mans 25, 67
L'Equipe newspaper 194, 307, 323
Lewis, Carl 384
Ligier 98, 185, 203
Lotus 18-19, 96-97, 100, 108, 119, 122,
    138, 179, 211, 263, 353
Louis, Joe 384
Lundberg, Linus 29
Luther, Martin 351
Luxembourg GP 1997 217; 1998 251

Macau 50-51, 61, 63, *130*
Magny-Cours 91-92, 95, 111, 215, *333*
Mail On Sunday, The 120
Malaysian GP 1999 264, 272-276, 282;
    2000 293; 2001 304; 2002 314, 316; 2003
    339-340; 2004 352; 2005 359; 2006 365
Manheim kart track 22-24
Mansell, Nigel 43, 51, 75, 80, 82-86, 88-
    100, 104, 124-125, 128, 148, 150, 153-
    154, 157-158-159, 162, 176-177, 199,
    211, 228, 245, 288-289, 302-303, 306,
    310, 312, 314, 324, 358
Maranello test track 201, 324
Marlboro McLaren 41, 74
Marlboro 59, 118, 211, 221, 269; Press
    Service 201; Switzerland 59
Marriott Harrison legal advisors 142
Martinelli, Paolo 325, 341
Martini, Pierluigi 139
Marx, Karl 341, 351
Mass, Jochen 41, 51-52, 54-59, 65, 80, 96

Massa, Felipe 7-8, 10, 13, 317, 362, 371,
    374, 377
Matra 18
McEnroe, John 384
McLaren 10, 18, 41, 43, 74-75, 82-83, 87,
    93, 99-100, 104, 108, 111, 113, 118, 139,
    161-162, 183, 188, 197, 199, 205-206,
    208, 211, 229-232, 237-239, 241-243,
    248-250, 254-255, 262, 270, 282-285,
    290-291, 293, 296-297, 303, 308, 311,
    315, 323, 327, 338-339, 342, 353-354,
    358, 373
McNish, Allan 21, 24-26, 28-29, 32, 36, 50,
    323
Melbourne 12, 183-184, 202-203, 230-231,
    255, 261, 287, 289-290, 304, 315, 340,
    365
Mercedes-Benz 51-54, 65-69, 76-77, 80, 92,
    108; Junior Team 55, 64, *130*, 379
    C11 57
    C291 66
Merzario, Arturo 19
Mexico City 59, 80, 83
Michelin tyres 346, 358, 361, 374
Mild Seven 127, 147
Minardi 139, 211, 253, 362-363
Miracle of Berne film 383
Modena, Stefano 92
Monaco GP 45; 1984 194; 1992 90; 1994
    120-122; 1995 170; 1996 191; 1997 208-
    210, 212-214; 1998 232, 234; 1999 256;
    2000 291; 2001 306; 2002 314, 320; 2003
    341; 2004 355; 2005 360; 2006 365-367,
    369, 391-392
Monte Carlo 159, 208, 214, 262
Montoya, Juan Pablo 303, 306, 311-312,
    314, 316, 318, 320-323, 339, 341-343,
    345-347, 353-355, 357-358
Montreal 91, 170-171, 385
Monza 11, 14, 18-20, 66, 75, 78, 114, 147-
    148, 160, 174-175, 197, 217, 250-251,
    263, 266-268, 293, 304, 311-312, *336*,
    342, 344, 356, 362, 369, 371-372, 387
Morbidelli, Gianni 27, 42, 288
Moreno, Roberto 78-79
Moseley, Max 121, 147, 168, 225
Moss, Stirling 387, 391-392
Motoring News 119
Mount Fuji 61, 63
Mugello circuit 266-268, 271-273, 275
Muller, Gerd 277
Muller, Yvan 25-26
Munkholm, Gert 28-29, 33

Nakano, Shinji 253
Naspetti, Emanuelle 29
Neerpasch, Jochen 51-52, 64, 69, 75-77, 79
New Zealand GP 1969 18
Nicklaus, Jack 384

Nivelles kart track 22
Norisring 57
Nürburgring 19, 41, 45, 47, 56-58, 68-69,
    75, 177, 186, 188, 194, 217, 251, 269-270,
    291, 307, 320, 342, 355, 361, 366, 378

Observer, The newspaper 144, 355
Olympic Games Berlin 1936 384
ONS 46
Opel Lotus Challenge 42
Opel-Lotus 41, 52
Oppenrod kart track 29
Orsini, Massimiliano 25, 31-32
Österreichring 40
Owens, Jesse 384

Pacific GP 1994 116
Paletti, Riccardo 385
Panis, Olivier 213, 215, 253, 303, 315, 346,
    349
Parker, Steve 123
Parma kart track 26
Patrese, Riccardo 75, 82, 84-86, 90, 92, 94-
    97, 99, 104-105, 109, 112, 115, 175, 362
Paul Ricard circuit 54, 65, 161, 385
Pele 384
Peugeot 905 68
Phillips, Ian 68, 71, 76
Piggott, Lester 384
Piquet, Nelson 74-75, 78, 80-81, *132*, 199,
    301, 358
Pironi, Didier 22, 24, 175, 288-289
Porsche 38
Portuguese GP 1985 100, 194; 1989 128;
    1992 96; 1993 114; 1994 146-148; 1995
    177; 1996 198
Postlethwaite, Harvey 103-104
Price, Dave 54, 69
Proaction publicity company 153
Prost 213, 228, 252, 307-308
Prost, Alain 15, 43, 51, 66, 87, 89, 99-100,
    104-105, 108, 110-114, 117, 125, 175,
    182, 194, 199, 203, 211, 222, 246, 289,
    291, 301-304, 308, 311, 315, 324, 353
Pukekohe 18

Räikkönen, Kimi 10, 12-13, 315, 322-323,
    336, 339-348, 350, 354, 356-357, 361-
    362, 366, 372, 378
Ralt 44, 50, 62, 67
    RT34 59
Ralt-Spiess VW 63
Ramirez, Jo 308
Ratzenberger, Roland 119-120, 159
Redgrave, Steve 384
Regazzoni, Clay 19
Renault 7, 175, 315, 339, 354, 358-359,
    363, 365, 370, 372-374, 377
Rensing, Otto 27, 44, 50, 55-58, 60-61, 63

Reutemann, Carlos 20
Reynard 42, 44-46, 49-50, 62-63
Reynard-Spiess VW 61
Richards, Gordon 384
Rindt, Jochen 19
Rives, Johnny 194-195
Robertson, Steve 63
Rodriguez, Pedro 19
Roppes, Michael 44
Rosberg, Keke 36, 68-69, 87, 90, 100, 285,
    358, 368, 375-376, 387
Rose, Pete 384
Rossi, Valentino 384
Rosso, Victor 45
Rothmans 125, 157
RTL television 221, 270
Ruth, Babe 384
Rydell, Rickard 50

Salo, Mika 40, 264-268, 270-271, 273, 283-
    285, 288
Salzburg 40, 42
San Marino GP 1982 24; 1983 175; 1994
    119, 137, 167; 1996 189; 1997 208; 1998
    255; 2002 317, 340
Sao Paulo 15, 105, 117, 207, 231, 316, 376
Sato, Takuma 348, 354, 358, 362
Sauber 108, 138, 176, 212, 317, 349
Saward, Joe 74
Schattling, Wolfgang 45, 64
Scheckter, Jody 20-22, 51, 160, 174, 221-
    222, 225, 261, 269, 277, 288
Schiffer, Claudia 341
Schlesser, Jean-Louis 51-52, 57, 59, 64-66
Schmalgemeier, Detlef 43
Schmickler, Frank 44-46
Schroder, Gerhard 301, 301
Schubel Reynard 49
Schumacher, Corinna (wife, née Betsch)
    44, 90, 109, 111, *132*, *134*, 164-165, 174,
    178, 205, 259, 272, 277, 345, 350, 365
Schumacher, Elisabeth (mother) 17, 19,
    98, 221, 340
Schumacher, Gina-Maria (daughter) *134*,
    205, 273
Schumacher, Michael
    admitting to mistakes 58, 95, 225, 257
    appearance 12, *129*, 137
    apprenticeship in garage 28
    bikes and scooters 111, *131-132*
    birth 17, 19
    championship wins:
        European karting 32, 379
        Formula Koenig 38
        German Formula 3 58, 60, 63, 66
        German Juniors karting 24, *129*
        German Senior karting 33
        World F1 11, 15, 290, 350; 1994 *135*,
        158-159; 1995 177; 2000 300-301, 309,

332; 2001 311, 313, *332*; 2002 314, 323, *333*, 342; 2003 350; 2004 *335*

charity work *330*

contracts 306

crashes and collisions 14-15, 41, 46, 57-58, 92, 98, 115, 155-156, 159, 163, 165, 168-169, 176-177, 196, 224-225, 232, 249, 257-260, 264, 273, 285, 303-304, 313, *329-331, 335-336*, 342, 366, 371, 386

disqualifications and penalties 56, 146, 163, 174, 217, 236, 239, 276, 322, 340

diving incident 164-165

driving in the wet 15, 92, 97, 106, *132*, 151, 173, 180, 191, 194, 209, 213-214, 216-217, 230, 249, 263, *329*, 340, 346, 388

driving skills and style 15, 27, 35, 51, 71, 88, 180, 194, 236, 274, 305, 368, 387, 392

fastest laps 10, 15, 92, 188, 196, 242, 244, 256, 303-304, 310, 314, 346, 348, 352, 357

first F1 race 9, *131*

first race led in a Ferrari 190

first time in single-seater 35-36

fitness 6, 15, 148-149, 183, 227, 275-276, 376

football 6, 15-16, 20, 24, *132*, 273

holidays and relaxation 6, 109-110, *132, 134*, 164, 286, 365

homes: Switzerland *334*; Monte Carlo, Monaco 100, 108-109, 111

interviews/press conferences 6, 13-14, 112, 264, 270, 277-280, 319, 323, 376

judo 24

karting 12, 19, 22-35, 39, 43-44, 50, 64, 80, 99, 182-183, 205, 257, 379

knee and leg injuries 11, 14, 111, 196, 259, 280, *331*

lap records: F1 98; karting 27

marriage 174

mental alertness 276

nice guy 14, 27, 35, 388-389

pole positions F1 8, 12, 15, 120, 124, 143, 151, 168-170, 189, 191, 196, 214-216, 236, 250-251, 274, 291, 293, 297, 302, 304, 309, 312, 314, 316-317, 324, *331*, 339, 341, 353-355, 357, 362, 370; F3 47, 55-56; karting 29-30

race wins: FF1600 40; F. Koenig 38; F1 14, 15, 98, 118, 120-121, 163, 170, 240, 303, 306, 314, 316-318, 320-321, 323-324, *329*, 340-341, 352-353, 355, 357, 366, 370, 372; F3 46, 63

records 324, 326, 328, 341, 357; most: fastest laps 303-304, 357; laps led 357; points 15, 302, 312, 324, 356-357, 391; pole positions 12, 15, 302, 312, 324, 357;

race wins 14-15, 302, 306, 308, 320, 323-324, 357, 391; races for Ferrari 317; wins in a season 323; World Championships 311, 320, *333*, 357, 391; on podium every race of the season 323;

retirement from racing 6, 11, 14, *336*, 369, 371, 375, 377, 386-387, 389, 391

sports car racing 57, 65

testing 12, 35, 41, 54, 65, 105, 121, 128, 179-181, 184, 202-203, 229, 255, 265-269, 271-273, 275, 290, 303, 317, 321, 342-343, 358, 364, 375

track records 310

wealth 7, 39, 172

Schumacher, Miki (son) *134*

Schumacher, Ralf (brother) 19, 101, 205-206, 212-213, 215, 217-218, 253, 255, 257, 279, 281, 290, 303, 305-307, 311, 315-318, 320-321, *332*, 338-340, 343, 349, 354, 360-361

Schumacher, Rolf (father) 17, 19, 21, 23, 32, 39, 44, 221-222

Schumacher, Toni (goalkeeper) 23

Schwitalla, Helmut 38, 42

Senna, Ayrton 10-15, 22, 41, 51, 55, 75, 82, 84-88, 91-94, 96-97, 99-102, 105-107, 110-111, 113-120, 123, 125, *136*, 149-150, 158-159, 162, 173, 179, 181, 187, 194, 199, 226, 228, 236-237, 246, 263, 274, 282, 301-302, 312, 314, 324, 326, 353-354, 357-358, 362, 378, 386; fatal crash 12, 101, 119, 167-168, 258

September 11, 2001 311

Shanghai 357, 363, 372

Sheene, Barry 152

Shell 364, 376

Shoemaker, Bill 384

SID news agency 265

Sieber, Peter 35, 39-40

Silverstone 14, 56, 66, 75-78, 89, 92-93, 95, 101, 117, 125, 128, *132*, 137, 143-144, 146, 149, 172, 176, 196, 216, 262, 264, 273, 279, 291, 313, 321, 324, 328, 337, 362, 370, 386

Simon, Gilles 341

Simtek 119

Soccer World Cup 1954 383

South African GP 1993

Spa 68, 70-74, 76, 79, 96, 98, *131*, 145-146, 173 197, 267, 282, 284-285, 292, 311, 355-356, 362, 376, 380-381, 385, 388

Spanish GP 358; 1991 80; 1992 85, 87, 96; 1993 108; 1994 121, 125; 1995 169; 1996 191, 195, 214, *329*; 1997 214; 1999 257; 2000 291; 2001 306; 2002 317; 2003 341; 2004 352, 355; 2006 366

Spitz, Mark 384

Sportscar World Championship (SWC) 51, 56, 59, 68, 80, *130*

Stepney, Nigel 179, 182, 184, 187, 195, 209, 211, 214, 244, 261-263, 273, 283
Stewart 207, 270, 289
Stewart, Sir Jackie 194, 301, 385, 387, 392
Stewart, Paul 50
Sugo 67, 69
Sunday Times 368
Suzuka 66, 151-152, 177, 199, 219, 251, 282, 286-287, 289, 294-295, 297-298, 312, *332*, 347, 350, 363, 373, 375; earthquake 295
Suzuki, Aguri 109
Symonds, Pat 169

Takagi, Toranosuke 253-254
Tambay, Patrick 24, 175, 256, 288
Tark Aleco-Spiess 45
Tasman Series 18
Tauranac, Ron 67
Team orders 319, 321, 324
Theodore 50
Thorpe, Jim 384
Tifosi 175, 190, 198, 269, 317
Times, The newspaper 391
Todt, Jean 12, 178, 187, 200-204, 209, 238-240, 249, 254, 259-261, 267, 271, 275, 283, 290, 300, 308, 321, 325-327, *330*, 340-341, 346, 354, 360, 369, 372-373, 377, 388
Toleman 87, 100, 237
Tomba, Alberto 'The Bomba' 202
Tour de France cycle race 384
Toyota 323, 343, 349, 358, 361, 374, 390-391
Traction control 109-110
Trulli, Jarno 252-253, 290, 303, 305, 315, 339-340, 354-355, 374
Tuero, Esteban 253-254
Turkish GP 2005 362; 2006 371
Tyrrell 36, 87, 100, 120, 253

UN *Make Roads Safe* campaign 12-13
United States GP 2000 293; 2001 311; 2004 355; 2005 361
Ustinov, Peter 380

Valencia 358
Valkenburg, Robert 30
van de Poele, Eric 74
Van Diemen 36
Van Eglem, Frank 28
Ventimiglia kart track 183
Verdegay, Joaquin 367
Verstappen, Jos 125, 138-139, 144, 147-148, 306, 362

Villadelprat, Joan 128, 143
Villeneuve, Gilles 20-22, 24, 87-90, 100
Villeneuve, Jacques 176, 180, 183-184, 188-189, 191-193, 196-197, 207, 209, 214-220, 222-225, 230, 234-235, 241-242, 250-251, 263, 288, 303-304, 308-309, 315, *330*, 339, 375, 386
von Trips, Wolfgang 18

Walkinshaw, Tom 76-78, *135*
Walldorf kart track 33
Walters, Martin 123-124
Warwick, Derek 67-69
Watkins, Prof Sid 12, 14, 259, 274
Watson, John 124, 182
Webber, Mark 348, 358, 362, 366
Weber, Willi 41-43, 68-69, 71-72, 75, 82, 120, *130*, 164, 178, 220, 261, 264-265, 379
Welt-am-Sonntag newspaper 147
Wendlinger, Karl 28, 43-51, 54, 64, 66, 68, 80, 101, 120, 159
Werner, Marco 48-49, 52
West Surrey Racing 59
Whiting, Charlie 143
Williams 9, 51, 75, 82, 84, 91, 96-97, 99, 104, 111, 113, 116, 125-126, *134*, 144, 148, 150, 152, 154-157, 161, 163-164, 166, 169, 174, 176, 180, 183-184, 186, 188, 190, 197, 206-209, 219-220, 222, 224-225, 230, 255, 290, 303, 311, 315-316, 322, 338-339, 342, 344, 353-354, 358
Williams, Frank 235, 318
Wilson, Justin 347-348
Woods, Tiger 384
World Karting Championship 75
World Motorsport Council 128, 137, 143, 147, 225, 321
WTS Racing 41, 62, 379
Wunstorf 47, 56
Wurz, Alexander 230, 232-233, 238, 253, 255, 290, 299

Yipp, Teddy 50
Young, Eoin 103

Zakowski, Peter 47-49, 55, 58, 60
Zanardi, Alessandro 28-29, 31-32, 108, 138, 255
Zandvoort 40
ZDF television's Greatest German 340-341
Zeltweg 46, 57
Zolder 38, 42, 55, 72
Zonta, Ricardo 292, 299